AF854799

TREATISE

ON THE

CONTRACT OF SALE,

BY R. J. POTHIER.

TRANSLATED FROM THE FRENCH

BY L. S. CUSHING.

THE LAWBOOK EXCHANGE, LTD.
UNION, NEW JERSEY
1999

ISBN-13: 978-1-886363-82-3
ISBN-10: 1-886363-82-X

Third printing 2007

The Lawbook Exchange, Ltd.
33 Terminal Avenue
Clark, New Jersey 07066-1321

Please see our website for a selection of our other publications and fine facsimile reprints of classic works of legal history:
www.lawbookexchange.com

Library of Congress Cataloging-in-Publication Data

Pothier, Robert Joseph, 1699-1772
[TraitJ du contrat de sociJtJ. English]
Treatise on the contract of sale / by R.J. Pothier ; translated from the French by L.S. Cushing.
p. cm.
Originally published : Boston : C.C. Little and J. Brown, 1839.
Includes bibliographical references and index.
ISBN 1-886363-82-X (alk. paper)
1. Sales—France. 2. Sales. I. Title.

KJV2320.P68 1999
346.4407'2—dc21 99-10260
CIP

Printed in the United States of America on acid-free paper

TREATISE

ON THE

CONTRACT OF SALE,

By R. J. POTHIER.

TRANSLATED FROM THE FRENCH

By L. S. CUSHING.

BOSTON:
CHARLES C. LITTLE AND JAMES BROWN.
MDCCCXXXIX.

Entered according to act of Congress in the year 1839, by L. S. Cushing, in the Clerk's Office of the District Court of the District of Massachusetts.

PRESS OF THE AMERICAN JURIST,
FREEMAN AND BOLLES.

PREFACE

BY THE TRANSLATOR.

THE name of Pothier is so well known to the English and American lawyer, and his character as a jurist so justly appreciated in other countries as well as in his own, that nothing need now be said of his life or history, by way of introduction to a translation of a portion of his works.

The writings of this celebrated author relate either to the Roman or to the French law. In the department of the former, they consist of his arrangement of the whole body of the Roman law, under the title of *Pandectæ Justinianeæ in novum ordinem digestæ*, originally published in three volumes, folio. The treatises on French law are devoted to matters of the customary law, then in force in France,—to the subjects of obligations and contracts,—the nature and transmission of various kinds of property,—the law of persons, of things, and of possession,—and to civil and criminal procedure. The most valuable of these works are the treatises on obligations and contracts.

The treatise on obligations has for many years been familiar to the profession, in the translation of sir William D. Evans; and has become a standard work, without which even a moderately sized law-library would scarcely be considered complete. In the course of his labors on the Roman law, and, particularly, in arranging the titles concerning pacts and obligations, for his Pandects, Pothier had remarked, that, whilst every contract possesses a character which is peculiar to it, all contracts have certain relations in common. He undertook, therefore, to collect together all the doctrines possessing this general character, and to form from them a kind of prototype, applicable to all particular agreements, and to the obligations derived from them. The result of these labors was the treatise on obligations. In this work, he considers agreements in themselves,—in their elementary formation,—in their different modalities,—in their execution,—and, finally, in their manner of dissolution; and, in treating all these matters, he considers them, as he expresses it, according to the rules of the forum of conscience, as well as of the exterior forum. "Thus," continues his editor, Dupin, from whom the above description is taken, "this immortal work is not only a good book of law, but an excellent book of morals; a work of all countries and of all nations; a book, to which antiquity can present no rival but the Offices of Cicero, and which has no superior but the Gospel, and that because the gospel is the very word of God."

In the treatise on obligations, the general rules relating to all contracts are treated of. It was immediately followed by treatises on particular contracts, in which those general rules are applied. The work on obligations, therefore, and those on contracts, are the complements of each other; and neither without the other can be said to be complete. It is the purpose of the present undertaking to furnish the American lawyer with the necessary supplement to the work on obligations, in a translation of the treatises on those contracts, which are known in our legal system, and which may be supposed to possess some value to a student of the English and American law.

It would not be difficult to show the importance of a knowledge of these works, by reasons drawn from considerations of the utility of the study of the Roman law, in general; but, waving all these, a further inducement to this publication is presented by the fact, that the existing laws of all that part of the United States, which was purchased of France during the administration of Mr. Jefferson, as well as the laws of the British province of Lower Canada, have their foundation in the laws of France, prior to her revolution; so that the works of Pothier possess an authority, in these portions of the American continent, analogous to that of the books of the common law, in others.

The treatises on contracts, of which it is proposed to publish a translation, are the following, namely: sale, letting to hire, exchange, partnership, beneficence, (including loan for use, loan for consumption, deposit, mandate, &c.) insurance, bottomry, play and pledge; together with the author's general observation on the treatises on obligations and contracts. The late edition of Pothier's works, published by Dupin, has been followed in the translation.

The present volume contains the treatise on the

contract of sale. If the reception of it shall be such as to warrant the belief, that the plan of this publication meets with the favor of the profession, a second volume will follow, containing the contracts of letting to hire and of partnership. The other contracts mentioned above will be comprised in two or possibly three additional volumes. If the plan should be executed, the last volume will also contain a glossary of those terms and phrases of the Roman and French law, which occur in the translated works, and a bibliographical account of the works referred to or cited by the author.

The style of Pothier, though somewhat diffuse, is characterized by great clearness, simplicity and precision; and, in the translation, it has been found impossible to condense the language materially, without, at the same time, obscuring the meaning in an equal degree.

The author's mode of referring to the several parts of the Corpus Juris Civilis has been changed for that now more generally in use, whenever the change could be made without inconvenience; and where the old mode has been preserved, the references have been rendered more intelligible, by the addition of the book, title, &c., of the text referred to, nserted in a parenthesis.

It has not been thought worth while to translate the Latin quotations, which so frequently occur, for the reason, that, besides the difficulty of rendering these isolated passages into English with the desirable exactness, the author himself almost always precedes or follows them with a paraphrase in his own language.

The orderly arrangement and scientific division and treatment of subjects, by which the works of Pothier are almost pre-eminently distinguished, render it quite unnecessary for one who has read them, to look beyond the table of contents, in order to refer to any part that he may be in search of; but, for the convenience of those, who may desire to consult the works now proposed to be published, without the trouble of a previous perusal, copious indexes will be added to each volume.

The writings of Pothier differ in one respect, which has already been alluded to, from those of all other writers on municipal law. He considers every subject, both in conscience and in law; or, as he most frequently expresses himself, as well according to the rules of the forum of conscience, as of the exterior forum; and many doctrines, which were promulgated by the Roman jurists as obligatory in law, are stated by Pothier as obligatory only in conscience, and not susceptible of application in the civil tribunals. This distinction, which seems to have been sometimes overlooked, by those who have cited Pothier's works in our courts, should be constantly kept in mind by the reader. The expressions, "forum of conscience," and "exterior forum," are not used by Pothier in a sense so entirely metaphorical, as might at first seem to be the case. His works were intended for the use of both the clerical and legal professions,—for the ecclesiastic, as well as the lawyer; and, by the forum of conscience he sometimes means the confessional, as by the exterior forum he intends a legal tribunal. The following extract from the treatise on the contract of letting to hire affords a very clear example of the author's use of both these terms. "The letting of masks and ball dresses is a valid contract in the exterior forum, the use for which these things are let not being prohibited by the secular laws. But the severity of the maxims of the gospel not permitting balls and other similar diversions, there can be no doubt, that, in the forum of conscience, the business carried on by persons who let these sorts of things is improper and unlawful, and that the gain derived therefrom is an unlawful gain, of which they ought not to profit. Such persons, therefore, should not be absolved, but upon their promise to renounce the business, and to employ in alms the gain which they have made by it."

The translator hopes that his work will be found to be exact; he very early in his professional life began the study of these writings; he has devoted to it some portion of the leisure hours of many years; and he has aimed, in the following pages, to furnish his professional brethren with a translation, which shall not be unworthy of their approbation or of the fame of the author.

L. S. C.

Boston,
March, 1839.

TABLE OF CONTENTS.

PART THIRD.

OF THE ENGAGEMENTS OF THE BUYER.

PART FOURTH.

PART FIFTH.

OF THE EXECUTION AND DISSOLUTION OF THE CONTRACT OF SALE.

PART SIXTH.

OF PROMISES TO SELL AND TO BUY; OF EARNEST; AND OF SOME PARTICULAR KINDS OF SALE.

PART SEVENTH.

OF ACTS AND CONTRACTS RESEMBLING THE CONTRACT OF SALE.

* According to the division made by the author of part sixth (p. 292) what is here inserted as Article II. of the third chapter should have been entitled Chapter IV. and the following chapter should have been Chapter V. The mistake is so entirely harmless, that, in order to avoid confusion, it has been thought best to follow the original.

CONTRACT OF SALE.

PRELIMINARY ARTICLE.

The contract of sale is a contract, by which one of the contracting parties, called the seller, enters into an obligation to the other, *to cause him to have freely by a title of proprietor*, a thing, for the price of a certain sum of money, which the other contracting party, called the buyer, on his part, obliges himself to pay.

I have said, *to cause him to have by a title of proprietor.* These terms, which answer to the *præstare emptori rem habere licere*, of the Roman law, comprise an obligation to deliver the thing to the buyer, and also an obligation, when it has been delivered, to defend him against all claims, which may deprive him of his possession, or prevent him from making use of the thing as his own; but they do not, in strictness, import an obligation to transfer the property: *Hactenus tenetur ut rem emptori habere liceat, non etiam, ut ejus faciat;* l. 30, § 1, D. *de act. empt.* (19, 1, 30, § 1). And therefore, if a buyer discovers, that the seller was not the owner of the thing sold, and consequently that the property in it has not been transferred to him, he cannot, on that account, so long as his possession remains undisturbed, complain that the seller has not fulfilled his obligation.

It is indeed of the essence of the contract of sale, that the seller should not intend to retain the right of property in the thing, when he is the owner of it; and that in such case, he should be bound to transfer it to the buyer: *Nemo potest videri eam rem vendidisse de cujus dominio id agitur, ne ad emptorem transeat: sed hoc aut locatio est, aut aliud genus contractus*, l. 80, D. § *fin. de contr. empt.* (18, 1, 80, § 3). But when the seller is not the owner, if he in good faith believes himself to be so, he is bound only, as above stated, to defend the buyer against those, who seek to deprive him of his possession, or to prevent him from exercising the rights of ownership.

The following Treatise is divided into seven parts, viz.: *first*, of the nature of the contract of sale and of that which constitutes the substance of it; *second*, of the obligations of the seller, and the actions which result therefrom; *third*, of the obligations of the buyer; *fourth*, at whose risk the thing sold remains during the intermediate time between the contract and the delivery; *fifth*, of the execution and dissolution of the contract of sale; *sixth*, of some particular kinds of sale; and, *seventh*, of some contracts and transactions resembling or preparatory to the contract of sale.

PART FIRST.

OF THE NATURE OF THE CONTRACT OF SALE, AND OF THAT WHICH CONSTITUTES ITS SUBSTANCE.

SECTION FIRST.

Of the nature of this contract.

2. This contract is entirely of natural right; for not only does it owe its origin to that right, but it is governed solely by rules drawn therefrom. It is of the number of those, which are called *consensual* contracts; for it is formed by the mere consent of the contracting parties: It is a *synallagmatic* contract, that is to say, it contains a reciprocal engagement of each of the contracting parties, one towards the other, according to the definition above given: And it is a *commutative* contract, in which the intention of each of the parties is to receive as much as he gives.

SECTION II.

Of that which constitutes the substance of the contract of sale.

3. Three things are necessary to the contract of sale; a thing which makes the object of it, a price agreed, and the consent of the contracting parties.

ARTICLE FIRST.

Of the thing.

4. In the first place, there must be a thing, which may be sold, and which may make the object of the contract; and, therefore, if I, being ignorant that my horse is dead, sell

him, there will be no contract of sale, in such case, for want of a thing which may be the object of it. For the same reason, if I, being with you at Paris, sell you a house situated at Orleans, both of us being ignorant that it is then destroyed by fire, either wholly or for the greater part, such contract is void, because the house, which makes the object of it, does not exist; the ground upon which it stood and the part of it which is not destroyed not constituting the thing about which we contracted, but rather the remains of that thing; l. 57, D. *de contr. empt.* (18, 1, 57). If the greater part of the house escape from the flames, so that it cannot be denied, that the thing about which we contracted is in existence, though somewhat diminished; the contract, in such case, is valid, at least in strictness of law, and provided the seller makes a deduction from the price, in proportion to the part destroyed, which the parties believed to exist; *dict. l. 57.* Nevertheless, upon the supposition that the buyer would not have been willing to make the purchase, if he had known that the house was not entire, equity requires that he should be permitted to demand a dissolution of the contract; *arg.* l. 58, *dict. tit.*

5. There cannot, in truth, be a contract of sale, without a thing sold; but it is sufficient that the thing sold may exist, though it has no present existence. Thus, it is common, before harvest, to sell the wine, which we may make; and, in such case, there is a sufficient thing to constitute the object of a valid contract, though as the thing sold does not yet exist, the contract depends upon the condition of its future existence; and if it should not happen to exist, that is, if no wine should be made, there will be no sale.

6. It is not necessary, that the thing sold should be a physical being. An incorporeal thing, a moral being, a credit, a right, &c., may be the object of this contract. So, even a mere expectation may be sold; and, therefore, if a fisherman, for an agreed price, sells the casting of his net,

this will be a true contract of sale, even if there should be no fish taken; for the expectation of those, which might have been taken, is a moral being, capable of appreciation, which may be the object of a contract; D. 18, 1, 8, § 1.

This kind of sale gave rise to the famous controversy related by Plutarch, in his life of Solon. Some Milesians, being at the island of Chios, purchased of some fishermen there, the casting of their net. The fishermen drew up a golden tripod, and the buyers laid claim to it. In this case, the claim of the buyers was not well founded, for they did not intend to buy, nor did the sellers intend to sell, any thing except the fish which might be taken. The tripod, which was not in the contemplation of either of the parties, and could not consequently make a part of their agreement, was a piece of good luck, of which the fishermen alone ought to have the benefit. This decision is more conformable to justice than that of the oracle, which, being consulted on the occasion, adjudged the tripod to the wisest of mortals; in order, that as neither party would dare to lay claim to that quality, it should remain with the priests.

7. A valid contract of sale may be made, not only in relation to a thing, which belongs to the seller, but also to one which does not belong to him, and even without the consent of the owner. It is true, that, in the latter case, the seller cannot transfer the property in the thing, according to the rule of law: *Nemo plus juris ad alium transferre potest quam ipse haberet;* D. 50, 17, 54. But the contract of sale does not consist in a transfer of the property in the thing sold. It is sufficient, in order to render it valid, that the seller should be legally bound to cause the buyer to have the thing, which he undertakes to sell to him; and his obligation to that effect is equally binding upon him, though, by reason of the refusal of the owner, to consent to the sale, he may not have it in his power to perform it; for, if the promise of the seller be to do an act, which is possible in

itself, the promise is valid, though he may be unable to perform it; and it is his own fault, if he rashly oblige himself beyond his power; Treatise on Obl. n. 133, 136. This decision agrees with that of Ulpian, in the law 28, D. *de contrah. empt.* (18, 1, 28,): *Rem alienam distrahere quem posse nulla dubitatio est: nam emptio est et venditio: sed res emptori auferri potest.*

8. A valid sale cannot be made of a thing which belongs to the buyer: *Suæ rei emptio non valet, sive sciens, sive ignorans emi;* D. 18, 1, 16. The reason is, that the contract of sale, according to the definition above given, consists in an obligation on the part of the seller, to cause the buyer to have the thing; or, in other words, it consists in rendering the buyer a creditor of that thing; but it is evident, that this cannot take place, in regard to a thing, which belongs to the buyer; for no person can be a creditor of his own property; nor can the buyer require the seller to cause him to have a thing, which he already has.

Though a man cannot buy a thing of which he is owner, yet if his title be defective, he may buy that which is wanting to make it perfect. In like manner, if another person have some right in reference to a thing which belongs to me, as, for example, if he be my creditor for it, a sale of it by him to me will be valid, and will be considered as a sale of his right merely.

From this principle, results the decision of the following question. A testator, whose heir I am, devises a house, which belongs to me, to James, and before a delivery of it, James sells it to me. This estate, which I believed to belong to me in full property, was in fact reversible, and at the end of the time of the reversion, I suffer an eviction thereof. Am I, in this case, entitled to an action of warranty against James? I am not; for James, in selling me my house, which had been bequeathed to him by one whose heir I am, has sold me the right, which he had in reference to my house, rather than the house itself, which he could not properly sell to me *quum rei suæ emptio esse non possit;* and the eviction, therefore, is not properly an eviction of the thing sold, and consequently does not give rise to the action *de evictione* against him. Nevertheless, as the reversionary claim, of which we were ignorant, was an incumbrance upon the estate, which, by lessening its value, lessened also the value of James's right in relation to it, which I have purchased; I am entitled to the action *ex empto* against him, to compel him to reduce the price to the sum for which I might have purchased his right, if I had known of the incumbrance.

When I purchase a thing, which already belongs to me, of one to whom I am the debtor of it, it has been observed, that it is his right rather than my own property, which I am considered as purchasing; because, during the subsistence of my title as owner, I cannot buy it, nor can the seller bind himself to cause me to have that which is already mine, according to the rule of law: *Non ut ex pluribus causis idem nobis deberi potest, ita ex pluribus causis idem possit nostrum esse;* D. 50, 17, 159. *Dominium non potest nisi ex una causa contingere;* D. 41, 2, 3, § 4. But when my title as owner is destroyed, though I still remain the proprietor, as it were, until the redelivery which I am bound to make to him, to whom the thing reverts by the extinction of my title, a sale by him to me will be a true sale of it; for the title, in virtue of which it previously belonged to me, being destroyed, such sale becomes the title, in virtue of which, it will from that time belong to me; and, therefore, if you make me a donation of an estate, which donation subsequently becomes revoked by the birth of a child, and before a re-entry on your part, you sell me the same estate; such sale, though in some sort of my property, is a true and valid sale of the estate, and constitutes the title, in virtue of which, it will, from that time, belong to me, my former title being destroyed by the contingency to which the donation was subject.

9. Though a man cannot unconditionally become the purchaser of his own property, yet he may buy a thing which is his own, upon condition and in case that it cease to belong to him: *Existimo posse me id, quod meum est sub conditione emere, quia forte speratur meum esse desinere;* D. 18, 1, 61. For example, if I am the owner of a house, included in a substitution with which I am charged in your favor, I may purchase it upon the condition and in case of the opening of the substitution, though until that event, I am the proprietor. But if I unconditionally buy my own property, the contract is void, and will not become valid, though it afterwards cease to belong to me.

10. We are not at liberty to sell those things, which, by their nature, are out of commerce, as a church, a cemetery, a public place, a benefice, an office not venal, &c. When things, which are *divini juris*, as a chapel, or a right of patronage and of presentation to benefices, make a part of the dependencies of an estate, they cannot indeed be sold alone and *per se;* but they may be sold with the land to which they belong, whether expressed in the contract, or included under the general expression of dependencies; *arg.* D. 18, 1, 22 & 24.

11. There are also certain things, the sale of which is prohibited by the laws, on account of their being injurious to health. For example, grain, which has been covered by an inundation, is not allowed to be sold; and, upon the information of a physician, that it is unwholesome, may be destroyed. Butchers, poulterers, and victuallers are prohibited from selling measled pork, or the flesh of an animal, which has died of disease; vintners and taverners are also prohibited from selling adulterated wines, or beer made of bad materials.

By a declaration of the king, made March 23, 1728, the

sale of poinards, knives in the shape of poinards, pocket pistols, sword-canes, and other secret offensive weapons, was prohibited. By an edict of July, 1682, the sale of poisons, not used in the composition of medicine, was prohibited; and, in regard to those, which were used in that manner, they were allowed to be sold only to those persons, who were in a situation and of the proper profession to employ them, and who were required to write their names, quality, and residence, together with a memorandum of the quantity of the article taken, in a book kept by the seller.

12. There was a law of police among the Romans, which prohibited the sale of any kind of materials, united and incorporated with the privileges of a city, so long as they were so united; and, consequently, a sale of such things was void; D. 18, 1, 52. This regulation does not exist in our laws.

13. We are not permitted, either by ourselves or by the interposition of other persons, to buy those things, which we hold in trust; thus, a tutor cannot buy the property of the minor under his care; nor can an administrator become the purchaser of any of the goods of which he has the administration: *Tutor rem pupilli emere non potest, idemque porrigendum est ad similia: id est ad curatores, procuratores, et qui aliena negotia gerunt;* D. 18, 1, 34, § 7.

A sale of this description is not absolutely void, like that of things which are out of commerce, or which are forbidden to be sold; but it may be avoided, against the tutor or other administrator, and for the benefit of the minor or other person, to whom the property belongs, who alone is entitled to avoid the sale; for if he find the contract advantageous to him, he may abide by it, and, in that case, the other party, who has made the purchase, cannot object.

This rule is established only for the purpose of preventing those frauds, by means of which a tutor for his own advantage might either purchase the property of his ward at a mean price, or might become the purchaser of things which it is not for the interest of his ward should be sold; and its operation ceases, when there is no interest on the part of the tutor to lead to a suspicion of such fraudulent intention; and, upon this ground, it is decided, that a tutor may bid upon and become the purchaser of goods seized by a creditor of the minor under his care: *Si creditor rem pupilli distrahat, tutor emere bona fide poterit;* D. 26, 8, 5, § 5. *Tutor nihil ex bonis pupilli comparare palam, et bona fide prohibetur;* C. 4, 38, 5.

14. Among things which cannot be sold, are reckoned also the inheritances and other immovables of minors, of persons under an interdict, of the church, and of corporations (*corps*) and municipal bodies (*communautes*). Property of this kind cannot be sold, except for just cause, in virtue of a judicial decree, and attended by a due observance of certain preliminary formalities.

A sale of property of this description is, in like manner, not absolutely void. It is valid as against the buyer, but may be annulled at the election of the minor, the person interdicted, the church, corporation or community, for whose benefit the prohibition exists. If, however, the minor, after his arrival at full age, the interdicted person, after the interdict is removed, or their heirs, ratify the contract, either expressly, or impliedly by not taking out letters of rescission within the time prescribed by law, the sale will then become binding upon them.

15. Domat improperly reckons among things, which cannot be sold, those which are charged with a substitution. It is true, that when such things are sold, they cannot pass to the buyer in any other manner, than as subject to the substitution, since the seller cannot transfer any other or greater right than he himself has. But the sale is valid, and the more so, because the substitution may become void, by the previous decease of those who are named in it. The law

fin. Cod. de re. alien. non alienand. (4, 51, 7,) cited by Domat, does not refer to all substitutions, but only to those which result from a testamentary prohibition, made by a testator, against the alienation of a particular thing out of his family; and it does not say that the sale of such a thing is not valid. It merely declares, that the alienation of it is not valid, that is to say, that the sale does not transfer the property to the buyer, because it is itself the condition which opens the substitution, and causes the property to pass to those who are named in it.

ARTICLE II.

Of the Price.

16. The second thing requisite to the formation of a contract of sale is, that there should be a price agreed upon between the parties: *Sine pretio nulla venditio est;* l. 2, § 1, D. *de contrah. empt.* (18, 1, 2, § 1). And, therefore, if a man sell me a thing, for the price which it cost him, and it in fact cost him nothing, but was given to him, there will be no sale, because there is no price; l. 37, *dict. tit.*

17. The price necessary to a contract of sale ought to have three qualities; 1, it ought to be a serious price; 2, it should be certain and determined, or, at least, capable of determination; and, 3, it should consist of a sum of money.

§ 1. Of the first quality of the price.

18. The price must be a serious price and agreed upon with an intention that it shall be exacted; and, therefore, if a man sells me a thing for a certain sum, which, by the contract, is remitted to me, this act is not a sale, but a donation: *Quum in venditione quis pretium rei ponit, donationis causa non exacturus, non videtur vendere;* D. 18, 1, 36.

The reason is, that the price, requisite to the existence of a contract of sale, is a serious price, which the buyer obliges himself to pay, according to the definition already given of the contract of sale, *supra*, n. 1; but, in this case, as the buyer is never obliged to pay the price, which is supposed to be remitted to him, at the time of the conclusion of the act, there is no real price, and consequently no contract of sale.

It would be otherwise, if the release of the price were made *ex intervallo;* for, in that case, there would once have been a price, really incumbent upon the buyer to pay, which is sufficient to constitute the contract: *Non (enim) pretii numeratio, sed conventio perficit emptionem;* D. 18, 1, 2, § 1.

19. A price, which bears no proportion to the actual value of the thing sold, is not a real price; as if one sells a considerable tract of land for a crown; for, as the price is only the estimation of the parties in regard to the value of the thing, a sum, which bears no proportion to that value, cannot pass for a serious estimation, nor consequently for a real price. Such a contract is not a sale but a donation falsely called a sale, which ought to be subjected to all the formalities required in donations; and cannot be valid, unless made between persons, who may legally make and receive donations.

20. It is not necessary, however that the sum agreed upon as the price should be exactly equal to the just value of the thing. For the price in this contract is not the true value of the thing; but the sum at which the parties estimate it, and it may happen that their estimation is too low. For this reason, if the sum agreed upon is not merely nominal, or one which bears no proportion to the value of the thing, though it is below it, the contract will be a real contract of sale, of which that sum is the price.

21. Thus, if the seller is willing to do the buyer a favor, by consenting that the price shall be estimated at a sum

below the just value, this will not prevent the contract from being a true contract of sale: *Si quis donationis causa minoris vendat, venditio valet: toties enim dicimus in totum venditionem non valere, quoties universa venditio donationis causa facta est: quoties vero viliore pretio res donationis causa distrahitur, dubium non est venditionem valere;* D. 18, 1, 38. It must be remarked, however, that in this case, the contract is not purely and wholly a contract of sale, but one of a mixed nature, which partakes in some degree of a donation, but which, nevertheless, in regard to the principal intention of the parties, is a sale rather than a donation.

In like manner, inferiority of price does not prevent the contract from being a true contract of sale, when the parties are ignorant of the actual value, or when the seller, though he knows the real value, is obliged, by his need of money, to sell the thing at any price, however small, which may be offered him. But the contract, in the last case, though valid in strictness of law, and accompanied by all the obligations, which result from a contract of sale, is nevertheless unjust; and the buyer ought, in the forum of conscience, to repair its injustice, by supplying what is wanting to make the price a just one. And even in the exterior forum, the laws sometimes come to the assistance of the seller by letters of rescission, to rescind the agreement, when the lesion is enormous, as we shall see in the fourth part of this treatise.

22. It must be observed, that, to the validity of a contract of sale, which is made for a mean price, it is necessary, that the buyer should be a person to whom the seller is not prohibited from making a donation; for, otherwise, the meanness of the price will always create a presumption, that it is the intention of the parties to make a donation, and will render the contract void.

§ II. Second quality of the price.

23. The price, which is of the essence of the contract of sale, must be certain and determined. It is not necessary, however, that it should be absolutely determined, provided it is capable of determination, and not left in the power of one of the parties.

24. For this reason, a valid sale may be made for a price to be fixed by a third person, provided, however, that such person make the estimation; for, if he die or refuse to act, there will be no sale, according to the decision of Justinian, in the last law of the Code, *de contrah. empt.* (4, 38, 15,) because there is no price. The parties being agreed only upon the price, which shall be established by this person, it cannot be said, that they are willing, on his default, to submit themselves to the estimation of another. They repose their confidence only in him. In accordance with this principle, by a decision of the parliament of Bordeaux, cited by Automne, *ad leg. fin. Cod. de contrah. empt.* (4, 38, 15,) a seller, in a similar case, was discharged from the claim, brought against him by the buyer, to compel him to agree upon another estimator.

If the third person agreed upon makes an estimation which is manifestly unjust, there will be no sale. Such an estimation is the same as none at all; for the parties, in submitting to his opinion, did not intend an arbitrary but a just estimation, *tanquam boni viri.* This is the opinion of the Gloss, *ad. dict. leg.* (C. 4, 38, 15,) and is more equitable than that of Despeisses, who, relying upon these terms of the law, *Omnimodo secundum æstimationem pretium solvatur*, considers the parties to be bound by the estimation whatever it may be.

If either of the parties thinks the estimation unjust, he may require a new one to be made, at his own expense, by skilful persons (*experts*) appointed by the court; and, if, by their estimation, the first appears to be unjust, it will be void, and there will be no contract of sale. Inasmuch, however, as the valuation of things admits of some variation, the difference between that of the person agreed upon by the parties, and that made by the order of court, must be not merely trifling, but very considerable, in order to cause the former to be declared unjust. Ought this difference to be equal to the half, according to the rule in the Gloss, or the third, or the fourth part? I think it should be left to the discretion of the judge.

25. There may also be a sale of a thing, for such a price, as may be determined by experts, to be appointed by the parties; and, in such case, though the price is not certain, at the time of the contract, yet it is capable of being made so, by the estimation. Some interpreters pretend that such a contract is innominate, giving rise to an action *præscriptis verbis*, and similar to but not itself constituting a contract of sale. But these subtle distinctions are not recognised in our law, and are not used in practice.

26. There is more difficulty in the case of a sale, *for the price which a thing is worth.* Nevertheless, as agreements are to be construed, *magis ut valeant, quam ut pereant*, the parties must be considered, by these terms, as agreeing upon a price, equal to the value to be estimated by experts appointed by themselves, as in the preceding case.

27. Fabian de Monte, in his treatise *de empt. vend.*, which is to be found in the first part of the sixth volume of the grand collection,[1] folio 53, *recto*, proposes the following question, namely, whether an agreement purporting to

[1] The collection of law tracts, referred to by the author, in the above passage and elsewhere, as the "grand collection," bears the following title, in Dupin's edition of Camus's *Bibliothequé Choisie des Livres de Droit:*

Tractatus universi juris, duce et auspice Gregorio XIII. P. M. in unum congesti .... XVIII. materias 25 voluminibus comprehendens. Venetiis, Fr. Ziletus, 1584, 22 vol. in fol.

This collection contains 715 tracts, the names of the authors and the titles of which are given by Dupin. T.

be a sale by one of the parties, of a certain thing, for such a price as shall be offered him for it, constitutes a valid contract of sale? And, upon the authority of the law *fin. Cod. de jur. emphyt.*, (4, 66, 3,) which has no application to the question, he decides it in the affirmative. I do not think that such an agreement ought to be received in our courts, as a contract of sale. It would give rise to too many frauds. The buyer, in order to obtain the thing for a small sum, might bring forward a person, to offer a mean price; and the seller, with a view to obtain a large sum, might interpose an offer of a high price, in the same manner. Besides, if the seller should become unwilling to abide by the contract, he might conceal from the buyer the offers, which had been made him. Such an agreement, therefore, ought not to be considered as containing a contract of sale; but should rather be regarded as equivalent to a contract, by which the owner of an estate obliges himself, to give a particular person the preference, if he should conclude to sell it; and this obligation will bind him not to sell to any other person, until he has informed the other party of the offer made him, and required him to determine, within a short time, whether he will become the purchaser upon the terms proposed.

28. It is a mode of sale much used in our province of Orleans, for a man to sell the wine of his next harvest, at the price for which his neighbors may sell theirs. This contract is valid; for, though the price is uncertain at the time of the contract, it will be made certain by that which the neighbors may sell for; and it will not be the less certain, if they sell at different prices; for the parties, in that case, will be considered as having agreed upon the average price.

29. If a thing is sold for a price, to be fixed afterwards by one of the parties, the sale is void; D. 18, 1, 55.

§ III. Of the third quality of the price.

30. The price ought to consist of a sum of money, to be paid by the buyer to the seller; and if it consists of any other thing, the contract will not be a contract of sale, but rather of exchange: *Emptionem rebus fieri non posse pridem placuit;* C. 4, 64, 7. Yet, if, besides the sum of money agreed upon as the price, the buyer is bound, in addition thereto, to give or to do some other thing, the contract will not thereby be prevented from being a contract of sale: *Si vendidi tibi insulam certa pecunia, et ut aliam insulam meam reficeres, agam ex vendito, ut reficias; si hoc solum ut reficeres eam, convenisset, non intelligitur emptio venditio facta;* D. 19, 1, 6, § 1. It remains to be observed, that, if the parties agree upon a price in money, and the buyer afterwards gives something else in payment, and does not in fact pay any money, the contract will notwithstanding remain a contract of sale: *Non enim pretii numeratio, sed conventio perficit emptionem,* as has already been observed.

ARTICLE III.

Of the consent.

31. The consent of the parties, which is of the essence of the contract of sale, consists in a concurrence of the will of the seller, to sell a particular thing to the buyer, for a particular price, and of the buyer, to buy of him the same thing for the same price. How ought this consent to intervene, and in relation to what? These subjects are now to be examined.

§ I. Of the manner in which the consent ought to intervene.

32. In this contract, as in others, the consent of the parties may be manifested not only between those who are present together; but also between those who are at a distance

from each other, by means of letters, or through the intervention of an agent, *per epistolam, aut per nuntium.*

In order that the consent of the parties may take place, in the last mentioned case, it is necessary that the will of the party, who makes a proposition in writing, should continue until his letter reaches the other party, and until the other party declares his acceptance of the proposition.

This will is presumed to continue, if nothing appears to the contrary; but, if I write a letter to a merchant living at a distance, and therein propose to him, to sell me a certain quantity of merchandise, for a certain price; and, before my letter has time to reach him, I write a second, informing him that I no longer wish to make the bargain; or if I die; or lose the use of my reason; although the merchant, on the receipt of my letter, being in ignorance of my change of will, or of my death or insanity, makes answer that he accepts the proposed bargain; yet there will be no contract of sale between us; for, as my will does not continue until his receipt of my letter, and his acceptance of the proposition contained in it, there is not that consent or concurrence of our wills, which is necessary to constitute the contract of sale. This is the opinion of Bartholus and the other jurists cited by Bruneman, *ad* l. 1, § 2. D. *de contrah. empt.* (18, 1, 1, § 2), who very properly reject the contrary opinion of the Gloss, *ad dictam legem.*

It must be observed, however, that, if my letter causes the merchant to be at any expense, in proceeding to execute the contract proposed; or if it occasions him any loss, as, for example, if, in the intermediate time between the receipt of my first and that of my second letter, the price of that particular kind of merchandise falls, and my first letter deprives him of an opportunity to sell it before the fall of the price; in all these cases, I am bound to indemnify him, unless I prefer to agree to the bargain as proposed by my first letter. This obligation results from that rule of equity, that no person should suffer from the act of another: *Nemo ex alterius facto prægravari debet.* I ought therefore to indemnify him for the expense and loss, which I occasion him by making a proposition, which I afterwards refuse to execute.

For the same reason, if the merchant, on the receipt of my first letter, and before receiving the second which contains a revocation of it, or being in ignorance of my insanity or death, which prevents the conclusion of the bargain, charges to my account and forwards the merchandise; though, in that case, there cannot properly be a contract of sale between us, yet he will have a right to compel me or my heirs to execute the proposed contract, not in virtue of any contract of sale, but of my obligation to indemnify him, which results from the rule of equity above-mentioned.

33. The contract of sale may be made between persons who are present together, verbally and without writing; but care should be taken, that what is said expresses a sale and not a mere discourse in relation to a sale, which is not binding, and leaves them both at liberty to change their minds.

The doctors have agitated the question, whether a discourse, in which one of the parties says, "I am willing to sell you such a thing for such a price," and the other answers, "I am willing to pay the price," constitutes a perfect contract of sale. Cynus pretends, that this is nothing more than a mere discourse; because, that *to be willing to sell* is not to *sell,* any more than to be willing to climb a tree is actually climbing. Fabian de Monte (p. 54), on the contrary, maintains, with more reason, that this discourse expresses a perfect sale. He answers to the objection, that it is very true, that, to be willing to do a thing is not actually doing it, when that thing is some external act; as to be willing to climb a tree is not actually climbing it. But to be willing to do a thing, which is in fact done by the will to do it, without any external act, is actually doing it; and therefore, *to be willing to sell,* is the same thing as *to sell,* when the will of him, to whom I am willing to sell concurs with my own, and to say *I am willing to sell* is the same thing as to say *I sell.*

The same author observes, *ibid.*, that the decision ought to be different, if I express myself by the imperfect time, and, instead of saying, "I am willing to sell," should say, "I might be willing to sell you such a thing for so much:" because, says he, *verbum imperfecti temporis rem adhuc imperfectum significat:* and, therefore, in this case, though you answer, that you are willing to pay the price; there is yet no contract of sale, and I may change my mind, at least, if I do not reply to you, that *it is a settled affair*, or use some other equivalent expression.

§ II. In relation to what things there must be a consent.

34. The consent, necessary to the formation of a contract of sale, must intervene; 1, in relation to the thing which makes the object of the contract; 2, in relation to the price; and, 3, in relation to the sale itself.

In the first place, it must intervene concerning the thing, which makes the object of the contract. There is, therefore, no contract of sale, if one of the parties intend to sell one thing, and the other to purchase another; D. 18, 1, 9. In like manner, there is no contract of sale, if one sells me a sack of barley, which I take for corn; or a snuff box of pinchbec, which I take for gold: for, though, in these cases, we agree concerning the body which is sold, yet we do not agree concerning the matter of its substance; and, consequently, we cannot, with propriety, be said to be agreed in relation to the thing sold, according to Ulpian: *Nullam esse venditionem puto, quoties in materia erratur;* D. 18, 1, 9, § 2.

35. If the error relates only to some accidental quality of the thing, as if one sells cloth for *good*, which is in fact *bad;* this does not prevent the parties from being truly agreed, in respect to the thing sold; and, consequently, in such case,

there is a contract of sale; D. 18, 1, 10. An error in name only is of still less importance, and furnishes no obstacle to the consent necessary to the validity of the contract: *Nihil facit error nominis, quum de corpore constat;* D. 18, 1, 9, § 1.

36. The consent must also be manifested in reference to the price; and is wanting, when one of the parties intends to sell for a sum greater than that for which the other intends to buy. In that case, there can be no contract of sale for want of consent.

On the contrary, if one of the parties, by mistake, intends to buy for a sum greater than that for which the other is willing to sell; this is a valid contract of sale, for the sum for which the seller is willing to sell, and the parties are really agreed upon that sum; for it is included in the greater sum, for which the buyer is willing to buy; and he, who is willing to buy for the greater sum, is willing to buy for the less which is included in it.

37. Lastly, there must be a consent to the sale itself: *Si in ipsa emptione dissentiant, emptio imperfecta est;* D. 18, 1, 9, that is to say, one of the parties must be willing to sell, and the other to buy. But if the one party intends to sell a certain house for a certain price, for example, for nine thousand livres, and the other thinks only of hiring the house for nine years at that price; in this case, there is neither a contract of sale nor of letting to hire, for want of consent; for, one of the parties is willing only to sell, and the other is not willing to buy but to hire. It cannot be said, that he, who is willing to hire, must be much more willing to buy at the same price; for, not knowing that the other is willing to sell, he does not think of buying. It is true, only, that he might have been willing to buy, if he had known the other's wish to sell; which is quite different from being really willing to buy. This error is not like that, where one party is willing to buy for ten crowns, what the other is willing to sell for nine; for nine being contained

in ten, he who is willing to buy for ten is, without doubt, willing to buy for nine.

38. The consent of the parties, in relation to the sale itself, consisting in the concurrence of the seller's will to sell and that of the buyer to buy; there can be no contract of sale, if it appears from circumstances, that the intention of the parties is neither to buy nor to sell, but rather to disguise another contract under the false appearance of a contract of sale.

An example of this kind occurs in the famous contract, vulgarly known under the name of *mohatra*, by which one of the parties sells a thing to the other upon credit, and, immediately, or soon after, either by himself or by means of an agent, buys it back for a less sum, in ready money, than the price for which he sold it, for which the other party still remains his debtor. It is evident, that, in this case, there is no real intention to sell or to buy, but rather to disguise, under the false appearance of a sale, an usurious loan of the sum of money paid; and, therefore, if the seller demands the price, due in virtue of the pretended sale, the other party, (without regard to the contract, which is void,) will be entitled to be discharged from his demand, by paying the sum which he received.

A transaction of this nature may, under some circumstances, give rise to a prosecution against the seller, for usury; as, for instance, if there is a great difference between the price, for which the thing is sold upon credit, and that for which it is resold in ready money, so as to constitute enormous usury.

If contracts of this kind are to be considered usurious and to be condemned in a court of law, they are not the less so in the forum of conscience. The intention of the seller, not to be willing to lend the buyer, upon interest, the sum of money, which he needs, but to be willing to sell him an article upon credit, and to repurchase it for a less sum in ready money, is a mere delusion of avarice, which may deceive the parties, but cannot deceive God, who searches the bottom of our hearts, and who does not judge of our will by what we falsely imagine it to be, but by what we really determine upon in our hearts. Now, it cannot be doubted, that, in the case supposed, the real will of the seller, however he may deceive himself, is to get an usurious profit from the money which he pays the other party, by disguising a loan under the cover of false contracts of sale and resale of a commodity of which the latter has no need: *Deus non irridetur.*

39. When a sale is made for a mean price, to a person to whom the laws do not permit the seller to make a donation; the presumption is, that it is not his intention to sell, but to make a donation, under the false appearance of a contract of sale. Upon this principle, if a husband, for an inadequate price, sells an estate to his wife, whose property is separate and distinct from his, his heirs are admitted to reclaim the estate, without regard to the sale (which is to be considered as void), by merely offering to repay the purchase money to the wife.

Neratius, who was of the sect of the Proculeians, was of opinion, however, that we ought to inquire whether the husband really intended to sell, or to make a donation to his wife; that, in the latter case only, the sale ought to be considered void; and, that in the other, the heirs of the husband ought to be entitled to recover back so much only of the estate, as the purchase money falls short of a just price, the transaction, in that case, being considered as a donation only so far as a just price is wanting. This distinction of Neratius is good in theory; but, *in praxi*, and in the tribunals, to avoid the proceedings, to which an examination and discussion of the husband's intention would give rise, I think we should prefer the opinion of Julian and the Sabinians, who indirectly decide, that a sale made by a husband to his wife, for a mean price, should be considered as fraudulent and void. These two opinions are referred to in the law § 5. D. *de donat. int. vir. et ux.* (24, 1, 5, § 5). It appears, that that of the Sabinians prevailed; for, Ulpian, in the law 38, D. *de contrah. empt.* (18, 1, 38), after having said: *Si quis donationis causa minoris vendat, venditio valet,* says expressly, *hoc inter cæteros: inter virum vero et uxorem, donationis causa venditio facta pretio viliore, nullius momenti est.*

According to the same principle, if a father, for a mean price, sells an estate to one of his children, who afterwards comes to the succession, with his brothers and sisters; the sale is considered void, as a disguised donation, and the son is consequently obliged to bring the estate into the common stock, upon the condition of an allowance, out of the succession, equivalent to the price paid by him.

PART SECOND.

OF THE ENGAGEMENTS OF THE SELLER, AND OF THE ACTIONS WHICH RESULT THEREFROM.

40. The engagements of the seller result from the nature of the contract of sale; from the good faith, which ought to be observed in all contracts; and from the particular clauses of the contract.

CHAPTER FIRST.

Of the engagements of the seller which result from the nature of the contract.

41. The seller, according to the definition already given of the contract of sale, becomes thereby bound to the buyer, to cause him to have freely by a title of proprietor the thing sold; and, from thence, result: 1, an obligation to deliver the thing to the buyer, and, until the delivery, to watch over its preservation; 2, an obligation of warranty against evictions; 3, an obligation of warranty against real charges not declared by the contract; and, 4, an obligation of warranty against certain defects, which are called redhibitory.

SECTION FIRST.

Of the obligation to deliver the thing, and, until the delivery, to watch over its preservation.

The subject of this section is considered under the following divisions, namely: 1, what is comprised in the obligation to deliver the thing; 2, when and where it ought to be delivered; 3, what care the seller is bound to take in its preservation until the delivery; 4, when the extinction or loss of possession of the thing will discharge the seller from his obligation to deliver it; and, 5, of the action which results from this obligation.

ARTICLE FIRST.

What is comprised in the obligation to deliver the thing.

42. The seller is bound to deliver the thing to the buyer, if it is not already in his possession; and, as a necessary consequence of this obligation, to do, at his own expense, whatever may be necessary to enable him to perform it. If, therefore, the thing is pledged to a creditor of the seller, who has it in his possession, the seller is bound to redeem it at his own expense, in order to make the delivery. It is thus, that the law 5, C. *de evict.* (8, 45, 5), ought to be understood: *Ex his prædiis quæ mercata es, si aliqua a venditore obligata, necdum tibi tradita sunt, ex empto actione consequeris, ut ea a venditore liberentur.*

43. It follows, also, from the same principle, that, as the seller of wine of his own growth is not permitted to deliver it, without obtaining a license from the office of excise, he is bound, in order to put himself in a situation to perform his obligation, to procure the license at his own expense and to deliver it to the buyer, at least, if it is not expressly agreed that it shall be at the expense of the latter.

44. For the same reason, the seller of grain, at so much the *mine* (six bushels), ought to cause it to be measured at his own expense, according to an ancient ordinance of Saint Louis, of 1258, unless it is expressly agreed, that the measuring shall be at the expense of the buyer; for, as the delivery cannot take place, until the grain is measured, the seller must cause it to be done at his own expense, in order to put himself in a situation to make the delivery.

45. For the same reason, also, if one sells goods, which

are in a certain place, he is bound, either to cause the keys to be delivered to the buyer, or to provide some person to be at the place to open the warehouse to him, in order that he may take and carry away the merchandise.

46. The buyer must carry away the thing at his own expense; for the seller fully satisfies his obligation to deliver the thing, by doing what is incumbent on his part, to enable the buyer to carry it away when he pleases. The carrying it away is the business of the buyer.

47. The obligation to deliver a thing includes also that of delivering every thing which makes a part of or is an accessory to it. As to what things are considered as making a part of an estate in the country or of a house in the city, the reader is referred to the general introduction to the Custom of Orleans. The title deeds and all the evidences which relate to an inheritance are accessories, which the seller is bound to deliver to the buyer. The seller ought also, with the thing itself, to deliver its fruits, natural as well as civil, born and received subsequent to the payment of the price; Paul, *sentent.* 11, 17, 7; Cujas, *obs.* XXI. 15. This restitution of the fruits is due *ex natura contractus;* and, in order to establish the buyer's claim thereto, it is not necessary that the seller should be put in delay to deliver the thing sold. But the seller, before a delay, is bound only to account for the fruits, which he receives; whereas, after a delay, he is bound also to account even for fruits which he does not receive, provided the buyer might have received them.

48. Lastly, the delivery, to which the seller is bound, is one, which ought to transfer to the buyer all the right, which the former has in and in relation to the thing sold.

But the seller is not bound, in strictness, to transfer the property, if he is not the owner; but only to put the buyer in possession, and to defend him against all who may afterwards attempt to deprive him of it, or to set up any rights in the thing: *Hactenus tenetur ut rem emptori habere liceat, non etiam ut ejus faciat;* D. 19, 1, 30, § 1. And, therefore, if one, in good faith, sells and puts me in possession of an estate, of which he is not the owner, and I afterwards discover his want of title, yet I am not entitled to an action against him, so long as I remain undisturbed.

Against this opinion, it is common to quote the authority the last law D. *de condict. caus. dat.*, (12, 4, 16,) the answer to which is, that the paragraph referred to does not relate to a contract of sale, but to another kind of contract, *do ut des*, in which one of the parties is under an express obligation to the other, to transfer to him the ownership of the slave Stichus, which is the object of the contract.

Caillet, who was a professor at Poitiers, near the beginning of the seventeenth century, in an excellent commentary, *ad tit. Cod. de evict.*, (8, 45,) which is to be found in Meerman's Thesaurus, vol. ii., *ad* l. 5, *dict. tit.*, says, that the doctrine of the Roman jurists, that a seller is not, in strictness, obliged to transfer the property of the thing, is a purely arbitrary principle adopted by them, which has no foundation in nature, and which ought not to be adopted in our practice. But he cites no authority for this opinion. The principle, however, seems to me to be founded in the nature of the contract, and in the terms which we are accustomed to apply to it. We say that the seller *sells;* and, to explain this term, we add, that he *yields, quits and delivers*, and promises to warrant and defend the buyer against all disturbances. These terms do not import any other obligation contracted by the seller, than that of yielding to the buyer all the right which he has in the thing, by delivering it to him, and of defending him against all disturbances, to which his possession may be subjected. They do not express any obligation to transfer the property of the thing.

ARTICLE II.

Of the time and place of delivery.

§ I. Of the time.

49. In order that the seller may perform his engagement, it is not sufficient that he should be merely ready to deliver the thing; he must actually deliver it, at the time and place, when and where it ought to be delivered.

If the parties by the contract agree upon a term, within which the delivery is to be made, it must be made accordingly; and, if the buyer, in consequence of the seller's neglect to deliver it within the term, suffers any inconvenience, he will be entitled to recover his damages (*dommages et intérèts*) against the latter. If, however, the seller is prevented, by any unforeseen accident, from making the delivery at the time, he will not be liable; as, for example, if a carpenter sells me a wine press, which is to be made and delivered for the next vintage, and he is prevented by sudden and severe sickness, from making the delivery at the appointed time, and also, from giving me notice, in order that I may furnish myself elsewhere, he will not, in such case, be liable for the damage which I sustain; Dumoulin: *de eo quod int. n.* 187.

Though, according to the principles of law, the lapse of the term alone is sufficient to put the seller in delay, and to subject him to the buyer's claim for damages; yet, in our practice, the seller ought to be called upon by a judicial interpellation, that is to say, by an assignation or summons.

50. When there is no time agreed upon by the contract, the seller is bound to deliver the thing immediately, upon demand and payment, or an offer of payment, of the price, by the buyer; unless there is some just cause for delay.

§ II. Of the place.

51. When the place of delivery is agreed upon, it must be made at that place. The buyer is not obliged to receive the thing, nor the seller to deliver it, elsewhere.

52. If no place is agreed upon, the delivery must be made at the place where the thing is. The buyer must send and take it. The seller cannot, without just cause, after the sale, remove the thing to another place, where the delivery is more incommodious and expensive to the buyer; and, if he does so, he will be bound to indemnify the latter, for the additional trouble and expense, which he may be thereby obliged to incur.

ARTICLE III.

Of the obligation to keep the thing until the delivery.

53. The obligation contracted by the seller, *præstare emptori rem habere licere*, manifestly includes an obligation to watch over the preservation of the thing, until the delivery.

54. What degree of diligence is he bound to exert? It is sufficient if he uses common and ordinary diligence. The most exact is not required of him. This is decided by the law 35, § 4, D. *de contrah. empt.* (18, 1, 35, § 4), and is conformable to the principle: *In contractibus in quibus utriusque contrahentis utilitas versatur, levis culpa, non etiam levissima, præstatur; arg.* D. 13, 6, 5, § 2.

55. This obligation, to watch over the preservation of the thing, ceases when the buyer is in delay to carry it away; for, as it is a consequence of the obligation to deliver the thing, it is terminated by a delivery; and the seller ought therefore to be discharged from it, when it is not his fault, that the thing is not delivered. It ought not to be in the power of the buyer, by wilfully delaying the delivery, to prolong the seller's obligation to keep the thing.

Though the seller, in such case, is discharged from his

obligation to keep the thing, yet he is not thereby liberated from the requisites of good faith in relation to it: *Quum moram emptor adhibere cœperit, jam non culpam, sed dolum tantum prœstandum a venditore;* D. 18, 6, 17: and, therefore, if the seller, after the buyer is in delay to carry away the thing, maliciously suffers it to perish or be destroyed, he will be liable for the loss. He will also be responsible for gross negligence or fault, which is equivalent to malice, and is contrary to good faith: *Lata culpa dolo comparatur;* D. 11, 6, 1, § 1: *Dissoluta negligentia, prope dolum est;* D. 17, 1, 29, *in pr.* For example, if a merchant, to whom I have made a sale of wine, is in delay to receive it, and, in consequence, my obligation to keep it is discharged, and it becomes at his risk; yet, if I am informed that it is in imminent danger of loss, and, being on the spot, and having the means, I neglect to preserve it, this is such deliberate negligence on my part, as is equivalent to malice, and will render me liable for the loss.

ARTICLE IV.

When the extinction or loss of possession of the thing will discharge the seller's obligation to deliver it.

§ I. Of the loss or extinction of the thing.

56. According to the principles established in the Treatise on Obligations, part 3, ch. 6, if one sells a specific thing, the obligation to deliver it is an obligation of a thing certain, and will be extinguished, if the thing perishes without the fault of the seller, and before he is put in delay to deliver it; for, there can be no debt, when there is no longer a thing which is due. If any part of the thing remains, the seller will be bound to deliver that part.

57. If the thing perishes by the act or fault of the seller, his obligation is not discharged; but he becomes liable for

the damages resulting from the loss; this is a consequence of his obligation to preserve the thing, which is accessory to that of delivering it. He is also liable, if it perishes by the act of another person, for whose acts he is responsible, as, for example, if it perishes by the act of any of his domestic servants; Tr. on Obl. n. 456. But if it is destroyed by the act of a stranger, which it is not in the power of the seller to prevent, the latter is discharged from his obligation; and is only bound to substitute the buyer in his rights and actions against the wrong doer.

58. These principles prevail, if the thing perishes before the debtor is in delay to deliver it; but if it perishes after he is put in delay, even without any fault on his part, and by an irresistible force, he will, notwithstanding, be liable in some cases for the loss; for, if the thing would not equally have perished in the possession of the buyer, if it had been delivered to him, at the time the seller was summoned to deliver it, the latter will be bound to pay the value to the buyer. The reason, as is explained in the Treatise on Obligations, n. 663, is, that a creditor ought not to suffer from the delay of his debtor: *Mora debitoris non debet esse creditori damnosa;* and, therefore, if, after I am in delay to deliver a horse which I have sold you, my stable is struck by lightning, and the horse is killed, I am responsible for the loss; for it would not have happened, if I had delivered the horse.

But, notwithstanding the thing perishes after a delay, if it would have equally perished, in the possession of the buyer, the seller is not liable for the loss, but is equally discharged from his obligation; for, it cannot be said, in that case, that the buyer sustains any injury by the delay; as, for example, if a horse, which is sold, after the seller is in delay to deliver him, die of a colic or other disease, which he would equally have had, in the possession of the buyer; Tr. on Obl. n. 664.

Nevertheless, if the buyer were a dealer, who purchased the horse to sell again, the seller would be liable, even in the case above stated, for the loss of the horse; for the buyer might have sold him before his sickness; and, consequently, it cannot be said, that he would have perished equally in the possession of the buyer; *Ibid.*

§ II. Of the case in which the thing sold ceases to be an article of commerce.

59. When the thing sold, after the contract, ceases to be an article of commerce, as when a piece of land, which I have purchased, is taken by public authority to make a highway, the obligation to deliver it ceases and becomes extinct; and the seller is only bound to substitute me in his right of indemnification against the king, provided the king think proper to grant one; Tr. on Obl. n. 650.

§. III. Of the case, in which the seller loses possession of the thing sold, subsequent to the contract.

60. Though the thing sold remains in existence and is not out of commerce, yet, if the seller loses possession of it, after the contract, by means of some newly occurring cause, which he is not able to prevent, as if it is taken from him by violence, his obligation to deliver it ceases, and he is bound only to substitute the buyer in his right of action, to recover possession, to be carried on by the latter at his own risk; Tr. on Obl. n. 656.

But when the seller of a thing is not in possession of it, at the time of the contract, or is subject to eviction for some cause existing at that time, against which he is bound to warrant the buyer, even after a delivery; though, in such case, the seller has no possession and cannot deliver the thing, yet, if it exists, his obligation to deliver it subsists, and he is liable for the damages resulting from the non-performance. It is no objection, that no one can be held to perform an impossibility. This maxim is true only in regard to an impossibility, which is absolute, and not to one which is merely relative; as is explained in the Treatise on Obligations, n. 133, 136.

ARTICLE V.

Of the action, which results from the obligation to deliver the thing, and of the damages to which the buyer is subject, in case of the non-performance of his obligation.

61. The obligation to deliver the thing gives rise to the action *ex empto*, which the buyer is entitled to maintain against the seller, in order to cause him to deliver possession of the thing, with its titles and fruits, and every thing dependent upon it.

In this article, we shall consider, 1, the nature of the action *ex empto*; 2, what the buyer must do, in order to be allowed to commence it; 3, whether he can, in virtue thereof, put himself in possession of the thing sold by force, if the seller refuses to deliver it; 4, into what the action resolves itself, in default of delivery; 5 and 6, of the damages to which the seller is liable.

§ I. Of the nature of the action *ex empto*.

62. The action *ex empto* is merely personal, and can only be brought against the seller and his heirs; but not against a third person, to whom the seller may subsequently sell and deliver the thing, contrary to the faith of the contract of sale between him and the buyer. This results from a principle, established in the Treatise on Obligations, n. 151, and 152, that an obligation to deliver a thing does not confer any right in the thing itself, upon him, in whose favor it is contracted.

This personal action *ex empto* is movable or immovable, according to the nature of the thing sold, which makes its object.

§ II. What the buyer must do in order to be allowed to commence this action.

63. The buyer cannot regularly commence this action, without offering to pay the price, if it is not already paid; for, he cannot be permitted to require the seller to perform his engagement, if he is not also ready, on his part, to perform his own.

The buyer ought to offer to pay the whole price agreed upon; and, if he offers only a part of it, he will not be allowed to demand a delivery of the thing sold, or even of the least part of it; the seller having a right to retain it, as a pledge for the entire payment of the agreed price. For this reason, a buyer is not allowed to demand the smallest part of the thing sold, until he pays the whole price, in the same manner, that a debtor is not allowed to demand the least part of the thing pledged, until he pays the whole sum for which it is in pledge. This is the doctrine taught in the law 13, § 8, D. *de act. empt.* (19, 1, 13, § 8): *Offeri pretium venditori ab emptore debet, quum ex empto agitur; et ideo et si pretii partem offerat, nondum ex empto est actio; venditor enim, quasi pignus, retinere potest eam rem, quam vendidit.*

64. This principle is applicable, not only so long as the action *ex empto* remains undivided, but even after it becomes divided by the death of the buyer leaving several heirs. Neither of them can commence this action, to recover his share of the thing, without offering to pay the whole price; in which case, his co-heirs will be bound to account to him for the part which they are bound to pay; D. 18, 1, 78, § 2.

65. The judge may sometimes, however, moderate the rigor of this rule, when equitable circumstances seem to demand it, as in the following case, namely; a taverner purchases a cellar of forty tuns of wine, for a certain sum payable on delivery; but, not having the whole on hand (which he expects to have within eight days), he demands

permission to carry away two tuns, which are necessary for the supply of his tavern, in the mean time, and offers to pay, on account of the price due, a sum much greater than the value of those two tuns. In this case, it would clearly be inhuman, to refuse to listen to the buyer's request, on the ground of a too scrupulous regard for the rule, which does not permit a buyer to demand a part of the thing sold, before payment of the whole price.

66. If the buyer brings his action for the thing sold, without offering to pay the price, and, by a sentence in the last resort, which does not impose, upon the buyer, the condition of a previous payment of the price, the seller is condemned to deliver it, can the buyer pursue the execution of this decree, without offering to pay the price? The question is discussed by Fabian de Monte, in his treatise *de empt. vend.*, which is in the grand collection, volume vi. page 1, 61. He quotes the opinion of some ancient doctors, in the affirmative, who think that the seller cannot prevent the execution of the sentence, by objecting the non-payment of the price; since even peremptory objections ought to be set up before judgment, and cannot be taken advantage of afterwards. The contrary opinion, embraced by this author himself, is the more correct. Though the sentence, which condemns the seller to deliver the thing, does not contain an express condition, that the buyer shall first pay the price, yet this condition must be understood; for it results from the nature of the action *ex empto*, upon which the sentence is founded; and, in reference to things which do not tend to aggravate but to moderate the sentence, the judge is considered as pronouncing it conformably and in relation to the nature of the action, upon which it is founded. In regard to what is alleged in favor of the other opinion, that exceptions cannot be set up after a judgment, the answer is, that this rule relates only to those, which impugn the judgment itself, and not to those, which merely concern its exe-

cution. It is upon this ground, that the exception called *competentiæ*, to which, by the Roman laws, certain persons were entitled, *ne ultra quam facere possent ab eis exigeretur*, might be taken even after condemnation; l. 41, § 2, D. *de re jud.* (42, 1, 41, § 2,); and, it is upon this ground also, that if I am condemned to pay you a certain sum of money which I owe you, I may, notwithstanding the sentence, set against it the sum which you owe me; Tr. on Obl. n. 625. In the present case, the exception taken by the seller, tending to compel the buyer to pay the price before the thing is delivered to him, is an exception of the latter kind. The seller does not thereby impugn the sentence, which condemns him to deliver the thing, which he is ready to execute; but, he maintains, with justice, that the buyer ought first to satisfy the obligation on his part, by paying the price.

67. The principle above established, that the buyer is not allowed to commence his action for a delivery of the thing, until an offer on his part to pay the price, does not apply, when, by the contract, he is entitled to a term of credit, which is not yet elapsed.

But if the affairs of the buyer subsequently become deranged, so that the seller runs the risk of losing the price, the latter may defend himself against a delivery of the thing, notwithstanding the term of credit given, at least, if the buyer does not offer payment, or to furnish a sufficient surety for the payment of the price.

It is only a term of right, contained in the contract, which authorizes the buyer to demand the thing sold, before payment of the price; a term of grace is not sufficient. For example, if a buyer obtain letters of respite, or letters of state, which grant him a term of time, for the payment of his debts, the seller is not thereby bound to deliver him the thing sold, without payment of the price. The only effect of such a term is to prevent the commencement of suits against the debtor to compel payment; *arg.* D. 19, 1. 50.

§ III. Whether the buyer, in virtue of the action *ex empto*, can take the thing sold by force.

68. The question has been agitated, whether a seller, who is condemned to deliver a thing, and who has it in his possession, can be literally constrained to deliver it; or, whether, upon his refusal to do so, his obligation and the sentence against him are not converted into an obligation and a condemnation for damages only. Many interpreters of the Roman law, and, among others, Schulting and Noodt, are of the latter opinion. They rest themselves, first, upon the law 4, *Cod. de act. empt.* (4, 49, 4), which declares expressly, that a seller, who, through malice and obstinacy, does not deliver the thing, ought to be condemned to make good the damages to the buyer: *Si traditio rei venditæ procacia venditoris non fiat, quanti interesse compleri emptionem fuerit arbitratus præses, tantum in condemnationis taxationem deducere curabit.* They say, secondly, that as the seller remains the owner of the thing sold until a delivery, it would be uncivil to despoil him of his own property by force. Lastly, they allege, that it is a maxim of law, that *nemo potest cogi præcise ad factum;* from which they conclude, that *nemo potest cogi ad traditionem.*

The contrary opinion has also illustrious defenders. I believe it to be the correct one, and I think, that, in case of a refusal by the seller to deliver the thing sold, which he has in his possession, the judge may permit the buyer to seize and carry it away, if it is a movable, or to put himself in possession of it, if it consists of a piece of land or a building, and to expel the seller, if he refuses to quit, by the ministry of an officer. It is easy to answer the reasons above-mentioned in favor of the first opinion. The answer to the paragraph quoted from the Code is, that, it indeed furnishes the buyer with the action *in id quod interest,* against the seller, if he refuses unjustly to deliver him the thing sold; but it does not say, that that action is the only means, which he has to do himself justice. Paul, *sent.* 1, 13, 4, says expressly, that the seller may be literally constrained to deliver the thing, *potest cogi ut tradat;* but, as it is not always easy for the buyer to put himself in possession of the thing sold, *manu militari*, since the seller may convey away and conceal it; the law above cited permits him to have recourse to the action *in id quod interest.* The buyer has therefore his choice of these two remedies. In regard to what is said in the second place, that, as the buyer remains the owner of the thing sold, it would be uncivil to take from him by force that which belongs to him, I answer, that there is no more incivility in this, than there is in seizing the goods of a debtor, who refuses to pay what he owes. As to the argument that *nemo potest cogi ad factum*, and that obligations, which consist in doing something, resolve themselves *in id quod interest actoris*, I answer, that this maxim is applicable only, when the act included in the obligation is an act purely of the debtor's person, *merum factum;* as, if one undertakes to copy writings or to dig a ditch for me, it is evident that I cannot make him write, or work, against his will, and that his obligation, if he refuses to perform it, must necessarily be resolved into a claim for damages. It is not so, in regard to the act of delivery. This act is not *merum factum, sed magis ad dationem accedit;* and the debtor may be constrained by a seizure and carrying away of the thing. This is the opinion of Cujas, *ad* l. 1, D. *de act. empt.* (19, 1, 1), of Zoesius, *parat. ad dict. tit.;* of Perez, *Cod. ad dict. tit.;* and of Devesan, *Tr. de empt. vend.*

Amongst those, who think the first opinion most conformable to the Roman law, there are some, who agree, that, in that respect, the Roman jurists departed from the natural law. This is the sentiment of Barbeyrac. It seems, indeed, that the opinion, which is above adopted, is followed in practice, as is agreed by Wissembach, though he is himself of the contrary opinion.

There are some cases, however, in which, for particular reasons, this rule admits of an exception. For example, if one, who is about to take down his house, sells me a certain beam or some other part of it; though the Roman laws, which prohibit the sale of things united to buildings, are not in force with us; and, though, in other respects, the sale is valid; yet, if the seller changes his mind, and, being no longer willing to demolish his house, refuses to deliver me the thing sold, I cannot be permitted to demolish it, in order to put myself in possession of my purchase; and the obligation of the seller must consequently be converted into a claim for damages. The public interest is opposed to the destruction of a building; and, besides, as the debtor must, from the execution of his obligation, suffer a damage much more considerable, than any which the creditor can receive from its non-performance, it is equitable, that the latter should be content with an indemnification in damages; and that in this case he should not constrain the debtor to a precise execution of his obligation. This results from the second precept of that law, which requires us to love our neighbor as ourselves.

§ IV. Into what the action *ex empto* is resolved in default of delivery.

69. Those interpreters of the Roman law, who wrote before Dumoulin, admit but a single object in the secondary conclusions of the action *ex empto*, in case of non-delivery, or of eviction, namely: a condemnation for the sum, in which the present interest of the buyer, in having the thing, which is not delivered to him, or of which he suffers an eviction, ought to be estimated. From this principle, they infer, that if the estimation of the buyer's interest, having regard to the present situation of the thing, which, since the contract, has become considerably diminished in

price, is reduced to a sum less than the price, the seller is bound only to pay that sum, and may retain the surplus. Domat, book 1, title 2, of the contract of sale, sect. 10, n. 15, though he wrote a long time after Dumoulin, has embraced this opinion. It is also followed by Caillet, in his elegant commentary upon the title of the code *de evict.* Dumoulin, who has gone more profoundly into this subject, in his treatise *de eo quod interest*, n. 68, 69, *etc.*, than any of the interpreters, refutes this doctrine, and holds, that the action *ex empto in id quod interest*, in case of non-delivery, as in case of eviction, has two objects, the principal of which is a restitution of the price paid, or a discharge from it, if it remains due; and, the other, a payment of all that the buyer suffers over and above, by means of the non-delivery or eviction. These two objects are clearly to be distinguished in the law 43, *in fin.* D. *de act. empt.* (19, 1, 43): *Non pretium continet tantum, sed omne quod interest emptoris.*

And, therefore, if a thing, which I have purchased, is afterwards considerably injured and depreciated, either through my negligence or by accident; as, for example, if I purchase a house for 20,000 livres, and afterwards a part of it is consumed by lightning, so as to reduce the value to 10,000 livres, and consequently my present interest, in having or retaining it, becomes less than the price of 20,000 livres; yet, I have a right, in case of non-delivery or eviction, to demand a restitution of the whole price. The reason is, that, according to the nature of all commutative and reciprocal (*synallagmatique*) contracts, like the contract of sale, the engagement of each of the parties depends upon the condition of a performance on the part of the other; and, therefore, as I contract no engagement to pay the price, but upon condition that the seller shall not fail in the engagement on his part; and, as he fails in the performance of his obligation, by the non-delivery, or by not defending me against the eviction; the obligation, which I contracted to pay him the price, and also the right resulting to his benefit, from his own obligation, are dissolved. The seller, from that time, ceases to have any right in the profit, to be derived from my obligation to pay him; from which it follows, that he cannot demand it; that if it be paid he cannot retain it; and that I may reclaim the whole, *condictione sine causa.* Besides, it is manifestly contrary to equity, that a seller, who is himself in fault, and deceives me in selling me a thing which does not belong to him, should take advantage of his own wrong, and make a profit out of me of a part of the price. Against this opinion, its opponents cite, but without effect, the law 23, *Cod. de evict.* (8, 45, 23), which declares, that there is due to the buyer in case of eviction, *quanti tua interest, non quantum pretii nomine dedisti;* but which must be understood in this sense, *non* (*solum*) *quantum pretii nomine dedisti.* They also cite the law 8, D. *de hær. vend.* (18, 4, 8), where it is said, that, in the case of an action brought against the seller of rights of succession, as belonging to him, of which he is not the owner, the value of such rights is to be estimated. Dumoulin very well answers this objection, by saying, that the estimation in this case is made only for the benefit of the buyer, and against the seller, who ought to be condemned to pay the whole value of the rights, in case they are worth more than the price, and, who, at all events, ought to pay the entire price, even if they are worth less.

In regard to the law 70, D. *de evict.* (21, 2, 70), upon which Domat relies, in which Paul says: *Evicta re, ex empto actio, non ad pretium duntaxat recipiendum, sed ad id, quod interest, competit; ergo, et si minor esse cœpit, damnum emptoris est;* Dumoulin answers, that these terms, *damnum emptoris est,* do not refer *ad pretium recipiendum,* as the price, in case of eviction, is always to be wholly restored to the buyer; but that they refer only *ad id quod interest emptoris;* for, in the same manner, that *id quod interest emptoris non habere licere* increases, in proportion as the thing increases in value, so, it is diminished and reduced to nothing, as the thing diminishes in value; and, in this sense, *si res minor esse cœpit, damnum emptoris est.* The same answer may be made to the law 45, D. *de act. empt.* (19, 1, 45), which is also cited by Domat in support of his opinion. The expression therein, that *minuitur præstatio, si servus deterior apud emptorem effectus sit, quum evincitur,* must not be understood in this sense, *ut minuatur præstatio quantum ad restitutionem pretii,* but only, *ut minuatur præstatio ejus quod ultra pretium interesse posset emptoris;* because this *hoc quantum interest* is regulated by regard to the situation in which the thing is at the time of the eviction, and not to that in which it was, at the time of the delivery.

The law *ex mille,* l. 64, D. *de evict.* (21, 2, 64), which is also cited by Domat, does not apply to this question. It does not refer to a thing, which is simply deteriorated or depreciated, but to one, of which a part is wholly destroyed, and of which part, consequently, the buyer cannot be evicted, since it does not exist; from which it follows, that if the buyer afterwards suffers an eviction of a part of what remains of the thing, the seller is bound to a restitution of the price, for that part only of which the buyer is evicted, and not for that part, which does not exist, and of which there can be no eviction. See Dumoulin's explanation of this law, quoted *infra,* n. 154. Lastly, no argument against the doctrine of Dumoulin can be drawn from the law 66, § *fin.* D. *de evict.* (21, 2, 66, § 3), which relates to the warranty of divisions; for that kind of warranty is regulated by different principles from those which govern in the case of a sale, as will be seen, *infra,* part 7, art. 6. Besides the arguments drawn from the laws above-mentioned, Caillet objects also that the opinion of Dumoulin is contrary to that principle of the law, which requires that a diminution, subsequent to the contract of sale, should fall upon the buyer.

Now, says he, it will not fall upon him, if, notwithstanding the diminution, he has the right, in case of eviction, to reclaim the whole price. The answer is, that, according to the principles of law, a diminution happening to the thing sold ought to fall upon the buyer, so long as it remains in his possession, and provided the seller does not contravene his obligation; but, if the latter fails to perform the obligation on his part, these principles do not prevent him from being liable to restore the entire price. On the contrary, the principles of law as well as of good sense declare, that if the seller does not fulfil his engagement, the buyer is discharged from that contracted on his part, to pay the price. Caillet insists further, that the reasoning of Dumoulin is applicable only to a seller in bad faith; and that a seller in good faith fully satisfies his engagement, by offering the damages. To this, the answer is, that the obligation for damages is a secondary obligation, which supposes the non-performance of the principal obligation; and, if there is a non-performance of the principal obligation on the part of the seller, it is sufficient to discharge the buyer from that which is incumbent on him. Caillet also incorrectly asserts, that Dumoulin has expressed a different opinion in n. 124, of the same treatise. The question, which he there treats of, does not depend upon these general principles, as will be seen hereafter, *infra*, n. 164, in the discussion of that question.

§ V. Of the damages for which the seller is liable in default of delivery.

70. The damages for which the seller is ordinarily liable, in default of delivery, as in case of eviction, are all which the buyer loses or fails to gain, in relation to the thing which makes the object of the contract, over and above the price paid, *id quod interest propter ipsam rem non habitam.*

71. All that the thing sold costs the buyer, over and above the price, makes a part of his damages, such as the expense of the contract, of the hundredth penny, of seignorial dues, of a journey to see the estate, &c.

72. Any increase of value also, in consequence of an augmentation in the price of articles of the same kind, makes a part of the buyer's damages; and, therefore, if one sells me a tun of wine, the price of which afterwards rises, and neglects to deliver it according to his contract, he is bound to pay me the difference; for, by the non-delivery, I lose a profit which I should otherwise have made; D. 19, 1, 21, § 3.

73. The action *ex empto* is not ordinarily extended, as has already been remarked, beyond the damages which the buyer sustains, in relation to the thing itself; for, it is these only, which are foreseen, and to which the seller expects to subject himself; and, therefore, this action does not ordinarily extend to the damages which the buyer sustains otherwise, *extrinsecus*, and of which the non-performance of the contract is only a remote cause. This is the doctrine of Paul: *Quum per venditorem steterit, quominus rem tradat, omnis utilitas emptoris in æstimationem venit, quæ modo circa ipsam rem consistit;* D. 19, 1, 21, § 3.

For example, if one sells oats to a husbandman, and neglects to deliver them according to his contract, the damage, which the non-delivery occasions the buyer in his horses, which, not being properly fed, grow thin, and in his lands, which he is unable to cultivate on account of the weakness of his horses, cannot be claimed against the seller; since it is not a damage suffered by the buyer, *circa ipsam rem venditam*, and the want of delivery is only an occasional or remote cause of it. The law above cited contains some similar examples.

74. The action *ex empto* is sometimes extended, however, to the damages which the buyer suffers *extrinsecus*, and in his other goods; and this takes place, whenever it appears from circumstances, that such damages were foreseen at the time of the contract, and were agreed to by the seller, at least, impliedly, in case of the non-performance of his engagement. The following is an example of this kind. A

carpenter, who is informed that my house is in imminent danger of falling, sells me some props, and agrees to deliver and put them up, in the course of the day, to prevent the accident. If he, through negligence, fails to deliver the props within the time, and, for want of them, the house falls and is demolished on the next day, the carpenter is liable for the loss; for, though the damage does not concern the thing itself, yet it is one which was foreseen at the time of the contract, and to which the seller tacitly submitted, in case of non-performance of his engagement; since he was informed of the danger, which threatened the house, and to avoid which was the principal object of the contract; and, it was for that purpose, that he contracted to deliver and put up the props at the appointed time.

The reader is referred to the Treatise on Obligations, n. 159, *et seq.* for the general rules concerning the damages, which result from the non-performance of an obligation to give a thing, These rules are as much applicable to the contract of sale as to other contracts.

§ VI. Of the damages which may be claimed by the buyer on account of a delay in the delivery.

75. When the seller has been put in delay to deliver the thing sold, within the time agreed; if he afterwards offers to deliver it, he will not, always, by so doing, be discharged from his obligation; for, if the buyer suffers from the delay, the seller must be condemned to pay the amount of his damages.

These damages consist in indemnifying the buyer, as well against the losses which the delay causes him to suffer, as for the gains of which he is deprived in regard to the thing sold. Thus, in the first place, if the thing which you sell me becomes deteriorated, though by irresistible force, after you are in delay to deliver it, you are bound to account to me for the diminution of value in consequence of such deterioration.

This rule holds, when the accident, by which the thing becomes deteriorated, would not have happened to it, if it had been delivered. It also takes place, sometimes, even if the accident would have equally happened; as, for instance, when it appears, from my being a dealer, that I purchased the thing to sell again, and that time enough elapsed before the accident, for me to have resold it, if it had been delivered to me at the appointed time.

But it is not applicable, in case the loss arising from the deterioration would have equally happened to me, if there had been no delay in the delivery. For example, if, after you are in delay to deliver me a farm, an inundation carries away a considerable portion of it, I have no claim against you for the loss; for I should have suffered it equally, even if you had not been guilty of any delay in the performance of your obligation. It is not a damage which results from the delay.

76. In the first two cases, in which the seller is liable for the deterioration which happens to the thing, subsequent to the delay, the buyer may not only require the seller to account for the difference in value, as above stated, but, instead thereof, in some cases, may even refuse to take the thing, and may claim a restitution of the price and his damages; as in case of non-delivery. This takes place when the deterioration is considerable, and of such a nature that the buyer would not have been willing to purchase the thing, if it had been in the same situation at the time of the contract.

77. Secondly, it is also an incident to the damages, which result from a delay on the part of the seller, to execute his obligation, that he should be held to account to the buyer, for any loss which he may suffer, or for any gain which he may fail to make, by reason of a diminution in the price of the thing sold, subsequent to the delay. For example, I sell my wine at the rate of a hundred livres a tun. Subsequently to the making of the contract, the price of wine rises to one

hundred and twenty livres; and, after I am put in delay to deliver it, the price of this wine, which might have been sold for one hundred and twenty livres, if it had been delivered according to agreement, again falls to one hundred livres; I ought to be condemned to account to the buyer for the gain of twenty livres the ton, which the delay prevents him from making.

78. Thirdly, the expense of carriers, sent by the buyer to take away the merchandise, at the time agreed upon for the delivery, and which return empty, in consequence of the seller's neglect, is also a loss suffered by the buyer from the delay, for which the seller is responsible.

79. In general, if the delay occasions the buyer any necessary expense, which he would not have otherwise incurred, the seller is bound to indemnify him. For example, while at Paris, I purchase of you two horses for my carriage, and after you are in delay to deliver them, I am under the necessity, in order to attend to my affairs, to hire carriages, which I should not have been obliged to do, if I had had the horses, which I purchased; in this case, you are bound to indemnify me, by a payment of the excess of the expense of the carriage hire, over what the keeping of the horses would have amounted to, during the time for which you are in delay to deliver them.

For the same reason, if I purchase a house in a city, where I am going to establish myself, and the seller contracts to deliver me the keys at a certain time; and, if I am there at the time, and he fails to put me in possession; he must indemnify me for the expenses I incur, during the time he is in delay, in keeping myself elsewhere, and storing my goods in another place.

It is to be observed, that the expenses, which the buyer alleges to have been occasioned by the non-delivery, ought to be estimated with moderation, and to be allowed only so far as they appear probable and necessary.

80. Lastly, it is an effect of the delay, that the seller, who, before the delay, is bound to restore the fruits which he receives, is liable afterwards to account, not only for those which he receives, but even for those which he neither receives, nor is able to receive, provided the buyer might have received them, if the thing had been delivered to him according to his demand. For example, if I sell a horse to a letter of horses, and delay to deliver the animal, I am bound to indemnify the buyer for all the gain, which he might have made by letting the horse, during all the time, that I am in delay.

81. It remains to be observed, that the damages which result from a delay do not ordinarily include any thing more than what the buyer suffers or fails to gain, in relation to the thing sold, and not what he suffers *extrinsecus.* But above all, they do not include losses, of which the delay is only a remote cause. We may here apply the principles mentioned in the preceding paragraphs, and which are established more at large in the Treatise on Obligations; n. 159 *et seq.*

SECTION II.

Of the obligation to warrant the buyer against evictions.

82. The obligation of the seller is not entirely fulfilled by a delivery of the thing. He still remains bound, after the delivery, to defend and warrant the buyer against all evictions, in relation to the thing. This obligation is called the obligation of warranty, and results from this maxim of Pomponius, in the law 3, D. *de act. empt.* (19, 1, 3): *Ratio possessionis quæ a venditore fieri debet, talis est, ut si quis eam possessionem jure avocaverit, tradita possessio non intelligatur.*

The subject of this section is treated of under the following divisions, namely: 1, what is an eviction; 2, what evictions give rise to warranty; 3, from whom the eviction must be made; 4, what thing must be evicted, in order to give rise to the warranty; 5, of the action which results from the obligation of warranty; 6, of the exception which results from it; and, 7, of cases in which there is no obligation of warranty.

ARTICLE FIRST.

What is an eviction.

83. To evict is, properly speaking, to take something from a person, in virtue of a sentence. *Evincere est aliquid vincendo auferre.* An eviction is the abandonment, which one is obliged to make, in pursuance of a sentence, by which he is condemned to do so. The term eviction is also applied in practice, both to the sentence which orders the abandonment, and to the demand which is brought to obtain it; and, therefore, demands in revendication and demands in the hypothecary action, brought against any one, are, in legal phraseology, called evictions.

It is in this sense, that the seller is said to be obliged to defend and warrant the buyer against all evictions, in relation to the thing sold; that is to say, he is bound to defend him against all demands, whether in revendication, in the hypothecary action, or others, which may be brought against him by any person whatever, to compel him to abandon the thing; to warrant the buyer against all condemnations, which may pass against him upon the said demands; and, if he should be unable to prevent the buyer from being constrained to abandon the thing, to pay him his damages in consequence thereof.

84. The sentence is called an eviction, not only when it condemns the party to an unconditional abandonment of the thing, but also when it condemns him in the alternative, to

abandon the thing, or to pay or to be bound to some thing; and, therefore, if the buyer of an estate, who is condemned in the hypothecary action, pays the sum due in virtue of the hypothecation, to prevent an abandonment of the estate, which is worth as much or more than the debt due the demander; the buyer, in this case, is deemed to suffer an eviction of the thing sold, which he is unable to preserve but by paying the money; and the seller is bound to warrant him against the eviction, by paying him the money which it costs him to preserve the estate.

85. The sentence is also called an eviction, not only when it condemns the buyer to abandon the thing to a third person, but also when it debars him of a demand in revendication, which he might have brought against a third person, who was in possession.

The law 16, § 1, D. *de evict.* (21, 2, 16, § 1), includes all these kinds of evictions: *Duplæ stipulatio committi dicitur tunc, quum res restituta est petitori, vel damnatus est* (*emptor*) *litis æstimatione, vel possessor ab emptore conventus absolutus est.*

86. The term eviction is applicable, strictly speaking, to those cases only in which the buyer is deprived of the thing sold by a sentence. It is used, however, though in a sense less proper, to include cases in which the buyer is deprived, without any sentence, of the power to retain the thing, in virtue of the sale; and these cases give rise to warranty, as will be seen in the following article.

ARTICLE II.

What evictions give rise to warranty.

FIRST MAXIM.

87. The seller is liable for evictions, of which there is a cause or at least a germ existing, at the time of the contract, whether they do or do not proceed from his act.

For example, if one sells a thing which does not belong to him, or which is hypothecated either for his own or the debt of another, or which is subject to a right of some sort, either absolute (*ouvert*) or contingent (*non encore ouvert*), which may or must, at some future period, give some one an action against him to compel him to abandon it; in all these cases, the seller is liable for the evictions, which may pass against him, either on the part of the owner, of the hypothecary creditors, or of those who at the time of the contract had an absolute or even an imperfect right to compel him to abandon the thing; for, in all these cases, the cause, from which the eviction proceeds, existed at the time of the contract.

88. This principle admits of an exception, in regard to those cases of eviction, which the buyer is subjected to, either by the municipal law, or by a particular clause of the contract of sale.

For example, if a buyer suffers an eviction of an estate, upon a demand in lineal or feudal redemption, though the law, which is the cause of these kinds of eviction, is a cause which existed at the time of the contract, the seller is not liable for them, because, by the municipal law, they are made a charge upon the buyer, who is deemed to purchase subject to the conditions of the custom. In like manner, if it is stated, by a clause of the contract, that the estate, which one sells, is charged with a right of reversion (*retour*) or of redemption (*reméré*), or a right of reversion after a certain time, &c., and the buyer is obliged to abandon the inheritance, upon the action of the party to whom the right belongs; though this eviction is the result of a cause, which existed at the time of the contract of sale, the seller is not liable, because the buyer charges himself with this kind of eviction, by the clause of the contract, in which the seller declares to him that the estate is subject to it.

89. This principle admits also of an exception, in regard

to evictions, which remain without effect; and, therefore, if a sentence condemns me *to abandon* to a third person an estate, which you have sold me, the eviction, resulting from this sentence, will not give rise to any warranty against you, if I always remain in possession of the estate, in consequence of the non-execution of the sentence; as, for example, where the party, for whose benefit it is rendered, dies shortly after, in a state of insolvency, and no one is willing to embarrass himself, by pursuing the rights belonging to his succession. This is the case of the law 57, D. *de evict.* (21, 2, 57).

90. A third exception is, when the eviction is one, against which the buyer is himself obliged to defend the seller. For example, after having purchased an estate of Peter, I sell it to you, and you are obliged to abandon it to James, to whom it belonged not only before my sale to you, but before my purchase of Peter, of whom you become the sole heir; you cannot commence an action of warranty against me, on account of this eviction, because, being the heir of Peter, you are yourself bound to defend me against it.

91. The principle above stated admits of a fourth exception, when the eviction proceeds from the act of the buyer, though the cause exists anterior to the contract. For example, you consent to a hypothecation of your estate for a debt of Peter's; afterwards, you make a donation of the same estate to James, who sells it to me, and I resell it to you. If you suffer an eviction, on the part of Peter's creditor, though the cause is anterior to the sale by you, you are not allowed to commence an action of warranty against me, on account of such eviction, because it proceeds from your own act; you yourself imposed the hypothecation, when you were first the proprietor of the estate. In this case, you are not, in truth, my warrantor, on account of the eviction, as in the preceding case, since you are not the seller of the estate, and James, who is so, holds it of you by a donatory

title, which does not import a warranty. But it is sufficient, that the eviction proceeds from your own act, to prevent you from complaining of it, and from commencing an action of warranty against me.

SECOND MAXIM.

Those evictions, the cause of which does not begin to exist, until after the making of the contract, create a warranty, when the cause proceeds from the act of the seller, otherwise not.

92. The first part of this maxim is evident. For example, if you sell me an inheritance, and, after the contract of sale and before the delivery, you hypothecate it to another person, upon whose hypothecary action, I suffer an eviction of the estate; though the hypothecation, which is the cause of the eviction, does not exist until after the contract of sale, yet it is evident, that you ought to be responsible; for, by contracting the hypothecation, which prevents me from retaining the estate, you contravene the obligation, which you contracted in my favor *præstare mihi eum fundum habere licere.*

93. The second part of the maxim is not less evident. As the thing sold becomes at the risk of the buyer, from the time of the contract, it follows, that he has no claim of warranty against evictions, the cause of which begins to exist after that time, and does not proceed from the act of the seller. According to this principle, if I purchase an inheritance, a part of which is afterwards taken, by public authority, to make a public road, the seller is not my warrantor against this eviction, the cause of which does not exist, until after the contract.

94. For the same reason, if the buyer suffers another to usurp possession of the thing, and to keep it until he obtains his discharge, by a right of prescription, from a demand in revendication, brought against him; the seller is not liable

to the buyer, for the eviction which he suffers in consequence of this sentence; for, as the cause of the eviction is the usurpation permitted by the buyer, subsequent to the sale, it has no cause which existed at the time of the contract. Besides, as it is the result of the buyer's own neglect, he is not allowed to complain of it.

95. If the buyer is condemned to abandon the thing, through the injustice of the judge, upon a demand which is not well founded in law; this is an eviction, without any cause existing at the time of the contract; and, consequently, the seller is not bound to warrant against it; D. 21, 2, 51; C. 8, 45, 8.

This question only arises, when the buyer, upon the demand brought against him, omits to summon the seller in warranty; for, if he summons him, the seller must take his act and cause, and the sentence will be rendered against him and not against the buyer.

THIRD MAXIM.

An abandonment of the thing sold by the buyer, though without sentence, to a third person, who, at the time of the contract, was the owner of it, or, who, at that time, had at least an inchoate right to compel the buyer to abandon it, gives rise to a warranty, provided the buyer can prove, that the person, to whom he abandoned, really had the right which he claimed.

96. For example. You sell me an inheritance, which was given to you by a man who had no children, without declaring to me from whence you derive your title; after the contract, your donor marries, and has issue, which, of full right, annuls the donation, and, without waiting to be condemned, or even summoned, I abandon the estate to him. I am not the less entitled to my action of warranty against you; for, it is sufficient for me to prove, that the party, to whom I abandoned the estate, had, in virtue of the dona-

tion, made by him to you, and, consequently at that time, and at the time of the sale made to me, an inchoate right to compel an abandonment of the estate, whenever issue should be born to him.

The equity of this maxim is evident. Though the term eviction, in its proper sense, is applicable only to the abandonment, which one is condemned to make, by a sentence of the judge; yet, when it is proved, that the party, to whom the buyer without any sentence makes an abandonment of the thing, has a right to compel it, and that it is made only for the purpose of forestalling and avoiding the expense of a sentence, it is manifest, that in this case, it is not in the power of the buyer to retain the thing; and, consequently, that the seller does not fulfil his obligation, *præstare ipsi rem habere licere,* which gives rise to the warranty.

Notwithstanding an abandonment, made without sentence, gives rise to warranty, when it is proved that the party, to whom it is made, has really a right to compel it; yet, it will be prudent on the part of the buyer to suffer himself to be assigned to abandon the thing, and to signify the assignation to the seller, so as not to charge himself with the justification of the right of the party, to whom he might have abandoned the thing too hastily.

FOURTH MAXIM.

It is a kind of eviction, which gives rise to warranty, when the buyer, subsequent to the sale, succeeds to the thing sold, by a universal, particular, or even lucrative title, derived from a third person, who was the real owner.

97. This maxim is founded upon the doctrine of several texts of the law. Ulpian, in the law 13, § 15, D. *de act. empt.* (19, 1, 13, § 15), says: *Si fundum mihi alienum vendideris, et hic ex causa lucrativa meus factus sit, nihilominus ex empto mihi adversus te actio competit.* Julian, in the law 29, D. *dict. tit.*, says likewise: *Cui res sub conditione legata*

erat, is eam imprudens ab hærede emit, actione ex empto poterit consequi emptor pretium, quia nunc[1] *ex causa legati rem habet.* To these texts may be added the law 84, § 5, D. *de legat.* 1°, (30, 1, 84, § 5, I); l. 9, l. 41, § 1, D. *de evict.* (21, 2, 9 & 41, § 1).

The reason is this. If I purchase of you a thing which is not yours, or in which you have no permanent title, and afterwards succeed to the owner, by some title, whatever it may be; it is in virtue of this new title, that I thenceforth retain the thing, and not in virtue of the sale from you; from that time, therefore, you cease to perform your obligation towards me, *non jam præstas mihi rem habere licere;* and, consequently, you are bound to restore the price.

It is to be observed, that, by the Roman law, this and the preceding maxim apply only in relation to the action *ex empto*, and not in relation to the action *ex stipulatu*, which, being an action *stricti juris*, admits no other eviction, than that properly so called, which results from a sentence. This distinction does not exist in the French law, in which the distinction of actions into those which are *stricti juris*, and those which are *bonæ fidei*, is not in use, and in which, also, no other action is known, in case of warranty, than the action *ex empto.*

ARTICLE III.

From whom the eviction must be made.

98. To entitle the buyer to his action of warranty, it is immaterial whether he himself, or his successor in the thing, suffers the eviction; and, therefore, if I sell you an estate, which you resell to Peter, and Peter suffers an eviction of it, you are entitled to an action of warranty against me, in

[1] This is a correction of Ant. Faber, who substitutes the word *nunc* for *non*, which is the common reading; the sense demands the correction.

the same manner as if you yourself suffer the eviction; for I sell the estate to you and to all having your rights; I am bound to cause you and those having your rights to enjoy it; and you are interested that I should defend Peter against the eviction, against which you are yourself bound to warrant him.

If you give or bequeath the estate to Peter, will the eviction give rise to a warranty against me or my heir? It will not: for, the eviction, which the successor of the buyer suffers, gives rise to the action of warranty, so far only as it affects the interest of the buyer or his heirs; *arg.* l. *Pater*, 71, D. *de evict.* (21, 2, 71). Now, as you are not the warrantor of Peter, in regard to the thing of which you make him a donation, and as your heir is not his warrantor in regard to the legacy bequeathed to him, neither you nor your heir are interested in the eviction which he suffers, and, consequently, it does not give rise to the action of warranty.

But if, by the act of donation, you cede all your rights and actions in relation to the thing, which include those resulting from my obligation of warranty; in this case, Peter, as being in your rights, may bring an action of warranty against me; for you are interested, that the eviction should give rise to a warranty, inasmuch as you are under an obligation to cede this action to him. This results from the law 59, *dict. tit.: Si res quam a Titio emi, legata est a me, non potest legatarius conventus a domino rei, venditori meo denuntiare, nisi cessæ ei fuerint actiones.*

99. You sell me an estate which I resell to Peter; I afterwards become his heir, and find the same estate in the succession, and subsequently suffer an eviction of it. The question has been raised, whether, in this case, I am entitled to an action of warranty against you. The reason of doubt is, that it is not in my own right, but as the heir of Peter, that I suffer the eviction; for, having resold the estate to him, it is only in my quality of his heir that I am the

possessor of it; and, therefore, properly speaking, it is his succession that is evicted. Now, in order that this eviction may give me an action of warranty against you (which I cannot have in my own right, since it is to me and not to Peter that you are bound), it is necessary that in my own right I should have some interest that the succession should not suffer the conviction. But it is not easy to see wherein I have such an interest. It cannot be said, as in the preceding case, that I have an interest that the second buyer or his succession should not suffer the eviction, on account of my obligation of warranty in his favor in case of eviction; for, being his heir, I cannot be under an obligation to myself. Notwithstanding these reasons, Paul, in the law 41, § 2, *dict. tit.*, decides, that, in this case, I am entitled to an action of warranty against you and your sureties in the warranty; and, as the foundation of his opinion, he gives the following reason, which serves at the same time to answer the doubt above suggested, and, which, though subtle, is not the less solid and true: *Quoniam*, says he, *et quum debitor creditori suo heres exstiterit, ratio quædam inter heredem et hereditatem ponitur, et intelligitur major hereditas ad debitorem pervenire; quasi soluta pecunia quæ debebatur hereditati et per hoc minus in bonis heredis esse.* It is as if the jurist were to say: Putting out of the case the fact that I am the heir of Peter, his succession has a credit, for instance, of 10,000 livres, on account of the eviction, for which credit, I, as the seller of the inheritance, am the debtor; now, if it were another myself, who was the heir of Peter, it would cost me 10,000 livres, which I should take from my own goods, to satisfy the debt to this heir; and, in the same manner, as I am myself the heir of Peter, I must be considered as paying myself, in that capacity, the same sum, of which my own estate, as distinguished from the succession, becomes so much diminished. If this sum, in fact, remains in my possession, it is no more a part of my own proper goods, but of the succession, to which it was due, and of which I hold it. It is therefore true, that I pay in my own right and out of my own estate, the damages resulting from the eviction, which I suffer as the heir of Peter; from which it follows, that I am entitled, in my own right, to an action against you, as my warrantor and against your sureties, for an indemnification.

The same rule holds also, in the opposite case, in which Peter, to whom I resell the estate, becomes my heir, and afterwards suffers an eviction; for, he is deemed to pay the damages resulting from this eviction, out of the goods belonging to my succession; *et sic minus in hæreditate videtur, tanquam ipsa hæreditas hæredi solverit; dict.* l. 41, § 2. Now, you are bound, as my warrantor, to indemnify my succession against the eviction; and, consequently, Peter, as my heir, is entitled to an action of warranty against you for his damages.

ARTICLE IV.

What thing must be evicted, in order to give rise to the warranty.

100. The warranty results not only from an eviction of the entire thing, but also from an eviction of any part of it, either aliquot and undivided, as when the buyer is condemned to abandon the third or fourth part, &c. or integral, as when the buyer of a farm is condemned to abandon a certain piece of land belonging to it. This is the case, even when the part remaining is worth much more than the price paid for the whole; D. 21, 2, 47.

101. But if one sells rights of succession, and the buyer suffers an eviction of some particular thing, which is found among the goods belonging to the succession, this does not give rise to a warranty. The reason of the difference is, that he, who sells a piece of land, sells all the parcels of

which it is composed, and of which he is in possession at the time of the contract; but he, who sells rights of succession, does not sell the different substances which appear to belong to the succession, but only the right, which includes those things merely, to which the succession really has a right. See *infra*, part 6. ch. 3.

102. The warranty results, not only from an eviction of the thing sold or of a part of it; but even from an eviction of what arises from it, or of what remains of it after an extinction. For example, if one sells me a beast, which does not belong to him, and, after the death of the animal, the true owner causes me to be condemned to restore the skin; though the skin does not, in strictness, make a part of the animal, which is no longer in existence, yet the seller is liable for the eviction, and is bound to restore the price of the skin. It is the same in regard to the young of the animal.

The reason of all this is, that the obligation of the seller, to cause the buyer to have the thing by a title of proprietor, includes that of causing him to have every thing, which may remain of it, or which may arise from it. This results from the law 8, D. *de evict.* (21, 2, 8). The laws 36, 42, and 43 of the same title seem to decide the contrary; but they speak only of the action *ex stipulatione duplæ*, which, in this respect, is different from the action *ex empto*. This is the explanation of Dumoulin, in his treatise *de eo quod int.* n. 148, and of all the interpreters. The action *ex stipulatione duplæ* is not known in our law, as has already been remarked.

ARTICLE V.

Of the action which results from the obligation of warranty.

From the obligation of warranty results the action of warranty, which is considered in this article under the following divisions: 1, of the action itself and of that which gives occasion to it; what is its primitive and what its secondary object; and, in what manner the heirs of the seller are individually liable; 2, when it ought to be commenced; 3, against whom; 4, of the taking of the act and cause by the seller and of his refusal to do so; 5, of the general rules concerning the amount in which the seller ought to be condemned, if he fails in the action of warranty; 6, of the amount in which the seller ought to be condemned, in the particular case of an eviction of a part, whether undivided or integral, of the thing sold, or of some thing which arises from it; 7, of the amount in which the seller ought to be condemned, when it is a second buyer, who suffers the eviction; 8, of the effect upon the action of warranty, which results from an agreement, on the part of the seller, to restore the price and a certain sum over and above the price, in case of eviction; and, 9, of some particular cases of eviction, which give rise to questions in regard to the action of warranty.

§ I. Of the action of warranty, and of that which gives occasion to it: what is its primitive and what its secondary object; and in what manner the heirs of the seller are individually liable.

103. The action of warranty is a branch of the personal action *ex empto*, which results from the obligation contracted on the part of the seller to the buyer, by the contract of sale, *præstare ei rem habere licere.*

This obligation includes that of defending the buyer against all troubles and evictions: and, therefore, not only an eviction, that is to say, the abandonment, which a buyer is constrained to make of the estate to a third person, but even a mere trouble, that is to say, a mere demand brought against the seller, by a third person, claiming a right existing at the time of the contract, to compel him to abandon the estate, gives occasion to this action.

When the buyer is not in possession of the thing, the trouble consists in the refusal of the person who is in possession to deliver it to him.

104. The immediate and primitive object of this action is the taking of the act and cause for the buyer, that is to say, the defence of his cause, with which the seller is obliged to charge himself, *factum defendendi.*

105. This act is indivisible, *quia respicit unicam et integram totius controversiæ defensionem, quasi certam quandam formam; Tr. de div. et. indiv.* p. 2, n. 496; from which it follows, that this action is indivisible; and, therefore, when the seller of a divisible thing dies leaving many heirs, though the obligation which he contracted, *præstare emptori rem habere licere,* having a divisible thing for its object, is a divisible obligation, which passes to each of the heirs only for the part of which he is heir; yet the action of warranty, which results from it, having an indivisible act for its object, may be instituted for the whole against each of the heirs of the seller; and, the buyer may conclude against any single one of the heirs, that he should be held to take his act and cause, and charge himself, in his stead, with the entire defence of the cause.

By defending only for his part, the heir would not even satisfy his part of the obligation *præstandi ei rem habere licere;* for, as the buyer purchases the thing to have it entire, the obligation *præstandi ei rem habere licere,* though divisible *obligatione,* is indivisible *solutione ;* and, therefore, no one of the seller's heirs can defend the buyer to any good purpose unless he defends him for the whole.

106. If the heir, summoned in warranty, refuses to take the act and cause of the buyer, as, for instance, because he thinks there are no means of defending it; or, if he takes the act and cause, and fails in the defence; in both these cases, his obligation to defend the buyer is converted into a divisible obligation to pay him the damagés resulting from

the eviction, which binds the heir only for the part of which he is the heir. This is what is decided by the law 85, § 5, D. *de verb. obl.* (45, 1, 85, § 5) : *In solidum agi oportet, et partis solutio adfert liberationem, quum ex causa evictionis intendimus; nam auctoris hæredes in solidum denuntiandi sunt omnesque debent subsistere, et quolibet defugiente omnes tenebuntur; sed unicuique pro parte hæreditaria præstatio injungitur.* The same thing is also decided in the law 139, D. *dict. tit.*, and these decisions are very just; for the obligation to defend is derived from the obligation *præstare emptori rem habere licere,* which, though indivisible *solutione*, is divisible *obligatione.* The heir, who, by not defending, fails to perform this obligation *præstandi rem habere,* is, therefore, held only to the extent of his part, for the non-performance and the damages resulting from it.

107. There is one case, in which an heir in part of the seller, being summoned alone, and being charged alone with the defence of the buyer, if he fails in the defence, ought to be condemned, for the whole, to a payment of the buyer's damages, saving his right of recourse against his coheirs: and this happens, when the heir in part conducts himself as sole heir, and thereby prevents the buyer, whom he leads into error, from prosecuting his warranty, at the same time, against the other heirs of the seller, who may consequently oppose to the buyer, that if they had been summoned in warranty before the judgment, they would have had good means of defence against it.

§ II. When the action of warranty may be commenced.

108. There is in this respect a difference between the Roman law and our practice, which is very well pointed out by Caillet, *ad tit. Cod. de evict.* (8, 45). By the Roman law, the buyer, when he is troubled, either by a demand in revendication, or by any other demand, has only the right

of denouncing or notifying to the seller the action which is brought against him, in order that the seller may take the defence of it upon himself, if he thinks proper; but it is not until after a condemnation passed against the buyer in that action, that he becomes entitled to commence his action of warranty against the seller, to procure an indemnification from him against the condemnation; and, it is before the judge of the domicil of the seller, that the action of warranty must be commenced. In our practice, this circuity of action is avoided. The buyer, at the same time, that he notifies the seller of the action in revendication or other action, by which he is troubled in his possession, and summons him to take his act and cause, and to defend him against the said action, may also, at the same time, commence his action of warranty against the seller, before the judge who has the original demand pending before him, though he is not the judge of the domicil of the seller, and may conclude against the seller, that in case he fails in the defence, and the original demander obtains judgment, the said seller shall, at the same time and by the same sentence, be condemned to indemnify him.

109. Although the buyer has the power to commence his action of warranty, as soon as he is troubled by a demand brought against him; yet, if he fail to do so, he is always in time to commence it, not only until the sentence of condemnation, but even afterwards. The ordinary prescription of thirty years is the only one which can exclude this action; and it begins to run from the day of the trouble occasioned by the demand brought against the buyer.

It is to be observed, that if the buyer delays, until after the suit is terminated with the original demander, to commence his action of warranty, it must then be brought before the judge of the domicil of the seller.

In like manner, when the buyer commences his action against a third person in possession of the thing, though, upon the refusal of the defender to abandon the thing, he may immediately summon the seller to take his act and cause, and may prosecute his warranty against him, yet he is always in time to do so, even after the termination of the suit by a discharge of the defendant.

110. Although the buyer may prosecute his action of warranty, without limitation of time, it is greatly for his interest to prosecute it, as soon as he is troubled in his possession; for, otherwise, he will have no claim against the seller, for all the expenses incurred in the intermediate time, between the trouble which he suffers and his demand in warranty; the seller being responsible only for the expenses incurred after he becomes a party to the cause, and for the cost of the commencement of the original demand.

The buyer is especially interested to prosecute his action of warranty before a definitive sentence; for, if he waits until afterwards, he is bound to prove the right of the party who obtains it against him; whereas, if he commences his demand in warranty, before the end of the process, that question must be settled between such party and his warrantor.

Besides, when the buyer waits until after the sentence, to commence his action of warranty, though he may establish the right of the original demander, to whom he is obliged to abandon the thing, yet the warrantor, in order to obtain his discharge from the demand in warranty, may sometimes object successfully to the buyer's demand, that he had means and exceptions, whereby he might have defended against the original demand, if he had been summoned at the time. It is not however sufficient for him merely to say so; he must establish and prove his means of defence.

§ III. Against whom the action of warranty may be brought.

111. The action of warranty must be brought against the seller or his heirs, or other universal successors.

If the seller dies leaving several heirs, the buyer may bring his action against all, or only against one of them; but he has a great interest in commencing it against the whole; for, if he brings it against one, though he may be held for the entire defence of the cause, yet if he does not defend it, or fails in the defence which he undertakes, he will be liable personally only for the part of which he is the heir of the seller; and the buyer will be obliged to proceed anew for the remainder, against the other heirs of the seller, and to establish against them his claim of warranty, and that he has been justly condemned to abandon the thing; for, as the sentence is rendered only against one of the heirs of the seller, it is not evidence against the others, who are not parties to it.

When the buyer summons only one of the heirs of the seller, he, who is summoned, has himself an interest in summoning his coheirs into the cause, in order that they may be held to defend jointly with him, and that they may divide with him the expense attending the defence of the cause; otherwise, if he defends alone, without summoning them, he must bear the expense alone.

112. In regard to the sureties of the seller, the buyer, who summons the seller in warranty, is not obliged also to summon the sureties: *Auctore laudato, si evicta res est, fidejussorem, etiam si agi causam ignoraverit, evictionis nomine conveniri posse non ambigitur;* l. 7, *Cod. de evict.* (8, 45, 7). It is the seller, rather than his sureties, who ought to be considered as informed of the means of defence, which may be set up to maintain the buyer in his title; the sureties, by becoming bound for the seller, accede not only to the principal obligation on his part to defend the buyer, but also to the secondary obligation, for the payment of the damages and interests, for which the seller is liable, if he fails in the defence. See the Treatise on Obligations, n. 405.

113. The only persons liable to this action are the seller and his heirs or other universal successors or his sureties. One who merely consents to the sale of a thing, is not liable as warrantor. Such consent binds him not to bring any trouble upon the buyer, by his own act; but it does not oblige him to defend the buyer against that, which may be brought upon him by the act of others; hence this rule: *Aliud est vendere, aliud vendenti consentire;* D. 50, 17, 160.

It is a question of fact, whether one is a seller, or merely consenting to the sale. The decision will depend upon the terms of the act, and upon circumstances; one who shares in the price is easily presumed to be a seller; *arg.* D. 21, 2, 12; Despeisses, *ibid.* n. 21.

§ IV. Of the taking, and of the refusal to take, the act and cause of the buyer.

114. When the seller or his heirs, summoned in warranty, declare that they take the act and cause of the buyer, the buyer, if he requires it before the contestation, may be put out of the cause; Ordinance of 1667, tit. 8, art. 9; and the process, commenced upon the demand of the original demander against the buyer, may be pursued between the original demander and the warrantor, as having taken the act and cause of the buyer, and being charged with the defence of his cause. Nevertheless, the buyer, though put out of the cause, may assist in the conducting thereof, for the preservation of his rights; art. 10.

115. Although the buyer is put out of the cause, yet the cause, which his warrantor is charged with defending, is really that of the buyer; and, therefore, the judgment which intervenes between the original demander and the warrantor is for the benefit of the buyer, when it is rendered in favor of the warrantor; and, *vice versa,* when it is rendered against the warrantor, it is executed against the buyer. The original demander, by merely notifying the buyer of

the judgment, which condemns the warrantor to an abandonment, may constrain the buyer to make it accordingly; Ord. tit. 8, art. 11; D. 42, 1, 4.

It is to be observed, that the judgment rendered against the warrantor, who takes the act and cause of the buyer, is only executed against the latter in relation to its principal object, that is to say, for an abandonment of the estate, which the warrantor is condemned to cause to be abandoned, and for a restitution of the fruits received by the buyer, when that is contained in the sentence. The judgment for the expenses, to which the warrantor is condemned in favor of the original demander, is not executed against the buyer, but against the warrantor. It is the penalty for an unsuccessful defence, which ought to be borne by the party who undertakes it; and, in this case, it is the warrantor, who does so, by taking the act and cause of the buyer, which he ought not to take, if the original demand is well founded.

116. In fact, the obligation, contracted by the seller to the buyer, to defend him, and to take his act and cause, in all demands which tend to trouble him in the free possession of the thing sold, is not limited to that precise object, but is contracted, with liberty on the part of the seller, to discharge it by offering to restore the price to the buyer, and indemnifying him against the eviction. From the primitive obligation, which the seller contracts, *præstandi emptori rem habere licere*, results the obligation to defend the buyer against evictions, by taking his act and cause, or by paying him his damages. The seller ought not to take the act and cause of the buyer, unless he has good means to defend it, and to procure a discharge from the demand of the original demander; but if that demand is well founded, he ought to declare, that, having no good means of defence against it, he submits to a restitution of the price and a payment of the buyer's damages. The obligation which he

contracts to the buyer does not extend so far as to require him to sustain an unjust defence on his behalf.

117. When the seller, being summoned in warranty, declares, that he has no means of defence, and offers to restore the price to the buyer, and to indemnify him against the eviction, the buyer is permitted, if he thinks proper, to carry on the defence himself; but, in this case, he proceeds at his own risk; and, if he fails, he cannot demand of the seller a reimbursement either of his expenses incurred in conducting the suit, or of those, which he is condemned to pay to the original demander. He can demand nothing more of the seller, than a restitution of the price, and the damages which have been offered him, the expense of the summons in warranty, and a reimbursement for the cost of the commencement of the original demand.

If the buyer succeeds, and obtains a discharge from the original demand, it will be for the advantage of the warrantor; for, as in that case, the buyer does not suffer an eviction, but preserves the thing, he is neither entitled to damages nor to a restitution of the price.

118. When the seller is dead, leaving several heirs, who are all summoned in warranty, one alone may take the act and cause, and carry on the suit, at his own risk; though the others declare that they have no means of defence, and that they submit to the payment of the damages and interests. If he succeed in his defence, his coheirs may take advantage of the judgment in his favor.

§ V. General rules concerning the amount in which the seller ought to be condemned, if he fails in the action of warranty.

The seller, who does not defend the buyer, or who fails in the defence which he undertakes, ought to be condemned in case of eviction, 1, to a restitution of the price; 2, to acquit the buyer from judgments in favor of the original demander, for a restitution of the fruits, or on account of degradations committed upon the estate; 3, to acquit the buyer from the expenses; 4, to pay the buyer his damages resulting from the eviction over and above the price.

FIRST OBJECT OF CONDEMNATION.

119. The seller, in case of eviction, ought to be condemned to restore to the buyer the price which he has received.

This condemnation ought to take place, as in case of non-delivery, even if the thing sold, subsequent to the contract, becomes considerably deteriorated, either by the buyer's negligence, or by accidents resulting from irresistible force, so, that, at the time of the eviction, it is worth much less than the price. We have established this principle, *supra*, part 2, n. 68.

120. Sometimes it is necessary to make a deduction from the price, which the seller is bound to restore to the buyer in case of eviction.

(1.) If, previous to the demand, upon which the buyer is evicted, there has been a suit between the seller and the buyer, either on account of a defect in quantity, or on account of some real charge not declared by the seller, and in that suit, the latter has been condemned to pay a certain sum to the buyer; the seller, if he is afterwards summoned in warranty, in reference to the demand, upon which the buyer is condemned to abandon the estate, has a right to deduct from the price, which he is bound to restore to the buyer, the sum which the buyer has already received, by reason of the defect in quantity or charge not declared; for that sum is a restitution of a part of the price, already made by the seller, who is consequently bound only to restore the residue; D. 21, 2, 48.

121. (2.) If the seller, before the contract of sale, makes improvements upon the estate which he sells, and the buyer receives the price of such improvements from the owner to whom he abandons the estate, the seller may deduct the

sum so received from the price which he is bound to restore to the buyer; for the price of these improvements makes a part of the price, for which the estate is sold; which being already received by the buyer, the seller is consequently bound to restore only the surplus.

122. (3.) When the buyer has committed degradations upon the inheritance, to his own profit; as, for example, by selling a wood, without being obliged to account for it to the party to whom he is condemned to abandon the estate; there ought to be a deduction in such case, of what he receives on that account, from the price which the seller is bound to restore to him; for, to that extent, he is already reimbursed.

123. The seller has no right to make a deduction, from the price which he is bound to restore, of the sums which it has already cost him to put an end to preceding evictions, unless those sums have been received by the buyer. This may be illustrated by the following example. You sell me as your own an estate which belongs to Peter. Upon a demand in revendication brought by Peter against me, I summon you in warranty, and you make a compromise with Peter, who, for a sum of money paid by you, relinquishes his demand. Afterwards I am obliged to abandon this estate to James, who is named in a substitution thereof, after the death of Peter. You cannot make a deduction of the money paid by you, from the price which you are bound to restore me in consequence of the eviction, for I have not received that sum. It cannot be said, that you have paid it to Peter, for me and in my discharge; for I owed nothing to Peter; you were bound to put an end to the eviction; and, to discharge your obligation to do so, you have paid the money. But by defending me against an eviction, on the part of Peter, you do not become the less obliged to defend or indemnify me against evictions, which I may suffer on the part of other persons. James having evicted

me of the entire estate, I am entitled to a restoration of the whole price; Caballinus, *de evict. in addition.* to the grand collection, fol. 104, 105.

SECOND OBJECT OF CONDEMNATION.

124. When the buyer is condemned to restore the fruits, which he has received, his warrantor, the seller, is bound to acquit him from this condemnation.

Nevertheless, if the seller, summoned in warranty, declares to the buyer that he has no means to defend him, and offers to restore the price, and to indemnify him wholly against the eviction, and, the buyer, notwithstanding these offers, elects to carry on the process; the seller, by paying the price into court, may discharge himself from his obligation to acquit the buyer from a restitution of the fruits received subsequent to the offers made during the pendency of the process; for the seller, having offered to the buyer all that is due to him, ought not to suffer, because the buyer, without regard to those offers (which he ought to accept), is willing to carry on an unjust defence against the suit of the original demander. But the seller, in order to discharge his obligation, ought to pay into court the price of which he offers a restitution; for, so long as he does not pay it into court, but retains the enjoyment of it, he ought to cause the buyer to have the enjoyment of the thing, which, on his part, stands in place of the enjoyment of the price, on the part of the seller. And, therefore, the seller ought to acquit the buyer from a restitution of what he receives by means of such enjoyment, when the latter is condemned to restore it to the original demander.

125. In like manner, when the buyer is condemned to account to the original demander for degradations committed by his act or fault, the seller ought also, in certain cases, to acquit him from this condemnation. I say, in certain cases, for, in this respect, some distinctions must be made.

126. For example. You sell me an estate for the price of 50,000 livres. I cut down a wood which is growing on the estate, and sell it for 10,000 livres. I am condemned to abandon the estate, and to pay the original demander the sum of 10,000 livres, received by me as the price of the wood. You ought not, upon my action of warranty, to be condemned to pay me the said sum of 10,000 livres, in addition to the restitution which you are bound to make to me of the entire price of 50,000 livres; for, if so, it is evident, that I should make a profit of 10,000 livres at your expense, which equity does not permit.

Further, you are not only not obliged to pay this sum for me, but if I am condemned to abandon the estate without restoring it, as, for instance, upon the demand of a hypothecary creditor, who has no right to the estate, in any other condition, than that in which it is at the time he exercises his hypothecary right, you have a right to compel me to deduct from the 50,000 livres paid you as the entire price of the estate, the 10,000 livres, which I receive as the price of the wood, and which I should otherwise twice receive; for the price total of 50,000 livres is the price of all the things, which composed the estate, at the time of the sale, and, consequently, the price of the wood, which was then comprised in it.

127. In regard to degradations, of which the buyer makes no profit, the question can scarcely arise as to a buyer in good faith; who ought not to be held liable, in favor of the original demander, for degradations committed before he has knowledge of such demander's right. Every one is allowed to neglect his own property; and, it cannot be regarded as a fault, that a man does not take proper care of a thing, of which he has reason to believe himself the real owner, though, in fact he is not so: *Qui quasi suam rem neglexit, nulli querelæ subjectus est;* D. 5, 3, 31, § 3. Yet, if the judge condemns me, by an error in point of law, though

a buyer in good faith, to account for degradations committed upon an estate, which I am condemned to abandon, the seller, if he is summoned in warranty, ought to be condemned to acquit me; for, being obliged to take my act and cause, he ought to defend it at his own risk, and consequently to acquit me from all condemnations, whether just or unjust. But if I suffer myself to be condemned, without summoning him in warranty, the seller may defend himself against my claim for an acquittal from this condemnation, by objecting that it is through my own fault, and by means of my bad defence, that I am condemned, and that if I had put him into the cause, he would have defended me better, and have prevented the sentence.

But, in order that the seller may be allowed to take this exception, it is necessary that he himself should be a possessor in good faith; for, if he is an usurper, though he is not summoned in warranty, he cannot defend himself against his obligation to acquit me from this condemnation; since, whether I am condemned or not, he is personally liable; as an usurper is liable not only for waste done by himself, but also for that committed by his successors.

128. The case remains to be noticed, in which the buyer is condemned for degradations committed after he knows that he is not the owner of the estate or not irrevocably so, and of which he makes no advantage; as, if he pulls up good vines for the purpose of making a pleasure garden, or pulls up vines which are in bad condition from not being properly dressed and cultivated, &c; in such case, his warrantor, the seller, must acquit him from the condemnation; for, though the buyer, as it regards the proprietor, does wrong in committing this degradation, yet, as it regards the seller, his warrantor, he does not, and the seller cannot reproach him with these acts. He has a right in doing them to rely upon the seller's warranty, and that the seller will prevent an eviction, as he is bound to do, by purchasing the

estate of the proprietor. The warrantor therefore can have no pretext for refusing to acquit the buyer from this condemnation.

The seller ought to acquit the buyer, in this case, even if he is not summoned in warranty; for, as the latter must be condemned on account of the waste done, the warrantor cannot object, as in the preceding case, that if he had been summoned in warranty, the condemnation would not have happened. It must be observed, however, that if it appear, that the degradations were committed maliciously, at a time when the buyer has reason to expect a demand in eviction, with a view to increase the obligation of the warrantor, the buyer can have no claim against him on account of such waste; for, *malitiis non est indulgendum.*

After the demand, and pending the process, the buyer even in good faith ought not to commit degradations; and, if he does so, and suffers a condemnation, he is not entitled to any recourse against his warrantor.

THIRD OBJECT.

129. The seller ought to be condemned, in case of eviction, not only for the expense of the buyer's demand in warranty against him, but also for the expense of the original demand, as well on the part of the buyer, as of the original demander, when the buyer is condemned. He is liable however only from the time when he is summoned in warranty. In regard to costs incurred before the summons in warranty, the warrantor is liable only for the first summons in the original demand; for, otherwise, a seller might be ruined without his knowledge, and without being able to prevent it; and, therefore, as soon as a buyer is summoned to deliver an estate, he ought to make no delay in summoning the seller in warranty.

130. When the seller, summoned in warranty, signifies to the buyer, that he has no means of defence, and offers to

pay the price received, and to indemnify the buyer fully against the eviction; if the latter, notwithstanding these offers, carries on the suit and fails in it, he has no claim against the warrantor for expenses incurred afterwards; for, as the seller offers to do all which he is bound to do, the buyer should be content; and it ought not to be in the power of the buyer, to load the seller, in spite of himself, with the expense of an unjust cause.

FOURTH OBJECT.

131. The seller, in case of eviction, ought to be condemned for the damages, when the buyer suffers any over and above the price paid, *in id quod supra pretium interest emptoris.*

When the sale is made in good faith, and the seller is ignorant that the thing does not belong to him, or does not belong to him irrevocably, the damages to which the seller ought to be condemned, in case of eviction, as in case of non-delivery, are, in ordinary cases, those only which the buyer suffers in relation to the thing itself, *propter rem ipsam non habitam*, and not those, which the eviction occasions him, *extrinsecus*, in his other goods.

132. These damages which the buyer suffers in case of eviction, in relation to the thing itself, *propter rem ipsam*, are, (1), as has already been observed, in the first section, n. 69 *et seq.*, all the legal costs incurred by the buyer, in the acquisition of the thing; for, by the eviction, all these costs become a dead loss to him. Such are the expenses of making the contract, and of feudal duties and profits paid on account of the transfer. The seller must reimburse the buyer for all these things.

Even when the eviction gives rise to a repetition of these profits, the seller is not discharged from reimbursing them to the buyer, saving a right on his part, to prosecute the buyer's claim for a repetition. The reason is, that the seller is bound to indemnify the buyer entirely against the eviction. But the buyer will not be wholly indemnified, if he is obliged to bring an action for a repetition of these profits; for, besides, that the receivers may be insolvent, this is not to be indemnified, but to have an action to maintain.

133. (2.) When the thing sold, subsequent to the contract, becomes increased in price, by the lapse of time, such increased value constitutes a loss, which concerns the thing itself, and for which the buyer is entitled to an indemnification; as, for example, if a house, which I purchased eleven years since, for 20,000 livres, becomes worth at the time of my eviction 30,000, the *id quanti mea interest eam habere licere,* is the value of 30,000 livres, and consequently of 10,000 more than the price, for which the seller is bound to indemnify me.

If, however, by reason of circumstances, which could not have been foreseen at the time of the contract, the thing sold becomes immensely increased in value, the seller in good faith ought not, in case of eviction, to be condemned to pay the entire sum, which the estate is worth at that time, and to which the damages resulting from the eviction consequently amount; but only to pay the highest sum, which the parties, at the time of the contract, could have had in contemplation as the amount of damages resulting from an eviction. See the Treatise on Obligations, n. 164; and Dumoulin, *Tr. de eo quod int. n.* 57, *et seq.*

134. When the highest value of an estate, which I have purchased, is the result of improvements, which I have made; and I am condemned to abandon the estate, upon condition that the original demander pay me the value of these improvements; it is evident, that I cannot claim against my warrantor any damages on account of this increased value; for, being entitled to receive it of the original demander, I ought not to demand it a second time of my warrantor. This is what is taught by Paul, in the law 45,

§ 1, D. *de act. empt.* (19, 1, 45, § 1): *Si mihi alienam aream vendideris, et in eam ego ædificavero, atque ita eam dominus evincit; quia possum petentem dominum, nisi impensam ædificiorum solvat, doli mali exceptione summovere, magis est, ut ea res ad periculum venditoris non pertineat.*

But if the original demander is not subjected by the sentence to account to me for meliorations; as, for example, if they are compensated by the enjoyment; in that case, my warrantor is bound to indemnify me. It is of this case, that we are to understand the law 9, *Cod. de evict.* (8, 45, 9): *Sin evictum fuerit, a venditore consequeris, quanti tua interest; in quo continetur etiam eorum persecutio, quæ in rem emptam a te, ut melior fieret, erogata sunt.*

This rule is subject to the modification above-mentioned, namely, that if the augmentation of price, which results from meliorations made by the buyer, is immense, the buyer, if he does not obtain a reimbursement for these meliorations against the party from whom he suffers the eviction, cannot claim, against a seller in good faith, a greater sum than that which the parties, at the time of the contract, had in contemplation, as the highest amount of damages resulting from an eviction. This is the decision of Paul in the law 43, D. *in fin. de act. empt.* (19, 1, 43): *Si in tantum pretium excessisse proponas, ut non sit cogitatum a venditore de tanta summa, veluti si ponas agitatorem postea factum vel pantomimum, evictum esse eum qui minimo væniit pretio, iniquum videtur in magnam quantitatem obligari venditorem.*

The above modification is admitted only in regard to a seller in good faith; and therefore Paul adds: *In omnibus tamen his casibus, si sciens quis alienum vendiderit, omnimodo teneri debet;* l. 45, § 1, *dict. tit.*

135. In the same manner, that the warrantor is held in case of eviction, to reimburse the buyer for meliorations made by him, when the sentence of condemnation does not order the party who evicts him to pay for them; so, for the

same reason, if the sum, in which the estate is augmented in price by the meliorations made by the buyer, exceeds the expenses incurred in making them, the original demander in this case not being obliged to reimburse the buyer for any sum over and above the expense, the warrantor ought to be condemned to indemnify him for the surplus; for example, I purchase an estate for 20,000 livres, and incur upon it an expense of 3,000 livres, which increases the annual income 200 livres, and consequently raises the value in the sum at least of 4,000 livres. An eviction of this estate, which is now worth 24,000 livres, after deducting the 3,000 livres, which I am entitled to be reimbursed, by the party evicting me, causes me a loss of 21,000 livres, and consequently of 1,000 livres beyond the price, for which I purchased; for which sum, I am entitled to an indemnification from my warrantor, who is liable to me, *in omne quanti mea interest supra pretium.*

136. What ought to be the decision in the opposite case, in which the sum expended by the buyer exceeds the increased value of the estate? For example, I purchase an estate for 20,000 livres, and expend 10,000 upon it, which increases its value only four thousand livres, and am evicted by the true proprietor. It is certain, that he is not obliged to account to me for more than the real increased value; and the question is, whether the warrantor is obliged to account to me for the remaining sum. He is not; for, as the estate is supposed to be worth no more than the sum of 24,000 livres, the damages resulting from the eviction, being nothing more than the *id quanti interest eum fundum habere licere,* consequently do not exceed that sum. The buyer, being reimbursed the 4,000 livres by the demander, suffers nothing beyond the price of 20,000 livres, which the seller is bound to restore to him. The additional sum of 6,000 livres, expended by him, is a loss; but it is not a loss resulting from the eviction; and, consequently, it cannot be considered to

make a part of the damages resulting from the eviction, for which the seller is liable. It is a loss, sustained by the buyer before the eviction, independent of, and not caused by it. Nor is the contract of sale the cause, but merely the occasion of the loss. The loss has no other cause than the fault of the buyer, who incurs an expense, which he is under no obligation to incur, and for which he alone ought to suffer.

137. In the preceding cases, the damages which the buyer is in a situation to suffer, in relation to the thing, of which he is evicted, *propter rem ipsam*, have been alone considered. The seller, in good faith, as has already been observed, is ordinarily liable only for the damages of this kind; and not for the loss, which the eviction causes the buyer, *extrinsecus*, and in his other goods. For example, if I establish an inn in a house, which I purchase without any such intention at the time, the loss, which I suffer from an eviction, in the derangement of my business as an innkeeper, makes no part of the damages for which my warrantor is liable; because it does not concern the thing of which I am evicted. I do not suffer it *propter rem ipsam*, but *extrinsecus*, and in my other property.

The reason of this decision is drawn from a principle, which cannot be too often repeated, viz.; that the obligation for damages, contracted by the seller in good faith, being formed merely by his consent, comprehends those damages only to which he gives his consent to be bound; and, he cannot be considered as consenting to be bound to those, of which he cannot be presumed to have thought. In the contract of sale, the parties ordinarily regard those only, which concern the thing itself; and they cannot foresee an infinity of kinds of damages, which the eviction may in other respects cause the buyer. For example, in the case supposed, the seller could not imagine that I would make an inn of the house, and consequently he could have no regard to the

6

damage, which the eviction would cause me in my business of an innkeeper. He ought not therefore to be liable for it.

138. The decision ought to be otherwise, in the case of one, who, in bad faith, sells me, as belonging to him, a thing which does not. He is liable, in case of eviction, for all kinds of losses and damages occasioned and caused by the eviction, though they do not concern the thing sold, and are suffered in relation to my other property. The reason is, as has been already stated in the Treatise on Obligations, n. 166, that, in this case, it is not the will merely, which he manifests to bind himself, but his bad faith, which binds him, even against his will, to a reparation of all the damage occasioned by it.

It must be observed, however, that the seller in bad faith is only liable for those damages suffered by the buyer, of which the eviction is the immediate and proximate cause, and not for those of which it is a remote cause, and which may have some other cause. The principles, which are established, in reference to this subject, in the Treatise on Obligations, n. 167, may be here applied.

139. The seller, in good faith, is sometimes liable, in case of eviction, for certain kinds of damages caused by the eviction, which do not concern the thing sold itself, and which the buyer suffers *extrinsecus* and in his other goods. This takes place, when it appears by particular circumstances, that such damages were foreseen at the time of the contract, and consequently that the seller may be considered as having tacitly submitted himself to them. For example, if I sell a house for an inn, to a person who is an innkeeper by profession, I ought in such case to be liable for the damages he sustains, in the derangement of his business as an innkeeper, in consequence of the eviction; for, as I sell the house for the purpose of being used as an inn, and as I know the buyer to be an innkeeper by profession, this kind of damage is clearly in view, and cannot be considered as one which could not have been provided against by the contract.

In the liquidation and estimation of these damages, we should be much more indulgent to a seller in good faith than to one in bad faith.

§ VI. Of the amount in which the seller ought to be condemned, in case of an eviction of a part of the thing, or of something which arises from it.

140. When the buyer suffers an eviction of a portion only of the thing sold, if this portion be an undivided and aliquot part of it, the seller ought to be condemned to restore him, (1.) a portion of the price equal to the part evicted. For example, if he suffers an eviction of the half or third part of the thing sold, the seller must restore the half or third part of the price. All that is said in the preceding paragraph, concerning the obligation to restore the whole of the price, in case of an eviction of the whole thing, is equally applicable to the obligation to restore a part of the price, in case of an eviction of a part of the thing sold.

141. (2.) The seller, as in case of an eviction of the whole, ought to acquit the buyer from condemnations against him, either for a restitution of the fruits of the part evicted, or in consequence of degradations committed; and, in short, against the expenses; the whole according to the distinctions laid down in the preceding paragraph.

142. (3.) Lastly, the seller ought to be condemned for the damages of the buyer, if the eviction causes him to suffer any in addition to the price. The inconvenience of becoming an owner in common with the party evicting him may be comprised and estimated in the damages. The rules laid down in the preceding paragraph, concerning the damages resulting from a total eviction, may, in like manner, be applied to the case of a partial eviction.

143. When the portion evicted is not an undivided but an integral part of the estate; as, for example, if I suffer an eviction of a meadow or a vineyard, dependent upon a farm which I purchased of you; in this case, to determine the

part of the price, which you ought to restore, an estimation must be made of the value of the meadow or vineyard, having regard and in proportion to the price, for which the whole farm was sold.

144. As the price, which ought to be restored in case of eviction, is that for which the thing is sold, and not its value at the time of the eviction, as is established in the preceding paragraph, it follows, that the estimation ought to be made, in reference to the situation, not only of the part evicted, but of the other parts of the farm at the time of the contract, and not to their situation at the time of the eviction; according to the law 13, D. *de evict.* (21, 2, 13): *Bonitatis æstimationem faciendam quum pars evinceretur, Proculus recte putabat, quæ fuisset venditionis tempore, non quum evinceretur.* But, in order to ascertain the damages which may be due to the buyer beyond the price, the estimation must be made in regard to the situation, in which the part evicted is at the time of the eviction, and to its value at that time. For example, if the vineyard, of which I am evicted, was worth 12,000 livres at the time of the contract, having regard to the value of the whole farm, and is worth 15,000 at the time of the eviction, the seller ought to be adjudged to pay, besides the 12,000, as a restitution of the price, the increased value of three thousand: *nam tanti mea interest eam habere licere;* Dumoulin, *Tr. de eo quod interest, n.* 67, 68, 69.

145. It remains to be observed, that an eviction of a part may sometimes give a right to the buyer to claim against the seller an entire rescission of the contract; and this happens, when it is probable, that, without the part evicted, the buyer would not have been willing to purchase the residue.

146. When the eviction is not of an undivided and aliquot nor of an integral part of the thing sold, but of something which arises from it; as, if one sells me an animal which

does not belong to him, and, after the death of the animal, I am evicted of the young, which it has brought forth; in this case, there is no ground for the first object of the action *ex empto*, which concerns a restitution of the price of the thing sold, because it is not the thing sold which is evicted, but only something which has arisen from it. But there is ground for the second object of the action *ex empto*, which concerns the *quod interest emptoris habere licere*, which must be determined according to the value of the thing, at the time of the eviction; Dumoulin, *Tr. de eo quod interest*, *n.* 149.

§ VII. Of the amount in which the seller ought to be condemned, when it is a second buyer who suffers the eviction.

147. When it is not the first buyer, who suffers the eviction, but a second buyer, to whom the first resells the thing, the damages which are due in this case, by the first seller to the first buyer, besides the restitution of the price, consist in any sum, over and above that price, which the first buyer, in the action of warranty brought by the second buyer, is condemned to pay him. For example, if I purchase an estate for 8000 livres, which I resell to Peter for 10,000 livres, and Peter being evicted, I am condemned to restore him the sum of 10,000 livres, and to pay him his damages, which are liquidated at the sum of 2,000 livres; the party of whom I purchase will be condemned in my favor to discharge me from the 12,000 livres, which I am condemned to pay to Peter, and consequently from the 4,000 livres, over and above the price, for which he sells me the estate.

148. *Vice versa*, suppose that I purchase an estate for 10,000 livres, and sell it to Peter for 6,000, and Peter being evicted, I am condemned to pay him the price, and his damages liquidated at 1,500 livres; is it sufficient for my warrantor to acquit me for the 7,500 livres, which I am

obliged to pay the second purchaser, and ought he not to render me the entire sum, for which he sold me the estate? It appears, according to the principles of Dumoulin, that he ought to pay the entire sum of 10,000 livres; not in virtue of the second object of the action *ex empto*, namely, that which the buyer suffers beyond the price, since what he suffers from the eviction is, on the contrary, much less than the price paid; but the warrantor is bound to this restitution, in virtue of the first object of the action *ex empto*, which consists in a restitution of the price, which the seller, in case of eviction, has no right to retain, in consequence of his neglect to perform the obligation on his part, that I and my successors should enjoy the estate.

149. Can the second buyer, by offering to discharge me from what I owe him, be permitted to sue the first seller, in my place, and for his own benefit, for a restitution of the price of 10,000 livres? The question may be decided in the affirmative; for, when I sell a thing to any one, I am considered as selling and transferring to him all the rights and actions, which tend to cause him to have the thing, and, consequently, the action *ex empto*; which I am entitled to bring against the seller, *ut præstet rem habere licere.* This appears to be included in the obligation, which I myself contract in his favor *præstandi emptori rem habere licere.*

§ VIII. **Of the effect upon the action of warranty, resulting from a clause of the contract on the part of the seller, to restore the price and a certain sum over and above the price, in case of eviction.**

150. The clause, by which, in a contract of sale, the seller is obliged, in case of eviction, to restore to the buyer the price and a certain portion of the price in addition, is very different, in our French law, from the stipulation *duplæ*, which was in use in the Roman law, by which the seller was obliged, in case of eviction, to restore double the price to the buyer. This stipulation was a contract accessory,

in truth, to the contract of sale, but separate and distinct from that contract, and which produced a separate action, very different from the action *ex empto;* and it was in the election of the buyer to commence either of these actions. On the contrary, this clause, which is inserted, at the present day, in a contract of sale, makes a part of that contract, and does not produce an action distinct from the action *ex empto;* but serves to determine the amount which the buyer is entitled to demand by the action *ex empto*, in case of an eviction foreseen by the clause.

151. The parties, by this clause, agree upon the damages, as a penalty which may be claimed by the buyer, in case of eviction; in such a manner, as if, for example, it is agreed, that the seller shall render to the buyer a third of the price in addition, the buyer cannot claim a greater sum, even when he can prove that the damages amount to more; and, *vice versa*, the seller cannot avoid the payment of the third part of the price in addition, even when the buyer does not suffer any damages beyond the price; Dumoulin, *Tr. de eo quod. int. n.* 120.

152. This rule admits of the following exceptions, namely: (1), when it is agreed, that the seller shall pay to the buyer, in case of eviction, a third part of the price in addition, *without prejudice to his right to recover greater damages;* or, when the contract, which contains the obligation to pay a third of the price in addition, in case of an eviction, contains also an obligation for damages: *Si adjectum sit sine præjudicio damnorum majorum; vel si nihilominus promissa sunt damna et interesse;* Dumoulin, *ibid. n.* 120.

(2.) If the eviction proceeds from the bad faith of the seller, or from some new act on his part; as, if, after a contract of sale, in which this clause is contained, and before the delivery, the seller, in prejudice of the sale, hypothecates the estate to a creditor, who afterwards evicts the buyer.

(3.) When this obligation to restore, in case of eviction, a third part of the price, or some other thing in addition, is contracted by the seller, as a penalty, *nomine pœnæ*, for the non-performance of the principal obligation; for the rule above-mentioned applies only when the clause makes a part of the principal provision of the contract, and is intended by the parties to regulate the object and extent of the principal obligation, in case of eviction. But when it includes a penalty, it is accessory to the principal provision. The obligation which results from it is a secondary obligation, and is termed a *penal obligation;* the nature of which is to accede to without diminishing the principal obligation, as is explained in the Treatise on Obligations, n. 342, to which the reader is referred; Dumoulin, *ibid. n.* 121.

153. It must be observed, that if this agreement is made only with a surety of the seller, it operates only as to him, and he is considered as thereby intending to restrain and limit his engagement to a third part of the price in addition, which does not discharge the seller, if the damages exceed that amount; Dumoulin, *ibid. n.* 120. But if the damages be less than this amount, the surety is notwithstanding liable only for their actual amount; it being of the essence of a surety's undertaking, that he shall be held liable for no more than the principal debtor; Tr. on Obl. n. 371. If there are several sellers, and this agreement is made with only one of them, it will operate only as to him; Dumoulin, *ibid. n.* 120.

§ IX. Of some particular cases, which give rise to questions concerning the action of warranty.

FIRST CASE.

154. A person, who is the owner of three undivided fourth parts of a meadow of one thousand acres, sells me the whole field, as belonging to him exclusively; subsequent to the contract, the river carries away two hundred acres, and the proprietor of the fourth part evicts me of a fourth part of

what remains of the field, namely, two hundred acres; the question is, for what part I am deemed to suffer an eviction, and for what part of the price, I am entitled to an action of warranty against the seller.

It seems, at first, that the eviction in this case is of a fourth part of the field, for the demander is really the proprietor of a fourth part. He reclaims a fourth part, and I am compelled to abandon it to him. I therefore suffer an eviction of a fourth, and consequently the seller ought to restore me a fourth of the price. It is true, that the loss caused by the river lessens the fourth part of which I am evicted; and, that, from two hundred and fifty acres of which it consisted, it is reduced to two hundred. But, according to the principles above established, the seller ought not to make a profit by a diminution of the thing sold, of which the buyer is afterwards evicted, and to be allowed on that account to retain any part of the price of the thing, which he has no right to sell, and which he cannot cause the buyer to enjoy. Notwithstanding these reasons, Papinian, in the law *ex mille* (D. 21, 2, 64), decides, that, in this case, I am considered to suffer an eviction of the fifth part only; and, consequently, that the action *de evictione* lies for the recovery of that part only of the price: *Stipulatio duplæ*, says he, *pro parte quinta, non quarta præstabitur; nam quod periit, damnum emptori, non venditori attulit.* The reason, which Papinian here gives, in his usual laconic style, for his opinion, has need of some explanation. The loss of the two hundred acres caused by the river is a loss by accident and irresistible force, which consequently falls upon the buyer, at whose risk the thing is after the contract of sale. The seller is not responsible for this loss, even for the fourth part which did not belong to him, in the two hundred acres carried away by the river; for, in order to give rise to the action *ex stipulatione*, it is not sufficient that the thing should be subject to eviction; it is necessary that the buyer should be really evicted. Now, the proprietor of the fourth part of the field, who brings against me his demand in revendication, does not by that demand and by the sentence passed upon it evict me of the fourth part belonging to him in the two hundred acres carried away by the river. As that which does not exist cannot be evicted, he evicts me only of the fourth part in the eight hundred acres remaining; and, as this fourth part amounts only to two hundred acres, it is only the fifth part of the field of a thousand acres which I purchased. It follows, therefore, that I am evicted only of the fifth part, and consequently that I can claim against the seller only a fifth part of the price. In this case, there is nothing opposed to the principles above established, that the seller ought not to profit by a deterioration and depreciation of the thing, when the buyer is evicted of it; and that he ought not on that account to retain a part of the price. These principles are applicable, if the river covers the whole field with sand, without carrying away any part of it. Though, in such a case, at the time of the eviction, the field is hardly worth the tenth part of the price paid for it, yet I am not the less entitled to reclaim the fourth part of the price, because I really suffer an eviction of the fourth part of the thing sold; and, as the seller does not fulfil his obligation, in relation to this fourth part, to cause me to enjoy it, he has no right to retain the price of it. But it is not contrary to the principles above stated, that the seller should profit indirectly, in the case supposed, from the destruction of the two hundred acres carried away by the river, because the fourth part, which his co-proprietor has in the thousand acres, being thereby reduced to a fifth part of the thing sold, it is only of a fifth part of the thing sold, that I am evicted, and for which consequently I am entitled to an action. The seller in this case profits indirectly from the loss, in the same manner, that he would profit indirectly from a total destruction of the field, as if it were wholly carried away, in which case, there could be no eviction.

155. This decision holds, when the seller of a thing belonging to another sells it in good faith, believing it to belong to him, which ought always to be presumed, until the contrary is proved; for, the seller is not held, in strictness, to transfer the property of the thing to the buyer, but only to defend him against evictions: *Venditor hactenus tenetur ut emptori rem habere liceat, non etiam ut ejus faciat;* D. 19, 1, 30, § 1: *Qui vendidit necesse non habet fundum emptoris facere;* D. 18, 1, 25, § 1. And, therefore, the seller, though he sells the property of another, does not fail in the obligation on his part, so long as the buyer does not suffer an eviction of the thing; and his obligation is considered as consummated, when, by the destruction of the thing, the buyer ceases to be in a situation to be evicted.

It would be otherwise, in case the seller, at the time of the contract, knew that a fourth part of the field, which he sold as his own exclusively, was not his own; in which case, the loss of the two hundred acres, caused by the river, would not discharge him from a restitution of an entire fourth part of the price. It cannot be said, as in reference to a seller in good faith, that he discharges his obligation in relation to the part which is destroyed; for, in this case, he fails in the obligation, which good faith imposes upon the parties to a contract of sale, by selling as his own that which he knows does not belong to him; and, from this bad faith, on his part, there results an action, which the buyer may commence before he suffers an eviction of the thing, D. 19, 1, 30, § 1, and which is not extinguished by a loss of it, since the seller ought not to make a profit of his bad faith, and to retain the price of a thing which he sells in bad faith.

SECOND CASE.

156. Papinian, in the law *ex mille* (D. 21, 2, 64), proposes another question. Retaining the same supposition of the

sale of a meadow of a thousand acres, of which the river carries away two hundred, he inquires, whether, in case of an eviction of all that remains of it, upon a demand in revendication by one who is the proprietor of the whole, I can maintain an action for the whole, or only for four fifths, against a seller in good faith. It seems, that, according to the reasoning employed in the decision of the preceding question, I ought to have an action to recover only the four fifths and not the whole; for the 800 acres which remain, and of which I am evicted, make only four fifths and not the whole of the 1000 acres, which I purchased, and I am not evicted of the other fifth part which the river carries away. The loss which I suffer cannot be attributed to any eviction, but to an irresistible force, which ought to fall on me as the buyer. Notwithstanding these reasons, Papinian decides that the seller is liable in this case for the whole: *Si totus fundus quem flumen diminuerat evictus sit jure, non diminuetur evictionis obligatio; non magis quam si fundus deterior factus sit;* D. 21, 2, 64. Dumoulin, *Tr. de eo quod int. n.* 111, 112, 113, 114, subscribes to this as well as the preceding decision. The reason which he mentions for the difference is, that the proprietor of the whole estate sold, being evicted of all that remains of it, such eviction must be considered a total eviction, which ought consequently to oblige the seller, *evictionis nomine*, for the whole: *Toto residuo, jure* TOTIUS, *evicto, verba stipulationis verificantur in toto, quia totum residuum est totus fundus, et totus evincitur; dict. n.* 113. (3.) If it is objected, that the eight hundred acres which remain, and of which I am evicted, are only a part of the thousand, which I purchased; it may be answered, that, though at the time of the contract, they were only a part of the whole field, yet they become the whole of it, by the loss of the surplus, and it is as of the whole and not of a part that I am evicted. On the other hand, in the preceding case, the eviction which I suffer is an eviction of a part, and consequently gives rise to the action *de evictione* only for a part: *Locus esse potest benignæ interpretationi in hoc casu*, says Caillet, *ad h. l.* Though the part belonging to the demander were, at the time of the contract, a fourth part of the thousand acres, yet, as it is reduced by the abrasion of the river, to an undivided quantity of two hundred acres, which is only a fifth part of the thousand, and as the eviction which I suffer is consequently only of a fifth part, the action *de evictione* ought to be permitted to be brought only for the fifth part: *Ex quo formula evictionis semel limitatur ad partem, necesse est ut limitetur ad partem realiter per evictionem ablatam;* Dumoulin, *ibid. n.* 113.

The distinction, which Papinian makes between these two cases, appears to me to be more subtle than solid. The same reason, which induces him to decide, in the first case of the law *ex mille*, that the seller ought not to restore the price of the fourth part, which the demander has in the two hundred acres carried away by the river, it seems to me, should also induce him in the latter case, to decide in like manner, that he ought not to restore the price of the two hundred acres; for, in both cases, we find the same reason, namely, that the buyer cannot be evicted of that which does not exist, and that the action *de evictione* lies only for that of which the buyer is actually evicted. The reason mentioned by Dumoulin for the difference has more of subtlety than of solidity in it.

157. Even though the decision of Papinian, in the second case, ought to be followed, it can be so only where the party, evicting me of the eight hundred acres which remain, is in fact the owner of the whole thousand. But if he is the proprietor only of the remaining eight hundred acres, and is not the proprietor of the part which the river carries away, there can be no doubt, that, in such case, the eviction cannot be considered a total eviction of the thing sold, which entitles me to an action for the whole against the seller; inas-

much, as the demander who evicts me is not the owner of the whole, but only of a part of that which I purchase, though that part is all that remains of it, he can evict me *jure hujus partis*, and not *jure totius*, as in the preceding case; and, consequently, the seller cannot be held, in this case, for such eviction, except in proportion to that part, that is to say, for four fifths; Dumoulin, *ibid. n.* 217.

158. If a person sells me, for one and the same price, of ten thousand livres, two separate fields of equal goodness containing five hundred acres each, one of which belongs to him and the other to a third person, and, after two hundred acres of that which belongs to such third person are carried away by a river, he evicts me of the three hundred acres which remain, there is no doubt, that, in this case, we ought to decide, as in the first question, and for the reasons there given, that, as these three hundred acres are only three tenths of the whole thousand which are sold me, the seller is liable on account of the eviction, for three tenths only of the price. But if these two fields are sold for separate prices, thereby constituting two separate sales, the eviction is a total one of the object of one of these two sales, and amounts to the case of the second question; Dumoulin, *ibid. n.* 118.

THIRD CASE.

159. Papinian, in the law *ex mille*, §1, (D. 21, 2, 64, §1), proposes a third question. He supposes that the field of a thousand acres is enlarged by alluvion so as to contain twelve hundred acres; and that the proprietor of an undivided fifth part of it evicts the buyer of that part, which, in consequence of the alluvion, is found to contain two hundred and forty acres. He inquires whether the seller, in this case, ought to be held *de evictione* only for the fifth part, or whether he ought to be held for a greater part, because the two hundred and forty acres evicted make more than a fifth part of the whole thousand sold. He decides that the seller is liable

only for the fifth. The reason is, that the buyer is not in fact evicted of any more than the fifth part. The remaining forty acres, which he is obliged to abandon, make a part of the accession to the field, rather than of the field itself. Now, as to what concerns the stipulation *de evictione*, and the obligation for a restitution of the price, the seller is liable only for an eviction of the thing sold, and not of that which accrues to it: *Alluvionis periculum non præstat venditor ;* D. 21, 2, 64, §1.

It must be observed, that, though this decision of Papinian, and the principle upon which it rests, *Alluvionis periculum non præstat venditor*, refer only to the action *ex stipulatione duplæ*, which is treated of in the law *ex mille*, they may also be applied to the first object of the action *ex empto*, which concerns the mere restitution of the price. But, in regard to the second object of this action, which lies against the seller *in id quod supra pretium pluris interest emptoris rem evictam non esse*, the loss which the buyer suffers of the forty acres, which make a part of the accession to the estate by alluvion, may be taken into the consideration, and it cannot be said, in this respect, that *periculum alluvionis non præstat venditor ;* for every augmentation of the thing may be considered in estimating the damages, as has already been established.

FOURTH CASE.

160. Lastly, Papinian, in the same law *ex mille*, § 2, proposes a fourth question. He supposes that the river carries away two hundred acres of a meadow containing a thousand; but, afterwards, on another side, adds a like quantity of two hundred acres by alluvion; and that upon a demand in revendication by one, who is a proprietor of a fifth part of the field, the buyer suffers an eviction of this fifth part amounting to two hundred acres. Papinian demands whether the seller, in this case, is liable for a fifth or a less part of

the field; and, he decides, in accordance with his previous decisions, that he is not liable for a fifth part, but only in the proportion of one hundred and sixty acres; because the other forty acres which are evicted do not make a part of the thousand acres of which the field consists, but only of the accession by alluvion of two hundred acres, *cujus alluvionis periculum non præstat venditor*, as he says in reference to the preceding question. Dumoulin subscribes to this decision, observing, however, as has already been remarked, on the preceding question, that this decision, like the former, relates only to the action *ex stipulatione duplæ*, and to the first object of the action *ex empto*, which concern a restitution of the price; and not to the second object of that action, which includes *quod supra pretium emptoris interest.*

This distinction between the two objects of the action *ex empto* may be illustrated by an example. Suppose, in the above case, that the field of one thousand acres is sold for one thousand livres, which is at the rate of a livre the acre; the buyer then becomes a creditor for one hundred and sixty livres, in virtue of the first object of the action *ex empto*, which concerns a restitution of the price; because a restitution of the price is due to him only for the one hundred and sixty acres, which make a part of the thousand sold, and not for the forty others, which make a part of the alluvion. Though the extrinsic or intrinsic value of these estates may be increased or diminished, yet it is only for this sum of one hundred and sixty livres, that the buyer becomes a creditor in virtue of the first object of the action *ex empto*, which concerns a restitution of the price; but, in regard to the second object of the action *ex empto*, which concerns the *id quod supra pretium emptoris habere licere*, the whole of the two hundred acres of which the buyer is evicted may be taken into the consideration, as well that part which belongs to the field sold, as that which makes a part of the accession by alluvion. Therefore, if, at the time of the eviction, these two hundred acres are worth more than the sum of one hundred and sixty livres, which is due as a restitution of the price, the buyer may recover the excess in virtue of the second object of the action *ex empto;* but if the field becomes diminished in value, so that at the time of the eviction, the two hundred acres are worth no more or even less than one hundred and sixty livres, the buyer is not entitled to recover any more.

161. Papinian, in the case put, supposes the accession by alluvion to take place on another side of the estate; ought the same decision to take place, if the accession happens on the same side, from whence the two hundred acres are previously carried away? Cujas, *in Papin.*, on this paragraph, inclines to the opinion, that, in this case, the seller ought to be liable for the fifth part, and that the two hundred acres of accession ought to be considered the same which the river previously carried away, and which it may be deemed to restore. But Dumoulin, *n.* 119, decides, with reason, that the rule should be the same, provided the increase is made *ex intervallo*, after an interval of time, and not *in continenti*, immediately after the two hundred acres are carried away by the river; for the accession formed by an alluvion *ex intervallo* is a new accession, and cannot be considered as formed of that which the river previously carried away.

FIFTH CASE.

162. I become the purchaser of the useful seignory (*seigneurie utile*) of a house, of which there remain thirty years only of enjoyment. It does not belong to the seller, and after twenty years of enjoyment, I am evicted by the owner, and am obliged to abandon it to him, without any restitution of the fruits. Have I a right to recover of the seller the whole of the price? The reason for doubting is drawn from the principle, that the situation, in which the thing evicted is found to be, is only to be taken into consideration in refer-

ence to the second object of the action *ex empto*, which is the *quod interest emptoris ;* but, that as to the first object, which is a restitution of the price, it cannot be regarded, and, that however deteriorated and depreciated the thing may be, the obligation of the seller, as to this first object, is not thereby diminished: *Non diminuetur evictionis obligatio, si incuria fundus, aut servus traditus deterior factus sit;* D. 21, 2, 64. We must decide, however, in this case, that the seller is bound to restore the price only in proportion to the term which remains at the time of the eviction.

It is true, that when the whole thing sold is evicted, however deteriorated and depreciated it may be, the seller is bound to a restitution of the whole price, because he does not, in any part, fulfil his obligation. For example, if one sells me an estate of which I am evicted, and after the contract, it is covered entirely with sand, by an inundation, so as to be worth not more than a tenth part of the price, the seller is not the less obliged to restore the whole price. But, in the present case, the thing sold being a successive interest, consisting of a certain term of enjoyment, namely thirty years, the enjoyment of the five last years, of which I am evicted, is not the whole thing, but is the sixth part of it; and it is for this sixth part, that the seller fails in his obligation to cause me to enjoy it. He performs it for the remainder; *præstitit mihi habere licere.* He ought therefore to be liable, on account of this eviction, to no more than a sixth part of the price; for, otherwise, I should have both the price and the thing.

It is to be observed, that if the seignory of which I am evicted for the remaining five years, by any extrinsic or intrinsic augmentation, becomes of greater value than the sixth part of the price, the seller, *ex secundo capite actionis ex empto*, is held liable for such increased value.

163. This decision, in the case of a seignory, may be applied to a right of usufruct. If, at the age of thirty years,

I purchase the right of usufruct of an estate, and after an enjoyment of fifty years, I am evicted at the age of eighty; it is certain, that the right of which I am evicted is but a small part of that which I purchased, and that the eviction ought not to give me a right of action to recover the whole price. We ought to estimate the value of the right for the uncertain term of my life, or the seller ought to be condemned to pay me, during my life, an annuity equal to the revenue of the estate.

If the revenue of this right of usufruct is diminished subsequent to the contract, the annuity which the seller ought to be condemned to pay me, instead of a restitution of the price of the remainder of the right, ought to be not only equal to the present value of the revenue, but to its value at the time of the contract; for the seller ought to restore the price which the thing evicted is worth at the time of the contract, and for which it is sold, though its value is diminished at the time of the eviction.

On the other hand, if the revenue is increased subsequent to the contract, the annuity ought to be equal to its present value, in consequence of the second obligation, by which the seller, in case of eviction, is liable to the buyer, *in id omne quod supra pretium emptoris interest habere licere.*

SIXTH CASE.

164. A master, by his testament, bequeaths their liberty to his negroes, when they arrive at the age of seventy years. The heir sells me one of these slaves, then forty years of age, without informing me of this testamentary disposition, which does not come to his knowledge until afterwards. Thirty years afterwards, the slave reclaims his liberty. This is an eviction which the seller is considered as warranting against. Must we decide, as in the preceding cases, that he is liable for a restitution of the price, in proportion only to the estimated value of the remainder of the slave's life? It

seems, at first, that we ought, on the contrary, to decide that he is liable for a restitution of the whole price, and that this case is very different from the preceding; for, in this, the thing sold is not, as in the other cases, a moral being, successive and divisible, which consists in a measure of a certain term of enjoyment. The negro is a physical and indivisible being. It cannot be said, that, at seventy years of age, at the time of the eviction, he is a part only of the negro, which I purchased. He is entirely the same that I purchased when forty years of age; and, consequently, it cannot be denied, that I suffer an eviction of the whole thing sold; from whence, it might be concluded, that the seller is bound to restore the whole price. Notwithstanding these reasons, Dumoulin very well decides, that the seller is bound only to restore a part of the price, in proportion to the estimated value of the uncertain time of the remainder of the slave's life. The reason is, that, though a man is in himself an indivisible being, yet he is a kind of property, the duration of which is not perpetual and without bounds, like that of a piece of land, or a house, but which is of a limited duration, coextensive with his life, by which the price is regulated. In the sale of a slave, therefore, as in the sale of an emphyteusis or of a usufruct, the price of the sale is the price of a limited time of possession and enjoyment of the slave, equal to the probable duration of his life; and, when I am evicted, after thirty years of possession and enjoyment, the seller fulfils, for the greater part, the obligation which he contracted in my favor, *præstare eum mihi habere licere.* He fails in his obligation only for the little time which remains of the life of the slave, and is consequently bound to a restitution of the price only in proportion to that time. This is what Dumoulin teaches, *n.* 128: *In servo vendito, ex natura rei quæ tempore finitur, constat non minus durationem vitæ verisimiliter consideratam, quam in venditione ususfructus vel emphyteosis temporalis; uterque ergo casus, temporis commensurationem et appreciationem recipit;* and, again, *n.* 127: *Quum non venderetur res perpetuo durabilis, certum est non esse actum ut habere liceret perpetuo, sed ad tempus vitæ quod verisimiliter prævisum et æstimatum fuit, et ad verisimilem durationem majus vel minus definitum pretium.... Quum ergo toto fere tempore vitæ prævisæ fruitus sit emptor, nec per evictionem absit nisi modicum et fere inutile tempus, non potest totum pretium repetere.* In this respect, such things are very different from land; for, in the sale of a piece of land, its duration which is perpetual is not taken into consideration in order to determine the price; and, when the buyer is evicted, whatever time he may enjoy before the eviction, such enjoyment does not diminish the entire price, which the seller is bound to restore; as that time, however long it may be, is infinitely small, in proportion to the perpetuity of the duration of the possession, which the seller is bound to cause him to have, and of which the eviction deprives him.

There is also another reason, given by Dumoulin, *n.* 129, for the difference, which is, that, in regard to land, if the buyer enjoys the thing for some time before the eviction, he is on the other hand deprived of the interest and revenue of the price paid, which the seller enjoys in his place, and which equals or even surpasses in ordinary cases the revenue of the estate; whereas, in regard to things of short duration, as the revenue generally much exceeds the interest of the price, the buyer, who enjoys the thing, would profit at the expense of the seller, if the whole price were restored to him.

165. The above decision, in regard to things of a limited duration, holds good not only in the case where the seller is the owner and transfers to the buyer a property which endures until the happening of the condition, which gives rise to the eviction; but, even in the case where he sells a thing which does not belong to him at all. In both cases, he is

discharged from a restitution of the price, in proportion to the time of the possession and enjoyment, which the buyer has; for, though the seller, at the time of the contract is not the owner of the thing which he sells, yet, in his quality of possessor, he has a right against every person but the real owner. He has a right to the enjoyment of the thing until an eviction, if he does not sell it; and, it is immaterial to the buyer, whether the seller is the proprietor or not. In order to render the buyer the debtor of the seller, for the price of the enjoyment which he has, it is only necessary that the latter should cause him to have that enjoyment; Dumoulin, 130, 131.

ARTICLE VI.

Of the exceptions of warranty, which result from the obligation of warranty.

166. The obligation of warranty, which the seller contracts in favor of the buyer, gives the buyer against the seller and his heirs who succeed to his obligation, not only an action but also an exception, according to the maxim, that he, who is entitled to an action, is also, for a stronger reason, entitled to an exception: *Cui damus actiones, eidem et exceptiones competere multo magis quis dixerit;* D. 50, 17, 156, § 1.

This exception arises, when he who sells me a thing which does not belong to him, and who afterwards becomes the owner of it by a right of succession or otherwise, brings a demand in revendication against me, for the same thing. His demand proceeds against me, since he is the owner and not I; for, he cannot, by the delivery, transfer to me an ownership which is not then his. But, as, by selling me the thing, he contracts in my favor an obligation to warrant it to me, that is to say, to cause me to have it, and to defend me against all troubles in my possession of it, there results from this obligation an exception which excludes his demand; for, his obligation to cause me to have the thing sold is manifestly opposed to the demand which he brings against me for it; his obligation to put an end to all troubles brought against me in relation to the thing obliges him to put a stop to that which he himself causes by his demand; and, since he would be subject to the action of warranty, if another person should make a demand against me, he ought not himself to be allowed to bring any demand against me. This is the signification of the maxim: *Quem de evictione tenet actio, eumdem agentem repellit exceptio.*

167. For the same reason, if you sell and put me in possession of a thing, of which you are not the owner, and, after becoming the owner, sell the same thing to a second buyer, who reclaims it against me, I may avail myself of the exception resulting from your obligation of warranty; for, though you are the proprietor of the thing which you sell and deliver to me, at the time of the sale to the second buyer, yet you do not transfer the property of it to him; as the property cannot be transferred without a delivery, which you cannot make, not being in possession; *infra*, part 5. By the sale, you only substitute him in your action of revendication, in order that he may prosecute it *tanquam tuus procurator in rem suam;* but you do not, by so doing, confer any greater right than you yourself have. This action is useless. It exists *sola subtilitate juris.* The exception of warranty renders it inefficacious.

168. This exception of warranty is equally good against the heirs of the seller, though they are proprietors in their own right; for, they succeed to this obligation as to all other rights and obligations of the deceased; and, therefore, if he, who is the true proprietor of, or has some hypothecary or other right in a thing, which is sold to me by one to whom it does not belong, becomes afterwards the heir of the seller, he is not allowed to maintain any action of revendication, or any hypothecary or other action against me, to compel

me to abandon the estate, by reason of the action of warranty to which I am entitled against the seller; for, having himself become the heir of the seller, and in that quality liable to my action of warranty, he cannot maintain actions against me in his own right, which, in his capacity of heir, he is bound to put a stop to, according to the rule: *Quem de evictione tenet actio, eum agentem repellit exceptio.*

169. This exception takes place also, even in regard to the estate of a minor which his tutor sells as belonging to him (the tutor), or with a promise to procure a ratification from the minor. If the minor becomes the heir of the tutor, the exception of warranty may be set up against him, and will prevent him from claiming the estate. This decision is not contrary to the law, which prohibits the alienations of the estates of minors; for, if the minor cannot reclaim the estate, it is not because the estate is legally alienated, but because the minor becomes the heir of the seller.

170. It would seem, that, for the same reason, we ought to decide, that a person substituted cannot, after the opening of the substitution, reclaim against a third person the goods comprised in the substitution, when such party substituted becomes the heir of the party charged with the substitution, who is the seller of the property to such third person. Notwithstanding this, the new ordinance of substitutions, tit. 2, art. 31, decides, that the party substituted may reclaim property so situated, by restoring the price of the sale.

The reason is, that the ordinance, the principal end of which is to assure the effect of substitutions, and to cause goods comprised in them to pass to the parties who are called, in order to produce this effect, provides by this disposition, that parties charged with a substitution cannot, by selling, oblige themselves to a warranty against the substitution, for fear that the obligation of warranty, which passes to their heirs, who are frequently the same persons called to the substitution, may, in this respect, form some obstacle to the execution of the substitution. In this, the ordinance does no wrong to the buyer, because the registering of the substitution making it public, he ought to know that the estate is burdened with a substitution, and if he purchases, he must impute it to his own fault.

171. This provision of the ordinance, in relation to the sale of a substituted estate, being a particular law, ought, according to the maxim which applies to laws of that description, to be confined to its own particular case, and consequently cannot be extended to the sale of the estate of a minor, who afterwards becomes the heir of the seller. Besides, there is a great difference between these two cases. The buyer of a thing, charged with a substitution, either knows or ought to know that fact, which is made public by the registry; but, one who buys of a tutor, as belonging to him, a thing belonging to the minor, cannot know that the thing belongs to the minor; and, therefore, in such case, it would not be just, that the seller should not be subject to a warranty in his favor.

172. From this enactment of the new ordinance, that the party substituted may, by offering the price, reclaim the estate substituted, though he is the heir of the seller, ought we to infer the general rule, that the ordinance does not permit the seller to oblige himself to a warranty against the substitution in favor of the buyer, even by an express stipulation to that effect? It seems to me, that the ordinance supposes this rule; for, if the sale of an article substituted obliges the seller to warranty, the obligation will necessarily pass to his heir, since an heir is merely the successor to the rights and obligations of a party deceased. When the party substituted becomes the heir of the seller, he becomes thereby bound to a warranty of the thing sold, and consequently cannot demand an abandonment of it; inasmuch, as it would be inconsistent that a party should require me to

abandon a thing, in the possession of which he is under an obligation to maintain me.

173. The law established by the ordinance, being a new law, ought not to operate against sales previously contracted; and, there is ground for the opinion, that, in this case, the party substituted, if he becomes the heir of the seller, will not be allowed, according to the provision of the ordinance, to demand a surrender of the thing, by offering a restitution of the price; for, the obligation of warranty being legally contracted by the seller before the ordinance, it necessarily passes to his heir, and as necessarily excludes the action, which, in his quality of party substituted, he might otherwise commence.

174. Is one, who is the heir in part only of the seller, to be wholly excluded from his demand to compel an abandonment of the estate, by the exception of warranty? It would seem, at first, according to the principles above established, that he ought to be declared not receivable in his demand for the whole, since, as the obligation to defend is indivisible, *supra*, n. 105, he is bound to defend against it for the whole. Nevertheless, it is decided in the law 14, *Cod. de rei vendicat.* (3, 32, 14), in express terms, that the heir of the seller, who is the owner of the thing sold in his own right, is excluded from his demand in revendication, as to that part only for which he is the heir of the seller. It is true, that this law refers to the case of a buyer, who has knowledge, at the time of the contract, that the thing sold does not belong to the seller; but, this circumstance is indifferent to the decision; for, the obligation, which the seller contracts to defend the buyer against all troubles, is not the less an obligation of an indivisible act, which each heir of the seller is bound to, for the whole, whether the buyer knows or is ignorant that the thing sold does not belong to the seller. We must therefore decide indifferently, according to this law, that, notwithstanding the reasons for

doubting above proposed, the heir of the seller, who is so only in part, is excluded only for the part for which he is the heir, from the actions, to which he is entitled in his own right, to compel the buyer to an abandonment of the thing sold. The reason is, that the obligation of the seller *præstandi emptori rem habere licere* being a divisible obligation when the thing sold is divisible, and each of the heirs of the seller being consequently a debtor of the thing sold only for his hereditary part, each of them entirely fulfils his obligation, by surrendering the thing to the buyer, as to the part for which he is the heir, and by prosecuting his action of revendication only for the surplus. If the seller dies without making a delivery of the thing, the buyer cannot demand it of each of the heirs, except for the part as to which he is the heir; for, the seller, by executing his obligation by a delivery, ought not to render the condition of his heirs worse than it would be, if it were in no manner executed. As to the objection drawn from the obligation to defend, which is indivisible, the answer is, that this obligation, as has been remarked in its place, is not precise and absolute, but one from which each heir of the seller, though held liable for the whole on account of the indivisibility of the defence, may discharge himself, by satisfying, as much as is incumbent on him for the part of which he is the heir, the principal obligation, *præstare emptori rem habere licere.* It is upon this principle, that the heir in part, if summoned in warranty by the buyer to defend him against the demand of a third person, may discharge himself from his obligation, by offering for his part the damages resulting from the non-performance of the obligation *præstandi emptori rem habere licere.* For the same reason, when the heir of the seller, who is so only in part, and who in his own right is the owner of the thing sold, fully satisfies, for the part as to which he is heir, his obligation *præstandi rem habere licere,* by surrendering the thing for that part of which he is the debtor of it, that is to say, for which he is the heir of the seller, he is from that time discharged from his obligation to defend the buyer against the demand in revendication, which he may bring in his individual capacity for the surplus. The obligation to defend the buyer is subordinate to the obligation *præstandi rem habere licere;* and, consequently, ceases in him who fulfils the latter.

It must be observed, however, that it is in the choice of the buyer, either to retain that portion of the thing sold, which the owner, as heir of the seller for that part, cannot claim in revendication, or to abandon the entire thing to the heir upon his action in revendication, and to cause him to be condemned to pay, for the part of which he is the heir, the damages resulting from the eviction; for, not having purchased the thing to have it only in part, he cannot be obliged to retain it only for a part. This is the doctrine of Dumoulin, *Tr. de div. et ind., p.* 2, *n.* 499, 500, 501. Henrys, t. 1, 4, 31, says, that the heir in part ought to be admitted in his individual capacity, to a revendication of the whole, by offering the damages for the part of which he is heir. This opinion is contrary to principles.

175. It is otherwise in the case of a beneficiary heir. The exception resulting from the warranty, to which he is liable in that capacity, cannot exclude him from actions to which he is entitled in his own right; the buyer can only obtain against him, in his character of beneficiary heir, a condemnation for damages to be executed upon the goods of the succession. The reason is drawn from the principles relating to the subject of beneficiary heirs. A beneficiary heir is not liable for the debts and obligations of the deceased out of his own proper goods, but only out of those which belong to the succession. The obligation of warranty, which is a debt of the succession, cannot therefore exclude him from actions, to which he is entitled in his own right, and which are his own proper goods.

176. The exception of warranty may be opposed not only to the heirs of the seller, but to all those who succeed to or participate in his obligation. For example, it may be opposed to a universal legatee or donee, either of the whole or of a part of the goods of the seller, against the actions, which such legatee or donee may commence in his own right. But as these persons are held for the debts, to the amount only of the goods comprised in the donation or legacy, they may avoid the exception, by offering to abandon and give up such goods. Besides, they have not the same right as the beneficiary heir; they cannot avoid the exception but by abandoning the goods; for, universal donees or legatees have not the right, which a beneficiary heir has, of not being liable for the debts of the succession, out of their own proper goods; they have only a right to discharge themselves by surrendering the goods comprised in the gift or legacy, because they are liable only to the amount of such goods.

177. The exception of warranty may, in like manner, be opposed to the sureties of the seller, against the actions, which they are entitled to bring in their own right against the buyer, for a surrender of the thing sold: C. 8, 45, 11. Despeisses, *p.* 1, 7, 55, says, that this decision takes place only where the surety, at the time of his becoming such, is the owner of the thing, because, by making himself a surety in the sale of the thing, he renounces the right which he has of reclaiming it; but, that it ought not to exclude him from his demand, when he does not become the proprietor until after he becomes the surety, because in the latter case, he cannot be considered to renounce a right which he has not. This distinction is good for nothing. The exception of warranty results from the obligation of warranty, which the surety contracts by acceding to that of the seller. This obligation consists in defending the buyer against all demands tending to an eviction, and consequently in defending him against the demand, which the surety has a right to

commence against him, and which therefore deprives him of his right to commence his action, whether he has the right at the time of becoming surety, or whether he acquires it afterwards; for, it implies a contradiction, if he may in his individual capacity bring a suit, which, in his character of surety, he is obliged to cause to be stopped.

178. Can a surety, to whom I oppose the exception of warranty, object, that in his quality of surety, his obligation of warranty is only subsidiary to that of the seller, who is the principal debtor of it; that he is entitled to the benefit of discussion; and that I ought to proceed against the seller before I oppose the exception of warranty against him? No: for a surety cannot set up the exception of discussion, except when the principal debtor may acquit the debt. But, in the case supposed, the obligation of warranty, of which the seller is the principal debtor, and to which the surety accedes, being nothing else than an obligation to defend me, and to put a stop to all actions which may be brought against me to compel an abandonment of the thing, is an obligation which cannot be discharged by the seller, who is the principal debtor of it, and which can only be discharged by the surety, since he alone can put a stop to the action, which he himself brings against me in his individual capacity, by abandoning his action.

It may be objected, that if it is not in the power of the seller to acquit his primitive obligation, it is in his power to acquit his secondary obligation, which consists in paying me the damages which result from an eviction, and, that, so far as it is in his power to acquit his obligation, I cannot prosecute my suit against the surety. The answer to this is, that the primitive obligation of warranty ought not to be converted into the secondary obligation for damages, except in those cases, in which it cannot be acquitted by all those who are liable to it; and, that as the primitive obligation, to which the surety is liable, may be acquitted on his part, by causing him to be declared not receivable in the demand which he brings in his own right, we ought to declare him to be thus barred of his action, rather than to convert his primitive obligation of warranty into the secondary obligation for damages.

179. The obligation of warranty, which the surety contracts, on behalf of the seller, passes to his heirs and other universal successors; and, consequently, the exception of warranty may be opposed to them against the actions, which they may bring, in their own right, against the buyer, to compel him to abandon the thing sold.

The law 31, *Cod. de evict.* (8, 45, 31), seems to declare the contrary: *Heredem fidejussoris rerum, pro quibus defunctus apud emptorem intercesserat pro venditore, factum ejus, cui successit, ex sua persona dominium vindicare non impedit, scilicet evictionis causa durante actione.* But, Cujas, by the explanation, which he gives of this passage, removes the difficulty. This law says, indeed, that the obligation of warranty, to which the heir of the surety succeeds, does not prevent him from prosecuting the action to which he is entitled in his own right, to compel the buyer to abandon the estate to him, when the buyer does not avail himself of the exception of warranty; but, it does not deny, that the buyer may, on his part, oppose against this action the exception which results from the obligation of warranty. It is necessary to suppose, in the case of this law, that the buyer, who might oppose the exception, does not in fact make it, but suffers himself to be condemned to abandon the estate. The question made is, whether the buyer, in such case, is entitled to the action *de evictione* against the heir. The reason for doubting is, that a party is not entitled to this action, when he may avoid the eviction, as the buyer may do, by setting up the exception of warranty; but the law decides, that, as the heir is the party who causes the eviction, he cannot object to the buyer, that he might have avoided it, and consequently that the buyer may have the action *de evictione* against him. This is the meaning of these last terms of the law; *Scilicet evictionis causa durante actione.*

For want of a knowledge of this solution, Despeisses, *loco citato*, has recourse to a distinction, which is not tenable, namely, that the heir of the seller is subject to the exception of warranty, because the seller is bound, *præstare emptori rem habere licere;* but, that the heir of the surety is not subject to it, because the surety is bound only *ad interesse;* as if it were not of the nature of the surety's obligation, that he should be deemed to bind himself to all the obligations of the principal debtor.

180. The exception of warranty may also be opposed to a married woman, between whom and her husband there exists a community of goods, as to the moiety for which she is liable to the debts of the community; and there is a proper case for the exception, when she reclaims her own goods, which have been sold without her consent, by her husband, during the community; for her character of owner in common (*commune*) causes her to participate in all the obligations contracted by her husband during the community, and consequently in the obligation of warranty contracted by him by the sale of her estate. The woman, therefore, as owner in common, being liable to the obligation of warranty, for one half, ought to be excluded from her action of revendication, as to one half, at least unless she offers to abandon, and to account for all the goods which she receives from the community, in virtue of the privilege, to which wives are entitled, of discharging themselves, by making a good and lawful inventory, from all the debts and obligations of the community, for which they are liable only to the amount of the goods in their possession.

181. In order that he, who claims the right of property or some other right in a thing sold, should be declared not receivable in the demand which he brings to recover it, it is necessary that he should be personally liable to the obliga-

tion of warranty. It is not sufficient that he detains the thing in virture of a hypothecation. It is only to him who is personally bound to the warranty, that I have a right to say: you are yourself obliged to defend me against the action which you commence against me, and therefore you are not receivable to commence it. It is only in regard to such an one that the maxim is applicable: *Quem de evictione tenet actio, eum agentem repellit exceptio.* As the right of hypothecation, which I have upon an estate of which the party evicting me is in possession, consists only in a right to receive my damages caused by the eviction out of the price of the estate, I can demand nothing more of him, than, that, by abandoning to him on my part the thing sold, he may on his part be condemned to abandon to me the estate hypothecated to the warranty of the thing, in order that it may be sold and that I may receive my damages out of the proceeds, unless he prefers to pay me the damages.

According to this principle, the heir in part only of the seller, though in possession of goods,—and also a wife owner in common, though in possession of property acquired during the community, which is hypothecated to my warranty, ought not to be barred of the actions, to which they are severally entitled in their own right against me, to compel me to abandon the thing sold, except as to the part for which they are personally responsible in warranty; and I ought to be condemned to abandon it to them for the surplus; saving, that, on their part, they ought to be condemned to abandon the goods hypothecated to my warranty, of which they are in possession, in order that I may receive my damages from the proceeds thereof, unless they prefer to pay the damages.

ARTICLE VII.

Of cases in which the obligation of warranty does not arise, at least in regard to the damages which the buyer suffers from the eviction over and above the price paid.

We may distinguish three different classes of cases, in which the obligation of warranty does not arise, at least, as to the object of the damages, which the buyer suffers from the eviction, over and above the price. The *first* class consists of those cases in which there is a derogation from the obligation of warranty: The *second* consists of those in which there is no warranty unless it is expressly stipulated: And, the *third* class includes those cases, in which there is no obligation of warranty, even if it is expressly stipulated.

§ I. First class of cases.

182. The law common to all contracts of sale, which obliges the seller to a warranty of the thing sold, in favor of the buyer, concerning only the particular interest of buyers, the parties are permitted to derogate from it, by particular agreements: *Pacisci contra edictum Ædilium omni modo licet*, D., 2, 14, 31. The obligation of warranty is indeed of the nature of the contract of sale, and is always understood, if it is not expressed; but it is not of its essence. There may be a contract of sale, without any obligation of warranty; and, consequently, it may be excluded from the contract by a particular clause.

183. The clauses which exclude the obligation of warranty may be more or less extended. Sometimes the warranty is excluded only in relation to a single kind of eviction; as, when the seller declares by the contract, that the estate is subject to a right of preëmption, or redemption, to such a hypothecation, or to such a substitution, &c. By such and other similar clauses, the seller is discharged from his

obligation of warranty, in reference to the kind of eviction only which is declared by the contract; but, he is not the less obliged to warranty, on account of evictions which the buyer may suffer from any other cause.

184. Sometimes the clause is of greater extent; as, when the seller stipulates that he will warrant only against his own acts. By such a clause, he is discharged from a warranty, whatever may be the cause of eviction, unless it proceeds from his own act, such, for example, as a hypothecary action, brought by a creditor in virtue of a hypothecation contracted by the seller himself.

185. If the seller stipulates generally, that he will not be held to any warranty, without making an express exception of evictions which proceed from his own act; the clause will not thereby be more extended than the preceding, nor will it differ from it; but the exception will be easily understood. It would be contrary to good faith, for the seller, who cannot be ignorant of his own acts, to expose the buyer to evictions, which may happen in consequence thereof, without giving him information.

186. The clause, by which the seller stipulates that he will not be liable to warranty, prevents any claim against him for the buyer's damages, resulting from his inability to defend him against evictions and to fulfil his promise to cause him to have the thing; but, it does not discharge him from his liability to a restitution of the price, *condictione sine causa;* for, as the buyer is not obliged to pay and does not in fact pay the price, but in consequence of the seller's promise to cause him to have the thing, if the seller does not fulfil this promise, the cause for which the buyer pays the price no longer subsists, and the seller, being in possession of it without cause, is consequently bound to restore it. This is the decision of the law 11, § 18, D., *de act. empt.* (19, 1, 11, § 18): *Et si aperte in venditione comprehendatur nihil evictionis nomine præstatum iri; pretium deberi, re*

evicta, utilitatem non deberi; nec enim bonæ fidei contractus hanc patitur conventionem, ut emptor rem amitteret, et venditor pretium retineret.

Some doctors, cited by Bruneman, *ad dict. l.*, think that in this respect it is necessary to make a distinction. They agree, that, according to the law above quoted, the seller is not discharged from his liability to restore the price in case of eviction, when he stipulates generally, that he does not warrant against any evictions but those which proceed from his own act; but, they think it ought to be otherwise, when he stipulates that he does not warrant against a certain particular kind of eviction. This doctrine they pretend to establish, by the law 69, D., *de evict.* (21, 2, 69), which declares, that if the seller of a slave except, from the warranty to which he obliges himself, the case in which the slave may claim his liberty, he is not liable for an eviction, whether the man be already entitled, at the time of the delivery, to his freedom, or acquire his liberty afterwards, by the event of a condition upon which it is granted to him. This distinction is very properly rejected by Bruneman. It is devoid of reason, and is not supported by the law upon which it is attempted to be established; for, this law says indeed that the seller is not liable for the eviction, that is to say, he is not liable *actione in duplum ex hac stipulatione, qua se evictionis nomine obligavit;* but it does not by any means declare, as they would make it, that he is not liable to a restitution of the price; concerning which no question is made in this law, which speaks only of the stipulation *de evictione.* See Mornac, *ad dict. l.*

187. There is one case, however, in which the seller is not liable even to a restitution of the price in case of eviction; and, this occurs, when it appears, that the sale is not so much of a thing as of some uncertain claim which the seller has in the thing. Such a sale is similar to that of the casting of a net; D. 19, 1, 11, § 18.

§ II. Second class of cases.

188. There is one class of cases, in which the seller is not liable, in case of eviction, to indemnify the buyer, unless he is expressly obliged to do so by the contract; and this is when the seller can prove, that, at the time of the contract, the buyer had knowledge of the cause which afterwards gave rise to the eviction. For example, if the seller can prove, that the buyer, at the time of the contract of sale, knew that the estate did not belong to the seller, or that it was subject to certain hypothecations; in such cases, the buyer, if condemned to abandon it, upon the demand in revendication of the true proprietor, or upon the hypothecary action of the creditors to whom the hypothecary rights belong, is not entitled to any remedy for his damages; for, if the buyer, who purchases with this knowledge, suffers any thing beyond the price, in consequence of the eviction, he must impute it to himself, since it is an eviction which he has reason to expect. He is not drawn into error by the seller.

189. Accursius and Bartholus go much farther. They maintain, that, in this case, the buyer is not even entitled to recover the price paid. This opinion is manifestly contrary to equity, which does not permit the seller to enrich himself at the expense of the buyer, by retaining the price of a thing, which did not belong to him, nor the buyer to be deprived both of the thing bought and of the price paid: *Iniquum emptorem carere re et pretio.* These doctors are deceived by the law 27, *Cod. de evict.* (8, 45, 27), which, in the sense in which it first presents itself, seems to agree with their decision: *Si fundum sciens alienum vel obligatum comparavit Athenocles, neque quicquam de evictione convenit; quod eo nomine dedit, contra juris poscit rationem.* But Cujas, *ad h. l.*, removes the difficulty, by observing, that the last phrase *quod eo nomine dedit* ought not to be understood as referring

to the price which Athenocles pays the seller, which would contain a manifest injustice, but to that which he is obliged to pay the original demander, in order to preserve himself in the possession of the estate. The terms which follow, *Nam*[1] *si ignorans, desiderio tuo, juris forma, negantis hoc reddi, refragatur*, prove the interpretation of Cujas to be correct, and that the phrase, *quod eo nomine dedit*, ought not to be understood to refer to the price which the buyer pays to the seller; for, there could be no necessity for the emperors to decide, that the price paid by a buyer ought to be restored to him, in case of eviction, which is a doctrine not susceptible of doubt. Caillet, *ad h. l.*, bears witness, that the opinion of Cujas is followed in practice, though it formerly met with some difficulty, as appears by a decision of division upon this question, reported by Louet, *l. A*, *chap.* 13.

190. It is necessary to decide otherwise, in regard to a receiver of stolen goods, who purchases of the thief a thing which he knows to be stolen. Such a buyer, in case of eviction, ought not to be allowed to bring his action against the thief, for a restitution of the price; but the price ought to be confiscated or applied to charitable purposes. The reason is, that the purchase of the thing stolen is a crime on the part of the receiver, and makes him an accomplice in the theft. A criminal contract cannot give rise to an action: *Nemo ex proprio dolo, ex proprio delicto consequitur actionem.* The price which the buyer pays for such a purchase is paid *ex turpi causa;* and, according to the principles established in the Treatise on Obligations, n. 43, there can be no repetition of that which is paid *ex turpi causa, quum dantis æque et accipientis turpitudo versatur.*

But, if there is no theft or other crime in which the buyer participates by buying, and if he cannot be charged with any thing more than a mere want of good faith, in purchas-

[1] *Nam* is here, and very frequently in the Digest, an adversative particle, and has the same meaning as *sed*.

ing a thing which he knows does not belong to the seller; as such want of good faith is not of sufficient importance to be subject to the animadversion of the laws, which do not punish light faults, it does not deprive the buyer of his action for a restitution of the price, in case of eviction. And, therefore, Cujas, *ad h. l.*, says there is a difference *inter simplicem malam fidem, et dolum.*

191. The knowledge of the buyer, that the thing does not belong to the seller, or that it is hypothecated, does not prevent him from being received to demand a restitution of the price in case of eviction; neither does it prevent him from being received to demand the damages which he suffers beyond the price, if the warranty is expressly stipulated by the contract; for, it is only in those cases, where it is not stipulated, that the buyer, who has this knowledge, is excluded from his demand for damages. The law above quoted declares it expressly by these terms: *Quum de evictione nihil convenit.* The law 7, *Cod. commun. utriusque judic.* (3, 38, 7), also decides the same thing still more formally, in these terms: *Si fundi scientes obligationem, dominium suscepistis; tantum evictionis promissionem solemnitate verborum vel pacto pomissam probantes, eos conveniendi (in id quod interest) facultatem habebitis.*

The law *fin.* § 4, 4, *Cod. commun. de legat.* (6, 43, 4, § 4), seems contrary to these decisions. Justinian there decides, that he, who purchases of an heir things comprised in a legacy or trust, with a knowledge of the same, is not entitled, in case of eviction by the legatary, to the action which results from the stipulation of warranty, but that he ought to be satisfied with a restitution of the price: *Emptor sciens rei gravamen, adversus venditorem actionem habeat tantum ad restitutionem pretii, nec ex duplæ stipulatione locum habeat, quum sufficiat ei pro pretii quod sciens dedit pro re aliena satisfieri.* Cujas, *ad dict. l.* 27, *Cod. de evict.* (8, 45, 27), answers, that it is on account of Justinian's particular favor towards legacies and trusts, that he established this rule, in order to procure their more faithful execution, and to prevent the sale of things comprised in them to third persons, by denying to buyers who have knowledge of the testament the action of warranty, even when it is expressly stipulated. From this consideration, he infers that the decision of this law is *jus singulare;* that, consequently, it ought not to take place except in the particular case for which it is made; and, that it ought not to be extended to other cases, in which a party buys a thing, which he knows does not belong to the seller, or does not belong to him irrevocably. In all these cases, except in the single one provided for in this law, a knowledge on the part of the buyer, at the time of the contract, of the cause which afterwards gives rise to the eviction, does not deprive him of his action of warranty for his damages, when such warranty is stipulated.

I think, however, that this decision ought not to take place, except when the seller has in this respect the same knowledge which the buyer possesses, as will be seen in the following paragraph.

§ III. Third class of cases.

192. There are some cases of a third kind, in which there is no obligation of warranty, even when it is stipulated. Three cases of this kind may be mentioned. The first is that of a receiver of stolen goods, which has been already considered.

The second is the case of those who purchase estates comprised in a substitution duly published and registered; who, in case of eviction, are only entitled to an action against the seller and his heirs, for a restitution of the price, even when a warranty is expressly stipulated. See *supra*, n. 172.

The third case is that of a buyer, who, having knowledge of the cause, which afterwards gives rise to the eviction, conceals it from the seller, who is ignorant of it, and takes a stipulation of warranty against it from him. In this case, as it is the buyer who draws the seller into error, by stipulating a warranty, which the seller would not promise, if the buyer did not conceal from him, that the thing was subject to eviction, equity does not permit the buyer to profit from the surprise put upon the seller, in order to exact from him the damages, which he suffers beyond the price; and, the seller, it would seem, may exclude him from his action of warranty, by the exception of fraud, and by offering only to restore the price paid.

193. The fourth case is when the sale is made for the price of a sum of money, which the seller owes the buyer, as a debt won at play. If the buyer suffers an eviction, he is not entitled to an action of warranty against the seller; D. 45, 5, 2, § 1; not even for a repetition of the price. This is the opinion of Caballinus, in his treatise *de evictione, n.* 78. The reason is, that it would indirectly authorize an action to recover play debts, which the civil laws prohibit. The seller, summoned in warranty, may, in reference to this subject, cause the buyer to be interrogated upon facts and articles.

SECTION III.

Of the warranty agáinst real charges upon the thing sold.

194. The seller, in obliging himself by the contract of sale, in favor of the buyer, *præstare ei habere licere*, binds himself to a warranty against every thing, which may diminish or injure this faculty. It is therefore a result of this obligation, that the seller should warrant the buyer against all demands on account of real charges, other than those which are declared to him, or of which he cannot be ignorant.

The subject of this section is considered under the following divisions, namely: 1, what are the charges, which it is not necessary to declare; and, 2, what is the effect of a warranty against real charges.

§ I. What are the charges which it is not necessary to declare.

195. The charges, which it is considered the buyer's business not to be ignorant of, and, against which, consequently, the seller is not bound to a warranty, though they are not expressly declared by the contract, are, *first*, all those which are of common right. Of this number is the charge of tithes. This is not properly a real charge, the tithe being a charge upon the fruits and a debt due from him who gathers them, rather than a charge upon the estate which produces them; for, the *cure* or other party entitled has no right in the estates out of which he receives the tithes; his claim is founded only in a legal custom of receiving the tithe of the fruits which are gathered in his parish.

196. The charges of the hundredth penny, of contributions for the roads, of taxes to the church, and others of a similar character, are also charges of common right, against which the seller is not bound to acquit the buyer, even if they are not declared by the contract.

197. Those seignorial rights and duties, which are regulated by custom, are also charges, which need not be declared by the contract, when the estates subjected to them are situated in provinces where the maxim "no land without a lord," (*nulle terre sans seigneur*) is established; the presumption being that they are held of some lord, either *à fief* or *à cens*. This takes place, when an estate is not charged with any other rights and duties, than those which are regulated by the custom of the place.

But if the estate is charged, by particular titles, with rights greater than those which are regulated by custom and used in the province, they must, even if seignorial, be declared by the contract; and, in default thereof, an action of warranty may be maintained against the seller, not only for the diminished value of the estate, by reason of such unwonted charges, but also for what the buyer is obliged to pay beyond the ordinary profits. It is not in the power of the buyer to foresee such unwonted rights, even if they are seignorial.

198. If the seignorial rights, with which an estate is charged, are rights authorized by the custom of the place, where they are situated, which expressly mentions them; though they are not such as result from common right, but from rights for the existence of which the custom requires that the lords should have particular titles in order to claim them, such, as, in the custom of Dunois, is the right of *quint* and *requint*, in case of the sale of fiefs; I think that the want of a declaration of these rights does not give rise to a warranty, when there does not appear to be any studied dissimulation, and the seller cannot have had any knowledge of them; for, these rights being known, and the custom making mention of them, though they are not such as are of common right, the buyer cannot say, that he could not foresee them; and, in purchasing at the charge expressed, or always understood, of seignorial rights, without any explanation of their quality, he is considered to submit himself to seignorial rights, such and of the quality which they may be found to be.

199. It remains to be observed, that the buyer is subject to those charges, which are of common right, only for the future. He is entitled to an indemnification by the seller against all such as accrue previous to his possession; and also against all ancient seignorial profits which become due previous to his acquisition.

200. A *second* kind of real charges, of which it is the buyer's business not to be ignorant, and against which consequently he cannot claim any warranty, though they are not expressly declared by the contract, consists of visible

servitudes, such as those of light and eaves-dropping; of which the buyer cannot be ignorant, since in visiting the house before purchasing it, he cannot avoid seeing the windows or the eaves.

201. Are we to include amongst the rights, which it is the buyer's duty not to be ignorant of, a right of *champart* not seignorial? The reason for doubting is, that the perception of the *champart* being public and known in the country, it is easy for the buyer to inform himself, and to ascertain before purchasing, whether the estate is subject to that charge. An argument may also be drawn from what is decided by the custom of Orleans, art. 480, that this kind of charge is not extinguished by a decree. This decision of the custom is, in fact, founded upon the principle, that the adjudicatary cannot be ignorant of the existence of this right, the perception of which is public.

Notwithstanding these reasons, we must decide, that the seller is bound to warrant against a *champart*, which is not declared by the contract. A buyer does not buy a house without visiting it in person, or sending some one on his part, nor, consequently, without perceiving the visible servitudes; but, he cannot be instructed of the charge of champart, except by being informed of it, and he may neglect to inform himself, or be deceived in the information, which he receives. As to the argument drawn from the custom of Orleans, the answer is, that the disposition referred to, which is peculiar to that custom, is a particular law, which consequently is not to be extended to any other case. Besides there is no parity of reason. If the custom decides that the right of *champart*, though not seignorial, is not extinguished by a decree, it is for the reason, that the cause of the proprietor of that right, *qui certat de damno vitando*, is to be favored. We can only reproach him, at the most, with the negligence of not having opposed the decree, of which persons are frequently ignorant. On the contrary, the cause of the seller, who does not declare the existence of this right, is not in the least to be favored; such concealment is always suspicious.

If the *champart* is a seignorial right, with which the estate is charged, known and authorized by the custom of the place, a want of declaration of it does not seem to give rise to a warranty, according to the principles above established, *supra*, n. 195.

§ II. Of the effect of the warranty against real charges.

202. The effect of this warranty is, that if any one claims in the estate a real right, with which the buyer is not charged by the contract of sale, the buyer, summoned to acknowledge or to suffer this right, may summon the seller or his heirs in warranty, in order that they may defend him against the demand, and take his act and cause.

This action is a branch of the personal action *ex empto*, like the action of warranty in case of eviction; and, all that is said in the preceding section, of the obligation to defend the buyer against demands in eviction, may be applied to the obligation to defend him against demands, by reason of real rights claimed in the estate, when he is not charged with them.

If the seller neglects to defend the buyer, this action resolves itself into and terminates in a diminution from the price, which the seller is condemned to make to the buyer, and which ought to be of such a sum less, as skilful persons may estimate that the thing ought to have been sold for. If the thing is so incumbered, that, in all probability, the buyer would not have purchased, if he had known of the charge upon it (which must be left to the discretion of the judge), the seller, in such case, may be condemned, upon the demand of the buyer, to take back the thing. This is called the redhibitory action, of which we shall have occasion to speak more fully, in the following section.

When the real charge is one, which is repurchasable in money, which is sometimes the case, with respect to annuities issuing out of land, the buyer may cause the seller to be condemned to furnish the money necessary for the purchase.

SECTION IV.

Of the warranty against redhibitory defects.

203. The seller, by the nature of the contract of sale, is bound to warrant the buyer, that the thing sold is exempt from certain defects (*vices*), which are of a nature to render either almost useless, or even sometimes hurtful, the using of the thing, for the purpose for which it is bought and sold (*dans le commerce*).

This obligation is a consequence of that, which the seller contracts to cause the buyer to have the thing sold; for, to be obliged *to cause him to have the thing*, in the intention of the parties, is to be obliged to cause him to have it usefully; and it is in vain for the buyer to have a thing usefully which cannot be of any use to him.

These defects, against which the seller is bound to warrant, are called *redhibitory*, because the action, which results from this warranty, is a redhibitory action, that is to say, an action by which the buyer concludes against the seller, that he should be held to take back the thing, and to return the price: *redhibere est quasi reddere;* D. 21, 1, 21.

The subject of this warranty is considered under the following divisions, namely: 1, in regard to what things the seller is bound to this warranty; 2, what defects give rise to it and in what cases; 3, the extent of this obligation; 4, of the redhibitory action which results from it; and, 5, of the action *quanto minoris*, which also results from it.

ARTICLE FIRST.

In regard to what things the seller is bound to this warranty.

204. The seller is bound to this warranty, not only in regard to the thing, which makes the principal object of the contract, but also in regard to those things which are included in it as accessory, provided they are specially comprised in it, *tanquam res singulæ*, and not under a generality. This results from the law 33, D., *de ædil. edict.* (21, 1, 33,): *Quod in venditione accessurum esse dictum est, tam integrum præstetur, quam illud præstari debuit quod principaliter venit . . Sed hoc ita, si certum corpus accessurum fuerit dictum; nam si servus cum peculio venierit, ea mancipia quæ in peculio fuerint, sana esse præstare venditor non debet . . . . Idem probat, et si fundus cum instrumento venierit, etc.*

According to these principles, if I sell you a farm, with so many horses, so many cows, and such and such things upon it, I am bound to a warranty, provided there are any redhibitory defects in any of the said horses, cows or other things; for, though they are sold only as things accessory to the farm, which makes the principal object of the contract, they are however specially comprised in it, *tanquam certæ et singulæ res.* On the contrary, if it is declared by the contract, that I sell you the farm with all the cattle and other movables upon it, I am not bound to warrant against redhibitory defects existing in any of the horses or cows which are upon the farm, for I sell you only the generality of the movables and effects upon the farm, and not any one in particular.

ARTICLE II.

What defects give rise to a warranty and in what cases.

205. In order that a defect in the thing sold may give rise

to a warranty, there must be a concurrence of four things: 1, the defect must be of the number of those, which, according to the local usage, are considered redhibitory; 2, it must not have been known to the buyer; 3, it must not have been excepted from the obligation of warranty, by a particular clause of the contract; and, 4, it must have existed at the time of the contract.

§ I. First Condition.

206. In order that a defect may give rise to warranty, it is necessary, in the first place, that it should be of the number of those, which, according to the local usage, are considered redhibitory. For example, according to usage, it is a redhibitory defect, in regard to horses, to be broken-winded, foundered, or to have the glanders. The custom of Bourbon, art. 87, contains a regulation on this subject. Pulmonary phthysis in the first degree (*pommelière*) is also a redhibitory defect in cows. Certain epidemic and contagious diseases, which at certain times prevail among cattle, are also redhibitory defects, in regard to such as are diseased.

207. It is a redhibitory defect in a piece of timber, if it is rotten and consequently not fit for use; in casks, when some of the staves are made of a wood, which communicates a bad odor to the wine contained in them; and, in new cloths, when they do not possess the qualities required by the commercial regulations. Holes also in cloth are a redhibitory defect. Ulpian, in the law 49, D. *de ædil. edict.* (21, 1, 49), mentions as a redhibitory defect in an estate, that it is situated in an infected atmosphere: *si pestilens fundus.* Diocletian, in the law 4, C. *de ædil. action.* (4, 58, 4), mentions another, namely: if a piece of pasturage land produces poisonous herbs, *si pestibilis, id est pestibiles herbas vel lethiferas habens.*

208. Those defects, which, though considerable, are easily

to be perceived, are not considered as redhibitory. For example, it is not a redhibitory defect in a horse, to be lame or blind, or in a house, to be ruinous, &c., because, as these defects may be easily known, the buyer is presumed to have knowledge of them, and to be willing to make the purchase, notwithstanding their existence, and consequently not to suffer any wrong, *nam volenti non fit injuria;* and, even if the buyer does not know of such defects, he cannot be allowed to complain of the wrong which he suffers, since he has only to examine the thing himself, or to cause it to be examined by some one for him, if he has not sufficient skill himself, before purchasing. A wrong, which a person suffers through his own fault, is not one which the laws ought to relieve against, the law not being made to assist the negligent: *Damnum quod quis culpa sua non sentit, non videtur sentire.*

209. Such are the rules in the exterior forum. But in that of conscience, every considerable defect, which would have prevented the buyer from purchasing, if he had known of it, ought to be considered as redhibitory; since the seller ought not to make a profit of the buyer's neglect to examine the thing sold.

§ II. Second Condition.

210. It is necessary, in the second place, in order to give rise to a warranty, that the buyer should not have knowledge of the redhibitory defect, at the time of the contract; for, if it can be proved, that he had such knowledge, his demand in warranty cannot be sustained; D. 21, 1, 48, § 4.

This rule holds only when the parties are silent in respect to the warranty. But if the buyer, though he has knowledge of the defect, expressly stipulates a warranty against it, he will be allowed in his demand. The seller, who expressly submits himself to such warranty, cannot be allowed to make the exception, that the buyer had knowledge of it. This is decided in the law 4, § 5, D. *de dol. et met. except.* (44, 3, 4, § 5).

If it appears, however, that the buyer, by concealing his knowledge of the defect from the seller, who is ignorant of it, thereby leads him into an error, the latter may defeat the buyer of his demand, by an exception of fraud.

§ III. Third Condition.

211. It is necessary, in the third place, that the defect should not, by a particular clause, be excepted from the good faith of the obligation of warranty. It is so excepted, when the seller, being ignorant of the thing which he sells, and fearing that it may be subject to some particular defect, of which however he has no knowledge, stipulates that he does not warrant against such defect. In such case, the clause ought to be executed; and the buyer has no claim against the seller, on account of such defect, if the thing sold is found subject to it. But if the seller, at the time of the contract, has full knowledge of the defect, and instead of declaring it, stipulates that he does not warrant against it, such concealment is a fraud (*dol*) on his part, which renders him subject to warranty, notwithstanding the clause; D. 21, 1, 14, § 9.

§ IV. Fourth Condition.

212. It is necessary, in the fourth place, that the defect which gives rise to this warranty should have existed at the time of the contract; for, if it does not begin to exist until afterwards, as the thing has then become at the risk of the buyer, as will be seen more particularly hereafter, part 4, the seller cannot be held liable; D. 21, 1, 54.

ARTICLE III.

Of the extent of the obligation of warranty against redhibitory defects.

213. In regard to the extent of this obligation, it is necessary to distinguish between the case, in which the seller is ignorant of the redhibitory defect, and that in which he has knowledge of it. In the first case, the warranty does not generally extend beyond the thing sold. The seller is bound to restore to the buyer the price paid, but he is not bound to a reparation of the damage, which the defect in the thing sold causes him in his other goods. In the second case, when the seller has knowledge of the defect, and does not inform the buyer of it, he is also further liable for all the damages which the defect causes him in his other goods; for, such a concealment of the seller is a fraud (*dol*) upon the buyer, and obliges him to a reparation of all the wrong which results from it.

The seller, though he has no express knowledge of the defect of the thing sold, is in this respect considered to have knowledge of it, if he has reasonable ground to suspect its existence, and does not say any thing of it to the buyer; for such concealment is a fraud. For example, if he sells an animal, which he knows is from a place, where a contagious disease prevails; though he has no express knowledge that the animal is really attacked by the disease, he ought to be punished equally, as if he had such knowledge, and consequently to be liable, in favor of the buyer, for all the damages which the animal causes him, by communicating the disease with which it is infected to his other cattle; for, it is a fraud on the part of the seller, to conceal from the buyer, that the animal is from a country where the sickness prevails.

214. There is one case, in which the seller, even if he is absolutely ignorant of the defect in the thing sold, is never-

theless liable to a reparation of the wrong, which the defect causes the buyer in his other goods; and this is the case, where the seller is an artisan, or a tradesman who sells the manufactures of his own trade, or of the kind of dealing of which he makes a business. The artificer or tradesman is liable to a reparation of all the damages, which the buyer suffers by a defect in the thing sold, in making use of it for the purpose to which it is destined, even if such artificer or tradesman were ignorant of the defect. For example, if a cooper or a dealer in casks sells me some casks, and, in consequence of a defect in any of them, the wine which I put therein is lost, the seller will be liable for such loss. In like manner, if the wood of the cask, by its bad quality, communicates a bad odor to the wine, the usage, in such case, requires, that the seller should be condemned to take the damaged wine on his own account, and to pay me for it, according to the price of that which remains uninjured. The reason is, that an artificer, by the profession of his art, *spondet peritiam artis*. He renders himself, in favor of those who contract with him, responsible for the goodness of his wares, for the use to which they are naturally destined. His want of skill, or defect of knowledge, in every thing that concerns his art, must be imputed to him as a fault, since no person ought publicly to profess an art, if he does not possess all the knowledge necessary for its proper exercise: *Imperitia culpæ annumeratur*: l. 132. D. *de reg. jur.* (50, 17, 132). It is the same in regard to a dealer, whether he is or is not the maker of the articles which he sells. By the public profession, which he makes of his trade, he renders himself responsible for the goodness of the merchandise which he sells, for the use to which it is destined. If he is the manufacturer, he ought to employ, in his business, none but good workmen, for whom he is responsible. If he is not the manufacturer, he ought to expose for sale none but good articles. He ought to have knowledge of his wares, and ought to sell none but good.

215. It must be observed, that, however defective the thing sold by an artificer or tradesman may be, if the buyer makes use of it for a purpose different from that to which it is destined, the seller is not liable for the damages, which result from a defect in it, to any greater amount than the buyer would have suffered at the most, if he had made use of the thing, for the purpose to which it is destined. For the seller, by the public profession which he makes of his art or his trade, only engages himself to the public, that his wares shall be proper for the use to which they are destined; and submits himself only to the damages which the buyer may suffer, by making such use of the thing, and to none other. He is nevertheless liable for the damages, at least to that amount, though the buyer makes use of the thing for another purpose; for, if he ought not to suffer in consequence of the buyer's making such use of the thing, neither ought he to profit by it.

According to these principles, if I purchase casks of a cooper of Normandy, who makes such only as are proper to hold cider, and I put wine or brandy into them, which is consequently lost, the cooper will not be liable to me for the price of the wine or brandy lost. But if the casks are so defective, that cider, if put into them, would have been equally lost, the seller will be liable for the loss of the wine or brandy, to the amount of a like quantity of cider. If the casks are sufficient to contain cider, though not suitable to contain a more violent liquor, they cannot be considered as defective; and it is a fault of my own to make use of them for another purpose; Dumoulin, *Tr. de eo quod int. n.* 60, 61.

216. Except in these cases of an artificer or a dealer, the seller, who has no knowledge or any just suspicion of the existence of a redhibitory defect, is liable to nothing more than to restore the price to the buyer, who is bound on his part to return the thing sold; and the seller is in no manner liable for any damage, which this defect causes the buyer

in his other goods. And, therefore, if, instead of purchasing my casks of a cooper or of a dealer, I purchase them of an individual, who sells me those which he has more than he is in need of, and some one of them proves defective, the seller will only be liable to a restitution of the price; but, he will not be liable for the loss of the wine occasioned by the defect in the cask.

217. Dumoulin, however, in his treatise *de eo quod int. n.* 53, very well observes, that such individual ought at least to cede to me his rights and actions, if he has any, against the cooper or dealer, from whom he purchased the defective casks, in order that I may prosecute them in his place and for my own account and at my own risk; for the sale from him to me ought not to profit the cooper who is in fault, and to discharge him from his obligation; and, the party who resells the casks to me is considered as selling me with them all his rights in relation thereto. But if I exercise the right of my seller against the cooper, I cannot demand of the former a restitution of the price.

ARTICLE IV.

Of the redhibitory action.

From the warranty against redhibitory defects, results the redhibitory action, to which the buyer is entitled against the seller. The subject of this action is examined under the following divisions, namely: 1, what the buyer has a right to demand by it; 2, what he must do to entitle himself to commence it; 3, of some differences between the seller and buyer in regard to this action; 4, whether the existence of a redhibitory defect in one of many things included in a single purchase gives rise to a dissolution of the contract for the whole or only as to that thing; and, 5, of the conclusions of non-reception (*fins de non recevoir*) against this action.

§ I. What the buyer has a right to demand by this action.

218. The buyer has a right, by the redhibitory action, to demand a dissolution and annulling of the bargain, and, consequently, that things should be restored to the same situation, as if the sale had not intervened: *Judicium redhibitoriæ actionis utrumque, id est venditorem et emptorem, quodammodo in integrum restituere debere;* D. 21, 1, 23, § 7. *Facta redhibitione, omnia in integrum restituuntur, perinde ac si neque emptio, neque venditio intercessit;* D. 21, 1, 60.

The buyer has consequently a right to demand, that the seller should be condemned to restore the price, and also the interest of it from the time of payment to the time of repayment, D. 21, 1, 29, § 2; unless the judge thinks proper to set the interest against the fruits which the buyer is bound to restore.

He has a right also to demand, that the seller should be condemned to reimburse him for all the expenses of making the contract, and for all such as he is obliged to incur in relation to the thing sold, such as the expenses of conveyance, of tolls, of customs, &c.; but not for those which he might have dispensed with incurring; D. 21, 1, 27.

In regard to the damages sustained by reason of the injury, which the thing sold causes the buyer in his other goods, he is only entitled to claim them according to the distinctions established in the preceding article.

219. The expenses of the keeping of an animal cannot be demanded, inasmuch as they ought to be compensated by the services, which the buyer is able to derive from it; D. 21, 1, 30, § 1.

§ II. What the buyer must do to entitle himself to commence this action.

220. The buyer, in order to be received to this action, must on his part offer to restore the thing, if it exist, together with its fruits, if he has received any; at least if he does

not consent to compensate the latter with the interest of the price. He ought also to offer to restore all the accessories which have been delivered to him with the thing.

221. If the thing does not exist; and it is without fault on the part of the seller that it has ceased to exist; as, if the horse which I purchase dies of the disease, on account of which I bring the redhibitory action; it is sufficient for me to restore what remains of the thing, as the skin. If it is sold with any accessories, as with a bridle and saddle, these must be restored.

If no part of the thing sold remains; as, when a cow dies of a contagious disease, and, according to the police regulations, is buried with the skin; I may bring the redhibitory action, without restoring any part.

222. If the thing sold ceases to exist through the fault of the buyer, shall he be excluded from his redhibitory action, because he thereby puts himself, by his own fault, out of a situation to fulfil the condition? It results from the law 31, §11, D. *de ædil. act.*, (21, 1, 31, §11,) that the buyer is not on this account to be excluded from the redhibitory action, but that he is only liable, in such case, to make a deduction in favor of the seller of the value of the thing sold, in the situation in which it would be, if it had not ceased to exist by his fault.

For the same reason, if, by his fault, the thing is deteriorated, he is not thereby excluded from the redhibitory action, but is only liable to account to the seller, to whom he returns it, for such depreciation; D. 21, 1, 24.

These decisions are all agreeable to equity; for it is sufficient, if the seller is indemnified against the fault which the buyer commits in relation to the thing; he ought not thereby to make a profit and to enrich himself, which would be the case if he were discharged from the redhibitory action.

223. Sometimes the buyer, however, who, by his own act, puts himself out of a situation to return the thing, ought,

by so doing, to be declared not receivable in the redhibitory action,—as when he disposes of the thing,—when he makes use of it,—and when he makes his profit of it in the same manner, as he would have done, if it had not been subject to the defect; *arg.* D. 21, 1, 47.

§ III. Of the differences between the buyer and seller in relation to this action.

224. There are some differences to be remarked, touching the redhibitory action, between the buyer to whom, and the seller against whom, this action is allowed.

On the part of the buyer, it is indivisible; and, therefore, if the buyer leaves several heirs, one of them cannot prosecute this action for his share only; but they must all join in the suit. The reason is, that the seller would suffer a damage, if he were obliged to take back the thing only in part; D. 21, 1, 31, § 5. On the contrary, this action is divisible on the part of the seller against whom it may be brought; and, therefore, if the seller leaves several heirs, the buyer may very well prosecute his redhibitory action against one of them only and not against the others; inasmuch as the heir against whom it is prosecuted, and who is condemned to take back the thing, for the part of which he is the heir, and to restore the price for the same part, does not thereby suffer any injury; for even when the action is brought against all the heirs, he is only entitled to that portion in the thing; D. 21, 1, 31, §10.

225. The above rule in regard to several heirs of a buyer, is also true in regard to several buyers, when the thing is sold to them *sub specie unitatis*, though they are not bound *in solido* to a payment of the price: for, in this case, there is only one contract of sale of a single thing, and consequently there can be but one redhibitory action against all the buyers. It is not so, where several persons purchase a thing, each for a certain portion. In that case, there are as many contracts of sale as there are buyers, who purchase

each a part; and, consequently, each of them may prosecute the redhibitory action separately for the part which he purchases; the seller cannot complain, but must impute it to himself, in having sold by portions; *ibid.*

226. There is also another difference between the seller and the buyer touching this action. The seller is bound strictly and may be constrained to a restitution of the price; the buyer is not strictly obliged to a restitution of the thing sold. If he does not restore it, the seller cannot constrain him to do so, he can only thereby obtain his discharge from a restitution of the price; D. 21, 1, 29.

§ IV. Whether a redhibitory defect, in one of several things included in a sale, gives rise to a dissolution of the contract for the whole or only for that thing.

227. In the decision of this question, it is necessary to make some distinctions. If the thing which has the defect is alone the principal object of the sale, and the others are sold as accessories merely, the redhibition of the principal thing will draw after it that of all the accessories. For example, if a horse is sold with all his equipage, the redhibition of the horse draws after it that of the equipage; the seller may be compelled to take back the whole; and, *vice versa*, the buyer cannot prosecute his redhibitory action for the horse, unless he returns the equipage together with the horse.

On the other hand, if the principal thing is not subject to redhibition, but only some one of the accessories to it; as, if one sells a farm with the horses which are on it, and one of the horses is subject to a redhibitory defect; the redhibition takes place only for the horse, and the buyer, by offering to return the animal, will obtain a restitution of the price paid for him.

228. When the things sold are all equally principal, it is necessary to inquire whether they are sold as making

together one whole, and are such that one would not have been sold without the others; as, when one sells a pair of horses for a carriage, or a pair of oxen, &c.; in this case, a redhibitory defect in one of the things gives rise to a redhibition of all, and the action cannot be prosecuted for a part.

But if the things sold are independent of each other, the redhibitory action takes place only for that which is subject to the defect, even if they are all sold for a single price; for, although that circumstance joined with others serves to create a presumption, that the things would not have been sold the one without the other, yet it is not of itself decisive; and, for this reason, the action may be brought for the single thing, and the seller is bound to restore the price of it, according to its value in proportion to the whole price. This is the doctrine of the D. 21, 1, 38, § 14, and of many other texts. See *Pand. Just. tit. de Ædil. Edict. n.* 63, 64.

229. On the contrary, though separate prices create a strong presumption, that the things are sold independently of each other, yet this circumstance is not always decisive; and the presumption which results from it must give way to the stronger presumption, which results from the quality of the things sold; as, in the case above-mentioned of the sale of a pair of carriage horses. If, in such case, the sale is made at a separate price for each horse, the action cannot be prosecuted except for the whole; D. 21, 1, 34.

§ V. Of the conclusions of non-reception *(fins de non recevoir)* against the redhibitory action.

230. There are two conclusions of non-reception against this action. The one results from agreement; the other from lapse of time.

When, by the contract of sale, it is agreed, that the seller does not warrant against any defects in the thing, or that he does not warrant against a particular defect, this agreement constitutes a conclusion of non-reception against the redhibitory action.

231. If, however, the buyer can prove, that the seller, at the time of the contract, had not merely a doubt concerning such defects, but a perfect knowledge of their existence; as, in such case, the seller is guilty of bad faith in concealing them, the buyer is entitled, notwithstanding the agreement, to his redhibitory action; and, if he is opposed by the exception resulting from the agreement, *exceptionem pacti*, he may destroy this exception, by opposing in his turn the replication of fraud, *replicationem doli;* D. 21, 1, 14, § 9.

232. There results a conclusion of non-reception against this action, from the lapse of time, which the buyer suffers to expire, without commencing it.

By the Roman law, the buyer was entitled to six useful months within which to commence his action. The usage of different provinces accords a much shorter time. It is necessary to follow, in this respect, that of the place where the contract is made. According to the usage of this country, we do not allow the redhibitory action, on acount of defects in horses and cows, to be commenced after the expiration of forty days from the delivery. Mornac, *ad* l. 19, § *fin.* D. *de ædil. edict.* (21, 1, 19, § 6), bears witness, that, in his time, it was subject to prescription by the lapse of nine days. The custom of Bourbon, art. 8, limits it to eight days. This action, in regard to defective casks, is also limited to a particular time, which is not well ascertained. There are some who pretend that it cannot be commenced after Saint Andrew's day.

ARTICLE V.

Of the action quanto minoris.

233. Redhibitory defects not only give rise to the redhibitory action; they also give rise to the action, which is called

in law *æstimatoria* or *quanto minoris;* and, of these actions, the buyer has his choice. The action *quanto minoris* consists in demanding against the seller, that he should make a diminution from the price, of the amount in which the thing may be estimated, by reason of the defect, to be worth less than the price.

This action, on account of redhibitory defects, takes place, in the same cases, in which the redhibitory action may be brought; and the same conclusions of non-reception, which exclude the latter action, also exclude this. Nevertheless, by the Roman law, the action *quanto minoris* was of longer duration, and could be prescribed against only by the lapse of a year; but, with us, it is subject to the same prescription as the redhibitory action. Mornac, *loco citato.*

CHAPTER II.

Of the engagements of the seller which result from good faith.

The engagements of the seller, which result from good faith, are examined and considered, in the following articles, namely: 1, whether good faith obliges the seller, at least in the forum of conscience, not only to refrain from false declarations, but even from omitting to declare, in relation to whatever concerns the thing sold, and to what such omission obliges him; 2, what omission to declare obliges the seller in the exterior forum, and to what; 3, whether the seller is obliged, at least in the forum of conscience, to conceal nothing, not even extrinsic circumstances, which the buyer has an interest in knowing; and, 4, whether the seller may, in the forum of conscience, sometimes sell for more than the just price.

ARTICLE FIRST.

Whether good faith obliges the seller, at least in the forum of conscience, not only to refrain from false declarations, but even from omitting to declare, in relation to whatever concerns the thing sold, and to what such omission obliges him.

234. Though the rules of good faith, in many of the affairs of civil society, extend no farther than to prohibit us from falsehood, but permit us to refrain from discovering to others that which they have an interest in knowing, when we have an equal interest in concealing it from them; yet, in contracts of mutual interest, of the number of which is the contract of sale, good faith prohibits not only falsehood, but all suppression of every thing, which he, with whom we contract, has an interest in knowing, touching the thing which makes the object of the contract.

The reason is, that justice and equity, in these contracts, consist in equality. Every thing which tends to diminish this equality is therefore contrary to equity. It is evident, that every suppression, on the part of one of the contracting parties, of any thing which the other has an interest in knowing, touching the thing which makes the object of the contract, diminishes this equality; for, when one of them has more knowledge than the other concerning the thing, he has an advantage over him in contracting, he knows what he is doing better than the other; and, consequently, there is no longer equality in the contract.

In making an application of these principles to the contract of sale, it follows, that the seller is obliged to declare all that he knows touching the thing sold to the buyer, who has an interest in knowing it; and, that by omitting to do so, he offends against the good faith, which ought to govern in this contract.

This is what is taught by Florentinus, in the law 43, § 2,

D. *de contrah. empt.* (18, 1, 43, § 2): *Dolum malum a se abesse præstare venditor debet, qui non tantum in eo est qui fallendi causa obscure loquitur, sed etiam qui insidiose obscure dissimulat.*

235. According to these principles, a seller is bound not to suppress any of the defects of the thing, which are within his knowledge, though they are not redhibitory, but of such a nature, that the buyer would not be allowed to complain of them, if the seller were ignorant of their existence. *Quum ex* XII *tabulis*, says Cicero, (*lib.* 3, *de Off.*) *satis esset cautum ea præstare quæ essent lingua nuncupata, a jurisconsultis etiam reticentiæ pœna est constituta; quicquid enim inest prædio vitii, id statuerunt, si venditor sciret, nisi nominatim dictum esset, præstare oportere.* The seller is liable, in such case, *in id quanti* (*emptoris*) *intererit scisse*, D. 19, 1, 4; and such suppression sometimes even gives rise to a rescission of the contract; D. 19, 11, 11, § 5.

236. This decision ought to take place, though the seller, who conceals the defect of the thing, does not sell it for more than what it is worth with such defect. The reason is, that he, who sells me a thing, has no right to exact the highest price of me, if I do not consent to purchase it for that price; he only has a right to exact the price for which I am really willing to purchase it; and he ought not to make use of any artifice, to induce me to consent to buy it for more than I should be willing to give, if I knew of the defect which he maliciously conceals from me.

237. Good faith obliges the seller, not only not to suppress any of the intrinsic defects of the thing, but, in general, not to suppress any thing concerning it, which may induce the buyer not to purchase, or not to purchase at so high a price. For example, the buyer is entitled to an action, if the seller conceals from him, that the estate which he sells is in a bad neighborhood, which fact would prevent him from purchasing, if he had knowledge of it: *Si quis in vendendo*

prædio confinem celaverit, quem emptor, si audisset, empturus non esset, teneri venditorem ; D. 18, 1, 35, § 8.

238. These principles of the Roman jurisconsults are more exact, and more conformed to justice, than the decision of saint Thomas, who permits the seller to conceal the defects of the thing, except in two cases, namely; 1, when the defect is of such a nature that it may cause some damage to the buyer; and, 2, when the seller takes advantage of such concealment to sell the thing for more than it is worth. It is this which he decides, 11, 2, 77, art. 3. This decision is found also in his quodlibetic questions. The opinion of this author does not appear to me to be just. As the seller is perfectly free to sell or not to sell, he ought to leave the buyer the same liberty to buy or not to buy, even for the just price, if that price is not agreeable to him. It is therefore unjust to set a snare for this liberty, which the buyer ought to enjoy, by concealing a defect in the thing from him, in order to induce him to buy that thing, which he would not have been willing to buy, for the price for which it is sold to him, if he had known of the defect.

ARTICLE II.

What suppression imposes an obligation upon the seller in the exterior forum and to what.

239. Though it is in reference to the exterior forum, that the Roman jurisconsults established the principles above stated, touching the obligation of the seller, to suppress nothing from the buyer, which concerns the thing sold, and, though these principles ought to be strictly followed in the forum of conscience; yet, we pay little attention to them in our tribunals, in which a buyer is not easily allowed to complain of a concealment of some defect in the thing sold, unless such defect is redhibitory. The interests of commerce not permitting parties to be readily admitted to demand a

dissolution of bargains which have been concluded, they must impute it to themselves, in not being better informed concerning the defects, to which the thing sold may be subject.

240. There are, however, certain concealments touching the thing sold, which have merited the attention of the laws, and which impose an obligation upon the seller, in the exterior forum; these are the cases, in which the seller conceals the knowledge he possesses, that the thing does not belong to him; that it does not belong to him irrevocably; or that it is subject to certain charges, annuities (*rentes*), or special hypothecations.

Henry the Second enacted a law against this sort of fraud, in the ordinance of 1553, art. 15, in which it is provided, that sellers shall be bound to declare the charges, annuities, and special hypothecations, to which estates by them sold are subject, under the penalty of being considered as false sellers, and as such liable to punishment.

This ordinance seems to declare, that the seller, in such case, may be prosecuted criminally, as for the crime of false, which is not the practice. The whole penalty of this fraud, at the present day, consists in this, that the buyer, as soon as he discovers that the thing sold did not belong to the seller, or that it was charged with some special hypothecation, or considerable annuity, may, immediately and without waiting for an eviction, commence his action against the seller, who has knowledge of the defect and has not declared it, for a rescission of the contract of sale, and may conclude against him, that he should be condemned by his body to a restitution of the price, and to the payment of all the buyer's damages. In reference to this action, there are two differences between the seller in bad faith, and one who is ignorant that the thing sold did not belong to him, or who had no knowledge of the charges to which it was subject; for, though the latter is indeed liable, in case of eviction, for the damages of the buyer, yet he is only condemned to the payment thereof civilly, and not by his body; and, in this, consists the first difference between such seller and the seller in bad faith. The other difference consists in this, that the seller in good faith, who is ignorant that the thing did not belong to him, or who had no knowledge of the charges to which it was subject, is only liable to the buyer from the time the latter is disturbed in the free possession of the thing sold. So long as the buyer is not disturbed, he cannot proceed against the seller, who is not strictly obliged to transfer to him the property of the thing sold, but only to cause him to have the free possession of it, *præstare emptori habere licere*, and to warrant him against all troubles; and, consequently, the seller fulfils his engagement, so long as the buyer is not disturbed, and so long as *habere ei licet.* On the contrary, when the seller has knowledge that the thing does not belong to him, or that it is subject to charges which he does not declare, the buyer, as has already been remarked, may immediately commence his action against the seller, because the fraudulent concealment on the part of the latter gives rise to this action, *in id quanti tua interest non esse deceptum;* which may extend, as is above remarked, even to a rescission of the contract.

241. It must be observed, that where there are several sellers, some of whom have knowledge of the defect and others have not, as those only who have such knowledge are guilty of bad faith (*dol, dolus*), they alone are liable in this action; and, though they do not sell *in solido*, they are liable *in solido*, each one for the whole, to a restitution of the price and for the damages of the buyer; Dumoulin, *Tr. de div. et indiv. p.* 3, *n.* 201, *et seq.* This is conformable to the general principle, that bad faith always imposes an obligation *in solido* upon those who commit it. In this respect, bad faith, as Dumoulin remarks, differs from simple fault, which only obliges those who are guilty of it, each

one for his own part, except in the case of obligations of indivisible things or acts, *ut in obligatione susceptæ custodiæ.*

ARTICLE III.

Whether good faith obliges the seller, at least in the forum of conscience, not to suppress any of the extrinsic circumstances, which the buyer has an interest in knowing.

242. Cicero, in his third book of Offices, has considered this question, in the case of a corn merchant, who, having arrived at Rhodes, in a time of scarcity, before a great number of other vessels laden with corn, exposes his own cargo for sale. Cicero inquires, whether this merchant is obliged to inform the buyers, that there is a great number of other vessels upon the point of arriving? Upon this question, he mentions the opinions of two of the stoic philosophers, Diogenes and Antipater. Diogenes thought that the merchant might suppress his knowledge of the vessels, which were upon the point of arriving, and might sell his corn at the current price. Antipater, his disciple, whose opinion Cicero appears to have adopted, thought, on the other hand, that such concealment was contrary to good faith. The reason, upon which his opinion is founded, is, that the union which ought to exist among men, and the love which we ought to bear towards one another, do not permit us to prefer our individual interest to that of others; from whence it follows, that though we may conceal certain things through prudence, we are nevertheless not at liberty, for our own profit, to conceal that, which those, with whom we contract, have an interest in knowing: *Hoc celandi genus*, says he, *non aperti, non simplicis, non ingenui, non justi, non viri boni: versuti potius, obscuri, astuti, fallacis, malitiosi, callidi, veteratoris, vafri.*

This question belongs only to the forum of conscience; for, there is no doubt, that, in the exterior forum, a buyer is not entitled to complain, that the seller has not informed him of circumstances extrinsic to the thing sold, however much he may be interested in knowing them. The decision of Cicero meets with much difficulty even in the forum of conscience. The greater number of those who have written upon natural law have regarded it as going too far.

These authors are of opinion, that the good faith, which ought to govern in the contract of sale, obliges the seller to nothing more, than to cause the buyer to know the thing for what it is, without concealing any of its defects, and not to sell it for more than the price, which it bears at the time of the contract; that he does not commit any injustice, by selling for that price, though he knows that it must be much diminished afterwards; and that he is not obliged to impart to the buyer the knowledge which he possesses of the circumstances which must cause such diminution, since the buyer has no more right to require him to impart this knowledge, than he has to require him to give up a part of his property. If the seller does so, it will be, on his part, a gratuitous act of beneficence, which he is under no obligation to exercise, except in favor of those who are in need. The Rhodians were not in that situation; they were only in want of corn, and had money wherewith to purchase that which the merchant sold them. The profit, which he made by selling his corn at its current value, though he knew that it would soon be worth much less, was not an unjust profit; but a just reward for the diligence which enabled him to arrive the first, and for the risk which he ran of losing his merchandise, if any of the accidents, to which he was exposed, should have prevented his arrival at the time. It is no more forbidden to sell a thing for the current price, without informing the buyer of circumstances, which must cause it to fall, than it is to buy for the current price, without informing the seller of circumstances, which must cause it to rise. Now, we never think of accusing Joseph of injustice, in taking advantage of the knowledge which he had of the years of barrenness, to cause Pharaoh to buy the fifth part of the corn of his subjects, at the current price, without informing them of those years of sterility which were about to come.

Notwithstanding these reasons and authorities, I should have some difficulty in excusing, from the charge of injustice, the profit derived by a seller from the concealment of some fact, which must cause the price to fall, when such diminution of price must be very considerable, and must happen at the end of a very short interval of time, such as the knowledge which the merchant had, that there was a fleet laden with corn ready to enter the harbor of Rhodes in a few days. In the contract of sale, as in all other commutative contracts, equity requires, that what each of the parties gives should be the equivalent of what he receives, and that neither of them should desire to make a profit at the expense of the other. Now, in the case of this merchant, who, by the concealment on his part, is enabled to sell his corn, at the current price of 100 livres the cask, can he persuade himself, without illusion, that the corn, which in two days time must be worth only 20 livres, is really the equivalent of the 100 livres which he receives? You will say, it is sufficient, if, at the time of the contract, it is worth the price for which he sells it. I answer: a thing which has in truth a present and momentary value of 100 livres, but which the seller knows must be reduced in two days to 20 livres,—can it, in regard to the knowledge which he possesses, be seriously regarded by him as truly equivalent to the money which he receives, which will be always worth 100 livres? Is not his inducing the buyers, by the concealment on his part, to buy a thing, of which it is certain that in two days they must lose the four-fifths, a willingness to make a profit and enrich himself, by means of such concealment, at the expense of the buyers?

ARTICLE IV.

Whether the seller may, in the forum of conscience, sometimes sell for more than the just price.

§ I. General rule, and what is the just price.

243. The just price of things is the price, for which things of a like nature and goodness are accustomed to be sold, in the places where they are situated, if they consist of estates, or in the place where they are exposed for sale, if they consist of movable things.

For example, the just price of a farm, composed of tillage and meadow land, must be determined, by the price of the acre of tillage land or meadow, of a like goodness, in the province, where the farm is situated.

The just price of a yard of cloth, of a certain quality, is that, for which stuffs of the same quality are accustomed to be sold in that place.

As these things are not always sold for precisely the same sum, but *circum circa*, more or less; their just price does not consist in a fixed and indivisible point, like that of things, which are rated by the judge of police; but it has a certain extent within which we distinguish the *pretium medium*, or that for which things are ordinarily sold, and the *pretium summum*, and *pretium infimum*, which are the prices for which they are sold above or below the *pretium medium.*

This extent of the just price is greater or less, according to the different nature of things. The price of things, the commerce in which is frequent and daily, such as the most common merchandise, is ordinarily of less extent; on the contrary, the just price of things, the commerce in which is not daily, is ordinarily of greater extent. The just price of a kind of things, all of which nearly resemble each other, has commonly less extent, than that of things of another kind which are different among themselves. For example, the just price of a cow of common goodness is ordinarily of less extent than the just price of a horse.

There are certain things, of which we cannot, without difficulty, determine the just price; such are certain precious things of extreme rarity; for, the just price of a thing, as was remarked at the beginning, being regulated by that for which things of a like nature and goodness, (and to which consequently that thing may be compared), are accustomed to be sold, it follows, that the just price of a thing *unique* in its kind and incomparable cannot be determined.

Those things, which have no determinate price, may be sold for the price, which any one is willing to give for them; whatever that price may be, it cannot be said, that they are sold too dear and for more than their just price.

In regard to things which have a just price, the parties may struggle about the price, and regulate it for themselves, provided they do not go beyond the limits of the just price. For example, when the just price of a horse which you sell me is from eighteen to twenty pistoles, you may lawfully sell him to me for twenty pistoles, if I consent to give you that sum for him; as I may lawfully buy him for eighteen pistoles, if you are willing to sell him to me for that price. But, ordinarily, you are not at liberty to sell him for more than twenty pistoles, which is the *summum pretium*, nor am I at liberty to buy him for less than eighteen, which is the *pretium infimum*.

This principle is acknowledged only in the forum of conscience; and is not followed in the exterior forum, in which a buyer is not ordinarily received to complain, that he has purchased a thing at a greater than the just price, it being for the interest of commerce, that parties should not be admitted with facility to set aside their bargains.

§ II. Two cases in which one may sell for more than the just price.

FIRST CASE.

244. We may sometimes lawfully, even in the forum of conscience, sell for more than the just price, namely, for the price, which is called the *price of affection.*

For example, I am the owner of an estate which suits your convenience, but which I have no design to sell. You propose to me to sell it to you for a sum which is more than the just price, and I consent to do so. This sale is lawful. The excess, in this case, over the just price, is not received without cause and unjustly. It is the price of the affection which I have for the estate; and of the interest which I have in keeping my property rather than selling it for money, of which I might perhaps make a bad use. I may lawfully receive the price of the affection which I have for my estate, and of the interest which I have in keeping it, which I am under no obligation to sacrifice to you, for your convenience and pleasure, without compensation.

245. In order that I may lawfully receive, as the price of affection, something more than the just price of the estate, which I sell, it is necessary, that, when the proposition is made me, I should not have a design to sell it. If the situation of my affairs requires me to sell, I cannot receive any thing more than the just price; for, it cannot be said, in such case, that the excess above the just price is the price of the affection and interest which I have in retaining the estate, since, by the supposition, I am not willing to retain it; I should consequently give nothing, in such case, for that which I receive beyond the just price, contrary to equity, which ought to govern in the contract of sale, as in all other commutative contracts.

It may perhaps be said, that what I receive in this case beyond the just price is not received without cause and for nothing; but that it is the price of the convenience and of the interest which you have in acquiring the estate. The answer is, that, in commutative contracts, the value of what I may lawfully receive is determined by the value of what I give, it being the nature of such contracts, that each party receives the just equivalent of what he gives. But, it may be added, that I do you a pleasure in selling you this thing, which you have a great interest in having; that I am under no obligation to do you this pleasure; that I may sell it to another person, who is as willing as you to give the just price; and am I not at liberty to sell you a pleasure, which I am not obliged to give you? No; for it is a rule of justice, that we cannot exact, for the pleasure which we do any one, any thing more than it costs us to do it. This rule is derived from the rule which obliges us to love our neighbor as ourselves. It is in consequence of this rule, that we are not permitted to exact any lucrative interest, as a recompense for the pleasure which we do to any one by lending him money. It is not sufficient, therefore, to enable me lawfully to receive something more than the just price of a thing which I sell, that you should have an interest in acquiring it, even for a sum greater than its just price; but, it is necessary, that I should have, on my part, an interest in retaining it, as where I abandon the affection and interest which induce me to retain it.

Saint Thomas, 11, 2, *q.* 77, *a.* 1, decides this question conformably to the principle above established. After having said, that, "to sell a thing for more, or to buy it for less than it is worth, is in itself unjust and unlawful," he adds: "We may speak in another manner of a sale, which, by accident, turns out to be for the benefit of one party and to the detriment of the other; as, for example, when any one is much in need of a thing which belongs to another, and the owner would be injured by the want of it; in such case, the just price is to be determined, in respect not only to the thing which is sold, but also to the damage which the seller incurs by selling; and so the thing may be lawfully sold for something more than it is worth in itself, though not for more than it is worth to the seller. If any one will be much gratified by the thing of another which he receives, and the other will not be damnified by the want of it; the latter ought not to sell it for more than the just price, because the advantage which thereby accrues to him does not result from selling, but from the condition of the buyer; no one indeed can sell to another that which is not his own, though he may sell him the damage which he suffers."

246. When I intend keeping the thing which you propose to me to sell you, I may in truth lawfully receive something more than the just price for it; but, it is necessary, in such case, first, that you have knowledge of the just price of the thing, and that what you give me in addition, you give knowingly as the price of the affection and of the interest which I have in keeping the thing, of which I am willing to deprive myself in your favor. But if you have no knowledge of the just price of the thing; if the whole sum which you give me is given as the just price of the thing in itself; if it is your intention to acquire the thing of me for what you believe to be its just price, and not to purchase the affection and interest which I have in retaining it; what I receive, in such case, more than the just price, I receive unjustly; for, I cannot be considered to receive it as the price of the affection and of the interest which I have in retaining the thing, since I cannot receive of you the price of that which you have no intention to buy.

247. It is necessary, secondly, that what I receive as the price of affection and of the interest which I have in retaining the thing, should not be immense, and exceed what I conscientiously think to be the value of such affection and interest. In order to make this estimation, it is necessary that I should descend into myself, and inquire what sum in

addition to the just price would induce me to consent to the sale, if the other party were willing to give only that price; for the sum thus ascertained is the true price of affection and of the interest which I have in retaining the thing; and, consequently, I cannot lawfully receive any thing further as the price of such affection and interest.

SECOND CASE.

The second case, in which it is permitted to sell for more than the just price, is when a merchant, who has determined to keep a certain thing, until a certain time, when he has good reason to believe the price of it will rise, consents, at the request of some one who has need of it, to sell it to him. He may, in such case, lawfully stipulate for a sum exceeding the just price, equivalent to the price of the interest which he has in keeping it; and which he is not obliged to sacrifice to the buyer for nothing. But, it is necessary, that this sum should not exceed the value of the interest which the merchant has in keeping his merchandise. This interest is estimated at more or less, according to the greater or less degree of probability of the profit which he is expecting; the mere expectation of a profit never being entirely certain, nor consequently of the same value as a profit which already exists.

§ III. *May a sale be made upon credit for more than the just price?*

248. When goods, which are sold upon a certain term of credit, have, according to the current price, a certain price, which is greater than that of those which are sold for cash, or of those which are sold upon a shorter term, the merchant may lawfully follow these different prices. The reason is, that what he receives more than the cash price is an indemnification for the prejudice, which he would otherwise sustain from the credit afforded; for, being obliged, as fast as he sells his wares, to buy others to replace them and

to keep his shop furnished; when he sells them upon credit, those, which he buys to replace them, will cost him more than they would cost him, if he should sell his own for ready money, and thus enable himself to purchase others in the same manner; from whence it follows, that he must suffer a manifest prejudice, if he does not sell his goods for a greater price upon credit, than for ready money. The credit which he gives ought not to be prejudicial to him; *officium suum nemini debet esse damnosum.* He may consequently indemnify himself, by augmenting the price of the goods which he sells upon credit, in proportion to what he is himself obliged to pay, over and above the cash price, for those which he buys.

249. It is to be observed, that what the seller receives more than the cash price must not exceed the prejudice, which he suffers from the credit; for, though he may lawfully indemnify himself, he ought not to make a profit from the credit, or from the buyer's indigence. The seller above all has nothing wherewith to reproach himself, when he is in this disposition of will. If it is in his choice, he will prefer to sell for ready money, rather than upon credit for a price greater than the ready money price; for, it is plain, that, in that case, the addition to the price is not a profit, which he draws from the credit, but an indemnification against what he suffers from it.

250. When it is the usage, in a particular province, for individuals to give a certain term of credit to the merchants to whom they sell their wood or the wine of their harvest, the price for which they sell upon this term of credit is the just price, though it is dearer than that of some persons, who, having need of money, sell for cash; for, this term of credit being usual, and the sale made upon it being made upon the ordinary conditions, the price of such sale is the common and ordinary and consequently the just price. These individuals are not considered as drawing a profit

from the credit which they give, their bargain being made upon the ordinary conditions; it is rather the merchants, who purchase at a less price for ready money, who derive a profit from the payment of their money in advance; and this is a just profit to the extent only of what they suffer from advancing the price, before the expiration of the ordinary term of credit.

§ IV. Whether the buyer may sometimes complain, in the exterior forum, of an excess of price.

This subject is considered in part 5, chapter 2, section 3, to which the reader is referred.

CHAPTER III.

Of the obligations of the seller which result from particular clauses of the contract.

That which is expressed by the contract, touching the quantity and quality of the thing sold, the time and the place of delivery, constitutes a personal engagement on the part of the seller.

The time and place of delivery have already been considered, in the first part; and it now remains for us to treat of the clauses, which concern the quantity and quality of the thing sold. The engagement contracted by the seller, in the case of a sale upon trial, and the clause by which it is agreed that he shall make a particular use of the price, are also to be considered in this chapter.

ARTICLE FIRST.

Of the quantity of the thing sold.

251. When the thing sold is found to be of a less quantity than is expressed by the contract, the seller is obliged in

favor of the buyer to make him an allowance for such defect of quantity; as, if, for example, in the sale of a farm, it is declared to contain three hundred acres and is found to contain only two hundred and fifty; or, if one sells a vat, as containing fifteen casks of wine, and it contains only twelve.

252. In order to determine whether the buyer fulfils his engagements, in this respect, it is necessary to ascertain what ought to be included in the quantity expressed by the contract. It must be held as a rule, that we ought to include in the quantity that only which makes a part of the thing sold, at least, if it is not otherwise agreed; and, therefore, if one sells me a field, which is declared to contain ten acres, and it is crossed by a public highway, though the highway is included in the field, it ought not to be reckoned in the admeasurement, and the field ought to contain the ten acres without including the highway, at least, if it is not expressly declared that the field shall contain the ten acres including the highway; for the way being public cannot make a part of the thing sold; D. 18, 1, 51; D. 18, 6, 7, § 1.

253. When we sell a house and five acres of land dependent upon it, we ought to include, in the five acres, the hedges and ditches; for that which serves for the inclosure of the estate makes a part of what is sold, and, consequently, ought to be included in the purchase; at least, if it is not expressly said, that the estate contains five acres, exclusive of the hedges and ditches: *Quod venditur, in modum agri cedit, nisi id actum est ne cederet;* D. 18, 6, 7, § 1.

254. In declaring the quantity of an estate, we sometimes add these terms, *or thereabouts;* for example, five acres of vines, *or thereabouts;* one hundred acres of woods, *or thereabouts*, &c. The meaning of these terms is, that the seller will not be liable for a defect of quantity, when such defect is inconsiderable; for example, if, in the sale of five acres of

vines, there are wanting only eight or ten perches; for, five acres, wanting so little, are truly *five acres or thereabouts.* But if the defect be considerable, as, if the five acres fall short half an acre, the terms, *or thereabouts*, do not prevent the seller from being liable for such defect of quantity.

255. As the seller is liable to make the buyer an allowance for a defect in quantity, when it is found to be less than is expressed; *vice versa*, is the buyer liable to account for the surplus, when there is more than is expressed? This question must be decided in the negative. The reason is, that the field, for example, which is erroneously declared to contain ten acres, when it in fact contains eleven, is sold entire; and it is not the intention of the parties to make an exception of any part of it. The clause, by which the seller undertakes that it is of the quantity of ten acres, is inserted only in favor of the buyer; it is the seller only who promises and who undertakes. The buyer, by this clause, does not contract any engagement, and consequently cannot be liable to account for the surplus in quantity.

The buyer is not only not liable to account for such surplus, but if he is evicted of a small portion of the field, though that which remains contains the quantity declared by the contract, the seller will not, by such clause, be discharged from his liability for the eviction. This is the decision of the law 45, D. *de evict.* (21, 2, 45), and results from the principle above established. In fact, as the declaration of quantity, on the part of the seller, contains no reserve, it follows, that the portion which is evicted makes a part of what is sold, and that an eviction of that part ought to give rise to the action of warranty against the seller.

256. The rule, that the buyer is not liable to account for the surplus over the quantity expressed in the contract, takes place only in the case of sales made *per aversionem*, that is to say, in which the parties agree upon a single and only price for all that is sold; and not in those which are made

at the rate of so much the acre, so much the cask, &c. In the latter, it is evident, that the buyer ought to account for any surplus over and above the quantity specified in the contract.

257. When, by the same contract, and for the same price, there is a sale of two farms, or of two pieces of land, constituting one farm, with a declaration of the quantity of each, can the seller oppose to the buyer, in compensation of the deficiency of quantity in the one, the surplus of quantity in the other, when the two farms or pieces of land are of equal goodness, as, for instance, when it is declared that each contains one hundred acres, and one is found to contain only ninety and the other one hundred and ten acres? It would seem, if we follow rigorously the principle we have established, that the seller cannot be received to plead this compensation, since we can only oppose, in compensation of what we owe to any one, that which he reciprocally owes us, and, according to the above principle, the buyer owes nothing to the seller, on account of the excess of quantity in the farm of one hundred and ten acres. Paul nevertheless decides, D. 19, 1, 42, that, in this case, equity should be preferred to subtlety, and that the buyer has no claim on account of the deficiency in the piece which contains only ninety acres. The reason is, that, as these two farms or pieces of land are sold by the same contract and for the same price, and the buyer is only interested to have in the whole the same quantity which he expected to have, it follows, that, in the intention of the parties, the quantity which the seller promises is not so much that of each of the different parts, which make the object of the contract, as it is the entire quantity of all the parts which compose it, and, that as the buyer has this entire quantity, the seller ought to be considered as having satisfied his obligation.

This decision takes place, when the portion of the estate, which has the excess of quantity, is found to be better than, or at least, equal in goodness to, that which is deficient. It is necessary to decide otherwise, if it is inferior in goodness; for, in that case, the buyer being interested to have his quantity in the good piece of land rather than in the other, it cannot be said, as in the preceding case, that the intention of the parties is not so much to assure to him the quantity of each piece, as the quantity of the whole which they constitute.

258. The measure being different in different places, the quantity of estates must be determined according to the measure of the place where they are situated. Bartholus thinks it should rather be determined by the measure of the place where the bargain is made. I do not think this opinion reasonable; for, as estates are subject to the laws of the place where they are situated, they ought to be measured according to the law of that place. The buyer cannot set up the pretext that he does not know the measure; for, in going or sending to examine the estate, he is or ought to be able to inform himself concerning the measures which are there in use. If it appears, however, by what is said in the contract, that the parties have in view the measures of the place where the bargain is made, we must, in this respect, conform to the agreement of the parties.

Movable things having no locality or situation, it is evident, that their quantity must be regulated by the law of the place, where the bargain is made, or rather by that of the place, where they are to be delivered.

259. The action of the buyer, for a defect of quantity, consists in obtaining against the seller a proportionate deduction from the price.

This deduction is easily made, when there is a declaration, in general terms, of the quantity of the entire thing sold; as, if it be declared, that a lot of land contains ten acres, and it contains only nine; in which case, it is evident, that the tenth part of the price ought to be deducted.

But, if it is declared, that, in a farm composed of lands of different kinds, there is a certain quantity of such a kind, as, for example, so many vines, it is necessary to make a valuation, in order to estimate the defect of quantity in the vines, in proportion as they are more valuable than the lands of other kinds of which the farm is composed.

ARTICLE II.

Of the quality of the thing sold.

260. When the thing sold is not of the quality expressed by the contract, as, for example, if a wood is declared to be ten years old, and is, in fact, of a less age, the buyer is entitled to recover his damages, which consist in a deduction from the price.

261. Sometimes the buyer may be entitled to demand a rescission of the contract, if it appears, by circumstances, that the quality is such, that he would not have purchased the thing, if he had known of it; as, for example, if an estate is declared to be *en censive*, when it is in fact *en fief*, the buyer may sometimes demand a dissolution of the contract; as, where he is the father of several children, and is unwilling to make any considerable acquisitions of feudal property, lest his eldest son should have too great advantages in the succession.

262. It is necessary to observe, that the damages of the buyer, by reason of a defect in the quality of the thing sold, as expressed by the contract, may sometimes be differently estimated, according to the different circumstances and quality of persons. For example, when it is declared by the contract of sale of an estate, that it is *en censive*, and it is found to be *en fief*, the damages ought to be more considerable, if the buyer is a person subject to the right of *franc-fief*, than if he is a gentleman who is not subject to that

right. *Vice versa*, if it is declared by the contract, that the inheritance is *en fief*, and it is found to be *en censive*, the damages, resulting from the buyer's being deprived of the right to hunt, and from the *censual* being more considerable than *feudal* profits, (as in Dunois and Chartrain, where none but the *rachat* is due), are to be estimated with a deduction of the advantages resulting from the *censual* quality of the estate, which may extend so far as to amount to a compensation for those of which he is deprived; and, as one of the principal of these advantages is the not being subject to *franc-fief*, and as those who are exempt from that charge do not receive that advantage, it follows that the damages, resulting from an estate which is declared to be *en fief* being found to be *en censive*, will be much more considerable, when the buyer is not of a quality to be subject to the right of *franc-fief*, than when he is of a quality to be subject to it.

263. It remains to be observed, that the seller is obliged to indemnify the buyer, not only when he knows that the thing does not possess the quality declared by the contract, but even when he believes in good faith, that it has that quality. It is the same in regard to quantity.

264. What is above said, in regard to qualities expressed by the contract, must be understood of those, which are certain and determinate. The expression of vague qualities does not contain any engagement. For example, if, in the sale of a house, it is said to be a beautiful house, however ugly it may be, the buyer who might see it cannot complain. This is the doctrine of the law 43, D. *de contrah. empt.* (18, 1, 43): *Ea, quæ commendandi causa in venditionibus dicuntur, si palam appareant, venditorem non obligant.*

ARTICLE III.

Of the clause by which a thing is sold upon trial.

265. In sales of things, of which we cannot very well know the quality, but by trial, as a horse, a clock, or a watch; it is a clause quite common to be inserted, that they are sold upon trial, and that if the buyer be not satisfied the sale shall be void. Ulpian informs us that these sales are not conditional, and that the clause which they contain is only resolutory: *Si res ita distracta sit, ut si displicuisset, inempta esset; constat non esse sub conditione distractum, sed resolvi emptionem sub conditione;* D. 18, 1, 3. By this clause, which is entirely in favor of the buyer, the seller engages to take back the thing, if it shall not suit the buyer, and to restore him the price, if paid, or, if not, to discharge him from it. From this obligation, there results an action in favor of the buyer against the seller, for those objects; this action is a branch of the action *ex empto*, since it results from a clause, which makes a part of the contract.

266. When there is a time limited, within which the buyer is to have the thing upon trial, he may, during all that time, commence his action as above, but not afterwards. When there is no time limited, the Roman law limited the time, within which the buyer might demand a dissolution of the contract, to sixty days; D. 21, 1, 31, § 22. With us the time must be left to the discretion of the judge; it ought to be short.

267. The obligation, which results from this clause, is extinguished, when the thing perishes; for the buyer cannot then say, that the thing does not suit him, nor can he oblige the seller to take it back, when it no longer exists. This clause, as above observed, being only resolutory, the sale made subject to it is perfect, and the thing consequently becomes at the risk of the purchaser.

It would be otherwise, if, before there is a perfect sale, and while there is yet only a proposition for a sale, I give any one upon trial, for a certain time, the thing which I propose to sell him. In this case, if the thing perishes, it is my loss; and the other is not responsible for it, if there is no fault on his part; for, as there is yet no sale, *res perit domino.*

ARTICLE IV.

Of the clause by which the seller undertakes to make a particular use of the purchase money.

268. It happens very frequently, that when you sell me an estate, I stipulate with you, that the price which I pay shall be employed, either to discharge a certain debt, or, in general, to acquire other estates or annuities for the purpose of subrogating me to the privileges of your sellers or creditors; in the payment of whom you employ my money.

The effect of the engagement, which you contract by this clause, is, that if you fail to fulfil it, either by using the money for another purpose, or by dissipating it, or by omitting in the acquittances of payment, which you make to your creditor or to him of whom you purchase an estate, the declarations necessary to enable me to acquire the substitution, I am, in such case, entitled to the action *ex empto* against you, to the end, that, in default of the obligation being performed by you, the contract may become null, and you may be condemned to restore me the price, and also to pay me the damages resulting from its non-execution. You may ordinarily be condemned to do so even by your body; for it is a breach of faith and a kind of stellionate, on your part, to misuse the money which I gave you only upon the faith that you would make the agreed use of it.

269. As the buyer has no other interest in the performance of this clause, than to have his sureties for the warranty of

his acquisition, the seller may avoid the effect of this action, by procuring sureties otherwise, and thereby removing his interest. And, therefore, I think we ought to allow the seller the alternative, within a fixed time, to cause the estate to be sold by a decree at his own expense, in order to clear it of all hypothecations and real charges, with which it may be charged; provided he makes it appear that there is no reason to fear any right of dower, or other similar right, which the decree does not purge; or, if there is any such right, that it is an inconsiderable one, in proportion to the price of the estate, and gives sufficient sureties to be responsible for it.

CHAPTER IV.

Of the engagements which the seller of the property of another contracts in favor of the owner.

270. In the preceding chapters, the engagements and obligations of the seller, which result from the contract of sale, and which are contracted by him in favor of the buyer, have been considered. Besides these obligations, which he, who sells the property of another, contracts in favor of the buyer, he also contracts some in favor of the owner of the thing. The latter do not properly result from the contract of sale *per se;* contracts forming obligations only between the contracting parties; they result from a different thing, which is now to be explained.

271. In order to do this, it is necessary to distinguish between different cases. The *first* is when one sells a movable thing which he knows does not belong to him. There is no doubt, that, by selling and delivering such a thing, he commits a theft of it, against the owner, C. 7, 26, 1 & 7; and, consequently, he contracts in his favor the obligation which results from that species of offence; from which arises the action called *condictio furtiva,* by which the owner has a

right to demand a restitution of the thing, or, in default of that, the price.

The price, which he is bound to pay the owner, in default of restoring the thing, may be more considerable than that for which it is sold; for, if it is sold for less than its value, the owner, to whom the buyer is bound to restore the thing itself, is under no obligation to content himself with that price; in default of being able to restore the thing itself, the buyer ought to restore its true value.

The seller may even be liable for more than the true value of the thing; for, if the owner suffers or has suffered any damages from the want of the thing, he is entitled to an indemnification, according to the general rule, that he, who commits any kind of wrong (*delit*), whatever it may be, ought to indemnify the person against whom it is committed, for all that he suffers in consequence of it.

272. When he who sells a thing, which he knows does not belong to him, sells it for a very advantageous price, and, afterwards, by no matter what title, becomes the possessor of the same thing,—has the owner an election, to reclaim the thing, or the price for which it was sold, by offering to abandon it? I think he ought to be allowed this election; for the possessor in bad faith having committed a theft (*vol*) in selling and delivering the thing, which he knew did not belong to him, he ought not to be suffered to make a profit from his theft, nor consequently to retain the advantageous price for which it is sold. He, who unlawfully retains the property of another, is bound in favor of the proprietor, not only to a restitution of the thing, but to a restitution of the profit, which he makes in relation to it; such as that which he makes by selling it for an advantageous price; natural equity does not permit that any one should make a profit of his own wrong: *Fraus sua nemini opitulari debet.*

273. The *second* case is when one sells without right, and

as a thing belonging to him, an estate or incorporeal thing, which he knows belongs to me. In this case, he does not, properly speaking, commit a theft, these things not being susceptible of theft, *quum furtum non cadat nisi in res mobiles et corporales; arg.* D. 47, 2, 25; but he commits an injustice of a similar character; and, as natural equity does not permit any one to make a profit of his own injustice, in case I prefer the price for which the thing is sold to the thing itself, and desist from the exercise of my right to reclaim it, the seller is liable to me, *actione in factum*, to pay me the price, if it is already received; or to substitute me in his rights to recover it of the buyer, if it is not already received.

274. It is of no consequence, whether he, who sells as his own a thing which he knows belongs to me, is in possession of it without title, or in virtue of a just title; it is of no consequence, whether he possesses it by a lucrative or even by an onerous title; for, though he possesses it by an onerous title, and though he purchased it in good faith, he is equally under an obligation to restore it, as soon as he has knowledge that it belongs to me. The natural law not only prohibits us from taking but also from retaining the property of another; and, therefore, when, instead of restoring it to me, he disposes of it by selling it as his own, though he purchased it in good faith, he does not thereby the less commit a theft, if it is a movable corporeal thing, or if it is an immovable estate, an injustice similar to a theft, which imposes upon him all the obligations above mentioned.

275. The *third* case is when he, who possesses the property of another in good faith and by a title of donation or legacy, sells it in good faith as his own, and in ignorance that it belongs to another: If the thing so sold perishes or cannot be found, can the owner demand a restitution of the sum for which it is sold? This case is different from the two preceding; for the thing is sold in good faith; and, con-

sequently, I do not by selling commit any injustice towards the owner. Africanus, however, following Julian, decides, in the law 23, D. *de reb. cred.* (12, 1, 23), that even in this case, the owner of the thing is well founded to demand a restitution of the price of the buyer: *Si eum servum qui tibi legatus sit, quasi mihi legatum possiderim et vendiderim, mortuo eo posse te mihi pretium condicere Julianus ait.* This decision is founded upon that grand rule of natural equity, which does not permit one person to enrich himself out of the property of another; from whence it follows, that I ought not to make a profit out of the price of a thing belonging to another, which I have erroneously sold as my own. This is the reason, which the jurisconsult himself gives, in the law above quoted: *Posse te mihi pretium condicere, Julianus ait, quod ex re tua locupletior factus sim.*

276. The *fourth* case is when you sell in good faith the thing of another, which you have purchased in good faith of one who was not the owner of it; if it afterwards perishes or cannot be found, can the owner reclaim the price? The reasons, upon which the decision of the preceding case in the affirmative is founded, do not meet us in the present. You sell it in good faith, and it seems, we cannot say, as in the preceding case, that, by so doing, you enrich yourself with the price of a thing which belongs to another; for, by reselling, you recover the price which it cost you, rather than enrich yourself. It is only the case, where you resell for a price greater than that for which you purchase, which may in some sort seem like the preceding, and therefore to impose upon you the obligation to restore, not indeed the whole price, but only the excess of it over and above what the thing cost you. Notwithstanding these reasons, Pulveus, in his treatise *de rei alien. distract.*, *cap.* 20, thinks, that he, who, though in good faith, sells the thing of another, which he has purchased of one who was not the owner, is liable to restore the price to the latter, *utili actione negotiorum gesto-*

rum; because, in selling the thing, though believing it to be his own, he thought he was conducting his own business, yet, in truth, he was conducting the business of the owner of the thing rather than his own; and he is therefore obliged to account to the owner, *domino negotii,* for what he receives from such management. He is bound to do so, not according to the subtlety of law, since, meaning to sell his own property, he has no intention to contract any obligation to render an account of the sale; but, according to equity, because, by selling the thing, he really transacts the business of the party to whom it belongs. For this reason, *tenetur actione negotiorum gestorum, non quidem directa, sed utili.* Pulveus, in support of his opinion, cites the last law D. *de neg. gest.* (3, 5, 49), in which the case supposed is, that you purchase a slave of me, and in good faith, sell as your own, a thing which you find in his hands, and which was stolen from me by him. In this case, Africanus decides, that I am entitled to an action against you for a recovery of the price; *de pretio negotiorum gestorum actio mihi danda, ut dari deberet, si negotium quod tuum esse existimares, quum esset meum, gessisses.* This opinion of Pulveus seems to me to be liable to some difficulty. The law upon which he founds it is not decisive in his favor. In the case there supposed, you purchase the slave, but you do not purchase the thing which the slave has stolen, and which you sell; that thing does not cost you any thing. So this law proves only that he who sells, though in good faith, the thing of another, which he was in possession of by a lucrative title, is liable to render the price of it to the true owner; but it does not prove, that he is obliged to do so, when he is the purchaser of the thing. Perhaps it will be insisted, that the reason mentioned in this law, upon which the demand of the owner for a recovery of the price is founded, is, that, by selling the thing which belongs to me as your own, you really transact my business, though you think you are conducting your own; and, that this reason holds good, in all cases, where you sell, though in good faith and as belonging to you, a thing which belongs to me. The reason holds good equally, whether you possess the thing by a lucrative title, or by purchase, because it is always true to say, that it is a sale of my thing which you make, and that you consequently transact my business. To this reasoning we may answer, that, when you sell in good faith a thing which you have purchased, though it does not belong to you but to me, the sale is truly your own affair and not mine, *tuum negotium geris, non meum.* If, in the case of the law above quoted, it is decided, that you are obliged to account for the price of the thing which you sell for me, in the same manner, as if you had transacted my business, thinking to transact your own, it is not merely for the reason, that the thing belongs to me, but also because it is one which was stolen from me by the slave, whom I sold to you, which you have not purchased, which cost you nothing, and of the price of which, you ought not consequently to make a profit at my expense. The sale, which you make of this thing, being a sale, the price of which, according to the rules of equity, ought not to turn to your profit, but to mine, it follows, that, in making it, you conduct my business, thinking to conduct your own. It results from this explanation, that this law, as well as that quoted in the third case, is decisive only in that case, and does not prove any thing in favor of the opinion of Pulveus, in the fourth case. The law 3, C. *de rei vendicat.* (3, 32, 3,) and the law 1, C. *de reb. alien. non alien.* (4, 51, 1), prove still less for the opinion of Pulveus, as they refer to the case in which the seller has knowledge, in selling the thing, that it does not belong to him. The opinion of Pulveus, therefore, is not founded upon any text of the law. On the contrary, we may draw an argument against it, from the law 17, D. *de rei vendicat.* (6, 1, 17), in which it is decided, that if Mœvius, being the owner of a thing which I have purchased of Titus, bring his demand in revendication, and after this demand, and *post acceptum judicium*, I sell the thing to a second buyer, by whose act it perishes, I am liable to account to Mœvius, for the price for which I sell the thing. Ulpian, having in this case decided, that I am liable to restore the price, when I sell the thing *post acceptum judicium*; it follows, by a negative argument, that it would be otherwise, if I sell in good faith, before any demand. It is true that negative arguments are not always entirely conclusive.

PART THIRD.

OF THE ENGAGEMENTS OF THE BUYER.

277. The engagements of the buyer, like those of the seller, result from the nature of the contract, from good faith, and from particular clauses of the contract.

SECTION FIRST.

Of the engagements of the buyer which result from the nature of the contract.

278. The engagements of the buyer, which result from the nature of the contract, are: 1, to pay the price and the interest of it; and, 2, to carry away the thing sold, and to indemnify the seller against any expenses incurred in its preservation.

§ I. Of the obligation to pay the price.

279. The principal engagement, which the buyer contracts by the nature of the contract itself, consists in his obligation to pay the agreed price, from which there results an action in favor of the seller (*actio venditi*) to demand such payment.

280. When the contract contains no term of payment, the seller may immediately commence this action against the buyer, upon the offer which he ought to make him to deliver the thing, provided it is not already delivered.

If, after the contract, it ceases, without the fault of the seller, to be in a situation to be delivered, the seller is not thereby deprived of his right to commence his action for the payment of the price. But, whilst the seller is in delay to deliver the thing sold, he is not receivable to demand the price of it.

281. Even when the seller has delivered the thing, he cannot demand the price of it, if the buyer is troubled in his possession, by any demand in revendication, or by any hypothecary, or other demand, until after the termination of the process.

If, however, the process may last a long time, the seller may be received, after having taken the act and cause of the buyer, to demand the price of him; but it is necessary, in this case, that he should offer a good and sufficient surety, to return it in case of eviction.

If there is a strong presumption, that the demand brought against the buyer is brought by some trusty friend of his in order to vex the seller, and to prevent him from receiving the price, the surety, if the seller is unable to provide one, ought to be dispensed with. There is ground for such a presumption, if the demand appears to be destitute of foundation, and to be brought by a man from the very dregs of the people, who has nothing to lose.

282. The seller, who is not permitted to receive the price, for want of being able to provide a surety, may demand that the buyer should be held to deposit the price; but it is not always for the advantage of the seller to demand a deposit, because it puts a stop to the running of interest for his benefit; it is for his advantage to do so, when he is persuaded that the buyer has no money, and that the process is only a manœuvre to which the buyer has recourse in order to delay the payment. The buyer may also demand a deposit, in order to discharge himself from the interest.

283. The buyer may well defend himself from paying, when he is disturbed; but, if he has paid previous to the trouble, he can neither demand a restitution of the price, nor a surety, during the process. Even before he has paid, so long as he suffers no disturbance, he is not allowed to

require of the seller a surety for the price, the payment of which is demanded of him.

§ II. Of the interest of the price.

284. When the thing sold is not of a nature to produce fruits, as a library, or a suit of hangings, the buyer, like every other debtor of a sum of money, owes the interest of the price only from the day, that he is put in delay to pay by a judicial interpellation.

But, when the thing is of a nature to produce fruits, either natural or civil, as a piece of land, a house, a mill, or a herd of cattle, the buyer owes the interest of the price, of full right, and *ex natura contractus*, from the time that he enters into possession and enjoyment of the thing, whether interest is stipulated or not.

It may be legally agreed, that the interest shall be paid, at a rate less than the lawful rate, which is the twentieth part; for example, that it shall be paid at the rate of the twenty-second or twenty-fourth; but it cannot be legally agreed, that it shall be paid at a greater rate. For example, if the rate agreed upon is the sixteenth or eighteenth, the buyer, notwithstanding the agreement, is only liable for the twentieth; And. Gail, *obs.* 11, 15.

285. The buyer owes the interest of the price, not only before he is put in delay to pay, but even during the pendency of a process, upon a demand brought against him by a third person; though, during that time, he is not obliged to pay the price, unless the seller offers him a surety. He cannot, in such case, discharge himself from the interest, except by a deposit of the price, it not being just that he should enjoy the thing and also the price at the same time: *Quum re emptor fruatur, æquissimum est eum usuras pretii pendere . . . . . hoc enim solum spectare debemus, an habeat facultatem fructus percipiendi*; D. 19, 1, 13, §§ 20, 21.

286. When it is agreed by the contract, that the buyer

shall enter immediately into the enjoyment of the estate, and that nevertheless he shall have a certain term for the payment of the price, upon condition, that, during that time, he shall pay the interest; this agreement, though condemned as usurious, by some doctors, cited by Fachineus, *controv. lib.* 2, *cap.* 32, is lawful. The ground of their opinion is, that usury consists in drawing a profit from the loan or credit, which we make to our debtor. Now, say they, in this case, the interest is stipulated as the price of the credit, which the seller affords to the buyer; the buyer does not owe it, by the nature of the contract, since, having a term allowed him, he is not in any manner in delay to pay, *nec in mora regulari, nec in mora irregulari;* and, consequently, he cannot owe the interest in virtue of the contract.

The answer is, that, in this contract, the interest does not result from the delay to pay, but from the buyer's enjoyment of the thing, and from that rule of equity, which does not permit him to enjoy the thing and the price at the same time: *Hoc solum spectare debemus, an habeat facultatem fructus percipiendi;* D. 19, 1, 13, § 20. The interest which the seller stipulates is not a profit which he draws from the credit for the payment of the price; but rather the price of the enjoyment of the thing, which the seller is under no obligation to accord, before a payment of the price. Interest of this kind is not therefore *usura lucratoria*, which is unlawful, but *usura compensatoria*, which, by the acknowledgment of all, is permitted. The seller ought not to be in a worse condition, because he has the good nature to grant a term to the buyer for the payment of the price, than he would otherwise be in; he ought not to suffer from the favor which he confers on the buyer; and, if he does not grant a term, the interest will begin to run from the time when the buyer commences his enjoyment of the thing. The seller may, therefore, in granting a term, reserve the interest which would be due to him, if he did not grant it.

287. If, by the contract of sale, by which the seller grants a term for the payment of the price to the buyer, whom he nevertheless permits to enter upon the enjoyment of the thing, the parties do not explain themselves, whether the interest of the price shall run or not, can the seller claim it? For the affirmative, it would seem, that we might say nearly the same which we have said in regard to the preceding question. It may be said, that, in order to render the buyer liable for interest, it is sufficient if he has the enjoyment of the estate, since equity does not permit him to enjoy the thing and the price at the same time; *hoc solum spectare debemus; dict. l.* It is not necessary, therefore, in order that the interest may run to the profit of the seller, during the term, that the parties should make an express agreement to that effect. The seller, by granting a term for the convenience of the buyer, ought not to suffer from it; he ought not to be presumed thereby to renounce the interest, which belongs to him by the nature of the contract, from the time the buyer enters upon the enjoyment of the thing to the payment of the price, as no person ought to be easily presumed willing to renounce his rights: *Nemo res suas jactare, nemo quod suum est donare facile præsumitur.* Notwithstanding these reasons, the common doctrine is, that the buyer does not owe interest during the term which he grants for the payment of the price, though he has the enjoyment of the thing during that time. Fachineus, *controv.*, 11, 32, and Covarruvias, *var. res.*, 111, 4, so decide, in express terms, or rather take it for granted, and do not even make it a question. Though they do not mention the reason for their opinion, it is easy to perceive it. The enjoyment, which, by this clause, is granted to the buyer, before payment of the price, makes a part of what is sold him; he is considered as having paid for this enjoyment by the price stipulated in the contract; the parties are considered as having agreed upon a price greater than it would have been

without this clause. The seller cannot therefore exact the interest as the price of this enjoyment, since it is already paid for in the principal price itself, in which that of the enjoyment is included. Even when there is a doubt, whether the seller has included the price of this enjoyment in the price stipulated by the contract, or whether he intended to reserve to himself the right of compensating it by the interest, the contract ought to be interpreted against the seller, who ought to explain himself concerning such reservation; D. 2, 14, 39; D. 50, 17, 17; Tr. on Obl. n. 97.

288. If the term, for the payment of the price, does not make a part of the contract, but is granted afterwards, by an agreement between the buyer and seller, and it does not appear that the seller receives any thing for it; in such case, the seller is only to be considered as granting a delay of the action which he has a right to commence, in order to give the buyer time to procure the money, and not to intend a renunciation of his right to the interest, which is due by the nature of the contract, since no person is to be presumed willing to renounce his rights.

289. It is necessary to decide otherwise, if the term is granted by the testament of the seller. The heirs of the seller cannot, in such case, exact interest of the buyer during the term. The testator must be considered as having made a release of it, during the term which is granted by his testamentary disposition. Such a disposition, which, in its nature, imports a liberality, on the part of the testator, in favor of the legatee, ought to be favorably interpreted: *In testamentis voluntates testantium plenius interpretantur;* D. 50, 17, 12.

290. The interest being due by the nature of the contract, from the time when the buyer commences his enjoyment of the thing, the term granted by the contract, or by the testament of the seller, puts a stop to it only during the time thereby limited; after the expiration of the term, it accrues of full right.

§ III. Of the other obligations of the buyer which result from the nature of the contract.

291. One of the obligations, which result from the nature of the contract, is that, which the buyer thereby contracts, to carry away the merchandise which he buys.

When, by a judicial summons, he is put in delay to satisfy this obligation, he is liable for the damages, which the seller sustains from that time by being deprived of the use of his magazines, granaries, storehouses and cellars, in which the goods sold are stored.

The seller may, also, in this case, summon the buyer, to the end, that if he fails to carry away the goods within a short time, to be fixed by the judge, the seller shall himself be permitted to put them out at the expense of the buyer, notifying him of the day and hour appointed for that purpose.

292. When the contract does not import any time for the carrying away of the things sold, the buyer may be summoned immediately for that purpose.

There are however certain goods, for the carrying away of which, local usages accord a certain term. For example, in the wine country of Orleans, there is a custom, that the dealers, who make their purchases of wine at vintage time, shall be allowed until Martinmas-day for carrying it away.

Lastly, it is an engagement, which results from the nature of the contract of sale, that the buyer shall reimburse the seller for any expenses incurred by him, subsequent to the contract, in the preservation of the thing sold; for, as the fruits of the thing sold are due to the buyer, even before a delivery, as soon as he pays the price, so, as we have already seen in the preceding part, it is natural, that he should bear the expenses of it from that time, and, consequently, all the expense which is necessary for the support and preservation of the thing; D. 19, 1, 13, § 22.

293. If, by a particular agreement, or because the price remains unpaid, the seller continues, after the contract, to receive the fruits of the estate to his own profit, there is no doubt that the expenses of supporting it ought not to be reimbursed him, since they are a charge upon the fruits which belong to him. But is he entitled to be reimbursed the expense of large repairs? The reason for doubting is, that the seller, until a delivery, remains the owner, and that such repairs are a charge upon the property. I think, however, that they ought to be reimbursed to the seller, by the buyer. As to the remark, that repairs are a charge upon the property, it is true, when the question is between the owner and the usufructuary; but it is otherwise, when the question is between the seller and the buyer. The thing sold being, from the time of the contract, at the risk of the buyer, all the charges upon the fruits, which the seller still continues to receive, ought to rest upon the buyer.

SECTION II.

Of the obligations of the buyer which result from good faith.

294. The good faith, which ought to prevail in the contract of sale, obliges the buyer to two things; 1, not to make use of any bad faith to induce the seller to sell, or to sell for a less price; and, 2, not to buy the thing for less than the just price.

ARTICLE FIRST.

In what consists the bad faith which a buyer may commit and to what it obliges him.

295. There are two kinds of bad faith, which a buyer may commit, in the contract of sale. The first consists in falsehood and tricks (*manœuvres*) employed by him, to induce the seller to sell, or to sell for a less price; as, if, for

the purpose of inducing the proprietor of an inn situated upon a great road, to sell it to me, I practise any tricks to make him believe that a decree has passed for the making of a new road, which will divert the travel.

These tricks are not only condemned in the forum of conscience; but, when well proved, they may entitle the seller in the exterior forum, to letters of rescission against the contract.

296. The second kind of bad faith is when the buyer conceals from the seller the knowledge which he has of the thing and which the seller has not. For example, I am well acquainted with an estate, which you sell me, and I know that you are not so; that it is let to farm at a low rent; and that upon a renewal of the lease, it may be let to much better advantage; it is bad faith on my part to conceal from you the knowledge which I possess of the lowness of the rent of the estate.

The reason is, that good faith and equity, which ought to govern in the contract of sale, oblige the contracting parties not to conceal any thing within their knowledge touching the thing which makes the object of the bargain. The law 43, § 2, D. *de contrah. empt.* (18, 1, 43, § 2), considers every concealment, in this respect, to be bad faith; as we have already seen, *supra*, n. 234. It is true, that this refers to the case of a seller only; but it applies equally to the buyer, the obligations being reciprocal.

297. The buyer by such a concealment is guilty of an injustice, even when the price, for which he buys, is the just price; for, as he is perfectly free to buy or not to buy, and not to buy except for the price which he thinks the thing to be worth, he ought to allow the seller to enjoy the same liberty; the concealment, of which the buyer is guilty, in order to induce the seller to sell a thing, which he is unwilling to sell, or which he would sell for a higher price than he sells it for, if he had the knowledge, which is concealed

from him, is a snare spread for the liberty which he ought to enjoy, and consequently an injustice.

298. This kind of injustice, in the forum of conscience, obliges the buyer who is guilty of it, to declare to the seller the knowledge, which he concealed from him at the time of the contract, and to permit him to take back the thing, if he wishes; it also obliges him to be at all the expenses of the retrocession, as well as those of the sale.

299. This obligation concerns only the forum of conscience; in the exterior forum, a seller would not be allowed to complain that the buyer has concealed from him the knowledge which the latter possessed of his property. It is considered to be the seller's duty to know his own goods better than any other person; and, if he does not, it is a fault, which he can impute only to himself. The laws do not come to the assistance of the negligent. The freedom of commerce would be shackled, and persons would not dare to make contracts, in the fear of process, if the contracting parties were easily admitted to a hearing, for the purpose of setting them aside when made.

ARTICLE II.

Of the obligation not to buy for less than the just price.

300. The same reason of equity, which does not permit the seller to sell for more than the *summum pretium* of the just price, also prohibits the buyer from buying for less than the *infimum pretium* of the just price. See *supra*, part 2, art. 4.

301. However, in the case of the sale of a thing, which produces fruits either natural or civil, as an estate, or a herd of cattle, in the same manner, that the seller, who gives a credit to the buyer for the payment of the price, may lawfully add to the just price, the interest of the price, from the time he puts the buyer in enjoyment of the thing, to the

time of payment of the price, for the reason that the interest stands to him in place of the enjoyment of the thing, which he is not obliged to accord to the buyer, but upon receiving the price; so, when the buyer advances to the seller the price of a fruit-bearing thing, of which he is not yet put in possession, the buyer may deduct, from the just price, the interest from the day he advances it, to the day upon which the thing is to be delivered. The interest, which he deducts from the just price, is, in such case, a just equivalent for the enjoyment of the thing, which he is entitled to have, according to the ordinary rules of the contract of sale, from the time of payment of the price.

302. When the thing sold is not a fruit-bearing thing, as the seller cannot, in such case, exact any thing more than the just price for the credit, except only to the amount of what he suffers from it, as we have already seen, *supra*, n. 249; so, the buyer, who advances the price before the time of delivery, cannot deduct therefrom any more than what he suffers from the advance.

303. The buyer, however, is permitted to deduct something from the just price, in the following case, which is proposed by the authors, who have treated of moral theology. You propose to sell me a quantity of merchandise, of which you are not able to make a delivery, until the expiration of a month. To do you a favor, I purchase the goods now and pay you for them in ready money. If there is a moral certainty, or, at least a great probability, that the price of these goods will fall, I may lawfully deduct, from the price, which they are now worth, a sum equivalent to the loss, which I run the risk of losing in making the purchase.

The deduction, which may be made in this case from the just price, should be made, not only in regard to the quantity of loss, which there is reason to believe may take place, upon the goods, by the time of the delivery, but also in regard to the degree of probability there is, that there will be any loss at all. Consequently, the deduction may be of a sum more or less approaching the quantity of loss, which there is reason to apprehend, according to the greater or less degree of probability there is that the loss itself will happen; but it can never be equal to the entire quantity; for the risk of a loss, which has not yet happened, however probable it may be, can never be equal to the loss itself, when it happens; in the same manner that the hope of a gain is never of the same value as the gain itself when it accrues.

The estimation of this equivalent being difficult, since the buyer's desire of gain may induce him, even without perceiving it himself, to place it higher than it ought to be, and the seller's necessities may induce him to consent to every thing, it is much better, in such case, to make the bargain for the price of the goods at the time of the delivery, and that nevertheless the buyer shall pay a certain sum in advance, saving to the parties to account to each other for the difference of more or less, whenever the price shall be settled. If the buyer rejects a proposition of this kind, when made to him by the seller, it is a proof of the secret intention which he has to make an unjust profit at the expense of the latter.

ARTICLE III.

When meanness of price is considered in the exterior forum.

304. In regard to movable things, the seller is not allowed in our tribunals, to complain of a sale, which he has made for a mean price, upon the ground of meanness of price alone, however enormous may be the lesion which he suffers. The custom of Orleans, art. 446, contains an express provision to this effect, and it is a law generally received.

305. The laws of police, however, put a bridle upon the cupidity of traders, who take advantage of the necessities of

the country people, to buy produce of them before harvest, at a very mean price, which they advance. For this purpose, the laws prohibit, under very heavy penalties, purchases of growing corn and of other fruits, before they are gathered. They also for the same reason prohibit wool dealers from buying wool before it is sheared.

These regulations, however, are not observed with so much rigor, as to oblige us to consider as null, without distinction, all sales of fruit made before harvest; for, as the object of these provisions is to prevent the dealers from taking advantage of the pecuniary wants of the sellers, to purchase of them upon hard terms; whenever there is no suspicion of such a design, and the bargain appears to be made upon reasonable conditions, it ought to be confirmed. There is no ground for suspicion, when the buyer does not advance the price, which is not to be paid until the delivery. These regulations being made in favor of sellers, they alone, and not the buyers, are allowed to complain of bargains made in contravention of them.

306. In regard to estates (*héritages*), the lesion, which the seller suffers in the price, is not regarded in the exterior forum, when it is small (*modique*); but, when it is enormous, and when the price for which the estate is sold is less than a moiety of the just price, the laws grant the seller a rescissory action.

SECTION III.

Of the obligations of the buyer which result from particular clauses of the contract of sale.

307. Besides the engagements on the part of the buyer, which result from the nature of the contract and from good faith, which are treated of in the preceding sections, there are others, which may result from particular clauses of the

contract; for, if it is agreed, by a clause of the contract of sale, that the buyer, in addition to the price, shall give a certain thing to the seller, or that he shall or shall not do a particular thing, there results from this clause an obligation on the part of the buyer in favor of the seller, to execute the agreement, and also an action in favor of the seller to compel him to do so. This action is a branch of the action *ex vendito*. In regard to the effect of this obligation, we can only refer to the general principles established in the Treatise on Obligations, concerning the effect of obligations to give or to do.

In the contract of sale, the clauses, which most frequently include an obligation on the part of the buyer, are: 1, the clause of redemption, by which the buyer obliges himself to restore the thing to the seller, whenever the latter shall request it, upon condition that he shall indemnify the buyer, for all that it may have cost him to acquire the thing; 2, the commissory pact, by which the buyer obliges himself to a restitution of the thing, in default of payment of the price, within a certain time; and, 3, the clause, by which the buyer consents to a dissolution of the sale, in case the seller, within a certain time, shall find more advantageous terms upon which to purchase. A sale made with this agreement is what is called *addictio in diem*. As the engagements, which are contracted by these three clauses, tend to a dissolution of the contract of sale, these are treated of in the fifth part of this treatise.

PART FOURTH.

AT WHOSE RISK THE THING SOLD IS DURING THE INTERMEDIATE TIME BETWEEN THE CONTRACT AND THE DELIVERY.

308. It is a principle, established in the Title of the Digest, *de periculo et commodo rei venditæ*, (18, 6), that, as soon as the contract of sale is perfected, the thing sold is at the risk of the buyer, though it is not delivered to him; so, that if, during this period, it happens to perish, without the seller's fault, the seller is discharged from his obligation, while the buyer does not thereby become discharged from his, but still remains bound to pay the agreed price.

That the seller should be discharged from his obligation, when the thing sold perishes without his fault, is a consequence of another principle, that every obligation of a specific thing is extinguished, when the thing ceases to exist; Tr. on Obl. part 3, chap. 6. This principle results from the very nature of things; for the thing due being the subject of the obligation, it follows, that, when it ceases to exist, the obligation also ceases, since it cannot subsist without a subject.

The other branch of the rule, namely, that the obligation of the buyer remains, though that of the seller is extinguished by the extinction of the thing, seems to be attended with more difficulty. It is however true, and founded in the nature of the contract of sale. This contract belongs to the class of those, which we call *consensual*, and which are perfected by the mere consent of the contracting parties. The delivery of the thing sold is not necessary to the perfection of this contract. The obligation, which the buyer contracts to pay the price, being therefore perfect by the mere consent of the parties which intervenes and independently of a delivery, it ought to remain, notwithstanding the thing sold ceases to exist and can no longer be delivered. It is true, that, so long as the seller is in delay to deliver the thing, he cannot demand the price of it, because he cannot be allowed to require the buyer to perform his obligation, while he is in delay to perform his own. But when the obligation of the seller is extinguished, in one of the natural manners, in which obligations are extinguished, the buyer no longer has any thing to object, in order to defend himself against a performance of his obligation, which, having been legally contracted, continues to subsist, and cannot be extinguished, but in some one of the manners, in which obligations are extinguished.

Several moderns, who have treated of natural law, among whom are Barbeyrac, Puffendorf, &c. are of opinion, that the Roman jurisconsults have departed, in this respect, from the principles of natural law; and they maintain, on the contrary, that the thing sold is at the risk of the seller, so long as he remains the owner of it; that a loss, happening to the thing, though without his fault, ought to fall upon him, provided the buyer is not in delay to receive it; and, in like manner, that any accessions happening to the thing are for his benefit. Their arguments are, first, that it is an acknowledged maxim, even with the Roman jurisconsults themselves, that a thing is at the risk of the owner of it, *res perit domino*. The answer to this objection is, that the maxim is applicable, when the question arises between the proprietor and those who have the custody or use of the thing; in which case, the thing perishes to the loss of the owner, rather than to the loss of those who have the custody or use of it, who, by the happening of the loss without fault on their part, are discharged from their obligation to restore it. But when the question arises between the owner who is a debtor of the thing, and one who is a creditor of the same thing, and who is entitled to an action to compel a delivery of it, in such case, the thing perishes to the loss of the creditor, rather than the owner, who, by the loss, is discharged from his obligation to deliver it. In fact, each party loses the right which he has in a thing, or in relation to it, when it perishes by accident; the seller, who is the owner of the thing, loses his right of property, such as it is, that is to say, a right which he cannot retain, and which he is obliged to transfer to the buyer; the buyer, on his part, loses the right, which he has in relation to the thing, that is to say, the right which he has to compel a delivery of it to him.

These authors object, second, that the buyer's obligation to pay the price is dependent upon the condition, that the thing shall be delivered to him. I deny the proposition. The buyer is under an obligation to pay the price, not upon condition that the seller shall give him the thing, but rather upon the condition, that the seller is on his part obliged to cause him to have the thing; it is sufficient, therefore, if the seller is legally subject to such obligation, and does not fail in its performance, in order that the obligation of the buyer may have a cause and subsist.

Though the reasons in favor of the opinion of the Roman jurists, it appears to me, ought to prevail, yet it must be acknowledged, that the question is not without difficulty, and it seems even that the Româns themselves were not unanimous in their decision of it; for, Africanus, in the law 33, D. *locat. conduct.* (19, 2, 33), says expressly, that if the treasury seizes upon an estate, which I sell you, before I deliver it, so that it is no longer in my power to deliver it, I am not indeed liable for your damages, but I am liable to restore you the price of the sale. This text appears so decisive to Cujas, that, in his treatise *ad African.* upon this law, he goes so far as to maintain, that, according to the Roman law, the thing sold is not at the risk of the buyer, contrary to the express decision of other texts of the law, to the general opinion, and even to what he has himself written, *ad* l. 34, § 5, *alia caus.*, D. *de contrah. empt.* (18, 1, 34, § 5). The other interpreters imagine different modes of conciliation; the most plausible of which is that of Davesan, a professor of our university of Orleans, in his treatise *de contr.* He says, that in the case mentioned by Africanus, if the buyer is entitled to a recovery of the price, it is because the ordinances which require possessors to quit possession of their estates, on account of some public cause, probably contain this clause, *notwithstanding all sales previously made, which are to be null.* In such case, therefore, the sale being rescinded, the buyer is entitled to recover the price; but when the thing sold perishes, the sale is not thereby rescinded. Even if we should not admit this conciliation, but suppose that Africanus was really of a different opinion from our own, his opinion, which is mentioned in the Digest incidentally and in reference to another question, ought to yield to the express decisions of other jurisconsults, in the law 7, and in the law 8, D. *de peric. et comm. rei vend.* (18, 6, 7 & 8), and to the decisions of the emperors, namely, Alexander, in the law 1, and Gordian, in the law 4, C. *dict. tit.* (4, 48, 1, § 4), and, lastly, of Justinian, who, in the Institutes, *de empt. vend.* § 3, (I, 3, 24, 3), says expressly: *Emptoris damnum est, cui necesse est, licet rem non fuerit nactus,* PRETIUM SOLVERE.

309. Having established the principle, that the thing sold is at the risk of the buyer, as soon as the contract is perfected, it becomes necessary to inquire when the contract receives its perfection; and, generally, the contract of sale is considered to be perfect, as soon as the parties are agreed upon the price, for which the thing is sold. This rule holds, when the sale is of a specific thing, and is absolute (*pure et simple*): *Si id, quod venierit appareat quid, quale, quantum sit, et pretium, et pure venit; perfecta est emptio;* D. 18, 6, 8.

If the sale is of things, which consist *in quantitate*, and which are sold by weight, number or measure, as if one sells ten casks of the corn which is in a certain granary, ten thousand pounds of sugar, or one hundred carp, &c. the sale is not perfect until the corn is measured, the sugar weighed, or the carp counted; for, until such time, *nondum apparet quid venierit.* It does not yet appear, which is the corn, which is the sugar, or the carp, that makes the object of the sale, since that object can only be the corn that is to be measured, the sugar that is to be weighed, or the carp that are to be counted.

It is true, that, before the measuring, weighing or counting, and at the instant of the contract, the engagements which result from it exist. The buyer is then entitled to an action against the seller, for a delivery of the thing, and the seller is entitled to an action against the buyer, for a recovery of the price, upon offering to deliver it. But, though the engagement of the seller subsists from that time, it may be truly said, that it is not yet perfect, in this respect, that as yet it is only of an object which is indeterminate, and which can be determined only by the measuring, weighing, or counting. For this reason, until the thing is measured, weighed, or counted, it does not become at the risk of the buyer; for the risk cannot fall but upon some determinate thing.

This rule holds, not only when the sale is of a certain quantity of merchandise, to be taken from a magazine which contains a larger quantity, because, in such case, as we have seen, until the measuring or weighing, that which is sold does not consist of any determinate body or thing, upon which the risk may fall; it also holds, when the sale is of the entire quantity contained in a magazine or granary, provided it is made at the rate of so much the pound, or so much the measure, &c.

The sale, in this case, is not considered as perfect, and

the thing sold is not at the risk of the buyer, until it is measured or weighed; for, until that time, *non apparet quantum venierit.* The price, being constituted only for each pound, which shall be weighed, or for each cask which shall be measured, is not yet determined, before the weighing or measuring; and, consequently, the sale, before that time, is not so far perfect, that the risk of the thing may fall upon the buyer. He ought not to be charged with it, until after the goods are weighed or measured.

But if the goods are not sold by weight or measure, but *per aversionem,* that is, in bulk, and for a single and only price; in such case, the sale is perfect from the instant of the contract, and, from that time, these goods, the same as all others, are at the risk of the buyer. All these principles are drawn from the law 35, § 5, *de contrah. empt.* (D. 18, 1, 35, § 3).

310. The thing sold being, from the moment of the contract, at the risk of the buyer, when the sale is made *per aversionem;* and, on the contrary, remaining at the risk of the seller, when it is made by weight, or measure, until it is weighed or measured; it is important to know when the sale is considered as made *per aversionem,* and when it is considered to be made *by measure.* The following rules will enable us to determine this question.

First rule. There is no doubt that the sale is made *by measure,* when the price is expressly agreed upon for each measure; whether the contract imports, that it is of so many bushels of the grain, in such a granary, at the rate of so much the bushel; or of a heap of grain, which is in such a granary, and which contains a thousand bushels, at the rate of so much a bushel. All the difference is, that, in the first case, if the granary contains more than the quantity, the surplus is not sold; whereas, in the other, the entire quantity of grain is sold, though it exceeds the thousand bushels.

Second rule. When the sale is of so many measures of

such a thing, it is considered as made *by measure*, though the terms of the contract express only a single price; as when we sell ten bushels of grain for 500 livres; the price being regarded as the total of the prices for which each bushel is sold: *Non interest unum pretium omnium centum metretarum an semel dictum sit, an rei singulos eos;* D. 18, 1, 35, § 7.

Third rule. When a sale is made for a single price, not of so many measures of such a thing, but of such a thing, which is declared to contain so many measures, it is made *per aversionem;* as, where one sells, for the sum of 1000 livres, such a field, which he declares to be of the quantity of twenty acres; and consequently the thing sold, from the time of the contract, becomes at the risk of the buyer; D. 18, 6, 10, § 1. The expression of the number of acres has no other effect, in this case, than to oblige the seller to make an allowance for the defect of quantity, if the field is found to contain less, as has already been stated, *supra*, part 2.

311. There are certain things, which are sold subject to the condition of being tasted, as wine, oil, &c. These sales are still less perfect on the part of the buyer, until the things sold are tasted, than are sales by measure, until the things sold are measured; for, in the latter, from the moment of the contract, it no longer depends upon the buyer, that the sale does not take place. Before the goods are weighed or measured, he, as well as the seller, is bound to execute the contract, and the weighing or measuring intervenes only to fix and determine what is sold; whereas in sales made subject to the condition of tasting, the buyer may refuse to execute the bargain, if he does not find the goods to his taste: *Alia causa est degustandi, alia metiendi, gustus enim ad hoc proficit ut improbare liceat;* D. 18, 1, 34, § 5. These sales, therefore, until the tasting, are still more imperfect, than those which are made by weight or measure; and, con-

sequently, the things sold do not become at the risk of the buyer, until he is put in delay to taste them.

According to the practice in our tribunals, different from the Roman law, it is necessary in order to put the buyer in delay, that the seller should obtain a sentence, ordering the buyer to taste the goods, previous to such a day; and, in default of which, that the bargain shall be executed absolutely.

It is to be observed, also, that we must distinguish whether the buyer stipulates that he shall taste the goods, in order to know whether they are to his taste or not, or only to know whether they are good, lawful, merchantable, or undamaged. It is in the first case only, that he is at liberty to refuse the bargain, by declaring, after tasting the goods, that they are not to his taste; in the other, he cannot refuse the goods, provided they are found to be good.

312. When a sale is contracted, subject to a condition, the loss which happens by a deterioration of the thing, during the intermediate time between the contract and the existence of the condition, falls upon the buyer, if the condition happens to exist; for the seller is only bound to deliver the thing, such as it is, when the deterioration is not occasioned by his fault. But a total loss of the thing falls upon the seller; for a condition, which happens after a total loss of the thing, cannot confirm the sale of that, which is no longer in existence.

313. In the case of alternative sales, whether the choice be left to the seller, or be expressly accorded to the buyer, the first of the two things, which happens to perish subsequent to the contract, perishes to the loss of the seller; for that which is left remains *in obligatione*, and he is bound to deliver it. But if that which remains also perishes, it perishes to the loss of the buyer, who continues to be bound for the payment of the price, though neither of the two

things remains, and can be delivered to him. See what is said of alternative obligations in the Treatise on Obligations, part 2, chap. 2, art. 6. If they both perish at the same time, the seller is in like manner discharged from his obligation, and the buyer remains the debtor of the price; D. 18, 1, 34, § 6.

PART FIFTH.

OF THE EXECUTION AND DISSOLUTION OF THE CONTRACT OF SALE.

CHAPTER FIRST.

Of the execution of the contract of sale, and, in particular, of the tradition or delivery of the thing sold.

The contract of sale is executed on the part of the buyer, by the payment which he makes to the seller of the sum agreed.

It is executed on the part of the seller, by the tradition or delivery of the thing sold.

ARTICLE FIRST.

Of the different kinds of delivery.[1]

314. A delivery is real or feigned.

A real delivery is made, when the buyer is put in real possession of the thing sold.

[1] The doctrine of possession, according to the Roman law, is one of the most difficult subjects, within the whole range of juridical science. It has been elaborately treated by professor von Savigny, of Berlin, a celebrated living German jurist, and the head of what has been called the Historical School. An analysis of his work, prepared by professor Warnkönig, and originally published in the Themis, has been translated into English and published in the nineteenth volume of the American Jurist and Law Magazine. The following extracts from the analysis will give an idea of Savigny's doctrine, so far as relates to the delivery of a thing.

"The theory of Savigny differs essentially from that of all the other commentators, and his opinions on the nature of the fact of apprehension (of the

To *possess*, is to hold a thing by one's self, or by another person who detains it in our name; *est corporaliter rei insistere, vel per se, vel per alium.*

A feigned delivery is that by which the buyer is feigned to be put in possession of the thing sold, notwithstanding it remains in the possession of the seller.

This fiction results from the clause of constitution, by which the seller is constituted or appointed to hold the thing in the name of the buyer. By this clause, the buyer is considered as taking possession of the thing sold by the agency

thing of which one wishes to acquire the possession) are entirely new. Our author demonstrates, conclusively, that, in none of the fragments of the Corpus Juris, is a mere symbol or a fiction ever considered as capable of constituting this fact; but that the idea of the Roman jurisconsults was, that every fact, by which a person is put in a situation to dispose of a thing, whether movable or immovable, at his pleasure, must be considered as constitutive of the possession; and a great number of examples, drawn from the laws of the Digest, are here brought forward, to confirm the theoretical demonstration of the author. From this principle several consequences result, which are afterwards developed in the work; one of the most important of which is, that the Romans never had any knowledge of the *symbolical* delivery, so gratuitously imagined by the modern interpreters." Am. Jur. vol. xix. p. 21.

"Though nothing is more simple, apparently, than to determine wherein consists the material fact of the apprehension of a thing, this is nevertheless the point, in relation to which, the interpreters, who have treated of possession, have fallen into the greatest number of errors. They all teach that apprehension is the real and physical seizure of the thing, since, by this seizure alone, can we have the faculty of disposing of it at our pleasure. The numerous cases, in which the Roman law acknowledges a detention, without the occurrence of this real seizure, are regarded by the interpreters as particular cases, in which the detention is admitted only in virtue of a fiction, rendered necessary by considerations of public utility; and, the acts, which constitute this fictive apprehension, are considered as the symbols of a real seizure. The obscure theory of delivery, which is commonly received, and those ridiculous distinctions of the *traditio longæ manus, traditio brevis manus, traditio ficta*, &c. are all derived from this error." Same, p. 38.

The doctrines advanced by Pothier, in this and the succeeding article, are drawn from his treatise on possession, in which, according to Savigny, "he explains the ideas, which are the most generally received on that subject, with his ordinary talent." T.

of the seller, who, from that time, is no longer considered to possess it in his own name, but to hold it in the name of the buyer.

In the custom of Orleans, the simple clause of *dessaisine saisine*, which is inserted in acts passed in the presence of notaries, has the same effect as the preceding and is equivalent to a delivery, according to the two hundred and seventy-eighth article.

If the seller retains the usufruct of the thing sold, such reservation is also equivalent to a delivery; for, as one cannot be the usufructuary of his own thing, the seller, by making himself the usufructuary, sufficiently declares that he no longer possesses the thing as his own, and in his own name, but in the name of the buyer, from whom he holds it by a title of usufruct; C. 8, 54, 8.

It is the same, when, by the contract of sale, the buyer lets the estate sold to the seller, to hire or to farm; such letting stands in the place of a delivery, for, as the buyer no longer holds the estate as a thing belonging to him, but as the farmer or locatary of the buyer, he ceases to possess it, and the buyer begins to possess it by his agency: *et per colonos, et inquilinos, et servos nostros possidemus;* D. 41, 2, 25, § 1.

When the thing sold is in the possession of the buyer himself, who holds it from the seller, in virtue of a hiring, loan for use, deposit, or otherwise, the mere consent of the parties, that the buyer shall thenceforth possess it in his own name and as proprietor, stands in the place of a delivery. It has pleased the doctors to call this kind of delivery, *traditio brevis manus*, because, say they, *nihil brevius hac traditione.*

In the case of things of great weight, the permission which the seller gives the buyer, or to some one sent by him, to carry them away, stands in the place of a delivery, provided the permission be given *in re præsenti.* The buyer, or other person sent on his behalf, before it becomes his duty to carry away the thing, is deemed, by the permission given him, to take possession of it *oculis et affectu;* D. 41, 2, 21, § 1.

315. All the kinds of feigned delivery, above spoken of, are made *nuda voluntate*, by the mere consent of the parties. There are others also which operate by the means and intervention of some symbol, and, which, for that reason, are called *symbolical* deliveries. For example, the delivery of the keys of a house or other edifice, made by the seller to the buyer, stands in the place of a delivery of the house itself; the delivery of the keys being the symbol of a real delivery; D. 41, 1, 9, § 6. It is the same, in regard to the keys of a granary or magazine, which contains the things sold. A delivery of the keys stands in the place of a delivery of the goods. Papinian (D. 18, 1, 47) requires this delivery of the keys, in order to be equivalent to a delivery of the thing, to be made *in re præsenti, apud horrea.* I think, and it is also the opinion of Tiraqueau, *de jure contest. poss. p.* 2, that, according to our usages, it is not necessary. A delivery of the titles passes also for a symbolical delivery of the thing; C. 8, 54, 1.

316. The mark, which the buyer places upon casks, does not stand in the place of a delivery; but is considered as put there, *magis ne summutentur;* D. 18, 6, 1. It is otherwise in the case of things of great weight; D. 18, 6, 14, § 1.

317. Things incorporeal, *quæ in jure consistunt, quæ tangi non possunt*, which do not fall under the cognizance of the senses, cannot properly be possessed; and, therefore, it follows, that there cannot be a delivery, real and properly so called, of such things. But, as, in regard to these things, the enjoyment stands in the place of possession, it is a kind of delivery, in relation to them, when the seller suffers the buyer to have the enjoyment: *Usus et patientia in rebus incorporalibus pro traditione est.* For example, if I sell to the

owner of an estate adjoining mine, the right of pasturing his cattle on my land, the delivery of this right of servitude will be considered as made; when my neighbor begins, with my consent, to make use of it, by causing his cattle to be there pastured.

In the sale of credits and of actions, the notice of the assignment, which the buyer gives to the debtor, stands in the place of a delivery of the credit, as will be seen in the next part of this treatise.

318. When the seller is not himself in possession of the thing which he sells, it is evident that he cannot make any delivery of it, either real or feigned; for the delivery being *datio possessionis*, the seller, who is not himself in possession of the thing, cannot give it to the buyer: *Nemo dat quod non habet.* In this case, he can only substitute the buyer in the right which he has of reclaiming the thing by action. The demand, which the buyer brings, in consequence of such substitution, vests in him only a right to reclaim the thing by action, and not a right to the thing itself, which is sold him. It is only the abandonment, which is made to him upon such demand, which vests the thing in him, and which causes him to acquire the property of it, by causing the possession of it to pass to him.

ARTICLE II.

Of the effect of a delivery.

319. When the seller is the owner of the thing sold and capable of alienating it; or, if he is not the owner, when he has the owner's consent; the effect of a delivery is, to cause the property of the thing sold to pass to the person of the buyer, provided the buyer has paid the price, or the seller kept his faith.

The contract of sale cannot by itself produce this effect. Contracts can only form personal engagements between the contracting parties; and it is the delivery alone, made in pursuance of the contract, which can transfer the property of the thing constituting the object of the contract, according to this rule: *Traditionibus, et usucapionibus dominia rerum, non nudis pactis transferuntur;* C. 2, 3, 20.

320. From which it follows, that, if the owner of a thing, after having sold it to a first buyer, has the bad faith to sell and deliver it to a second, it is to the latter, that the property will be transferred; C. 3, 32, 15. The first buyer is only entitled to a personal action against the seller for the damages resulting from the non-performance of the contract; he cannot reclaim the thing against the second buyer, who purchases it in good faith, *inscius prioris venditionis.*

321. From the same principle, it follows, in like manner, that the creditors of the seller may seize the thing sold before it is delivered, even when the buyer has paid the price. The buyer, in such case, is only entitled to an action against the seller, and has no right in the thing.

But when the delivery is once made, and the property has thereby passed to the buyer, the creditors of the seller can no longer seize the thing, which no longer belongs to their debtor. In such case, hypothecary creditors have only their hypothecary action against the buyer or other possessor, if the thing sold is immovable. In regard to movables, they cannot be followed by hypothecary creditors, except in one case, namely, when a locatary or farmer sells movables, with which he furnishes the house or farm let to him; in which case, the custom permits the owner of the house or farm to follow the goods, which are regarded as in pledge to him; but, for such prosecution, he is only allowed the short term of eight days, if it is a house; or the term of forty days, if it is a farm, which is furnished with the movables sold.

Creditors, even those who are such in virtue of a private writing, may also, in one case, follow the movables of their debtor, which are delivered to a buyer, namely, when their debtor, being insolvent, makes a fraudulent sale of them, and the buyer, knowing the insolvency, thereby participates in the fraud; D. 40, 11, 27.

322. It is a question, agitated among the authors, whether a feigned delivery ought, in this respect, to have the same effect as a real delivery, and whether it is to be considered as transferring the property to the buyer, as against third persons. Let it be supposed, for example, that the thing is, in truth, remaining in the possession of the seller, that the buyer is not put into the real possession of it, but that the contract of sale contains a clause, by which it is said that the seller divests himself of the thing sold, and invests the buyer with it, declaring, that he holds it from that time, in the name of and for the buyer; or a clause, by which it is said, that the seller retains the thing as the tenant of the buyer, by a title of lease, for a certain yearly rent. They demand whether the buyer, in such case, is entitled to reclaim the thing, either against creditors, who seize it in the hands of the seller, or against a second buyer, to whom the seller delivers it, and who is in the real possession of it. Charondas, in his responses, decides in favor of the second buyer, and cites for his opinion two decisions, the one in 1498, and the other in 1569. Belordeau, *lib.* 1, *chap.* 18, cites also, in favor of the same opinion, two decisions of his parliament of Brittany. The reason they assign is, that as these feigned deliveries do not consist in any external act, but in a mere agreement intervening between the seller and the first buyer, they cannot have the virtue and efficacy to be considered, at least against third persons, as transferring the property of the thing sold to the first buyer, according to the rule, *traditionibus, et usucapionibus dominia rerum, non nudis pactis transferuntur*; C. 2, 3, 20. As agreements ought not to have any effect, except between persons who are parties to them, feigned deliveries, which do not result

from any external act, but merely from the agreement of the parties, cannot be considered, as against third persons, to transfer the property.

On the other hand, Guy Pape, *decis.* 112, maintains, that a feigned delivery transfers the domain and property of a thing, as really and as truly as a real delivery, even against third persons. By the feigned delivery, which results from the clause authorizing the seller to retain the thing, as a usufructuary, hirer, lessee, or from the mere clause of constitution, the buyer truly takes possession of the thing, and thereby truly acquires the property of it; for, we may acquire the possession and property of a thing, not only by ourselves, but by the agency of another person who takes possession of it in our name: *Animo nostro, corpore etiam alieno possidemus;* D. 41, 2, 3, § 12. *Generaliter quisquis omnino nostro nomine sit in possessione. . . . . nos possidere videmur;* D. 41, 2, 9. Now, by these clauses, the seller takes possession of the thing, in the name of the buyer. The buyer therefore acquires the possession, by the agency of the seller, in the same manner, that he would acquire it by the agency of any other person, who should take possession for him. This delivery has consequently the same effect as a real delivery, and ought in like manner to transfer the property. It is in vain to object the text, which says, *non nudis conventionibus, dominia rerum transferuntur*, and that agreements have no effect but between persons who are parties to them; for this maxim is true only of pure agreements; but those which are accompanied by feigned deliveries are not simple and nude agreements; and it is expressly decided in the law 77, D. *de rei vindic.* (6, 1, 77), that a similar feigned delivery, resulting from the retention of a thing as a lessee, by the donor of it, puts the donee in possession, and transfers the property of the thing, and consequently the right to reclaim it to him. From all these principles, Guy Pape concludes, that a first buyer, to whom a feigned delivery of the thing is made, may reclaim it against a second buyer, who is in the real possession of it; and he bears witness that this is the uniform rule in his parliament of Dauphiny. I think this second opinion more correct, with this limitation, namely, provided the proof of the delivery is established by an authentic act; or if the act is under a private signature, provided that the priority of its date to the real delivery made to the second buyer, or to the seizure made by the creditors of the seller, is sufficiently established; as, for example, by the death of some one of the parties who have subscribed it.

323. It is peculiar to the delivery, which is made in execution of the contract of sale, that it does not transfer the property to the buyer, except when the seller has paid or satisfied the price; Inst. 2, 1, § 41. The reason is, that the seller, who sells for ready money, is considered not to have an intention to transfer the property, except upon that condition. But when the seller intends to give a credit to the buyer, a delivery of the thing transfers the property to him, before payment of the price. And, therefore, Justinian, after saying, *Venditæ et traditæ res non aliter emptori acquiruntur, quam si is venditori pretium solverit, vel ei alio modo satisfecerit, etc.*, adds: *Sed si is qui vendiderit, fidem emptoris secutus fuerit, dicendum est statim rem emptoris fieri; dict.* § 41.

324. When there is a term expressly granted by the contract, for the payment of the price, the will of the seller to give a credit cannot be questioned; and there can be no doubt, that a delivery, made in pursuance of such contract, transfers the property to the buyer.

325. When there is no term agreed by the contract, if the seller delivers the thing, without declaring expressly, that he does so only upon condition that the buyer shall pay the price immediately, is such delivery sufficient to raise a presumption, that the seller intends to rely upon the faith of the

buyer, and consequently to transfer the property to him? Some doctors have supported the affirmative. Fabian de Monte, in his treatise *de empt. vend.*, very well refutes this opinion. The buyer, who maintains that the seller intends to give him a credit and to trust to his faith, ought to prove it. The credit is not to be presumed; on the contrary, in reciprocal contracts, each of the parties is presumed not to be willing to fulfil his engagement except so far as the other party shall, at the same time, fulfil his own. If the delivery alone and by itself creates a presumption of credit, Justinian would very improperly teach it as a principle peculiar to the contract of sale, that a delivery of things sold does not transfer the property of them, unless the seller trusts to the faith of the buyer, since he would be always presumed to do so. But if the seller, after delivering the thing, suffers a considerable time to elapse, without demanding the price of it, it is evident, in that case, that he trusts to the faith of the buyer; and, consequently, the property will be considered as transferred by the delivery.

326. When the seller sells and delivers the thing without the consent of the owner of it, it is evident, that he cannot transfer to the buyer a right of property, which he himself has not: *Nemo plùs juris ad alium transferre potest quam ipse haberet;* D. 50, 17, 54. The delivery however is not for this reason without effect. If it does not transfer the property, it gives the buyer the civil possession of the thing; and, this civil possession, when it is accompanied with good faith, gives the buyer, (1,) a right to receive the fruits, without being obliged to restore them to the true proprietor, who may afterwards reclaim the thing: (2,) the possession, in good faith, after a period of ten years, when the proprietor and possessor live in the same province, or, of twenty years, when they reside in different provinces, causes the buyer to acquire the property of the thing, which the seller was unable to transfer to him; this is called *prescription* or *usucapion.*

We call *good faith* the opinion entertained by the possessor, that the thing belonged to him from whom he acquired it, and that he had the power of alienating it. This opinion is presumed to exist in every possessor, who produces a title of possession, at least, if the contrary does not appear. Our custom of Orleans does not admit this prescription of ten or twenty years, but only one of thirty years. These prescriptions do not run against minors; and a lapse of forty years is necessary to prescribe against the church.

CHAPTER II.

Of the dissolution of the contract of sale.

The contract of sale may be dissolved by the mutual consent of the contracting parties, before it has been entirely executed. This kind of dissolution forms the subject of the *first* section of this chapter.

The contract, even after it has been entirely executed, may either be rescinded, by some rescissory action; or it may be dissolved for the future by some resolutory action.

The rescissory actions may be brought, either on account of minority, or even in regard to some transactions between persons of full age, on account of violence, fraud, enormous lesion, or some other just cause.

The rescissory action, on account of enormous lesion, that is to say, exceeding a moiety of the just price, constitutes the subject of the *second* section of this chapter. The rescissory actions which result from other causes, not being peculiar to the contract of sale, are not here considered, but are treated of separately, in a treatise concerning different actions. It is to be observed, that the rescission of a contract of sale may be demanded not only by one of the contracting parties, or by his heirs, but sometimes also by third persons; as when a sale is made by a debtor in fraud of his creditors, or by one accused of a capital crime, in fraud of the confiscation. In these cases, the creditors, or the seignor to whom the confiscation belongs, are entitled to a revocatory action, to cause the contract of sale to be declared null and fraudulent, and to reclaim the things sold.

The contract of sale, by the rescissory actions, is rescinded, as if it had never been made; the resolutory actions only dissolve it for the future. The latter actions result from resolutory clauses inserted in the contract. Sometimes the clause is inserted in favor of the buyer, as in the case of sales made upon trial, which have been already considered, *supra*, part 2, chap. 3, art. 3; but more commonly in favor of the seller. The most common are the clause of redemption, which is considered in the *third* section; that by which the seller stipulates for a dissolution of the contract, if, within a certain time, he shall find more advantageous terms, which is treated of in the *fourth* section; and the commissory pact, which makes the subject of the *fifth* section. In the *sixth* section, the question is considered, whether a mere non-performance of the contract, on the part of one of the parties, is sufficient, to authorize the other to demand a dissolution of it.

SECTION FIRST.

Of a dissolution of the contract by the mutual consent of the parties.

327. When the contract of sale is not yet executed, either on the one part or on the other, it may be dissolved of full right, by the mere consent of the contracting parties; D. 18, 4, 5, § 1. As it is the mere consent of the contracting parties which forms it, it may, in the same manner, be dissolved by a contrary consent. This is in conformity with that admirable rule of law: *Nihil tam naturale est, quam eo genere quidque dissolvere, quo colligatum est. . . . Ideo nudi*

consensus obligatio contrario consensu dissolvitur; D. 50, 17, 35, and with the law 80, D. *de solut.* (46, 3, 80)*: Quum emptio contracta est, quoniam consensu nudo contrahi potest, etiam dissensu contrario dissolvi potest.* It is the same, when the contract of sale is followed by a feigned delivery, which consists only in the intention of the parties; for a contrary intention destroys the first. Dumoulin, in Cons. Par. § 78, *gl.* 1, *n.* 32, *et seq.*

328. When the contract of sale of a thing is not executed, either on the one part or on the other, the parties are considered to abandon it, not only when they agree, that it shall no longer exist in fact, but also when they make between them another contract of sale of the same thing. This happens, when they agree upon a different price, either greater or less than that of the first agreement; in which case, they are considered to abandon the first contract of sale, and to make a new one for the price agreed upon by the new agreement; D. 18, 4, 2.

In like manner, if the parties make a sale dependent upon a condition, and afterwards by a new agreement, the seller sells the thing to the buyer absolutely, this agreement includes an abandonment of the first conditional sale, and a new absolute contract of sale.

Quid, vice versa, if, by one agreement, you sell me a thing unconditionally, and, by a second, you sell it to me for the same price, upon condition, that such a ship arrive safely? Paul, in the law 7, D. *de rescind. vend.* (18, 4, 7) is of opinion, that the second agreement is of no effect; and Cujas assigns the reason. It is, says he, *quia a priori perfecto contractu non receditur per imperfectum,* and because this pact, by which the parties, *ex intervallo,* add a condition to a contract of sale originally absolute, is, according to the principles of the Roman law, a simple pact, *quod prodesse non potest, ad parandam aut tollendam obligationem.* These principles, which are at variance with the simplicity of natural law, have no place with us, and there is no doubt, that such a pact has the effect to cause the contract of sale to depend upon the condition inserted into the new agreement.

329. When the contract of sale is executed in part only, as if the thing sold is delivered, and the price is not paid, or, *vice versa*, the parties may, also, by their mutual consent, abandon the contract. But the agreement in this case does not efface the contract of sale, as in the preceding; it only dissolves it for the future, and gives an action to the party who has begun to execute it, to recover either the thing sold and delivered, if he is the seller, or the price paid, if he is the buyer. The Roman laws, which, in this case, do not allow of an action, (C. 4, 45, 2,) because, *ex nudo pacto non dabatur actio*, have no application with us. From this principle, it follows, that when, by an agreement between the seller and buyer, the latter, who has been put in possession of the estate, but who has not entirely paid the price of it, abandons the purchase, and the seller re-enters into the estate, there is no second profit due; for it is an abandonment of the sale which has been made rather than a new sale.

From which, also, it follows, that if the estate was an estate proper (*propre*) to the seller, at the time of the sale, it will not become an acquisition; but will take back the ancient quality which it had; for the seller re-enters upon the estate, not in virtue of a sale of it to him, but by a dissolution of that made by him; it is not a new acquisition, but a cessation of an alienation made by him.

330. But if the contract is executed on both sides, an agreement that the buyer shall yield back the thing sold to the seller, for the same price, is not a dissolution of the contract of sale; for, it is not possible to desist from an act, which is entirely consummated: *Non potest intelligi discessio, nisi ab eo quod cœptum et nondum consummatum est.*

And, therefore, in such case, a new profit of sale will be due, and the estate will be an acquisition in the person of the seller to whom it is conveyed; Dumoulin, § 33, *gl.* 1, *n.* 19.

SECTION II.

Of a dissolution of the contract on account of enormous lesion in the price.

331. One of the cases, in which one of the parties may obtain, in spite of the other, a dissolution and even an entire rescission of the contract of sale, is the case, in which he suffers an enormous lesion. This is in conformity with the principles established in the Treatise on Obligations, part 1, chap. 1, art. 3, § 4; that, as equality is of the substance of commutative contracts, (to which class the contract of sale belongs), injustice and injury, sustained by one of the parties, render these contracts vicious and subject to rescission. It is in consequence of these principles, that the law 2, C. *de rescind. vend.* (4, 44, 2,) accords to the seller a rescissory action against the contract of sale, when he suffers a lesion which exceeds a moiety of the just price. In the *first* of the following articles, this action is considered; and, in the *second*, that to which the buyer is entitled.

ARTICLE FIRST.

Of the rescissory action of the seller in case of enormous lesion.

The subject of this action is considered under the following divisions, namely: 1, what is its nature; 2, for what things and in what cases there is a foundation for it; 3, how and against whom it may be brought; and, 4, of the effect of this action, and of the respective liabilities of the buyer and seller therein.

§ I. Of the nature of the rescissory action on the part of the seller on account of lesion.

332. The action, which the law 2, C. *de rescind. vend.* (4, 44, 2,) gives the seller, is a rescissory action, to cause the contract of sale and the alienation of the thing to be rescinded and declared null, provided the buyer does not prefer to supply what is wanting to a just price; in consequence of which rescission, the seller, by this action, reclaims the thing, as if it had never ceased to belong to him.

This action is an action *utilis in rem et non directa;* for the seller, who is entitled to it, is no longer, *in rei veritate*, the proprietor of the thing sold; he has transferred the property in it to the buyer by the delivery made with that intention. But as the effect of this action is to rescind the contract and the alienation or translation of property made in consequence of it, the seller is, by a fiction of law, reputed to have always remained the proprietor of the estate sold; and consequently reclaims it, by this action, as a thing which belongs to him, and which the buyer retains without any cause; the contract of sale, which was the buyer's title, and the cause in virtue of which he retained the estate, being rescinded.

333. The object of this action being to rescind the contract of sale, it follows, that when the seller by means of it causes the contract to be declared null, the buyer has a right to reclaim the price paid, in the same manner that the seller has a right to reclaim the estate; for the contract of sale being rescinded, there is no longer any cause, to give the one a right to retain the price, and the other the estate; besides, it is of the nature of all rescissory actions, that the parties should be placed in the same situation, in which they were before the act rescinded.

334. The rescission of the contract of sale, to which this

action tends, being founded solely upon the enormous injustice, which is found in the contract, it follows, that it ought to be left in the power of the buyer, to put a stop to the effect of the action, and to prevent the rescission of the contract, by making the offers permitted by the law above cited, to supply what is wanting to the just price, and thereby purging the injustice. This supplement deprives the buyer of all subject of complaint, and renders the contract valid, provided it is free from other vices; for if it is infected with fraud or violence, &c., an offer to supply the just price cannot prevent a rescission.

335. Dumoulin, *in Consuet. Paris.*, § 33, *gl.* 1, *n.* 41, observes, also, that this rule is peculiar to the contract of sale, and ought not to be extended to other commutative contracts. For example, in a contract of exchange, if I give you, in exchange for an estate worth 4000 livres, another estate which is worth 10,000 livres, you will not be allowed to offer, in order to exclude my rescissory action, to make me a return of 6000 livres: for, by such payment, the contract of exchange would degenerate into a contract of sale, contrary to the intention of the parties, which was to exchange and not to sell.

336. The just price, which the buyer is permitted to make up, is not the present value of the thing, but its price at the time of the contract; C. 4, 44, 8. This results from the principle, that the payment of the supplement is a remedy for the injustice contained in the contract.

337. It is a question, whether the buyer, who makes up the just price, ought also to pay the interest of the supplement, from the time that he enters upon the enjoyment of the thing sold. Cujas, *ad dict.* l. 2, (C. 4, 44, 2,) maintains the affirmative. The reason is, that the interest of the price is an equivalent for the enjoyment of the thing. The buyer cannot enjoy both the thing and the price at the same time; and, therefore, when he has the whole enjoyment of

the thing, he ought to account for the interest of what remains to be paid of the just price, for otherwise he would have, at the same time, the enjoyment of the thing and of the price, to the amount of that part of it which remains to be paid, which equity does not permit. Notwithstanding these reasons, many authors have embraced the contrary opinion. They found their opinion upon the fact, that the law 2, (C. 4, 44, 2,) above mentioned, only says, *vel si emptor elegerit, quod deest justo pretio recipias*, without adding *cum usuris;* and, consequently, that it does not subject the buyer to add interest to the supplement. In regard to the objection drawn from the principle, that the buyer cannot at the same time have the enjoyment of the thing and also of the price, they answer, that it only follows from this, that a buyer, who does not pay the whole of the price due, is liable for the interest of what remains; but, in the present case, the buyer, who pays the agreed price, pays all that is due, and he does not begin to owe what is wanting to supply the just price, until after the reformation of the contract. Though the contract of sale, in virtue of which he enjoys the estate, is a defective title; yet, as we ought not easily to presume that he has knowledge of the defect, so long as the seller does not complain and does not inform him of the lesion, he ought, until that time, to be considered as the possessor of the estate in good faith; and, as such, to have the right of enjoyment, without being obliged to pay for it by the interest of what is wanting to the just price. This is the opinion of Despeisses, who cites a case at Grenoble, reported by Expilli, which decides that the interest of the supplement is not due before the demand. It is also the opinion of Domat, part 1, book 1, t. 2, § 9.

If the lesion is so much beyond the moiety of the just price, that the buyer could not be ignorant of its enormity, or if this knowledge on his part appears from other circumstances, there can be no difficulty concerning the interest of the supplement. See, *infra*, § 4, the question whether the estate ought to be restored with its fruits, which is analogous to the present.

In regard to the forum of conscience, if the revenues, which the buyer receives, exceed the interest of the sum which he pays, it seems to me, that he cannot dispense with restoring the excess.

338. It remains to be observed, concerning the nature of the rescissory action, that, as its object is a restitution of the estate sold, which is a divisible thing, it follows, that the action is divisible; Tr. on Obl. n. 287.

And, therefore, if the seller leaves several heirs, neither of them can commence this action, nor claim a restitution of the estate, except as to the part of which he is the heir; and if the co-heirs do not complain of the contract, the buyer has the power to keep the other parts if he thinks proper.

Nevertheless, as the buyer purchased the thing, with an intention only to have it entire, and might not be willing to purchase it in part, if he is summoned by one of the heirs of the seller, with a view to a rescission of the contract of sale, as to the part of the demander, the buyer may, if he thinks proper, summon the coheirs of the demander, and require them to regulate the matter among themselves, in order to take back the estate entire, and to restore the price, or, if not, that he shall be discharged from the demand. The reason is, that it is of the nature of rescissory actions, that we cannot be received to prosecute them, but by remitting the parties to the same situation, in which they were, before the act of which the rescission is demanded; and the buyer cannot be remitted to the same situation, in which he was before the contract of sale, if he is obliged to keep a part of the estate, which he would not have been willing to purchase by itself. If the coheir of the demander, upon such summons, refuses to join himself to the latter, for the prosecution of the rescissory action with him, he cannot prevent the demander from being substituted in his rights for its prosecution. The heir, who is willing to prosecute it, may sometimes even obtain a sentence against his coheir, *judicio familiæ erciscundæ*, that it shall be exercised for the benefit and at the expense of the succession; namely, in case he proves that it is for the interest of the succession to prosecute it, and that there are sufficient funds for that purpose belonging to the succession.

This interest of the succession is susceptible of examination; for the estate, subsequent to the contract, may become so deteriorated and diminished in price, without the buyer's fault, that its present value may not be equal to the price for which it was sold.

It is to be observed, that the rescissory action has the same quality in the succession of the seller, that the estate, to which it puts an end, would have had, if it had not been sold. And therefore if the estate is proper, the heirs proper to the line from which it proceeds alone succeed to this action; and they alone are liable to the buyer for a restitution of the price; this restitution being rather a charge upon the rescissory action than a debt due from the succession of the seller.

What is said of several heirs is equally applicable to several sellers, who sell together by the same contract, *et sub specie unitatis*, an estate which they own in common. Though they do not sell *in solido*, no one of them is entitled to bring this action except for his own part only, where there is a lesion of more than the half; but the buyer may, in such case, if he thinks proper, require the action to be prosecuted for the whole.

It is otherwise, in case the coproprietors do not sell the estate, *sub specie unitatis*, but sell each one his portion, though by the same deed; in which case, there are as many contracts of sale as there are portions sold, and the buyer cannot claim that a rescission of the sale, in regard to one of these portions, should draw after it that of the other portions.

339. When the buyer leaves several heirs, there is no doubt that the seller may prosecute the rescissory action, against one of the heirs, and for the portion of such heir, without prosecuting it against the others; and it is the same, also, when the estate is sold to several buyers.

§ II. In what cases there may be a rescission.

340. In order that there may be ground for this rescission, it is necessary, *first*, that the thing sold should be an estate or an immovable right, the sale of movables not being subject to rescission, as we have already seen. Dumoulin, *in Consuet. Par.* § 33, *gl.* 1, *n.* 47, excepts from this rule precious movables, which are not goods of ordinary commerce, such as a precious stone, a production of the goldsmith's art, or of some other art of an excellent artist. He excepts also from this rule, the sale of the cutting of a wood, which includes the fruit of many years; and he disapproves a decision, which debarred a seller, in such case, from his letters of rescission. These exceptions are subject to much difficulty, especially in those customs, which, like that of Orleans, declare in express terms, that in the alienation of movables there is no ground for rescission.

341. There are certain sales of estates, and of immovable rights, which are not subject to this rescission; such are sales made by decree. The public faith, upon which these sales are made, places them beyond all suspicion; besides, the biddings and the different delays which take place in these sales make it evident, that the estate is sold for the highest price for which it can then be sold; from which it follows, that we cannot say the sale is made for less than

the just price, the just price being nothing more than that for which things can be sold: *Justum pretium est quanti res venire potuit.* The customs of Auvergne, of Marche, and of Bourbon, contain similar provisions concerning these sales; and Dumoulin, in his notes upon the last, observes that it is the common law, though some foreign doctors are of a contrary opinion; but when there is a contract of sale, the voluntary decree, by which it is confirmed, does not prevent the contract from being subject to this action.

342. It has been decided also, that the sale of rights of succession is not subject to this rescission. Soëfve reports a decision to that effect, of December 1654; and Automne, *ad dict. l.* 2, (C. 5, 44, 2) mentions one of the 7th of May, 1586, by which a waterman, who had sold for three hundred crowns the succession of a bailiff of the palace, which was estimated to be equal to 4,000 livres a year, was debarred of his letters of rescission. The reason is, that the great uncertainty, in regard to rights of succession, puts it out of the power of the parties to fix upon the just price, and, consequently, to prove that they have been sold for less than half the just price.

This decision admits of an exception, in the case of a sale, made of rights of succession by one heir to his coheir. Automne, *ad dict. l.* 4, C. *de hæred. vend.* (4, 38, 4,) reports a decision in red robes, which subjects such a sale to rescission if the buyer do not prefer to make up the just price. The reason is, that such an act stands in the place of a partition among the heirs, and, in acts of partition, still more than in others, equality ought to be observed. See the Tr. on Obl. n. 35.

343. Despeisses, *p.* 1, *tit.* 1, 54, *n.* 8, mentions among sales, which do not give rise to rescission, the sale of a thing which does not belong to the seller; and from thence he improperly draws the conclusion, that the seller, in order to be entitled to his action of rescission, must prove himself

to have been master of the thing. In fact, in the same manner, that every possessor is presumed to be the owner of the thing which he possesses, so long as the true owner does not reclaim it and prove his right, so the party from whom the possessor holds it is presumed to have been the owner, and to have transferred the property in it to him, so long as he does not suffer an eviction. And, therefore, if you sell me a thing, and commence the rescissory action against me, you have no need to prove that you were the owner of it; I am not allowed to object that you are not so; at least, unless I claim to have acquired the property myself, by a cause other than the sale, and the proof of this is incumbent on me.

344. In order that there may be ground for a rescission, it is necessary, *secondly*, that, by the contract, there should be a lesion in the price of more than one half of the just price. For example, if the just price of an estate is 20,000 livres, it is necessary, that it should be sold for a price less than 10,000 livres, in order to give rise to a rescission.

There being in the just price, the *pretium summum, medium, et infimum*, is it sufficient, to give rise to a rescission, that an estate should be sold for less than half the *pretium summum?* or must it be sold for less than half the *pretium infimum?* For example, if the just price of an estate is from 18 to 20,000 livres, and it is sold for 9,500 livres, is the seller entitled to this action, because the price is less than one half of 20,000, which is the *pretium summum?* or is he excluded from it because it is not less than one half of 18,000, which is the *pretium infimum?* It would seem that the price ought to be less than half of the *pretium infimum*; for the *pretium infimum* being a just price, that which is not less than half of it is not less than half the just price. Domat and some others think, on the contrary, with more reason, that it is sufficient, if the lesion is less than half the *summum pretium*, because this rescission is to be favored.

It would perhaps be more exact to say, that the just price, of which the law speaks, is the *pretium medium*, which is properly the just price, and which is the centre of it. This is the opinion of Scaccia, *Tract. de Comm.*

345. In order to know whether the contract includes a lesion sufficient to give rise to a rescission, we ought neither to regard the situation nor the present value of the estate; but we ought to estimate what the estate is worth, at the time of the contract, having regard to its situation, and to the value of estates at that time. And, therefore, this estimation ought to be made by experts, who have knowledge of the situation of the estate, at the time of the contract.

346. It follows from this principle, that, in the estimation of the estate, we ought not to regard the discovery of a treasure or a mine, made subsequent to the contract; for until such discovery, the value of the estate is not increased. When the buyer purchases the estate, for what it is worth before the discovery and at the time of the contract, the seller has nothing to claim. The discovery is a piece of good fortune, of which the buyer ought to profit, according to the rule: *Cujus est periculum rei, eum et commodum sequi debet.* This is the opinion of Fachineus, 11, 20, who cites the doctors on both sides of the question.

It is only by an estimation of experts, who have knowledge of the situation of the estate, at the time of the contract, that we ought to judge whether the lesion exceeds a moiety of the price. The disproportion, which is found to exist, between the price for which the seller has himself acquired the estate, and that for which he sells it, however great it may be, is not alone and by itself a sufficient proof of the lesion; for he may himself have purchased too dear: *Ad rescindendam venditionem, hoc solum non sufficit, quod magno pretio fundum comparatum, minoris distractum esse commemoras;* C. 4, 44, 4.

The just price of an estate, for the sale of which it is necessary to pay considerable seignorial dues, as the hundredth penny, &c., may be considered under two relations; either, in relation to the seller, as the just value of what the estate is worth in itself, and to him, to whom it will be no expense to retain it; or in relation to the buyer, as the price, for which it ought to be justly sold and bought. It is evident, that it ought not to be sold for the entire price, which it is worth in itself, and that the sum, which it will cost in order to acquire it, ought to diminish this price. For example, let us suppose that a feudal estate, subject to the profit of the fifth, in case of sale, is worth in itself 20,000 livres, the just price, for which it ought to be sold, ought not to be, having regard to what its acquisition will cost, but 16,000 livres or thereabouts. From hence, arises a question, namely, whether it is necessary, in order to give rise to a rescission of the contract, that the price, for which it is sold, should be less than half the just price, for which it ought to be sold? As in the case, above supposed, is it necessary that it should be less than 8000 livres? or will it suffice, if it is less than the half of what the estate is worth in itself and in relation to the seller? that is to say, in the case proposed, if it is less than 10,000 livres? Dumoulin, *Tr. de usur.* 14, *n.* 173, cites a decision rendered in red robes, December 31, 1557, which decides, that for this rescission, it is sufficient, if the price is less than the half of what the estate, at the time of the contract, is worth in itself, and in relation to the seller. For example, in the case proposed, if the estate is sold for only 9,900 livres, it is sufficient to constitute a lesion of more than the half. We pay no regard to what it costs the buyer, beyond the price of acquisition, for the seignorial profits, hundredth penny, etc; for it is not the less true to say, that, by the contract of sale, the seller suffers a loss of more than half of what the estate is worth as to him; and, it is in relation to him, that the lesion is estimated.

But if the charge or risk, from which the buyer is discharged, is a charge or risk for which the seller would be liable, if he retains the estate; for example, if the estate, which I sell, is in possession of an usurper, and I charge the buyer to reclaim it at his own risk, and without power to summon me into the cause; or if I charge him with a certain sort of eviction; in such case, in order to determine whether the price of the contract is or is not below the half of the just price, the sum, in which the charge or risk will be appreciated, ought to be added to the principal price, since the seller profits by it, being discharged from so much. Despeisses, *p.* 1, *tit.* 1, *s.* 4, *n.* 6.

347. Though the charge of suffering a redemption, imposed upon the buyer, is a charge appreciable in money, which makes a part of the price, and which ought to be taken into the account, to determine, in the forum of conscience, whether the buyer purchases for less than the just price; yet, when the sum, for which he purchases, though with this clause, is less than half the just price, which the thing is worth in itself, I think, contrary to the opinion of Despeisses, *ibid.*, that, in this case, in the estimation, to be made in order to determine whether there is ground for a rescission, we ought not to add any thing to the price, on account of this charge, which, in this case, is of no effect, and consequently of no value; since the seller, even when it is not added, is not the less entitled to re-enter upon his estate, not indeed in virtue of the action of redemption, but in virtue of that which amounts to the same thing, the rescissory action.

348. In order, *thirdly*, to give rise to this rescissory action, it is necessary that the seller should be within the time of restitution. This period is ten years, like that of all rescissory actions, for which it is necessary to take letters in

chancery. When the seller leaves an heir, who is under age, this time does not run against him, during his minority.

349. The question has been discussed, whether there is ground for this action, when the thing sold ceases entirely to exist, without the act or fault of the buyer, so that no part of it remains; for example, if one sells a meadow adjoining a river, which carries it entirely away. Some doctors, cited by Bruneman, *ad l.* 2, C. *de rescind, vend.* (4, 44, 2,) are of opinion, that the seller may, even in this case, commence this action, and demand what is wanting of a just price. The foundation of their opinion is, that they regard the obligation of the buyer, who purchases an estate, for a price less than the half of the just price, as an alternative obligation, either to restore the estate, or to make up the just price. Now, it is a principle, that when one of two things, due in the alternative, ceases to exist, the debt continues to exist in that which remains. See the Tr. on Oblig., n. 250. From whence they conclude, that if the estate sold ceases entirely to exist, the buyer remains the debtor for the supplement of the just price. The principle, which serves for the foundation of the opinion entertained by these doctors, seems to me to be false. The obligation of the buyer is only of a single thing, namely, a restitution of the estate; he is not in any manner the debtor of the supplement of the just price, being obliged only to the price, which his contract imports, and to nothing more. The choice, which the law gives him to make up the just price, is only a power granted him, to redeem himself from the obligation to restore the estate, by the payment of the supplement. This supplement is only *in facultate solutionis et luitionis;* it is not *in obligatione.* Now, according to the principles established in the Treatise on Obligations, n. 244, when a thing is due, with the power to pay another in the place of it, the

obligation is entirely extinguished by an extinction of the thing due, and no longer subsists in that which the debtor had the power to pay.

It should be added, that, in this case, however disadvantageous the contract may be, in itself, the seller, by the event, has no cause to complain of it, but rather to congratulate himself, since, if he had not made the sale, he would have lost the thing sold, and would not have had the price of it which he has received.

This opinion is that of Accursius, and of Bartholus, *ad dict l.*; of Covarruvias, *var. resol.*, *n.* 4; and of Fachineus, 11, 18.

350. There are two cases, however, in which the seller is allowed to demand a rescission of the contract, on account of a lesion of more than half the just price, though the thing ceases to exist, without any act, fault, or delay on the part of the buyer. The first case is, when the buyer resells the thing for a price greater than that for which he purchased it. The seller, in this case, has an interest in obtaining a sentence upon the validity of the contract; and is consequently allowed to prosecute the rescissory action; for, by causing the contract to be declared null, he entitles himself to reclaim of the buyer, the difference between the sum for which he purchased and that for which he resells the thing. The reason is, that, as the contract is rescinded, the thing is considered always to have belonged to the seller, and never to have lawfully belonged to the buyer; from which it follows, that the buyer, in reselling, puts himself in the situation of one who sells the property of another, who is not allowed to profit and enrich himself by the price for which he sells, as has been already stated, *supra*, 275, 276. This modification of the rule is followed by Fachineus, by Covarruvias, and by Pulveus, and is very improperly rejected by Antony Gomez, in his Treatise on Contracts, *cap.* 2, *n.* 22.

351. The second case is that in which one sells, for a price less than half the just price, a term for years, of which there remains no more than five or six years of enjoyment. The seller, after the expiration of this term, and consequently after the thing sold has ceased to exist, is not thereby deprived of his right to prosecute the rescissory action, for the purpose of recovering all the fruits, which the buyer has received, subject to a deduction of the price paid and interest.

The reason of this decision is, that the sale of such an estate is a sale of the enjoyment for the time which remains, rather than of the estate itself, the direct domain of which belongs to the owner of the reversion; from whence it follows, that as the enjoyment is the thing sold, the buyer, who receives and makes a profit of it, ought, in the case of this rescissory action, to account for it to the seller.

352. When it is by the act or the fault of the buyer that the estate is destroyed; as, for example, when in consequence of his having destroyed, or not having maintained a dike,—the sea, or a river, adjoining the estate, carries it away; in this case, the seller is not deprived of his rescissory action, to compel the buyer to restore the just value of the estate, subject to a deduction of the price paid. This decision is conformable to the general principle, on the subject of obligations, that a debt of a specific thing subsists after the extinction of the thing due, or at least is converted into a debt of the value of the thing, when the thing perishes by the fault of the debtor. According to this principle, the buyer, who purchases an estate for a price less than the half of its value, being the debtor for a restitution of the estate, is not discharged from the debt, and becomes a debtor for the value of the estate, in place of the estate itself, when it perishes by his fault.

353. It is made a question, whether the seller is entitled to his rescissory action, not only when he is ignorant, at the

time of the contract of the just value of the estate, but also, when it is established, that, at that time, he had an entire knowledge of it. All agree, that he, who sells an estate for less than a moiety of the just price, may easily be presumed ignorant of the just price; and this presumption ordinarily prevents the question from arising. But when this presumption ceases, and it is clearly established, that the seller could not have been ignorant of the real value of the estate, at the time of the sale; as, when it is one, which he has made valuable by his own labor for a considerable time, then this question arises. For the negative it is said, that rescissory actions are established in favor of those who are deceived in contracting; and, in this case, the seller cannot be said to be deceived, in selling for less than the just price, since he knows the value of the thing: *Nemo sciens fallitur.* If we are not permitted to complain of an injury, which we suffer through our own fault, according to the rule of law, *Quod quis ex culpa sua damnum sentit, non intelligitur damnum sentire*, D. 50, 17, 203, there is much stronger reason, that we should not be allowed to complain of an injury, which we are willing to suffer. This is not properly an injury; for *nulla injuria est, quæ in volentem fiat;* D. 47, 10, 1, § 5. And, therefore, when any one, having knowledge of the value of a thing which belongs to him, sells it for less than a moiety of the just price, it is an exercise of liberality on his part towards the buyer, rather than an injury done to himself, of which he is entitled to complain. This is the opinion of Boërius, *Decis. Burdig.*, 142, and of many other doctors cited by him. The contrary opinion, which is embraced by Covarruvias, *var. resol.*, 11, 4, by Pinell, &c., appears to me to be preferable. The reason is, that no one is to be easily presumed willing to give away his property. And, therefore, when one sells an estate for less than a moiety of the just value, of which he has knowledge, it ought to be presumed that he does so, rather to procure money, in his pressing need, *urgente rei familiaris necessitate*, than with a view to exercise a liberality in favor of the buyer. Now it is an injustice, on the part of the buyer, to take advantage of the pressing need of the seller, in order to buy for a mean price; and this injustice gives rise to a rescission of the contract. The maxim *volenti non fit injuria* is not applicable in this case; for, as the seller is presumed to be forced, by his great need of money, to sell the estate for less than a moiety of the just price, he cannot be said to sell for that price, of his own free will.

354. If it appears that it is not a want of money, which induces the seller to sell for less than the just price; as, if, by the contract, he is not to receive money, but allows the buyer to constitute him an annuity for the price; in this case, if it can be proved, that he had knowledge of the just value of the estate, it follows, that, in selling for less than the just price, he can have no other intention than to gratify the buyer. This is the true case of the maxim, *volenti non fit injuria*, which renders the buyer not receivable to demand a rescission of the contract.

355. It is also made a question, whether there is ground for rescission, when there is in the contract an express clause, by which the seller renounces the benefit of restitution, given him by the law 2, C. *de rescind. vend.* (4, 44, 2). Fachineus, *controv.* 11, 20, says, that the common opinion, to which he subscribes, is, that the seller is not, in this case, receivable to demand a rescission. The reason is, that it is permitted to any one to renounce laws established in his favor, which have regard only to a particular interest. Thus, sureties may legally renounce the edict of Adrian, which grants them the benefit of division, and the novel of Justinian, which gives them the privilege of discussion; so a buyer may renounce the right of warranty, which is provided in his favor by the edict of the ædiles; D. 2, 14, 31. Notwithstanding these reasons, I think we may decide, that

a renunciation of the restitution allowed the seller by the law above quoted, (C. 4, 44, 2), is of no effect; for the seller's ignorance of the just price, or his want of money which induces him to sell for a mean price, may induce him to make this renunciation, provided the buyer require it. And, therefore, he ought not to be the less entitled to relief against this renunciation, than against the contract of sale; otherwise the law, so wisely established to repress the injustice and cupidity of those, who take advantage of the necessities of others, to despoil them of their goods, by purchasing them for much less than their just price, would become illusory, and would be always evaded by these unjust buyers, who would not fail to cause a renunciation of the law to be inserted in the contract; which would become the established form. This is the opinion of Covarruvias, as above cited. Automne, *ad dict. leg.* 2, cites a decision of 1563, which establishes the same doctrine.

If the renunciation is made by an act posterior to the contract, and there is no ground to suspect that it is in pursuance of an agreement contained in it, it is valid; it is a voluntary renunciation, which the seller makes of a right which belongs to him, and of which he has the power to dispose.

356. A clause inserted in the contract, declaring that the seller makes a donation to the buyer, of what the estate may be worth more than the price, is not less a means of eluding the law, than the clause by which he renounces the benefit of it in favor of the buyer. The necessity, which obliges the seller to sell for less than a moiety of the just price, will also oblige him to consent to all these clauses. And therefore we ought not to pay any regard to them, especially when the buyer is a stranger to the seller, and there appears to be no reason to induce the latter to be willing to make a donation. Automne, *ad dict. leg.* 2, cites a decision of 1557, and Maynard cites another in the

parliament of Toulouse; both of which accord with our opinion.

§ III. How and by whom this action may be commenced.

357. The seller, in order to commence this action, ought to obtain letters of rescission; for, in France, persons capable of contracting cannot be admitted to prosecute actions to set aside their proper contracts, but by the authority of the prince, who alone can relieve them from the obligation which they have contracted. This action, as we have already seen, *supra*, n. 332, is *actio utilis in rem;* it ought to be brought against him who is in possession of the estate, whether he is the buyer, or a third person to whom it has passed.

§ IV. Of the effect of the rescissory action, and of the respective liabilities, to which the seller and the buyer are bound the one towards the other in this action.

358. First. The buyer ought to be condemned to restore the estate to the seller.

Second. He ought also to restore the fruits; but it is a question from what time he owes them. Cujas, *ad dict. leg.* 2, decides that the buyer is indebted for the fruits received by him, from the time he takes possession of the estate, subject to a deduction of the interest of the price received by the seller. The reason is, that the contract of sale, which constitutes the title, in virtue of which the buyer enjoys the estate, being annulled and rescinded by the rescissory action, the buyer is found to be in possession of the estate without title, and consequently he cannot be regarded as the true possessor in good faith, to whom the fruits may properly belong. To this it may be added, that, in the restitution on account of minority, the laws decide that the buyer is bound to restore all the fruits which he receives; D. 4, 4, 27, § 1. With how much more reason, it is said, the buyer ought to be obliged to do so, in the case of restitution on account of enormous lesion; for the greater the lesion, the less ground there is to discharge the buyer from accounting for the fruits, and from making an entire compensation for them, with the interest of the price. It is upon the same principle, Cujas decides that the buyer, who makes up the just price, in order to preserve the estate, owes the interest of the supplement, as we have already seen, *supra*, n. 337. Many other doctors, among whom are Mynsinger, Fachineus, Despeisses, &c., are of opinion, on the contrary, that the buyer is not liable to account for the fruits, except from the time of the offers made by the seller, upon the rescissory action, to restore him the price; and that the fruits, received previous to that time, ought to be entirely compensated with the interest of the price, even when the interest falls far short of the value of the fruits. In favor of this opinion, they employ nearly the same arguments, which they use to prove that the buyer does not owe the interest of the supplement of the just price. Though the title, in virtue of which the buyer is in possession, is rescinded and annulled, he is not, according to them, reputed to be the possessor in good faith, because, to give him that character, it is sufficient for him to possess the estate, in virtue of an apparent title: *Justus opinio tituli æquipollet titulo; arg.* D. 41, 8, 4 & 9, and 41, 10, 5, § 1. Now the contract of sale, in virtue of which the buyer is in possession, and of the defect of which we ought to presume him to be ignorant, is to him an apparent title, until the seller complains of it, and informs him of the lesion which renders it defective. If the buyer is liable to account for the fruits, in the case of a restitution on account of minority, it is because he ought to expect a rescission, since he cannot be ignorant that a sale made by a minor is subject to it; whereas, in the present case, as he has no reason to expect a rescission, he ought not to be obliged to account for the fruits.

If these reasons are sufficient to induce us to reject the opinion of Cujas, as a general proposition, it ought at least to be followed, when the lesion is so much beyond a moiety of the just price, that the buyer could not be ignorant of the vice of his contract; as when the buyer has for a long time been the farmer of the estate; or, when, for some other reason, it is certain, that the buyer could not have been ignorant of its value; for, in all these particular cases, he ought to expect a rescission of the contract; he cannot therefore pass for a possessor in good faith.

359. It remains to be observed, that the buyer, who is not obliged to an account of the fruits, is still bound to make a deduction, of the price of those which were pending at the time of the contract, from the price which the seller is bound to render him; otherwise he would, at the same time, have both the fruits and the price of them, which makes a part of the entire price to be restored to him.

360. Third. The buyer ought to render, with the estate, all that is accessory to it, saving the fruits. And, therefore, if the buyer, after he takes possession, discovers a treasure, the third part of it, which belongs to him, in his quality of proprietor, and *jure fundi*, ought to be rendered to the seller with the estate; for the treasure is to him a sort of accessory to the estate, and cannot be said to be a fruit of it.

361. In regard to degradations of the estate, there is no doubt, that the buyer, against whom the rescissory action is prosecuted, ought to account for those of which he makes a profit. For example, if he cuts down a wood of large trees (*haute-futaie*) which he sells, or if he takes down a house and sells the materials, there is no doubt, that he ought to account for the proceeds of such sales. As to degradations, from which he derives no benefit, and which are caused by his negligence, he is not liable to account, provided he is the possessor in good faith; for he may neglect an estate, which he believes to be his own, and which he does not

know is subject to restitution. If it appears, on the contrary, that he cannot be ignorant that his contract is subject to rescission, he will be liable.

362. The seller, who prosecutes the rescissory action, ought, on his side, to render the buyer the price, which he has received, and all that makes a part of it. In regard to interest, when the buyer is not condemned to an account of the fruits, it is compensated with the fruits, which the buyer is suffered to retain. If the buyer is condemned to an account of the fruits, it cannot be otherwise than subject to a deduction of the interest, as well of the principal sum, as of every thing that makes a part of it, and which turns to the profit of the seller.

363. The seller ought also to be liable to the buyer, for repairs of and erections which he has made upon the estate. Those, which are incurred for the support of the estate, diminish of full right the enjoyment, which is to be estimated subject to a deduction of them, when the buyer accounts; but when he does not account, the seller is not liable for any such expenses.

In regard to other additions, some doctors cited by Fachineus, *controv.*, 11, 20, are of opinion, that the buyer cannot exact a reimbursement for them of the seller, who prosecutes the rescissory action, because, as it is in his power to retain the estate, by supplying the just price, it depends only upon himself not to lose them. This reasoning has no solidity. It may be that the situation of the buyer's affairs does not permit him to supply the just price, in order to be able to retain the thing; ought he, for that reason, to lose his additions, and the seller to enrich himself and to make a profit at his expense? This opinion therefore has had but few followers.

364. In order to determine to what the seller is liable in favor of the buyer, on account of repairs and additions made by the latter, it is necessary to distinguish three kinds,

namely: the necessary, the useful, and those which merely give pleasure. The first class is attended with no difficulty; the seller is bound to reimburse them. Nevertheless, if the buyer, through inattention, pays much more than is necessary for the materials and labor, the seller, who ought not to suffer by his want of care, will be bound to reimburse him only to the amount of what the repairs and additions ought to have cost.

The seller ought to reimburse the buyer for such repairs, even when they no longer subsist, provided they are of such a nature, that he could not himself have dispensed with making them, if he had not sold the estate; as, where the buyer rebuilds a sheepfold which is afterwards destroyed by lightning; for such erections are deemed to be to his profit, in this respect, that he preserves the money, which he would otherwise have been obliged to expend, if he had not sold the estate: *Hactenus locupletior videtur, quatenus propriæ pecuniæ pepercit.*

365. It is not the same in regard to useful erections and additions; the seller, who might have dispensed with them, is not liable, if they do not subsist at the time he prosecutes his rescissory action; and, in case they do subsist, he is liable for them only to the amount, in which the estate is thereby rendered more valuable; for it is only to that amount, that he makes a profit of them, and it is only because he makes a profit of them that he is liable at all: *Quum æquum sit neminem cum alterius detrimento locupletari.*

Sometimes it is in the discretion of the judge not to subject the seller to a reimbursement of the sum in which useful additions, which are in no manner necessary, increase the value of the estate, and only to permit the buyer, in such case, to carry away such of his additions as are capable of removal. This ought to take place, when the expenses are very considerable; for it ought not to be in the power of the buyer, by incurring very considerable expenses, which the seller has no means of reimbursing, to prevent the latter from prosecuting his rescissory action. Besides, as the buyer has the power to preserve the estate, together with the meliorations, which he has made, by supplying the just price, he has no ground of complaint.

366. There can be no difficulty in regard to erections and additions which merely afford pleasure, and which do not augment the value of the estate. The seller is not bound to reimburse the buyer for them, but only to permit him to carry away such as are capable of being removed.

367. The useful erections and additions, for which the seller is liable to the buyer, must be estimated subject to a deduction of the deteriorations of the estate, which proceed from the act or fault, whichever it may be, of the buyer, and which the seller might have avoided, if he had not sold the estate; for an estate cannot be considered as improved, except so far as the meliorations exceed the deteriorations.

368. The seller is liable also for the interest of the sum, to which the expenses, whether necessary or useful, for which he is liable to the buyer, amount, when the buyer is liable to him for the enjoyment; for, since he derives a profit from the revenue, which these expenses produce, it is just that he should be liable to the buyer, for the interest of the price which they cost.

369. In regard to the expenses of the contract and other similar expenses, which the buyer incurs in making his acquisition, there is no doubt that he is not entitled to a repetition of them, the seller being liable only for that which is for his profit.

370. It remains to take notice of a difference between the liabilities of the seller and those of the buyer. The seller may constrain the buyer strictly to a performance of all to which he is liable in this action; whereas the buyer cannot constrain the seller to do what is incumbent upon him; he has only a right to retain the estate, until the seller fulfils

on his part, and to obtain a sentence, that in default of so doing, within a certain time fixed by the judge, the estate shall remain his irrevocably.

371. All that is above stated concerning the respective liabilities of the seller and of the buyer, when the rescissory action is commenced against the buyer himself or his heirs, is applicable also when the action is commenced against a third person who detains the estate.

There is no doubt that such third person ought to restore the estate to the seller; for he has no right except that which he derives from the buyer, whose rights he has; and this right is destroyed by the rescissory action.

In regard to a restitution of the fruits, in those cases in which the buyer, from whom such third person derives the estate, would be liable, *supra*, n. 358, the latter is not, in truth, liable directly for them, when he is the possessor in good faith, and acquired the estate in the belief, that he, from whom he acquired it, was the owner by length of possession; and, for a much stronger reason, he is not liable directly to account for fruits, which he does not himself receive, but which are received by the buyer, before the sale of the estate by him. But, though such tenant is not liable directly for a restitution of these fruits, he is liable indirectly, as well for those which are received by him, as for those which are received by the buyer, inasmuch as he is obliged to suffer a deduction of the amount, from the price which is to be rendered to him by the seller. In fact, if such third person has a right to reclaim of the seller the price received by him, it is not in his own right, since it is not paid by him; but it is in the right of the buyer, who, by selling or giving him the estate, substitutes him in all the rights which he has in relation to the estate, and, consequently in his right to receive the price of the seller, in case the latter causes the sale to be rescinded; now the buyer has no right to reclaim the price but with a deduction of the fruits; and, consequently, such third person, who has his rights, cannot reclaim the price, except upon the same condition of a deduction of the said fruits, according to the rule of law: *Qui alterius jure utitur, eodem jure uti debet.*

It is the same in regard to degradations, in those cases, in which the buyer is liable for them, according to what we have said, *supra*, n. 361. The third person, who is the possessor in good faith, is not liable directly for degradations, which are not to his profit, whether they are made by the buyer, from whom he acquires the estate, or whether they are made by himself; but he is liable to suffer a deduction of the value of such degradations, from the price, which is to be restored to him by the seller; the buyer in bad faith, whose rights he has, having no right to reclaim the price of the estate, except with a deduction of the price of the degradations, as well of those which proceed from his own act, as of those which proceed from the act of his successors, for whom, in this respect, he is responsible.

From all this it results, that the only difference between the buyer and the third person, in regard to their liabilities in this action, is, that the buyer, when he is in bad faith, is liable directly to account for fruits and degradations, and that the third person is liable for them only indirectly; from which it follows, that if the price, as well of the fruits which ought to be accounted for by the buyer, as of the degradations for which he is liable, exceeds the price paid and interest, the buyer, who is liable directly, ought to be condemned and may be constrained to the payment of this excess; whereas, the third person cannot be so condemned, since he is not personally a debtor for the said fruits and degradations.

From whence results a difference, which ought to be regarded, in the pronunciation of the judgment which intervenes in this action. When it is rendered against a buyer in bad faith, he ought to be condemned to restore the estate, account for the fruits, and pay for the degradations, upon condition that the seller renders him the price and interest. But when the judgment is rendered against a third person, who has acquired the estate from such a buyer, he ought to be condemned only to restore the estate, upon condition that the seller renders him the price and interest, after deducting the value of the fruits and degradations.

372. It remains to be observed, concerning the effect of a restitution against the sale of an estate, on account of enormous lesion, that the seller, in virtue of such restitution, re-enters upon the estate, such as it was at the time of the sale made of it, and discharged from any incumbrance of hypothecations, rights of servitude, or other real rights, which the buyer or his successors, whether universal or particular, have imposed upon it; for they are unable to confer any greater right, than they themselves have, upon the persons, to whom they give these rights of hypothecation, servitude, &c; consequently, as the right of the buyer and his successors is subject to be rescinded by the restitution, which the seller obtains against the contract of sale, so the rights granted by him or them are in like manner subject to this rescission. This is the true case of the maxim: *Soluto jure dantis, solvitur jus accipientis.*

This opinion, which we have embraced, is that of the greater number of the doctors, cited by Fachineus, *controv.*, 11, 23. Bartholus and some others are of the contrary opinion. Their reason is, that the rescission of the right of him, who incumbers the estate with servitudes or hypothecations, does not draw after it a rescission of those incumbrances, unless it is made *ex causa necessaria.* Now, say they, the rescission of the buyer's right is not made *ex causa necessaria*, in the case provided for by the law (C. 4, 44, 2), now under consideration, since it is in his power to retain the thing, by supplying the just price. The answer to this reasoning is, that it is true, that a rescission of the right of the proprietor does not draw after it that of servitudes and hypothecations, when it is not made *ex causa necessaria*, but *ex causa voluntaria*, and by some act which intervenes on the part of the owner, as when a donation is revoked on account of ingratitude; it not being just, that he should, in such case, by his own act, prejudice the rights of others, agreeably to the rule: *Nemo ex alterius facto prægravari debet.* But when the rescission of the owner's right is pronounced, without any intervening act on his part subsequent to his acquisition, which gives rise to it, and proceeds from a vice inherent in his title of acquisition, as in the present case, it may be truly said that the rescission is made *ex causa necessaria*, and that it draws after it a rescission of servitudes and hypothecations. Though the buyer is able to retain the thing, by supplying the just price, it cannot therefore be said, that his right is rescinded *ex causa voluntaria;* for it is not entirely in his power to retain it, since he cannot do so but by supplying the just price; it is sufficient, in order that the rescission may appear to be made *ex causa necessaria*, if there is no act on his part to give rise to it, and that he is constrained to abandon the thing; and he is actually constrained to do so, when he does not supply the just price.

To conclude, the hypothecary creditor of the buyer, having a right, for the preservation of his hypothecary claim, to exercise all the rights which his debtor is entitled to exercise, may come in upon the rescissory action, before it has been executed, and by paying to the seller the supplement of the just price, may prosecute his hypothecation against the estate; but he can no longer be admitted to do so, after the rescissory action has been executed by a restitution of the estate; for he cannot exercise the debtor's right of supplying the just price, when his debtor has ceased to have it.

ARTICLE II.

Of the rescissory action of the buyer.

373. It has been made a question, whether the buyer, when he suffers from enormous lesion in the price, is also entitled to an action to cause the contract to be rescinded.

Automne, *ad l.* 2 (C. 4, 44, 2), holds the negative; but his opinion is contrary to the principles of law, and to the sentiments of almost all the authors. Dumoulin, in his treatise *de contr. usur., quæst.* 14, supposes, as a thing settled, that the buyer may set aside the contract, on account of enormous lesion, and does not even raise the question. The rescissory action, on account of lesion, is not founded solely upon the law 2 (C. 4, 44, 2,); but also upon a principle drawn from the nature of commutative contracts, in which each of the contracting parties intends to give what he gives, only in order to receive an equivalent for it; from which it follows, that these contracts are vicious, and as such ought to be rescinded, when one of the parties suffers enormous lesion in the price, and does not receive any thing near an equivalent for what he gives. Now it is evident, that this principle is not less applicable in regard to the buyer, than to the seller. Automne, in favor of his opinion, says, that the injury which the buyer suffers, being an injury in the price, which is a thing movable, he ought not to be allowed to claim a rescission of the contract, which, according to the French law, is not allowed in the case of movables. This maxim, however, only declares, that there is no ground for rescission, in the case of alienations of things movable, that is to say, when the sale is of a movable; but when the object of the contract of sale is an estate, there is ground for the rescissory action on the part of either of the parties, who is injured.

This action is considered in the following paragraphs,

namely: 1, what is its nature; 2, for what things and in what cases it takes place; and, 3, what are the respective liabilities to which the seller and buyer are bound in this action.

§ I. Of the nature of this action.

374. This is a rescissory action, the principal object of which is to rescind the contract of sale and to cause it to be declared null. It cannot consequently be commenced, but by virtue of letters of rescission obtained in chancery, by which the prince directs a rescission of the contract, if the injury set forth by the buyer shall appear to the judge. From the rescission of the contract results the obligation, which rests upon the seller, to render to the buyer the price which he has received, as having received it without cause; upon condition that the buyer, on his part, render him the thing sold. This action, therefore, is a personal action, by which the buyer demands, that in virtue of the letters of rescission obtained by him, the contract should be declared null and rescinded, and that consequently the seller should be condemned to render him the price which he has received, upon the offer which he is bound to make to render him the thing sold.

375. As it is the injustice in the price, which vitiates the contract, and which gives rise to this action; in the same manner, that the buyer, when the injustice is on the side of the seller, may prevent a rescission of the contract, by reforming the injustice contained in it, by offering to supply what is wanting to the just price; so, when the injustice is on the side of the buyer, the seller ought in like manner to have the power to prevent a rescission of the contract, by offering to restrain himself to the just price, and to restore the excess without interest.

In this respect, the rescissory action, to which the buyer is entitled, on account of lesion in the price, differs from the redhibitory action, to which he is entitled on account of defects in the thing sold, and of which we have treated in the preceding part, which cannot be excluded by an offer on the part of the seller, to make a deduction from the price, equivalent to the diminished value of the thing, by reason of the defect which is found to exist in it. The reason of the difference is, that if the buyer had known of the defect, he would not have been willing to purchase at all; whereas his knowledge of the just price would only prevent him from purchasing so dear.

§ II. For what things and in what cases this rescissory action may be brought.

376. In the same manner that the seller is not admitted to demand a rescission of the contract, on account of lesion, in sales of things movable, in sales of rights of succession, and in judicial sales, as has been seen in the preceding article, the buyer is also in like manner excluded from his action in the same cases.

377. The lesion, which entitles the buyer to the rescissory action, must be similar to that which entitles the seller to the action on his part; and, as it is necessary that the seller should receive a price which is less than a moiety of the value of the thing which he gives, as, when he sells a thing worth twenty crowns, that the price should be less than ten crowns; so, it is necessary that the thing, which the buyer receives, should be less in value than a moiety of the price which he gives; as, for example, when he purchases a thing of the value of ten crowns, it is necessary that the price which he gives should be more than twenty crowns. This is the rule established by Dumoulin, *de cont. usur.*, *quæst.* 14, contrary to the opinion of those who think it sufficient, if the buyer purchases for a price greater than a moiety of the just price, over and above the just price; as,

if in the case supposed, he should purchase for sixteen crowns.

378. It is necessary, that the price, for which the thing is purchased, over and above the just price, should not be the price of affection; for, as has been seen, *supra*, n. 244, we may lawfully, in certain cases, in contracts of sale, add to the just intrinsic price of the thing the price of affection. For this reason, it is very rare that there is ground for this action on the part of the buyer, the excess of price being ordinarily the price of affection.

379. When the thing sold ceases to exist, the buyer is not thereby deprived of his rescissory action, though, in the like case, that of the seller ceases when the lesion is on his side, as we have seen in the preceding article. The reason of the difference is evident. The rescissory action of the seller includes a revendication of the thing sold, which cannot take place except during the existence of the thing; the action of the buyer, on the contrary, includes only the demand of a sum of money.

380. We may remark also another difference between the rescissory action of the buyer and that of the seller. We have decided, *supra*, n. 352 & 354, in reference to the latter, that it may be sustained, though it is proved that the seller, at the time of the contract, had a perfect knowledge of the value of the thing, and though he has expressly renounced his right to this action. The reason is, that poverty and pressing need frequently oblige people to sell their goods for a mean price; but this reason being peculiar to the seller, it is necessary to decide differently in regard to the rescissory action of the buyer.

§ III. Of the reciprocal liabilities of the buyer and seller in this action.

381. The seller, against whom the buyer brings the rescissory action, is liable to render to the buyer the price which he has received, and to discharge him from any part

of it which may remain due, upon condition that the buyer render him the thing. The seller, who has sold in good faith, is liable only to a restitution of the price, and not to a reimbursement of the expenses of the contract, and of what it costs the buyer to make the acquisition.

In this respect, the rescissory action of the buyer is different from redhibitory actions, of which we have treated, *supra*, n. 218. The reason is, that the latter is founded upon the obligation of warranty against redhibitory defects; an obligation contracted by the seller in favor of the buyer. This warranty obliges him for the damages and interests of the buyer, resulting from the existence of any of these defects, which damages and interests make a part of the indemnification for what it costs the buyer to make the acquisition. On the contrary, the rescissory action of the buyer, on account of mere lesion in the price, is not founded upon any obligation contracted by the seller by the contract of sale. This contract, which is null, not producing any obligation upon either party, the obligation of the seller, in this case, rests upon this foundation only, that as the contract is null, what he receives in virtue of it is received without cause. His obligation therefore is limited to what he receives, and cannot be extended to what the contract costs the buyer, and from which the seller derives no benefit.

382. The seller is also liable to reimburse the buyer for additions, which he has made to the estate, when the buyer restores it to him; for the seller ought not to derive a profit from these additions and to enrich himself at the expense of the buyer.

In regard to additions which are merely useful, for the same reason that no person ought to enrich himself at the expense of another, the seller ought to reimburse the buyer for them. He is not however liable to reimburse him the full amount of their cost, but only so far, as the estate, when it is restored, is thereby increased in value. He is not even bound to this extent, when the additions, useful indeed but not necessary, are very considerable; as it ought not to be in the power of the buyer to prevent him from being able to re-enter upon the estate, by making additions to it, at an expense, which the seller has not the means of reimbursing; it is sufficient, in such case, for the seller to permit the buyer to carry away all that is capable of removal *sine rei detrimento.*

It is the same in regard to additions for pleasure; the seller is not bound to reimburse the buyer for them; but if they are susceptible of being removed, he cannot prevent the buyer from carrying them away, if he does not prefer to retain them, upon condition of a reimbursement.

383. The seller is not liable to a reimbursement for additions, except when the thing sold exists, and is restored by the buyer; when it is not restored, he is not even liable to restore the whole price, but only the excess above the just price; for, having, as we have seen in the preceding paragraph, the power to put an entire stop to the rescissory action of the buyer, by restoring him the excess above the just price, he cannot be liable to any thing more, when he does not restore the thing sold.

384. In regard to the liabilities, to which the buyer is subject, when he brings the rescissory action against the seller, he is bound to restore the estate, in the condition in which it is found to be; and, consequently, with all the augmentations which it has received subsequent to the contract, whether natural, as alluvions, or artificial, as buildings erected upon the land sold; upon condition, however, that the seller make him an allowance for his erections, as is above explained. If the estate has been deteriorated by the fault of the buyer, he must be held to account to the seller for the deteriorations.

385. When the estate has been sold with the movables which were upon it, the buyer ought also to restore them,

if they are still in existence; if he has made use of them, and it is through his fault that they are not to be found, he ought to pay their value; for, in the rescissory action, the parties being remitted to the same situation in which they were before the contract, each one ought to take back all that he has given.

SECTION III.

Of the dissolution of the sale which is made in virtue of the clause of redemption.

386. The clause of redemption is one by which the seller reserves the right of repurchasing the thing sold.

By this clause, the buyer contracts an obligation to restore the thing sold to the seller, whenever it shall please him to repurchase it, the seller satisfying the conditions of the repurchase.

The sale, made with this clause, is different from the contract of engagement. He, who engages a thing preserves the property of it; he only transfers to the engagist, to whom he gives it by the engagement, a right to possess it until the repurchase, and to receive until that time all the fruits and enjoyment of it; but he, who sells a thing with the clause of redemption, transfers the property of it to the buyer, to whom he delivers it; he has only a right to repurchase it, resulting from the obligation of the buyer contracted by the clause of redemption.

This subject is considered in the seven paragraphs following, namely; 1, whether this clause is valid in the sale of an estate, when the buyer is a minor; 2, of the nature of the right of redemption; 3, of the nature of the action of redemption; 4, when and against whom the right of redemption may be exercised; 5, the respective liabilities of the parties in the action of redemption; 6, the effect of redemption; and, 7, of the ways in which the right of redemption is extinguished.

§ I. Whether the clause of redemption is valid in the contract of sale of an estate, when the buyer is a minor.

387. Fachineus, *lib.* 11, *controv.* 3, and several doctors cited by him, are of opinion, that the clause of redemption is not valid in the sale of an estate, when the buyer is a minor. They rest their opinion upon the ground, that the law ordains that the estates of minors cannot be alienated but by a decree of the judge, and consequently that it regards as null all agreements by which minors engage to alienate them. Now, say they, the agreement, by which a minor obliges himself to suffer the redemption, and consequently to alienate the estate, which he has purchased, and of which he has become the proprietor, is contrary to the laws, which prohibit the alienation of the goods of minors; for, by this agreement, the minor obliges himself to alienate an inheritance, which he has purchased, and of which he is become the owner. They cite, in confirmation of their opinion, the law 7, C. *de præd. et al. reb. minor.*, (5, 71, 7), which declares null an agreement by which a minor had consented to the dissolution of a donation which had been made him; and the law 1, § *fin.*, and law 2, D. *de reb. eorum qui sub. tit.* (27, 9, 1, § 4, and 27, 9, 2), which declare null the clause by which he, who had sold an estate to a minor, had stipulated that it should be hypothecated to him, for the price which was due; *Nam*, says the jurisconsult, *ubi dominium quæsitum est minori, cœpit non posse obligari.* Notwithstanding these reasons, we must decide that this agreement is valid in a contract of sale, though the buyer is a minor. The alienations of the goods of minors, which the laws prohibit, are those which are purely voluntary, and not those which are necessary, as are those made in virtue of a clause of the acquisition itself. Besides, we cannot say,

that the redemption of an estate, which is exercised against a buyer, is an alienation. It is not so much an alienation of the estate by the buyer, as a cessation and dissolution of the alienation made by the seller, and of the acquisition made by the buyer. It is for this reason, that no second profit of sale is due on account of a redemption; and that the estate returns to the seller, who exercises the redemption, with the ancient quality, which it had before the alienation. To these reasons, we may add, that sales, which are made with the clause of redemption, are made for a less price, on that account. It would be contrary to equity, that the buyer under age should avail himself of the good bargain and of the diminution of price, made in consideration of this clause, without being held by it. The minority well gives the minor a right to set aside a bargain which is not advantageous to him; but he ought, in such case, to reject it entirely; his minority cannot give him the right to divide it, by taking what is advantageous to him in the bargain and rejecting the surplus.

It is easy to answer to the texts relied upon, in opposition to this opinion. The law 7, C. *de præd. min.* (5, 71, 7), which declares null an agreement, by which a minor had consented to the dissolution of a donation made to him, must be understood of an agreement made *ex intervallo*, after the donation had been concluded and ended, and not of a clause contained in the act of donation itself; for a donor, who may refrain from giving at all, may impose such restrictions upon his donation as seem good to him: *Unicuique licet quem voluerit liberalitati suæ modum apponere;* and, consequently, he may make it with such a resolutory clause as he thinks proper.

In regard to the laws cited from the title *de reb. eor.* &c. the decision, which they import, is founded upon a mere subtlety. The jurisconsult acknowledges it himself, since he says, in the law 2, that, in this case, we have recourse to the prince, who, having more regard to good faith than to the subtlety of the law, confirms the agreement. The law cited cannot therefore receive any application in our practice, which does not regard the subtleties of the Roman law. The opinion which we have embraced is that of Baldus, of Pinell, of Tiraqueau, &c.

§ II. Of the nature of the right of redemption.

388. The right of redemption is not properly a right, which the seller has in an estate, which he sells with this clause; it is only a right in relation to that estate, a credit of the estate, which results from the obligation of the buyer, contracted by the clause of redemption, to suffer the repurchase of it, to the execution of which obligation, the estate is subjected; it is properly *jus ad rem* rather than *jus in re.*

389. This right of redemption is a right which is transmissible to the heirs of the seller. The Code (4, 54, 2) so decides expressly; and this decision is founded upon a general principle, that whatever we stipulate, we are considered to stipulate for our heirs, as well as for ourselves, at least, unless the contrary appears from the nature of the thing, which makes the subject of the agreement, or from particular circumstances.

390. When it is agreed, that the seller alone may exercise the redemption, Despeisses, following Tiraqueau, is of opinion, that this term *alone*, in this case, only prevents the right of redemption from being assignable, but not from being transmissible to the heirs of the seller. It may be said, as the reason of this opinion, that the heirs of the seller succeed to his quality of *seller*. But if it is said, that the right of redemption cannot be exercised but by the person of the seller, or by *the said such an one*, it is evident, that it will be restrained to the person of the seller, and that it cannot pass to his heirs.

391. This right is assignable; it is not a right which is

attached to the person of the seller, but one which makes a part of his goods, and of which he may dispose, as of his other goods; Fachineus, 11, 11; Tiraqueau, &c.

392. When the clause does not contain any limitation of time, within which the seller may exercise the right of redemption, some of the ancient doctors have pretended that the right is imprescriptible; because, say they, the redemption consists in a faculty which the seller reserves, and it is a principle, that what is of faculty is not subject to prescription. This opinion has, with reason, been rejected; and there is no doubt, at the present day, that the right of redemption is subject to the ordinary prescription of thirty years. The principle, that what is of faculty is not subject to prescription, is true only in regard to that which is of natural faculty, such as that which every one has of raising his house; or, in regard to that which is of faculty of public right, such as the faculty, which the municipal law accords to the laborers of Beauce, to pasture their cattle upon all the waste lands of the parish; or, lastly, in regard to a faculty, which proceeds from the nature and essence of the contract, from which it is derived, such as is the faculty, which he who gives a thing in pledge has of redeeming it; and that which the debtor of an annuity has of repurchasing it. But when the faculty proceeds from a clause, which is accidental to the contract, and does not belong to it, without a particular title, by which it is granted, such a faculty is a right subject to prescription, the same as all other rights. This is decided in the customs of Paris, art. 108, and of Orleans, art. 269, which declare: The faculty given by contract, to repurchase estates sold, or the rent of estates under a perpetual lease, is subject to the prescription of thirty years.

393. This decision takes place, not only when the clause of redemption does not express any time, but also, when it is declared that the seller shall have it *forever*, and that it shall not be barred by any lapse of time whatever; for, pre-

scriptions being of public right, individuals cannot derogate from them by their agreements: *Privatorum conventio juri publico non derogat;* D. 50, 17, 45, § 1. *Jus publicum privatorum pactis mutari non potest;* D. 2, 13, 38.

394. According to these principles, it would seem, that we ought to decide, where the clause of redemption expressly limits a time longer than that of the legal prescription, as, where it is said that the seller may exercise his right of redemption, during the period of forty years, that the legal prescription of thirty years is not thereby prevented from taking place; and that the whole effect of this clause is, that, if the prescription of thirty years is stopped by the minority of the heirs of the seller, who succeed to the right of redemption, and is not found to be elapsed at the expiration of the period of forty years, stipulated by the contract, these heirs, against whom the legal prescription does not run, may be excluded from the right of redemption, by the conventional prescription, which runs against minors, as will be seen hereafter.

395. In like manner, where the seller reserves the right of redemption, during his life, this clause does not avoid the law of prescription, nor prevent the right from being barred, after the expiration of thirty years subsequent to the contract; the whole effect of this clause is, that it prevents the right from passing to the heirs of the seller, if he does not commence his action during his lifetime.

§ III. Of the nature of the action of redemption.

396. From the right of redemption results the action of redemption. This action is a branch of the personal action *ex vendito;* for it arises from an obligation, which the buyer contracts in favor of the seller, by the clause of redemption, which makes a part of the contract of sale; and, consequently, it results from the contract of sale.

This action is personal-real, and may be brought against

third persons in possession of the estate sold under this condition; for the estate is subjected to the execution of the obligation, which the buyer contracts by the clause of redemption, inserted in the contract of sale, to render the estate to the seller, when he shall think proper to exercise his right of redemption; the seller having alienated the estate, only upon the clauses and conditions of his contract, he subjects it, by the alienation, to the execution of this clause.

It may be objected to what is above stated, that the action of redemption is a branch of the action *ex vendito*, which is only personal, and can be brought only against the buyer and his heirs, or other universal successors; and, therefore, that it ought to be the same in regard to the action of redemption. I answer, that though the action *ex vendito* is only personal, as to its principal object, which is a recovery of payment of the price, we are not therefore obliged to conclude that it cannot be personal-real as to other objects, such as that of redemption. There is nothing to prevent an action, which has several branches, issuing out of different engagements contained in the same contract, and which has different objects, from being merely personal in regard to one object, and personal-real as to another.

397. The action of redemption is divisible, when the thing sold is a divisible thing, as an estate; and, therefore, if an estate is sold, with this clause, to several buyers, or to a single buyer, who leaves several heirs, the action may be brought against each of them for his share in the estate.

Vice versa, if several sellers sell an estate with this clause, or if a single seller leaves several heirs, neither of the sellers can prosecute the redemption except for his own share; and, in like manner, neither of the heirs can prosecute it, except for the part as to which he is the heir. It is true, there are some authors, who are of the contrary opinion, and who think that any one of the sellers, or of the heirs, ought to be allowed to prosecute the redemption for the whole, by giving surety to the buyer, to defend him against the cosellers or coheirs, and saving to himself a right to adjust the matter with them, in case they are willing to take a part in the redemption; but the opinion of these authors is contrary to the principles established by Dumonlin, *Tr. de div. et ind.*, *p.* 3, *n.* 582, *et seq.*, whose opinion we follow. The action of redemption being divisible, since its object is an estate, which is a divisible thing, it necessarily divides itself among the heirs of the seller. Each of the heirs, succeeding to the action only for the part as to which he is the heir, can maintain it only for that part; and it ought to be in the power of the buyer, if he think proper, to preserve the other parts, when the other heirs do not exercise the right of redemption.

If the buyer, however, thinks it is not for his interest to retain any undivided portions, we cannot compel him to suffer a redemption, in part, of the estate, which he purchased only in order to have it entire; and, therefore, in such case, the buyer may conclude in bar of the demand of the heir in part, if the latter do not prefer to take back the estate entire, and reimburse to the buyer the entire price and legal costs of the acquisition. The heir, who may be thus obliged to redeem the estate entire, has a right to require his coheirs, in the division of the succession, to make him an allowance of the cost of the redemption, out of their shares; or otherwise, that the whole estate shall remain to him.

This decision is founded in the very nature of the action of redemption, which obliges the seller, or his heirs, who exercise the right of redemption, to indemnify the buyer against whom it is exercised, and to put him back into the same situation in which he was before his acquisition. Now, if the heir in part of the seller, who prosecutes the redemption for his part, is not obliged to redeem for the whole, when the buyer demands it, the latter would not be indemnified; he would not be put back into the same situation, in which he was before his acquisition, since he would be obliged to suffer the inconvenience of a tenancy in common, which, as he purchased his estate only to have it entire, he neither was willing nor intended to suffer, when he made the acquisition. The law 41, § 9, D. *de legat.* 3., (30, 1, 41, § 9, 3), which refers to the case of an heir, who is charged by the testator to sell a certain estate for a certain price to two legatees, is not opposed to our opinion. It says, indeed, that one of these legatees may require the estate to be sold to him for his part, though the other does not wish to purchase; which is agreeable to what we have said, that one of the heirs of the seller may demand the exercise of the redemption for his part; but it does not follow, that the heir, summoned upon this demand, may not, for his own indemnity, oblige the legatee to purchase the whole. This is a different question, which the law does not decide, or even agitate; and, therefore, this text does not impugn our decision.

§ IV. When the redemption may be exercised and against whom.

398. Zoannettus, a jurisconsult of Bologna, of the sixteenth century, in his treatise, *De emptione cum pacto retrovenditionis*, agitates the question, whether the seller can be admitted to prosecute the action of redemption, on the day after the contract of sale; which might occur, if the seller, immediately after the contract of sale, should receive a sum of money which he was not expecting, and which should place him in a situation to exercise the right of redemption. This author decides in the negative. He thinks that the seller ought to leave the buyer the enjoyment of the thing for a certain time, before being able to exercise the redemption, in the same manner, that he, who lends me a sum of money, is not admitted to prosecute me for the payment of it, so soon as the next day. This opinion of Zoannettus appears to be destitute of foundation. There is no analogy

between this case and that of a loan. If the lender, in the case of a loan, is not admitted to prosecute the debtor for payment, on the next day, it is for the reason, that he, who borrows a sum of money, borrows it only for the purpose of making use of it immediately in his business. If the lender should be admitted to prosecute the borrower for payment, as soon as he had made use of the loan, and before a sufficient time had elapsed, to enable him to get the money to repay it, it would happen, that the loan, which, in its nature, is a benefit, would become a snare laid for the borrower by the lender, to cause him expense, at a time when it is morally certain that he cannot have the means of repayment; which is contrary to this maxim of equity: *Beneficium nemini debet esse captiosum.* There is nothing analogous in the present case; the seller, by exercising the redemption the day after the sale, does no wrong to the buyer; on the contrary, it is frequently more advantageous to the buyer, that the seller, who intends to exercise the redemption, should exercise it soon rather than late, in order that the buyer may not lose any occasions which may present themselves, to make another advantageous employment of his money.

399. The action of redemption may be brought not only against the seller and his heirs; but, when they have alienated the estate, which is subject to the redemption, it may be brought even against third persons in possession, who have not made their acquisition upon that condition. When the usufruct of the estate is separated from the property, the action must be brought against the usufructuary as well as the proprietor.

§ V. Of the reciprocal liabilities of the buyer and seller in this action.

400. The buyer or the possessor, upon the action of redemption, must be condemned to render the thing sold.

In regard to this subject, the question has been agitated,

whether the seller, in this case, may constrain, *manu militari*, the buyer, who has the thing in his possession, to render it to him, by obtaining a sentence, when it is an estate, that he shall be permitted to put himself in possession of it, and forcibly to dislodge the buyer by the aid of an officer; and, when it is a movable, by obtaining a sentence, that he shall be permitted to seize and carry it away; or, whether the buyer ought only to be condemned for damages and interests, in default of satisfying his obligation. This question is very similar to one, which has already been discussed, in the second part of this treatise, n. 67, whether a seller, who is in possession of the thing sold, may be constrained *manu militari* to deliver it, or whether he is liable only for the damages and interests. The reasons which are there given at length, on both sides of the question, are equally applicable in the present case. The act of restitution of the thing sold, to which the clause of redemption obliges the buyer, like that of delivery, to which the contract of sale obliges the seller, is not a mere act of the person of the debtor, *non est nudum factum*, but an act, *quod ad dationem accedit*, to the execution of which he may be constrained *manu militari*. And, therefore, as we have decided that a seller may be constrained *manu militari* to deliver the thing which he has sold, when he is in possession of it; so we ought in like manner to say, that he, who has purchased a thing subject to a right of redemption, may be constrained *manu militari* to render it. This is the opinion of Fachineus, *controv.* 11, 8, as well as of Pinell, Zoannettus, and Chassanée. Tiraqueau adopts the contrary opinion.

401. The thing sold must be rendered to the seller, who exercises the redemption, in the situation in which it exists; provided, however, if it is deteriorated by the fault of the buyer, that he must be condemned for the damages and interests resulting from the deterioration.

The buyer is liable in this respect, for slight fault, according to the nature of the contract of sale, and according to the principle established in the Treatise on Obligations, n. 142, that, in contracts, which are made for the reciprocal benefit of each of the parties, like the contract of sale, they are reciprocally liable for slight fault, *de levi culpa.*

402. When the thing is found to be deteriorated without the fault of the buyer, the seller, who exercises the redemption, ought to take the thing as it exists, without any power to claim, on that account, a deduction from the price, which he is bound to reimburse; for the redemption including an entire dissolution of the contract of sale, neither of the parties can claim to retain any part of what he receives from the other in virtue of the contract. Besides, the clause of redemption includes the condition of indemnifying the buyer, against whom it is to be exercised. It is in vain for the seller to object, that the thing sold is no longer at his risk, after the contract, and still less after the delivery, and, consequently, that he ought not to suffer the loss which happens to the thing. The answer is, that, as it is in his power to exercise the redemption or not, if he thinks the thing is no longer worth the price for which it was sold, it is in his power not to bear the loss, but to leave it to be borne by the buyer.

403. Suppose, on the contrary, that the estate sold, with the clause of redemption, receives, subsequent to the contract, some natural augmentation, as by alluvion;[1] ought the seller, who redeems, to receive the benefit of it? Fachieus, *controv.* 11, 6, and the doctors cited by him, hold the negative. They found their opinion upon these rules of law: *Ubi periculum, ibi et lucrum collocetur.* C. 6, 2, 22, § 3. *Secundum naturam est commoda cujusque rei eum sequi, quem sequuntur incommoda;* D. 50, 17, 10. Now, after

[1] As alluvions in navigable rivers belong to the king, to the exclusion of the inhabitants of the banks, if the latter have no title, there is rarely any ground for this question.

the contract of sale, though made with the faculty of redemption, the thing is at the risk of the buyer; if it perishes either wholly or partially, he suffers the loss of it; and the seller may well refrain from exercising the redemption. Since the buyer would suffer the loss, he ought consequently, according to these rules of equity, to receive the benefit of the augmentation, and to retain the alluvion accrued subsequent to the contract. If it be objected, that, according to the principle above established, the buyer, against whom the redemption is exercised, ought not to retain any part of what is sold; that the accretion to the estate, by its union with it, becomes a part of it; and thus the buyer cannot retain it, for otherwise he would retain a part of the estate sold; I answer, that it is indeed true, that this accretion makes a part of the estate sold; but it is equally true, that, as it began to exist only subsequent to the contract, it has not itself been sold, and that the estate has not been sold as to that part. And, therefore, the buyer, in separating it from the estate sold, or in retaining it, does not retain any part of that which is sold; and the principle which is objected against us is not impugned. If it be objected also that there are many cases, in which the buyer is obliged to render not only the thing, but every thing which has arisen from or acceded to it; the answer is, that this takes place, when things are put in the same situation, as if the contract of sale had never intervened, as in the case of the failure of a suspensive condition, upon which it is contracted, or in case the nullity of the contract is pronounced upon some rescissory or redhibitory action. But the redemption has not this effect; it only dissolves the contract for the future, and suffers it to subsist for the past; it ought not therefore to prevent the buyer from retaining that which arises from the thing sold, or accedes to it, during the time that the contract subsists. This opinion of Fachineus appears the most correct; it is confirmed by a decision of the senate of Piedmont which he cites; and it is followed by Despeisses.

404. The buyer, against whom the redemption is exercised, may, by a much stronger reason, retain the augmentations, which he makes at his own expense, when they are capable of being separated, such as chimney pieces, wainscots, &c.; thereby remitting the estate in the situation in which he received it. In regard to augmentations, which cannot be carried away, such as plantations, buildings, &c., he ought to leave them, saving his right to an allowance as will be seen hereafter.

405. Upon the same principles, it appears to me, we ought to decide, that the buyer, who, in his quality of proprietor of the estate sold, has received the third part of a treasure, found in the estate, before the demand in redemption, is not obliged to render it to the seller who prosecutes the redemption. It is true that this treasure existed and was included in the estate sold, at the time of the sale, in which respect, this case may appear different from that of the alluvion; but though it then existed, it was a thing which then belonged to no person; the seller of the estate, in which it was buried, had neither the property nor possession of it, and it made no part whatever of the estate; D. 41, 2, 3, § 3; *glossa ad d. § in verbo Cepisse.* It cannot be said, therefore, that this treasure makes a part of what is sold; and consequently the seller, who has no right to reclaim, by this action of redemption, any thing more than what he has sold, cannot reclaim the part which the buyer has received in it *jure quodam accessionis; quia quamvis ille thesaurus non fuerit proprie pars fundi; tamen quum in fundo inventus fuerit, quodammodo ex fundo profectus, et ideo saltem pro parte, domino fundi addici debere visus est.* But it is not until the time of the discovery, and consequently after the contract, that this right comes into existence, and that the buyer acquires the third part of the treasure; and, consequently, he may retain it according to the principles above established.

It would be otherwise of a mine discovered by the buyer

in the estate; though it was unknown at the time of the contract of sale, and consequently did not increase the value of the estate, yet it made a part of the estate, at that time; and, therefore, the buyer ought to render to the seller, who exercises the redemption, what he has obtained from the mine, subject to a deduction of his expenses.

406. The buyer, against whom the redemption is exercised, is bound to render the fruits only from the day of the offers made him by the seller, to render him the price. This is a consequence of the established principle, that, as the redemption operates to produce a dissolution of the contract of sale only for the future, all that arises from the thing sold, until the redemption, ought to belong to the buyer. Besides, the seller having the enjoyment of the price, it is just that the buyer should have the fruits of the thing. We may draw an argument in favor of this opinion from what our customs decide in the case of lineal redemption.

407. Many doctors are of opinion, that, when a sale, made with a faculty of redemption, is also made for a very mean price, these two circumstances united ought to create a presumption of usury, and to cause the contract to be considered as a loan upon interest, disguised under the false appearance of a contract of sale, made by the pretended buyer to the pretended seller; and, consequently, that the buyer ought to apply in payment, all the fruits which he receives, and to deduct them from the price which is to be rendered to him. Fachineus, *controv.* 11, 12, cites more than forty-five doctors who are of this opinion; and he cites almost as many who are of the contrary opinion. Several of them require that other circumstances should concur; as, that the contract should not have been made until after the seller had solicited the buyer to lend him money, or that the buyer should be accustomed to lend upon usury. Covarruvias thinks, with reason, that this ought to be left to the discretion of the judge; and I think that the contract ought

not to be easily declared usurious, both because fraud ought not to be lightly presumed, and, because, as the seller is not compellable to return the price which he has received, since it is in his power not to exercise the redemption, such sale bears no resemblance to a loan upon interest.

408. The rule, that the buyer against whom the redemption is exercised, is not obliged to account for the fruits, admits of an exception, in regard to those which are pending and ready to be gathered, at the time of the contract of sale. These fruits augment the price of the sale; there is no doubt, that when we sell a quantity of vines, on the eve of the vintage, the price of the future vintage enters into consideration in the bargain and augments the price of the contract. The buyer, who receives the benefit of this vintage, and against whom the redemption is exercised, ought consequently to deduct the price of these fruits, from the price which is to be rendered to him by the seller; for otherwise he would have both the thing and the price at the same time, which equity does not permit.

409. In regard to fruits produced subsequent to the contract, and which are found pending, at the time of the exercise of the redemption, Fachineus, *controv.* 11, 14, and the doctors cited by him, are of opinion, that they ought to be divided, in proportion to the time of that year, between the seller who exercises the redemption, and the buyer; because it is equitable, that the seller, having enjoyed the price during a part of the time of that year, the buyer should retain as a recompense a part of the fruits of the said year, in proportion to that time. For example, if the sale and the payment of the price are made the first of November and the redemption is exercised the first of July, the seller having in such case enjoyed the price during the two thirds of the year, the buyer ought to retain two thirds of the fruits which are pending, at the time of the redemption. This opinion is equitable; and is followed by the custom of Poitou.

On the contrary, the customs of Auvergne, of Marche, and of Lodunois, which have also treated of redemption, reject the division, and adjudge to the seller, who exercises the redemption, the whole of the fruits, which are gathered subsequent to offers followed by consignation, upon condition of a reimbursement for his labor and seed.

The customs of Paris and Orleans have not treated of the right of redemption; but these customs, in the matter of lineal redemption, having rejected the division, and allowed the party redeeming all the fruits gathered subsequent to his offers, subject to the condition of a reimbursement for his labor and seed, we may, from these dispositions, draw an argument for deciding, that, according to the spirit of these customs, the seller, who exercises the redemption, is, in like manner, entitled to have all the fruits gathered subsequent to his offers, reimbursing the labor and seed, there being the same reason in both cases; saving the acquirer's right to be indemnified in another manner, as will be seen hereafter for the price which he has paid.

410. We have observed, that the seller, to whom the estate is rendered, with the fruits which are there pending, ought to make an allowance for the labor and seed. The seller cannot dispense with doing so, upon the pretext, that when the buyer entered upon possession, he in like manner found the fruits pending, as is very properly decided by Tiraqueau, *Tr. du Retr. conv.* § 5, *gl.* 4, *n.* 17; for the buyer has, in like manner, paid for the labor and seed, by purchasing at a price so much greater, regard being had to the fruits which were then pending; and he makes an allowance for them to the seller, by making him a deduction of the price of the fruits, from the price of the redemption.

411. There is another question concerning the offers, after the making of which, the fruits gathered belong to the seller who exercises the redemption. Many customs, which have treated of the right of redemption, require that the offers

should be followed by consignation; and it is not until after consignation, that they give the fruits to the seller who exercises the redemption. The reason is, that the seller is always considered to be in the enjoyment of the price, which is paid him, until he is divested of it by the consignation; and, that, so long as he enjoys the price, he ought not to have the fruits of the estate; equity not permitting him to enjoy at the same time both the thing and the price.

In the customs of Paris and Orleans, is it necessary, that the offers of the seller, who exercises the redemption, should be followed by consignation? For the negative, it is said, that in the matter of lineal redemption, these customs having accorded to the party redeeming all the fruits gathered subsequent to his offers, though they are not yet followed by consignation, it seems that we ought to decide the same thing, in the present case. It might perhaps be answered, that there is not entirely the same reason. In the lineal redemption, the customs have prescribed a certain short time, for the reimbursement or consignation of the price, which does not commence until after an adjudication or acknowledgment of the redemption. As this adjudication may be delayed a long time, by the chicanery of the other party, it would not be just that the party redeeming, who is obliged to have his money always ready for a reimbursement of the price, as soon as the redemption is adjudged or acknowledged, should be deprived of the fruits during the time, which the unjust delay caused by the other party may endure.

On the contrary, in the present case, as there is no time prescribed for the reimbursement or consignation of the price, the seller may, at the commencement of his demand, consign it, upon the refusal of the other party to receive it; and, when he does not consign it, there is ground to suspect him of not having it ready or of making use of it.

We may add, in order to strengthen this difference, and

to show, that we ought not, in this respect, to draw an argument from the lineal redemption to the present case, that many customs, which require the consignation, in the case of redemption, require only simple offers in the case of lineal redemption.

Notwithstanding these reasons, the common opinion is, that, in the custom of Paris, as in others, which contain no express disposition on the subject, there should be an allowance made to the seller, in the case of redemption, of all the fruits received subsequent to his offers, though they are not followed by consignation. The buyer ought not to make a profit of his delay, and of the unjust defence which he makes against the demand in redemption, in order to keep the enjoyment of an estate, which he is bound to abandon as soon as the demand is made. He cannot complain of being deprived, during the pendency of the process, of the enjoyment both of the estate and of the price, at the same time; since it depends only upon himself to receive the price which is offered him, and not to continue the process: *Damnum quod quis culpa sua sentit, non videtur sentire.*

412. The seller, who exercises the redemption, is also bound on his part to certain liabilites, in favor of the buyer or his successors, against whom it is exercised.

In the first place, the seller ought to restore to the buyer the price for which the estate has been sold, or to acquit him from it, if it has not yet been paid.

Some ancient doctors, whose opinion is reported by Zoannettus, *Tr. de empt. vend. sub. pact. de retr. n.* 111, held, that, when, by the clause of redemption, the parties were not explained concerning the price, it was the price which the thing was worth at the time of the redemption, which ought to be paid, rather than that for which the thing was sold. The foundation of their opinion was, that they regarded the redemption as a new sale, and the clause of redemption as a mere promise to sell; and they said, that when one has engaged to sell a particular thing to another, within a certain time, without any mention made of the price, he is considered as bound to sell for the price, which the thing shall be worth at the time of the sale, and not for that which it was worth at the time of the promise. This opinion has, with reason, been rejected; it rests upon a false principle. The redemption is not properly a new sale, which the buyer makes to the seller, but a simple dissolution of one previously made. The clause of redemption is a resolutory clause, subject to which the sale is made, and by which it is agreed that it shall be in the power of the seller to dissolve the contract. The redemption is *distractus potius quam novus contractus*, and each of the parties is, consequently, obliged to take back what he gives. This principle, that the redemption is rather *distractus quam novus contractus* admits of no question in our French law. It is in consequence of this principle, that it is held, that no new profit of sale is due on account of a redemption, which would nevertheless produce one, if it included a new sale. The custom of Poitou, art. 370, decides expressly, that it is the price of the contract, which ought to be rendered, when the seller avails himself of the privilege of redemption.

413. Ought the decision to be the same, when the power of redemption is granted to the seller, by an agreement posterior to the contract? Though this case is different from the first, and the redemption which is exercised, in virtue of this new agreement, is not a *distractus* but a new contract of sale, which gives rise to a new profit, yet I think, that the price, which ought to be rendered, is that for which the thing was sold, and not that which it is worth at the time of the redemption. It is true, that in the case of a promise to sell, which is absolute, and which has no relation to a preceding contract, the price, when the parties are not explained concerning it, ought to be that which the thing is worth at the time the sale is made, and not that which it is

worth at the time of the promise. But in this case, the agreement, which intervenes between the seller and the buyer, by which it is agreed that the seller may repurchase the estate, has an evident relation to the contract of sale which has intervened between the parties; and this relation raises the presumption, that it is the intention of the parties, that the resale, which the buyer is obliged to make to the seller, when he shall require it, shall be made upon the same conditions as the first sale, to which the agreement refers.

414. May it be agreed, by the clause of redemption, that the seller, when he shall exercise the redemption, shall pay a certain sum greater than that for which the estate has been sold? This agreement, in itself, contains nothing unlawful; the power of redemption not being due to the seller by the nature of the contract of sale, we may make him purchase it; and even when the sum, which he is bound to pay, in order to exercise the redemption, in addition to that for which the estate is sold, is excessive, the agreement, even then, does not import any prejudice to him. He cannot complain of it, since it remains in his power to avoid the payment of that sum, by refusing to exercise the redemption; and by not redeeming, he is in the same situation, as if the power of redemption, which the buyer, by the nature of the contract, is not obliged to grant him, had not been granted.

415. *Vice versa*, it may be agreed, that the seller may redeem for a less sum, than that for which the estate is sold. This clause contains a benefit and a liberality, which the buyer exercises in favor of the seller; and there is nothing unlawful in it, provided the seller is a person, to whom the laws do not prohibit the buyer from giving.

416. It remains to be observed, in regard to the price, that it may be rendered in a money different from that in which it is paid. If it is paid to the seller in gold, the seller may repay it in pieces of silver, or *vice versa*. In like manner, though, subsequent to the payment of the price, the pieces

in which it is paid are increased or diminished in value; though they are discredited, and at the time of the redemption, their place is supplied by new ones of better or worse alloy; the seller who exercises the redemption ought to repay in money, which is current at the time he redeems, the same sum or quantity which he received in payment, and nothing more nor less. The reason is, that, in money, we do not regard the coins which constitute it, but only the value, which the sovereign has been pleased that they shall signify: *Ea materia forma publica percussa usum dominiumque non tam ex substantia præbet quam ex quantitate;* D. 18, 1, 1. When the price is paid, the seller is not considered to receive the particular pieces, so much as the sum or value which they signify; and, consequently, he ought to repay, and it is sufficient for him to repay, the same sum or value in pieces which are current, and which have the signs authorized by the prince, to signify that value. This principle being well established in our French practice, it is sufficient merely to state it; it cuts off all the questions made by the doctors concerning the changes of money.

417. The seller repays the price without interest; the buyer not being liable to account for the fruits, *supra*, n. 406, which he receives, it is not just that he should account for the interest; it is compensated by the fruits.

418. *Quid*, if the buyer should offer to account for the fruits? He would not, even in that case, be allowed to demand the interest; for, as the redemption operates to dissolve the contract only for the future, the seller has a right to enjoy the price, in the same manner that the buyer has a right to enjoy the estate, and consequently the interest of the price cannot be demanded. If the fruits are abundant, and exceed the interest of the price, the buyer receives the benefit of them; he therefore ought to suffer the loss if they are less.

419. When the buyer does not receive the fruits of the

year, in which the redemption is exercised, because they are then pending and attached to the soil, the seller, who receives them, ought to make an allowance for the interest of the price for that year; otherwise he would at the same time have the enjoyment of the thing and also that of the price, which equity does not permit. This is the opinion of the new commentator upon the custom of Rochelle.

420. When, by the contract of sale, there is imposed upon the buyer, besides the price, some charge, which he acquits; the seller, who exercises the redemption, ought to repay to the buyer, in addition to the price, the sum in which such charge may be estimated. For example, if I sell you, with the power of redemption, a thing for a certain sum, and impose upon you the charge of copying a certain manuscript for me; I shall be bound, when I exercise the redemption, to render you, besides the price, agreed by the contract, the sum in which the price of such copy may be estimated, for this charge imposed by the contract, which you acquit, makes a part of the price.

421. The seller, who exercises the redemption, ought also to reimburse to the buyer, all that is paid by the latter, as presents to the wife, children, or domestics of the seller, when these presents are stipulated by the contract, for then they make a part of the price.

422. The seller, who exercises the redemption, ought also to reimburse to the buyer all the legal costs of his acquisition, such as the expenses attending the contract of sale, the hundredth penny, seignorial profits, and, generally, all that it costs the buyer to make the acquisition; for the power of redemption not being due to the seller by the nature of the contract, and, being, on this account, denominated in many customs, the *favor of redemption;* the buyer who grants this power to the seller, to do him a pleasure, is considered to grant it only upon condition that he shall himself be indemnified.

423. We go even the length of maintaining, that the buyer ought to be reimbursed for things due on account of his acquisition, as to the lord for fines of alienation, though they are released to the buyer, or he is exempted from payment of them by some privilege; because he ought to receive the benefit of the gift, which is made him, as well as of the privilege to which he is entitled, rather than the seller, who exercises the redemption against him.

424. Lastly, the seller, who exercises the redemption, ought to reimburse the buyer for necessary additions, other than those of simple maintenance; for the latter are charges upon the enjoyment, which ought to be borne by the buyer, who has the enjoyment.

425. In regard to additions, which are useful but not necessary, some customs, which have treated of the right of redemption, make, in this respect, a distinction between cases in which the redemption is granted for only one year, and those in which it is granted for many. In the first case, they refuse a reimbursement, the same as in the case of lineal redemption; but they accord it in the second case. This distinction is very equitable; and, as it seems to me, ought to be followed in those customs, which contain no provision on the subject. A buyer does not suffer much prejudice, by being prevented from meliorating the estate, during the short space of a year; but he would suffer a very great prejudice, and it would even be a thing contrary to the public interest, if he were prevented from doing so for a long time. It is therefore equitable, in this case, that the seller should reimburse the cost of additions, which, though not necessary, are at least useful, and render the estate more valuable; but he ought not to reimburse the cost of such additions to any greater amount, than what the estate is thereby increased in value; it is even sometimes sufficient, when they are very considerable, for the seller to permit the buyer to carry them away, if they are capable of removal.

In regard to additions for mere pleasure, the buyer cannot exact a reimbursement for them; he has merely the right to carry them away, provided they can be removed.

426. When the redemption is exercised against a third person in possession, the seller is subject to the same liabilities in his favor, as when the redemption is exercised against the buyer. And, therefore, if I sell you my estate, with a power of redemption, and you resell it to a third person, for a greater price, I am not obliged to reimburse to the latter, any thing more than the price for which I sold it to you; for you cannot, by your act, in reselling the estate, render the condition of my right of redemption more burdensome: *Nemo ex alterius facto prægravari debet.*

Vice versa, if such third person purchases the estate for a price less than that for which I sell it to you, I am notwithstanding bound to repay the entire price; for you are considered, in selling him the estate, to sell him all the rights, which you have in relation to it, and which may tend to retain the possession of it, and consequently that of reclaiming the entire price of me, in case of redemption.

427. When the buyer is condemned in the action of redemption, to abandon the estate to the seller, the latter cannot constrain him to such abandonment, provided he does not previously reimburse him for the price and legal costs which are liquidated. When the buyer refuses to receive the amount, it is necessary that the seller should make him offers to pay, by means of a summons, and that he should obtain a judgment declaring them valid, and permitting him to make a consignation. It is not until after such judgment, and the consignation made in consequence of it, and duly notified, that the seller may constrain the buyer to abandon the estate. In regard to the legal costs and expenses, which are not liquidated, the seller is not obliged to wait until a liquidation of them, in order to compel the buyer to abandon the estate.

428. There is no fatal term, within which the seller is bound to satisfy the liabilities to which he is subject. He is always in time to do so, until, by a judgment, he is declared to have forfeited his right, in default of having satisfied them; he owes only the expense of the prosecution against him by the buyer.

429. It is a question, whether the buyer, who acquiesces in the demand in redemption, or who, upon that demand, is condemned to abandon the estate, may compel the seller to exercise the redemption.

§ VI. Of the effect of redemption.

430. The effect of redemption, when the clause of redemption is contained in the contract of sale, is, to produce, for future, a dissolution of the contract. The seller, who, in execution of this clause, re-enters into the estate, which he has sold, does not properly acquire it anew; the redemption is a dissolution and cessation of the alienation previously made of the estate, rather than a new acquisition.

431. From this principle, are derived several corollaries: 1, that there is no new profit due on account of the redemption, since it does not include a new sale, but a cessation of the first; 2, that the seller, who re-enters into the estate, in virtue of this right of redemption, becomes the proprietor of it again, by the same title, by which he held it, previous to the sale; from which it follows, 3, that the estate, of which he again becomes the proprietor, takes back the same qualities which it possessed before the sale; if it was proper in a certain line, it takes back the same quality of being proper in that line; 4, if the seller, at the time of the sale, was in fealty for the estate, he is not obliged, when he again becomes the proprietor of it by means of the redemption, to renew his fealty to the lord of whom he holds it; for becoming again the owner by the same title, the fealty, in which he was received as proprietor, by that title, ought to revive;

and, 5, the seller, who exercises the redemption, takes back the estate, free from the charge of hypothecations and other real rights imposed by the buyer; for he does not hold the estate from him; he does not acquire it from him; he again becomes the owner of it, by a dissolution of the sale, and by a dissolution and extinction of the right of the buyer; from whence it follows, that all charges, imposed by the buyer, ought, in like manner, to be dissolved, according to the rule, *soluto jure dantis, solvitur jus accipientis;* the buyer, whose right is subject to be dissolved, cannot give to others any more right than he himself has.

432. It is necessary to decide entirely the contrary, when the power of redemption is granted only by an agreement posterior to the contract of sale, and *ex intervallo.*

The redemption is, in that case, a true resale, made by the buyer to the seller, in execution of a new agreement, which does not make a part of the first contract of sale; the seller acquires the estate anew; he holds it of the buyer, from whom he receives it, in virtue of this new agreement; and therefore there is a new profit of sale due. The seller, as the proprietor of the estate, in virtue of a new title, is obliged to bear fealty anew; the estate is an acquisition to him, though it was proper at the time of the sale; and he takes it subject to the charge of hypothecations and other real rights imposed by the buyer, from whom he acquires it.

433. Domat, book 1, tit. 2, § 12, n. 8, agrees, that when the power of redemption is not granted until after the contract, the seller, who exercises it, is subject to hypothecations imposed by the buyer subsequent to the contract; but he adds, that he is subject only to those, which are imposed previous to the act, by which the redemption is granted. This decision of Domat must be restrained to the case, in which the act, by which the power is granted, is an act passed before notaries, or acknowledged in court, and which

gives the seller a hypothecation upon the estate, for the execution of the obligation, which the buyer contracts in his favor by the act. Without this, even when the act has a date, which is made certain, either by the registry, or by the decease of some one of the parties, who have subscribed it, the seller will be subject to hypothecations imposed subsequent to the act; for as the seller acquires, by the act, only a personal credit against the buyer, to compel him to render the estate; the buyer, who remains the owner, until the seller exercises the power of redemption, always preserves, in his quality of owner, the power of alienating and hypothecating the estate. This act cannot give more right to the seller, than an act, by which the buyer should strictly resell him the estate. Now such an act cannot deprive the buyer of the power to alienate and hypothecate the estate to others, until after the delivery, as has been already established; *supra*, n. 319, 320.

§ VII. How the right of redemption is extinguished.

434. The agreement, which accords to the seller a power of redemption, either does or does not contain a time limited, within which the right is to be exercised. When it does not contain any, the right of redemption is extinguished by the ordinary prescription of thirty years, by which all other rights are extinguished, when he, to whom they belong, neglects to use them within the said time; and the minority of those, to whom this right belongs, prevents the time of this prescription from running.

435. When, by the agreement, there is a time limited, within which the redemption is to be exercised, the seller, or those who succeed to this right, must exercise it within the time agreed; and their minority does not prevent this time from running against them; for the buyer having limited a time, during which he consents to suffer the redemption, the minority of those, to whom this right belongs,

ought not to change the condition of the agreement, and to oblige the buyer to more than he is willing to oblige himself to; nor consequently to oblige him to suffer the redemption during a time longer than that during which he consents to suffer it.

436. From whence it follows, that an agreement of redemption, which contains no limited time, and one which limits it to thirty years, are different, the one from the other. It is true, that, in both cases, the right of redemption is prescribed against by the same period of thirty years; but, in the first case, which contains no limitation of time, the period of thirty years, being the legal time of prescription, does not run against minors, to whom the right of redemption belongs; whereas, in the second case, the period of thirty years, being limited by the agreement, the prescription, which results from the lapse of that time, is a conventional prescription, which runs against minors.

437. The jurisprudence has established a second difference between the legal and the conventional prescription; the right of redemption is extinguished, of full right, by the expiration of the time of legal prescription, when it is not interrupted; whereas, it is established in practice, that the right of redemption is not extinguished by the expiration of the time of the conventional prescription; and that in order to extinguish it, the buyer, after the expiration of this time, must obtain, against the seller or his successors, a sentence, declaring it to be foreclosed.

This jurisprudence commenced by a decision rendered *consultis classibus*, in the fifth chamber of inquests, in the month of March, 1650, which is reported by Leprestre, amongst the decisions of that chamber, and by Brodeau upon Louet, book 5, chap. 12. It has been followed by some other decisions; and all the subsequent writers have considered it as well established; it is founded upon this, that these sales are most commonly made under circumstances, which enable the buyer to take advantage of the necessity on the part of the seller to sell, in order to buy the thing for a mean price, and which therefore make the cause of the seller to be regarded with favor, and that of the buyer with jealousy. According to this jurisprudence, though the term, within which the redemption is to be exercised, is fixed and determined by the contract; yet, so long as the buyer does not obtain a judgment of foreclosure, the seller preserves the right of exercising the redemption, until it is foreclosed by the legal prescription of thirty years.

438. Though Leprestre, who reports the decision of 1650, says, that, according to the terms of it, the seller, against whom there is no judgment of foreclosure, after the expiration of the term limited by the contract, cannot be foreclosed but by the prescription of thirty years, reckoning from the expiration of the term; yet it appears to me, that this prescription ought to run from the day of the contract of sale, in which the power of redemption is stipulated, and not merely from the day of the expiration of the term; for the legal prescription, against any right whatever, runs from the day that the right is open and may be exercised. Now the right of redemption, which the seller reserves, is open from the time of the contract; and the seller, from that time, cannot be prevented from exercising it; it is, therefore, from the day of the contract, that the prescription ought to run. When the power of redemption, accorded by the contract, is unlimited, there is no doubt, that the prescription against it runs from the day of the contract. For what reason, then, should he, who only has a right of redemption limited to a certain time, be in a better condition, in this respect, than he, who has reserved to himself a right of redemption perpetual and unlimited?

439. The prescription of thirty years, which extinguishes the right of redemption, without the intervention of a judgment of foreclosure, being the legal and ordinary prescrip-

tion which the law grants against actions, does not run against minors; for the law accords it only against persons *who are of full age and not privileged.* Mr. Vaslin, who has given us a very good commentary upon the custom of Rochelle, is of the contrary opinion; he says that the prescription of thirty years, in this case, is only an extension of the conventional prescription, accorded by the jurisprudence to the seller, against whom no judgment is obtained; that it is of the same nature as the conventional prescription; and consequently that it ought to run against minors, as the conventional prescription runs against them. But upon what is this pretended principle founded? The jurisprudence may very well require the observation of some formality, in order to give effect to an agreement; but it cannot change the time limited by an agreement and prolong it; it cannot feign that the parties are agreed upon any other time than that which is expressed by the agreement. It is much more natural to say, that the rights and actions, which are subject to a conventional prescription, are not the less subject to the legal prescription of thirty years, which embraces generally all personal actions, without excepting any; and that consequently, as it is established that the conventional prescription remains without effect, when there is no judgment of foreclosure obtained by the buyer, the right of redemption, which is not extinguished by the conventional prescription, cannot be extinguished but by the legal and ordinary prescription of thirty years.

440. The same author advances another opinion, which does not appear to me to be any better founded than the first. He pretends, that this jurisprudence operates only against the seller himself, when he himself exercises the redemption on his own account, and not against a third person to whom the right is assigned; who, according to his opinion, ought to be declared not receivable in the action of redemption which is assigned to him, immediately upon the expi-

ration of the time accorded by the agreement, though the buyer does not obtain a judgment of foreclosure. His reason is, that as this jurisprudence is established against the strict principles of law, for the benefit of the seller, who is easily presumed to be compelled by the necessity of his affairs, to sell for a mean price, and consequently for a reason personal to the seller, it ought to operate only in favor and to the benefit of the seller himself, and not for the benefit of his assignee. I do not think this reason sufficient for embracing the opinion, which is besides destitute of authority. Though it is by a reason of favor towards the seller, that this jurisprudence has been established, yet it is sufficient that it is established, in order that the assignee of the seller may receive the benefit of it; it is sufficient, that it is established, that the expiration of the time contained in the agreement will not of itself, without a judgment of foreclosure, extinguish the action of redemption, in order that it may not of itself extinguish it, even after the action of redemption is assigned to a third person; for this action, though assigned, resides always in the person of the seller, of whom the third person, who is the assignee, is only the *procurator in rem suam*, and who ought consequently to enjoy the favor granted to the cause of him whose rights he exercises. The seller even has a great interest that his assignee should enjoy, as much as himself, the right of being able to exercise the redemption, after the expiration of the time, and until a judgment of foreclosure; for otherwise, it would follow, that the seller, who frequently has not the means of exercising the redemption by himself, could no longer, after the expiration of the time, assign his right to a third person. Vaslin is forced to agree, that the seller, who is not yet foreclosed, may, even after the expiration of the time, assign his right; and that the assignee may, in such case, exercise it, though after the expiration of the time; but he pretends that he cannot exercise it, when the assignment is made before the expiration of the time. These distinctions, which do not rest upon any authority, do not appear to me to be entitled to any weight.

441. According to a decision of the 27th of March, 1669, reported by Soëfve, *cent.* 4, *ch.* 36, this jurisprudence admits of an exception, in the case of a right of redemption, which, after the expiration of the time limited by the contract, is extended by a new agreement for a certain time, with an express clause, that the seller shall be foreclosed, after expiration of the time of the extension, without any judgment of foreclosure; the seller, having brought his demand, after the expiration of the time of the extension, was, by this decision, declared not receivable.

442. This jurisprudence, which requires a judgment of foreclosure, is not followed in Poitou, in consequence of article 367 of that custom, which declares, in express terms, that the redemption must be exercised within the time of grace; and, Vaslin, in his commentary upon the custom of Rochelle, reports a decision of the 18th of August, 1747, which, in this respect, confirms the usage of that province.

443. The right of redemption is extinguished also by all the different manners, in which all credits are extinguished, by release, novation, confusion, and by a loss of the thing happening without the act or fault, and before a delay, of the debtor.

444. The seller is considered to make a release of his right of redemption, when he gives his consent to a contract of sale, which the buyer makes to a third person, of the estate subject to redemption, by which contract the estate is not declared to be subject to it.

445. It is also a tacit renunciation of the right of redemption, when the seller, after having brought his demand to exercise it, and having consigned the price, withdraws the consignation.

SECTION IV.

Of the clause of dissolution of the contract of sale, if the seller shall, within a certain time, find more advantageous conditions of sale.

446. It was a clause, formerly much in use among the Romans, in contracts of sale, to stipulate that the contract of sale should not hold, if the seller, afterwards, and within a certain space of time limited by the contract, should find another buyer, who would make him a more advantageous offer. They called the sale made with this clause, *addictio in diem*. Paul, D. 18, 2, 1, describes it as follows: *Ille fundus centum esto tibi emptus, nisi si quis intra kalendas januarias proximas meliorem conditionem fecerit.* This condition, according to the different intentions of the contracting parties, was either a true condition, which suspended the contract, until its accomplishment, that is to say, until it appeared, by the expiration of the time, that the seller could not find a more advantageous offer; or it formed only a resolutory clause, which did not arrest the perfection of the sale, but only gave to the seller, at the time of the accomplishment of the condition, the right to demand a dissolution of the contract; D. 18, 2, 2.

This resolutory clause, and the action which results from it, are treated of in this section, under the following divisions, namely; 1, when is there ground for a dissolution of the contract, in virtue of this clause; and, 2, of the action which results from it.

§ I. When is there ground for a dissolution of the contract, in virtue of this clause.

447. In order to give rise to a dissolution of the contract, in virtue of this clause, and to the action, which results from it, it is necessary, that a second buyer should be found

who really purchases upon conditions more advantageous to the seller, and that such buyer should not be a fictitious buyer. For, provided such buyer is not fictitious, there is an opening to the action, even if the first buyer objects that the second buyer is not solvent; it is sufficient that the seller finds him good and solvent; D. 18, 2, 14, § 2. If the second pretended buyer is so notoriously insolvent, that the fact cannot be called in question, as when he is a mendicant, it creates a presumption, that the buyer, in this case, is fictitious; and there is no opening to the action.

448. It is necessary that the terms of the second bargain should be more advantageous; and they are reputed to be so, not only when the second sale is made for a price greater than the first, but also, when, being made for a price equal to that of the first, the conditions of the second sale include some advantage, whatever it may be, to the seller, which is not found to exist in the conditions of the first sale. Further; even when the second sale is made for a less price than that of the first, if the advantage, included in the conditions of the second, is of a greater value, than the sum, in which the price of the first sale exceeds that of the second, the second sale must be considered more advantageous; and, consequently, it gives an opening to the resolutory clause of the first. This results from the law 4, § *fin.* D. *de in diem addict.* (18, 2, 4, § *fin.*): *Et si nihil pretio addatur, solutio tamen offeratur facilior pretii, vel maturior, æque melior conditio allata videtur . . . Proinde si quis accedat ejusdem pretii emptor, sed qui levioribus emat conditionibus, vel qui satisdationem nullam exigat, melior conditio allata videbitur; ergo idem erit probandum, et si viliore pretio emere paratus sit, ea tamen remittat quæ venditori gravia erant in priore venditione.* For example, if I sell an estate, for the sum of $10,200 livres, with a clause that the buyer shall have the term of a year, within which to cause it to be decreed to him, during which time, he shall retain the price without interest,

and also with a clause, that the sale shall not hold, if I find, within a month, more advantageous terms of sale; I shall be considered as finding such terms, if, within the said time, I find another buyer, who purchases the estate for the price of 10,000 livres only, but payable in ready money, without waiting the decree; for the advantage, which I receive from the ready money price, without waiting the decree, is worth more than the sum of 200 livres, in which the price of the first sale exceeds that of the second.

449. *Vice versa,* though the second sale is made for a price greater than that of the first, it will not be considered as more advantageous, and will not give an opening to the resolutory clause, if the sum, in which the price of the second sale exceeds the first, is counterbalanced by the hardness of the conditions contained in the second sale, which do not exist in the first; D. 18, 2, 15, § 1. We may mention as an example the inverse case of that above proposed, namely; the first sale is made for the price of 10,000 livres only, payable in ready money and without decree; the second, though made for the price of 10,200 livres, will not be considered more advantageous, if it is made upon the condition, that the buyer shall retain the price without interest, during the year, to which he is entitled for the obtaining a decree.

450. In order that there may be ground for a dissolution of the contract, in virtue of this clause, it is not sufficient that a second buyer should present himself, and offer the seller conditions more advantageous than those of the first bargain; it is necessary that the seller should accept them; for this clause is presumed to be inserted only in favor of the seller; and as it is permitted to every one, not to make use of that which is established in his favor, however advantageous may be the conditions offered to the seller, he is at liberty not to accept them, and to hold to the sale which he has made; the buyer is not allowed to demand a dissolution of the contract, in virtue of this clause, which is not inserted

in his favor, but only in favor of the selller. This is the disposition of the law 9, D. *dict. tit.* (18, 2, 9): *Sabinus scribit licere venditori, meliorem conditionem oblatam abjicere, sequique primam quasi meliorem; et ita utimur.* These principles hold, at least, where the contracting parties are not expressly agreed to the contrary: *Si hoc erat nominatim actum, ut liceret resilire emptori meliore conditione allata; dicendum erit dissolutam priorem emptonem, etiamsi venditor sequentem non admittat; dict. l.* 9.

451. The acceptance, which the seller ought to make of the more advantageous conditions, which are offered him, being a condition requisite to the dissolution of the contract in virtue of this clause, and the performance of conditions being indivisible, as has already been seen in the Treatise on Obligations, n. 215, it follows, that when several persons sell a thing by the same contract and for the same price, with this clause, if one of these sellers rejects the more advantageous conditions, which are offered him by a second buyer, who presents himself, however advantageous these offers may be, and though they are accepted by the other sellers, there can be no dissolution of the contract in virtue of this clause, which, in this case, will be ineffectual, and the first bargain will hold: *Si tribus vendentibus, duo posteriori addixerint, unus non admiserit adjectionem .... si uno pretio vendiderint, dicendum est totam priori emptam manere;* D. 18, 2, 11, § *fin.*; D. 18, 2, 13.

452. If several sellers sell, with this clause, each one his part, for separate prices, there being, in such case, different bargains, those of them, who accept the more advantageous conditions offered by the second buyer, may demand, each one for his part, a dissolution of the contract; and the first contract of sale will hold only as to the part of those among the sellers, who reject these conditions; D. 18, 2, 11, § *fin.;* D. 18, 2, 12. It must be observed, however, that if it appears, from the circumstances, that the first buyer intended

to purchase the thing only to have it entire, such buyer, having suffered a dissolution of the contract, as to the parts of those of the sellers, who accept the terms proposed by the second buyer, may oblige those of the sellers, who reject them, to take back the parts which they have sold; D. 18, 2, 13. See *Pand. Just., lib.* 18, *n.* 13, *not. d.*

453. Lastly, in order that there may be ground for a dissolution of the contract in virtue of this clause, it is necessary that the more advantageous conditions, which are offered by the second buyer, who presents himself, should be notified to the first buyer, that he should be offered the preference to retain the thing upon those conditions, and that he should refuse to avail himself of them: *Licet venditori, meliore allata conditione, addicere posteriori, nisi prior paratus sit* PLUS *adjicere* (D. 18, 2, 7), that is to say, *plus quam ipse priori contractu promisit, et tantumdem quantum posterior emptor adjecit;* as appears by what Paul adds in the following law: *Necesse autem habebit venditor, meliori conditione allata, priorem emptorem certiorem facere, ut, si quid alius adjecit, ipse quoque adjicere possit;* D. 18, 2, 8; Cujas, *ad. h. l. lib.* 33, Paul, *ad edict.*

§ II. Of the action which results from this clause.

454. The action, which results from this clause, is a branch of the action *ex vendito*, by which the seller concludes against the buyer, to a dissolution of the contract, and, in consequence, to an abandonment and restitution of the thing sold, unless the buyer prefer to submit to the new conditions which have been offered to the seller.

455. The clause, from which this action results, making a part of the contract, and being a condition of alienation, the estate is subjected to the execution of this clause; from whence it follows, that the action, which results from this clause, is an action personal-real, and that the seller may consequently, in bringing his action against the buyer, to

cause a dissolution of the contract to be pronounced, bring it at the same time against a third person in possession, to cause him to be condemned, in consequence of a dissolution of the contract, to abandon the estate.

I think such third person ought to have the option, which the buyer has, to retain the estate, by submitting himself to the new conditions offered to the seller; for such third person, standing in the place of the buyer, ought to enjoy the same rights.

456. There is no doubt, that this action is transmissible to the heirs of the seller, and assignable, though it resides in the person of the seller.

The second buyer, as exercising, in this respect, the rights of the seller, ought to be received to this action against the first buyer, in order to avoid circuity of action.

457. All that is said in the preceding section, in treating of the action of redemption, on the subject of the respective liabilities of the buyer towards the seller, and of the seller towards the buyer, is equally applicable in regard to this action.

OBSERVATION.

458. Contracts of sale, with this clause, as used among the Romans, are very little in use with us. It is true, that in our judiciary sales, the delays, and adjudications with the reservation of a fortnight, give them much resemblance to this kind of sale. They are however different; as will be seen in the sixth part, in which judicial sales are treated of.

SECTION V.

Of the dissolution of the contract of sale, in virtue of the commissory pact.

459. The commissory pact is a clause or agreement, which is sometimes inserted in contracts of sale, by which the par-

ties agree, that if the buyer do not pay the price within a certain limited time, the contract shall be dissolved.

§ I. Difference between our own and the Roman law, concerning this pact.

460. Our jurisprudence is, in this respect, different from the Roman law. By the latter, the commissory pact produced, of full right, a dissolution of the contract of sale, when the buyer neglected to pay within the time limited by the agreement; in such manner, that the buyer could not prevent a dissolution of the contract, by offers of payment made after the expiration of that time. It was, however, necessary for this, 1, that the seller should do nothing to prevent the payment, D. 18, 3, 8; D. 18, 5, 10, § 1; and, 2, that he should be willing to make use of the right given him by this pact.

According to our jurisprudence, the commissory pact does not produce, of full right, a dissolution of the contract, by default of payment, within the time limited; it only gives the seller, in such case, an action to demand a dissolution of the contract, which is not produced at least irrevocably, but by the sentence, which intervenes in this action, and declares the contract null and dissolved, in default of payment by the buyer. The buyer may, therefore, until the intervention of this sentence, though after the expiration of the term, prevent a dissolution of the contract, by offers of payment.

§ II. In whose favor the commissory pact is considered to be made, and what is its effect.

461. The commissory pact is considered to be made only in favor of the seller, and acquires a right only to him; and, therefore, agreeably to the maxim: *Unicuique licet juri in favorem suum introducto renuntiare*, the seller, who is not paid, may refrain from taking advantage of this pact, and, instead of demanding a dissolution of the contract, may pursue the buyer for payment, without the buyer being able

to demand it. This is the decision of Ulpian in the law 3, D. *de lege commiss.* (18, 3, 3): *Legem commissoriam, quæ in venditionibus adjicitur, si volet, venditor exercebit, non etiam invitus.*

462. The seller has this choice, to make use of the commissory pact, or to constrain the buyer to a payment of the price, only so far as he has not yet adopted either course. When he has once concluded to a dissolution of the contract, he is no longer afterwards receivable to demand the price: *Papinianus scribit . . . non posse, si commissoriam elegit, postea variare*, D. 18, 3, 4, § 2. The reason is evident, according to the principles of the Roman law; for, according to those principles, the default of payment, within the time limited by the commissory pact, produces of full right a dissolution of the contract, provided the seller determines to avail himself of this pact. As soon, therefore, as the seller declares his will, in concluding to a dissolution of the contract, the sale is dissolved, the obligation to pay the price no longer subsists, and the seller cannot demand it, but can only reclaim the thing sold.

Even in our jurisprudence, which requires a sentence, in order to produce, at least irrevocably, a dissolution of the contract, in virtue of the commissory pact, I think we ought in like manner to decide, conformably to the law cited, that the seller, who has once concluded to a dissolution of the contract in virtue of the commissory pact, is no longer receivable to change his conclusions, and to demand the payment of the price, even in case the buyer has not yet signified any consent to the conclusions of the seller; for the buyer has sufficiently consented to them before hand, by the clause, which is in the contract of sale; and this consent, given before hand, to the conclusions of the seller for a dissolution of the contract, sufficiently produces a dissolution, in such manner, that the sentence only causes it to be declared and confirmed. It is true, that, before the sentence, this dissolution of the contract is not, in our jurisprudence, irrevocably produced, and that the buyer is admissible, until the sentence, to prevent the effect of it, by offering to pay the price; but this is purely a favor, which our jurisprudence accords to the buyer, and which ought not to be turned against him, when he does not choose to make use of it.

463. *Vice versa*, when the seller prosecutes the buyer, for payment of the price, after the expiration of the time limited by the commissory pact, he is considered to renounce the right which it gives him, and cannot, by abandoning his action, conclude to a dissolution of the contract: *Post diem commissoriæ legi præstitutum, si venditor pretium petat, commissoriæ legi renuntiatum videtur; nec variare, et ad hanc redire potest;* D. 18, 3, 7.

§ III. Of the action which results from the commissory pact.

464. The commissory pact being a clause inserted in the contract of sale, and which makes a part of it, the action which results from it is a branch of the personal action *ex vendito: Qui ea lege prædium vendidit, ut nisi reliquum pretium intra certum tempus restitutum esset, ad se reverteretur; si non precariam possessionem tradidit, rei vindicationem non habet, sed actionem* EX VENDITO; C. 4, 54, 3.

465. This action is personal-real, and may be commenced against third persons in possession; for the seller having alienated the estate only upon the conditions imported by his contract, by the alienation, he subjects it to the execution of the obligations, which the buyer contracts in his favor by the contract. See, *supra*, n. 386 *et seq.*, what is said concerning the action of redemption.

466. The seller, by this action, concludes to a dissolution of the contract, and, in consequence, to a restitution of the thing sold. The buyer ought to render, with the thing, the fruits which he has received, D. 18, 3, 5; for not having paid the price, he cannot retain the fruits of the thing, and enjoy at the same time both the thing and the price.

467. If the buyer has paid a part of the price, he is bound to render the fruits only in proportion to the part which remains to be paid; for example, if he has paid a fourth part of the price, he ought to render only three fourths of the fruits.

468. There is one case even, in which the buyer is not bound to render any part of the fruits; and that is, when it is agreed that the seller, who receives a part of the price, shall retain it by way of damages and interests, upon re-entering into the estate, for default of payment: *Interdum fructus lucretur emptor, quum pretium quod numeravit, perdidit;* D. 18, 3, 4, § 1. The reason of this decision is, that the part of the price, which he retains, stands to him in place of all the damages and interests, which he is entitled to claim for the non-execution of the contract, among which is included the want of enjoyment of the estate, until the re-entry. If the buyer, besides this, should make an allowance for the fruits, it would be a double use and a double indemnification. See, *infra*, n. 474.

469. Lastly, the buyer ought to make an allowance for deteriorations occasioned by his fault in the thing sold.

470. The seller on his part ought to render to the buyer what he has received of him, at least, when there is no agreement to the contrary, as will be seen in a subsequent paragraph, n. 474. He ought also to reimburse him for necessary additions made, in order to preserve the thing sold; he ought even to make him an allowance for augmentations and meliorations, to the amount in which the estate is thereby rendered more valuable; or at least to suffer the buyer to carry away and retain such meliorations.

471. In regard to the expenses incurred by the buyer, in making his acquisition, from which the seller derives no benefit, such as the expense of the contract, the hundredth penny, feudal or censual profits, which the buyer pays for his acquisition, the seller is not bound to an indemnity; on

the contrary, if these dues have not been acquitted by the buyer, and the seller, after re-entering upon the estate by him sold, is disturbed on account thereof, the buyer is bound to indemnify him.

In this respect, this action differs from those, which are treated of in the two preceding sections. The reason of difference is, that the dissolution of the contract, which is made in virtue of the commissory pact, is caused by the fault of the buyer, in not fulfilling the obligation contracted by him to pay the price; it is consequently upon him, that the loss of the expenses of acquisition ought to fall; the seller ought not to bear it. It is also for this reason, that the cost of the sentence, by which, upon this action, a dissolution of the contract is pronounced, together with the expenses incurred in obtaining and putting it in execution, ought to be borne by the buyer.

On the contrary, when the dissolution of the contract of sale is made in virtue of a clause of redemption, or in the case of an *addictio in diem*, which are considered in the preceding sections, the dissolution being then made for the sole advantage of the seller, without being occasioned by any fault on the part of the buyer, it ought to be made at the expense of the seller, who ought to indemnify the buyer, for all the legal costs of acquisition, and for the expenses of the demand and of the sentence, when the buyer does not make any defence.

472. The seller is not even obliged to render the sum which he has received by way of earnest: *Si per emptorem factum sit, quominus legi (commissoriæ) pareretur, et ea lege uti venditor velit; fundos inemptos fore, et id quod arrhæ, vel alio nomine datum esset, apud venditorem remansurum;* D. 18, 3, 6. The reason is, that the seller, who stipulates a dissolution of the contract, in default of payment, and also causes a sum to be paid him by way of earnest, is deemed to reserve the damages and interests re-

sulting from the non-execution of the contract, and to have fixed them at this sum which he is entitled to retain. It must be observed, that this decision takes place only, when the sum is not too considerable, and does not exceed the sum to which the damages and interests may probably amount.

§ IV. Of some particular kinds of commissory pacts.

FIRST KIND.

473. The law 4, § 3, D. *de leg. commiss.* (18, 3, 4, § 3) contains a particular kind of commissory pact: *In commissoriam, etiam hoc solet convenire, ut si venditor eumdem fundum venderet, quanto minoris vendiderit, id a priore emptore exigat.* This clause is an extension of the commissory pact; it is not in use with us in voluntary sales; but judiciary sales are deemed to be made subject to a clause somewhat similar; namely, that in default of payment by the buyer, the party, who pursues the sale, may cause the thing to be cried, and resold, on his account. These resales are treated of in the next part of this work. This clause is lawful; every debtor is liable for the damages and interests resulting from the non-execution of his obligation; and this clause does not import any thing more than the damages and interests, which result from the non-execution of the obligation of the buyer.

SECOND KIND.

474. We add sometimes to the commissory pact, this clause, that the seller, who has received a part of the price, may, in case of a dissolution of the contract, for default of payment within the time limited, retain, by way of damages and interests, this part of the price, taking back the thing sold. This clause is lawful, provided the sum is not too considerable, and does not exceed the highest sum, in which the damages and interests, resulting from the non-execution of the contract, may be estimated.

THIRD KIND.

475. The clause, by which we stipulate, without any limitation of time, that, in default of payment, the contract shall be dissolved, is a kind of commissory pact, which differs from the ordinary pact, in this, that in the latter there is a time limited, after the expiration of which there is ground for a dissolution of the contract, if the buyer has not paid. The want of a fixed time, in the former, does not prevent it from being valid. This is the opinion of Brunneman, *ad leg.* 4, D. *de leg. commiss.* (18, 3, 4), and of the doctors cited by him. Its effect is to entitle the seller to an action, by which he concludes against the buyer, that, in default of payment by him, within a time which shall be determined and signified to him by the judge, the contract shall be dissolved.

SECTION VI.

Whether the delay of either of the parties to execute his obligations is of itself sufficient to give the other a right to demand a dissolution of the contract.

476. According to the principles of the Roman law, a delay of one of the contracting parties, to satisfy his obligation, is not always a sufficient cause to give the other party a right to demand a dissolution of the contract. For example, if the buyer is in delay to pay the price, the seller is not thereby entitled to demand a dissolution of the contract, but can only exact, by means of the law, the payment of the price which is due to him. This is decided by the following law of the Code: *Si vineas distraxisti, nec pretium numeratum est, actio tibi pretii, non eorum quæ dedisti, repetitio competit;* C. 4, 30, 8. The following text declares in like manner: *Non ex eo, quod emptor non satis conventioni fecit, contractus constituitur irritus;* C. 4, 44, 14. These

principles were formerly followed in our French practice, as appears from what is said of them, by Despeisses, *tit.* 1, *sect. fin. n.* 19, and the authors to whom he refers.

But as we are most frequently unable, without great expense, to compel payment from our debtors, we have been obliged, in our tribunals, to depart from the strictness of these principles; and we admit a seller to demand a dissolution of the contract of sale, for nonpayment of the price, though the contract contains no commissory pact. There is only this difference, that when there is a commissory pact, the judge, upon the demand brought after the expiration of the time limited by the pact, immediately pronounces a dissolution of the contract, and permits the seller to re-enter into possession of the thing sold: whereas, when there is no commissory pact, the judge, upon the demand of the seller, renders a preliminary sentence, by which he fixes a certain time, which is left to his discretion, within which he decrees that the buyer shall be bound to pay; which time being passed, the seller shall be permitted to re-enter into possession of the thing sold; and if the buyer does not pay within the said time, the seller, after the expiration thereof, may obtain a second sentence, which, in default by the buyer of having satisfied the first, will declare the contract of sale null and dissolved, and will permit the seller to re-enter into possession. The buyer, even after the sentence which pronounces a dissolution of the contract, may prevent the dissolution, and preserve the thing sold, by appealing from the sentence, and by offering upon the appeal, to pay the price due, together with the interest and expenses.

We have so far treated the question, in the case of a sale made upon credit. If it is made for ready money, and the seller, in the confidence of receiving the price immediately, makes a delivery of the thing; as the delivery, in such case, does not transfer the property, *supra*, n. 323, there is no doubt, that the seller, in default of payment, may reclaim the thing, and demand a dissolution of the contract.

In regard to all the other obligations, either of the seller, or of the buyer, we must decide, according to the circumstances, whether their non-execution ought to give rise to a dissolution of the contract; it ought to cause a dissolution, when that which is promised me is of such a nature, that I should not have been willing to contract without it. Suppose, for example, that you sell me a piece of land, which contains no pasturage, though it cannot be made valuable without cattle, and, by the contract, you enter into an obligation to give me the right of pasturing the cattle, belonging to the land which I purchase, upon an adjoining territory of which you are in possession: if it afterwards happens, that you are evicted of this tract of land, and cannot consequently cause me to enjoy the right of pasturage, which you were obliged to cause me to have upon it, the non-execution of this obligation, which you have contracted in my favor, gives me a right to conclude against you to a dissolution of the contract of sale; for, it is evident, that, without this right of pasturage, I should not have been willing to purchase the land.

On the contrary, if there is sufficient pasturage dependent upon the land, which you sell me, for the cattle necessary to stock it, so that the right of pasturage, which you are obliged to furnish me upon the other tract, is not necessary but merely useful, inasmuch as it enables me to keep a greater number of cattle, and to make a greater profit; in this case, we cannot assert, as in the preceding, that I should not have been willing to purchase the land without the right of pasturage, but only that I should not have been willing to purchase it for so high a price; and therefore I cannot demand a dissolution of the contract, but only a deduction from the price.

PART SIXTH.

OF PROMISES TO SELL AND TO BUY; OF EARNEST; AND OF SOME PARTICULAR KINDS OF SALE.

This part is composed of five chapters. We shall treat, in the first, of promises to sell, promises to buy, and of earnest; in the second, of forced sales, licitations, and of judicial sales; in the third, of sales of rights of succession, or other universal rights; in the fourth, of the sale of a right of usufruct; and, in the fifth, of the sale of annuities and other credits.

CHAPTER FIRST.

Of promises to sell, promises to buy, and of earnest.

ARTICLE FIRST.

Of promises to sell.

§ I. What is a promise to sell, and when it is considered to be contracted.

477. A promise to sell is an agreement, by which one person is obliged in favor of another, to sell him a thing. For example, if, in the contract of sale, which I make to you of my library, there is a clause, which obliges me also to sell you the cases, if they suit you, and you are willing to buy them; this promise includes a promise to sell you the cases. There is a great difference between a promise to sell, and a sale itself. He, who promises to sell you a thing does not yet sell it; he only contracts an obligation to sell it to you when you require it.

478. We should be careful, not to take, for a promise to sell, a declaration which a person makes of his actual dis-

position to sell. Such a declaration does not include any obligation, and leaves him who makes it the liberty of changing his mind, until the conclusion of the bargain. For example, if, after making a verbal sale of my library, I do not say expressly and precisely that I oblige myself to sell you the cases, but only: *I will also sell you my cases, for the sum of so much, if they suit you;* this is only a simple declaration of the actual will in which I am, and not a true promise. It is necessary, in order to constitute a promise to sell, that when you say or write, that you will sell me such a thing, it should appear clearly, by the terms which you use, that you intend to oblige yourself, and that it is a true agreement, which intervenes between us; without this, it is a mere discourse, which does not include any obligation.

§ II. Difference between the contract of sale, and the simple promise to sell.

479. The contract of sale is a mutual contract, by which each of the parties is obliged to the other; but the promise to sell is an agreement, by which he only, who promises to sell, is bound; he, to whom the promise is made, does not, on his part, contract any obligation. He, who sells a certain thing, becomes the debtor of the thing to the buyer; the thing, from that time, becomes at the risk of the buyer to whom it is due, as we have already established in the fourth part of this treatise; but he, who promises to sell you a certain thing, is not yet the debtor of the thing itself; he is only the debtor of an act. And, therefore, the thing, which he promises to sell you, continues to be at his risk; if it perishes, it is his loss; you are not obliged to pay the price of it; you do not yet owe the price, not having yet purchased the thing.

§ III. Question concerning the effect of a promise to sell.

480. When he, who has promised to sell me a certain

thing, refuses to fulfil his promise, can I oblige him strictly to perform it, by obtaining a sentence, that, if he neglects to pass me the contract of sale, which he is obliged to pass me, the sentence shall be equivalent to a contract of sale, and that I shall be permitted, in virtue of the said sentence, to seize the thing, and put myself in possession of it? Or can I, upon his refusal, obtain against him only a condemnation for damages and interests to be estimated in a sum of money? On the one side, it is said to be a general principle, that obligations, which do not consist in giving but in doing, *quæ non sunt in dando, sed in faciendo*, are resolved into damages and interests, in default of performance by the debtor, because, that *nemo potest cogi præcise ad factum.* Therefore, say those who embrace this opinion, the obligation, which results from a promise to sell a thing, not having for its object the thing itself, but rather an act which is the sale of the thing, and being an obligation *quæ non in dando, sed in faciendo consistit*, it must, according to the principle stated, be necessarily resolved into a simple obligation for damages and interests. On the other side, it is said, that the rule, *nemo potest cogi ad factum*, and the rule, that obligations, *quæ in faciendo consistunt*, are necessarily resolved into damages and interests, are only applicable in regard to obligations of external and corporal acts, such as an obligation to copy a document; which acts cannot be supplied, but by a condemnation for damages and interests. But the act, which is the object of a promise to sell, is not an external and corporal act of the person of the debtor; it may be supplied by a judgment as above mentioned, decreeing, that, in default of the debtor's being willing to pass a contract of sale, the judgment itseif shall be equivalent to one. This opinion appears to be adopted in practice, as more conformable to the integrity which ought to govern men in the performance of their promises.

§ IV. **Of the different manners in which promises to sell may be made.**

481. Promises to sell may be made, in different manners: First, they may be made, either with or without limitation of time. When a party obliges himself to sell a thing within a limited time, he is of full right discharged from his obligation by the lapse of this time, if, during its pendency, he is not put in delay to perform his promise. This is conformable to the principles established in the Treatise on Obligations, n. 671. When I promise to sell you a particular thing, without any limitation of time, in order to be discharged from my promise, I ought to obtain a sentence, requiring you to declare, within a certain time limited by the sentence, whether you intend to buy; and, that, this period being passed, without any declaration of your intention, I shall be discharged from my obligation. Though I do not obtain a sentence, if I suffer a considerable time to elapse, it will create a presumption, that the parties have tacitly desisted from the agreement.

482. Second. A promise to sell a thing may be made, not only expressing the price, for which the party is obliged to sell, but also without expressing it; the debtor is considered, in this case, to be obliged to sell for the just price, to be determined by experts, agreed upon by the parties. This obligation is valid, in the same manner, that a legacy, by which a testator charges his heir, to sell a certain thing to some one, without making mention of the price, is not thereby prevented from being valid, and from obliging the heir to sell the thing *æquo pretio;* D. 30, 1, 49, § 8, 1. *Nec obstat* that there cannot be a sale, without a price agreed between the parties; for the promise to sell is not yet a sale.

483. When I promise to sell you a certain thing for the just price, or, which amounts to the same thing, without mentioning the price, is it for the price, which the thing is worth at the time of the promise, or for that, which it is

worth at the time of the contract of sale, which I make to you of it, that I ought to sell it? I think it is the latter; for it is only at that time, that the sale is made, and, consequently, it is in regard to that time, that we are obliged to determine, whether it is made *æquo pretio*. Yet if the thing is increased in value, after the promiser is put in delay to perform his promise, by a judicial demand, he will not be allowed to sell it for more than its value at the time of the delay; for you ought not to suffer from his delay; and still less ought he to make a profit by it.

484. When the price is determined by the promise to sell, whatever variation may take place, subsequent to the promise, in the price of things of the same kind, the seller is not allowed to demand for it a price greater than that which is agreed, and, on the other hand, he is not bound to sell it for a less price.

485. If the thing is much deteriorated by some accident; as if one of the rooms of a house, which the owner promises to sell you, is burned by lightning; have you a right to oblige the promiser to sell you the house, and to make you a deduction from the agreed price, proportioned to the deterioration? I think not; for the promiser is only obliged to sell you the house for the price expressed by his promise, and not for a different one. This decision is not contrary to what is above established, *supra*, n. 479, that he, who promises to sell you a thing, not being as yet either the seller or the debtor of the thing, it is at his and not at your risk; for, as it is in your power not to buy the thing, it is not at your risk, but at the risk of the promiser; since, by refusing to buy, you necessarily compel him to bear the loss.

486. If any augmentation happens to the thing, which you promise to sell me for a certain price, as, for instance, by alluvion, are you obliged to sell me the thing as it exists with the alluvion? The reason for doubting is, that this addition to the estate is considered to make a part of it.

Notwithstanding this reason, I think that you may retain the addition, at least, if I do not offer to pay its estimated value; inasmuch as the benefit of the augmentation ought to belong to him, at whose risk the thing is: *Ubi periculum, ibi et lucrum collocetur;* C. 6, 2, 22: *Secundum naturam est commoda cujusque rei eum sequi, quem sequuntur incommoda;* D. 50, 17, 10. Now the thing is at the risk of him who promises to sell it, so long as the sale does not ensue, since if it perishes or is deteriorated, he, to whom it is promised, may refuse to purchase and leave it with the owner. He ought therefore to receive the benefit of the augmentation, since he will be subject to the loss.

487. In regard to augmentations made to the estate by the owner, subsequent to a promise to sell it, he may, without doubt, carry away those which are capable of removal, thereby remitting the thing to the same situation in which it was at the time of the promise; but I do not think that he can require the party, to whom he promises to sell the estate for a certain price, to make him an allowance for the additions, though they render the estate more valuable. The rule ought to be the same in respect to him, as to the acquirer of an estate subject to redemption, to whom the customs refuse a reimbursement for useful additions; it ought not to be permitted to the one any more than to the other, to render the redemption or the purchase more difficult and more expensive.

488. It is not so in regard to necessary additions, which you make to a thing, after you promise to sell it to me for a certain price; as, for example, when you repair the side or roof of a building, the ruin of which is imminent, and which it is necessary to demolish and rebuild; there is no doubt, that, if you sell me the thing in execution of your promise, I am bound to make you an allowance for the addition, since it is one which you cannot dispense with making, of which I receive the benefit, and of which it would not be

just that I should profit at your expense; I am so much the more bound to make this allowance, that if you should not make the repairs, I should myself be obliged to make them.

489. For the same reason, if, when I sell you the thing which I promise to sell you, the fruits are pending, you ought to reimburse me for all the expenses of the culture and seed: for these expenses are charges upon the fruits, which ought to be borne by him who gathers them. There is no ground for any of these questions, when the promise to sell does not import any price for which the sale is to be made.

ARTICLE II.

Of promises to buy.

490. In the same manner, that we may make a promise to sell, which will not be equivalent to a contract of sale, we may also make a promise to buy. These promises to buy are common in judicial sales, whether of movables or immovables, which are made to the highest and last bidder; for the offer, made by a bidder, is a true promise to buy; by which he engages to buy the thing, for the price which he bids, subject to the condition that there shall be no offer higher than his own. This engagement is contracted in favor of the court or officer, or, to speak more accurately, it is contracted in court or to the officer, in favor of the pursuers and the opposers, and even in favor of the debtor. In licitations before notaries, the bid, of which the notary gives an act, in like manner, includes an engagement or promise to buy, which, in like manner, is extinguished, when a higher offer is received.

491. It is not by offers of this sort only, that we may contract promises to buy; we may, without this, engage ourselves to any one to buy a certain thing, by a simple promise, which will not be equivalent to a buying of the

thing. For example, if, being upon the point of purchasing a house ready furnished, I make an agreement with the seller, who has made an estimate of the movables, by which he engages to buy of me, in a year, all the movables, which I shall not wish to keep, for a price of two sous in the livre more than the estimated value, this agreement does not include a contract of sale, but a simple promise to buy. The seller alone is under an obligation to me; I contract none to him; I have the power to keep all and to sell none of the movables, which are in the house, and even to dispose of them to other persons.

492. The promise to buy either does or does not contain a time limited. If it contains a time, the promiser is discharged at the end of it, when he is not put in delay to perform his promise; if no time is limited, he must obtain a sentence, in order to be discharged, as we have already seen, *supra*, n. 481, in regard to a promise to sell.

In regard to the promise to buy, made by bidding, the bidder is considered to be willing to engage himself, until the time, when he has probable reason to expect that the adjudication will be made; and therefore if it is delayed for a very long time, by delays which he had no reason to apprehend, he may require the judge to discharge him from his offer; but until he is discharged from it by the judge, his engagement subsists.

493. The promise to buy either does or does not contain the price, for which you promise to buy a certain thing of me. If it contains no price, the sale ought to be made for the price, which the thing is found to be worth at the time of the sale, to be determined by experts, in the same manner, as we have decided in the preceding article, in regard to a promise to sell. If the price is determined by the promise itself, the sale must be made accordingly.

494. When the thing, which you promise to buy of me for a certain price, is deteriorated, though without my fault,

before you are in delay to buy, I cannot oblige you to buy for that price; for the loss, occasioned by the deterioration, ought not to fall upon you, who are not yet the buyer, but upon me, who am still the owner. The thing does not cease to be at my risk, because, though you are obliged to buy it, I have the power to refuse to sell it, and I am not the debtor of it to you.

It is upon this principle, that Lemaistre, in his treatise *des criées*, chap. 22, and Mornac, *ad leg.* 58, D. *de contrah. empt.* (18, 1, 58), decide, with Baldus, that if, after a bid is received, the estate is deteriorated by some accident, as, for instance, by fire, or by a tempest, which blows down a great number of trees, the bidder is well founded to claim a discharge from his bid, unless the other party is willing to make a deduction from the sum offered, of the amount, to be determined by experts, in which the estate is diminished in value.

If the degradation is such, that he, who engages to buy, not only would not have been willing to buy, at so high a price, but probably would not have been willing to buy at all, the thing not being capable of the use which he intended to make of it, he ought to be entirely discharged from his promise.

We have said, provided the thing is deteriorated before he, who promises to buy a thing of me, is put in delay to buy it; for if the deterioration happens afterwards, he ought to buy for the price agreed, or if there is no price agreed, for the price, which the thing is worth at the time of the delay; for I ought not to suffer from his delay; in this consist the damages and interests which result from it.

495. When you engage to buy a house of me, for a certain price, and, after the engagement, and before you are put in delay, great repairs become necessary; can I oblige you to buy the thing for the price agreed, and also, to make me an allowance, for the price of the repairs? No: if I

find, that, by means of the repairs, the thing is worth more than the price, for which you promise to buy it of me, I have the power to keep it; but I cannot require you to purchase for a price greater than that imported by the agreement, though, the house being repaired, you receive, in buying it, the benefit of the repairs; for as you are obliged to buy for that price only, having that sum only at command, I cannot require any thing more of you; and by refusing to buy, you do me no wrong, since I have the power to keep the thing.

496. In regard to expenses incurred on account of the fruits, which are pending at the time of the sale, if you are not willing to reimburse them, you ought to consent, that in selling the estate, I should reserve the fruits; for these expenses being a charge upon the fruits, which are estimated only *deductis impensis*, you cannot have the fruits without paying the expenses.

ARTICLE III.

Of earnest.

497. There are two kinds of earnest; the one, which is given at the time of a contract only projected; the other, which is given after the contract of sale is concluded.

§ I. Of the earnest given before the conclusion of the bargain.

498. The earnest, which is given at the time of a bargain only projected, and before it is concluded, forms the subject of a particular contract, by which he, who gives me the earnest, consents to lose it, and to transfer the property of it to me, in case of a refusal on his part to conclude the proposed bargain; and, by which I am obliged, on the other hand, to render him double the amount of the earnest paid, in case of a like refusal on my part; C. 4, 21, 17.

499. This agreement being of the nature of the contract

of earnest, it is not necessary, that it should be expressed; the act, alone, by which one of the parties, at the time of a bargain proposed, and not yet concluded, gives something to the other, by way of earnest, tacitly includes this agreement, though the parties do not explain themselves further in relation to the subject; *dict. l.* 17.

500. This contract is a real contract; for there can be no contract of earnest without an act, which is the delivery of the earnest.

501. By this contract, he only who receives the earnest obliges himself to the other; the party, who gives, does not properly contract any obligation; but he transfers, by the contract, the property of the earnest which he gives, in the case and upon the condition of a refusal on his part, to conclude the proposed bargain.

502. This takes place, when the thing, given by way of earnest, belongs to the giver, and of which he may consequently transfer the property; but if he gives, by way of earnest, a thing which does not belong to him, does he contract an obligation of warranty? This question depends upon knowing in what manner, we ought to regard the title of him, who receives the earnest. If it is a lucrative title, there is no ground for warranty: *Lucrativæ rei possessor ab evictionis actione ipsa juris ratione depellitur;* Paul, *sentent. v.* 10, 5. But can it be considered as a lucrative title? It is true, that he, who gives me earnest, receives nothing in its place; I pay nothing to have it; but if I do not pay any thing, I contract a reciprocal obligation in his favor, to render him double the amount, in case of a refusal on my part. It is in consideration of this obligation, which is equivalent to the value of the earnest, that I receive the earnest; and consequently I do not receive it by a lucrative title. The contract of earnest is not, in truth, properly of the class of commutative contracts; but belongs to the number of contracts of mutual interest. It is not a lucrative title; and it consequently gives rise to the obligation of warranty.

503. He, who receives earnest, is obliged, in case of a refusal, on his part, to conclude the proposed bargain, to render, to him who gives it, double the sum received, if it is a sum of money, or if any other thing is given, to render the thing, and its value besides, according to the estimation of experts to be agreed upon.

504. If it is by mutual consent, that the bargain does not take place, because the loss of the thing, or some considerable change happening to it, prevents it from being concluded, he who receives the earnest ought to restore it and nothing more. When the bargain is concluded, he ought in like manner to restore it; saving, however, if the earnest consists of a sum of money, that he may retain it, deducting the same amount from the price due.

505. Lastly, he, who receives a thing by way of earnest, is bound to take the care necessary to preserve it; and is liable, in this respect, for slight fault; the contract of earnest being made for the interest of both the contracting parties.

§ II. Of earnest given after the bargain is concluded.

506. Earnest is accustomed to be given by the buyer to the seller, in order to serve as a proof, that the bargain is concluded. And therefore Cujas defines it, *quod ante pretium datur, et fidem facit contractus facti totiusque pecuniæ solvendæ.* It is not of the essence of the contract of sale, which may be made without the giving of earnest, since the parties may agree upon some other mode of proof, than that which results from earnest. It is this kind of earnest, given *in argumentum contractus facti,* which is spoken of in the law 35, D. *de contrah. empt.* (18, 1, 35): *Quod sæpe arrhæ nomine pro emptione datur, non eo pertinet, quasi sine arrha conventio nihil proficiat; sed ut evidentius probari possit convenisse de pretio.*

507. The earnest given by the buyer sometimes consists of a sum of money; in which case, it is considered to be

given on account of and to be deducted from the price, which the buyer is obliged to pay. The people, in our province, call this kind of earnest, *money of adieu*, because it is a piece of money given by the buyer to the seller, when the parties, after having concluded their bargain, separate and say *adieu*. Sometimes the buyer gives some other thing than money, as earnest. The Romans had a custom of giving *a ring;* D. 14, 3, 5, § 15; Pliny, book 33, chap. 1. The seller, in this case, has a right to retain, as a sort of pledge, the thing given as earnest, until he is entirely paid. When he has been entirely paid, he ought to render it to the buyer. The law 11, § 6, D. *de act. empt.* (19, 1, 11, § 6), gives the buyer, in this case, the action which is called *condictio sine causa*, for a recovery of the earnest: *Certe etiam condici poterit, quia jam sine causa*, says the law, *apud venditorem esset annulus.* It adds that he may reclaim it by the action *ex empto.*

508. It is a question, among the doctors, when the seller receives earnest, after the contract of sale is concluded, whether each of the parties may compel the other to execute his obligation, and in default thereof, may cause him to be condemned in all the damages and interests resulting from its non-execution, in the same manner, as if no earnest were given; or whether it is in the power of the buyer to discharge himself from his obligation, by offering to lose the earnest; and in that of the seller, to desist, in like manner, from his own, by offering to pay double the earnest. Fachineus, *lib.* 11, *controv.* 28, and the doctors cited by him, have embraced the latter opinion. They rest themselves upon the ground, that Justinian, Inst. *tit. de empt. vend.*, *in princ.* (3, 24, *in pr.*) and in the law 17, C. *de fide instrument.* (4, 21, 17), declares, that the buyer, who refuses to execute the contract, ought to lose the earnest, and that the seller, when he refuses, ought to render double the amount. The law, say these authors, having fixed the damages and interests resulting

from the non-execution of the obligation on the part of the buyer, to be a loss of the earnest on his part, and a restitution of double the amount of the earnest, on the part of the seller, the parties are not at liberty to claim any thing more. By giving and receiving earnest, they ought to be considered to content themselves with this kind of damages and interests and to renounce all others, and even all other actions to which they might be entitled against each other, to compel the execution of the contract. Weissembach, *in parat. ad dict. tit.* D. *de contrah. empt.* (18, 1, 35), *n.* 9, and Vinnius, *ad dict. tit. inst.* (3, 24, *pr.*) with reason reject this opinion; they say that the texts, cited in its favor, must be understood to refer only to earnest given at the time of a bargain merely proposed, and not yet concluded. It appears to be sufficiently evident, that the text from the Code speaks only of this kind of earnest; it refers to the case of a contract not yet concluded, and which the parties delayed to conclude, until it should be put into writing. The text from the Institutes, though ambiguous and doubtful, can, in like manner, be understood only of this kind of earnest. The expression, *ita tamen impune recedere concedimus, nisi jam arrharum nomine aliquid fuerit datum,* clearly shows, that the contract, on account of which earnest was given, was one which the parties might with impunity refuse to execute, if it were not for the earnest; and, which, consequently, was not yet made and finished, but to be made and merely projected. And therefore the terms which follow, *sive in scriptis, sive sine scriptis venditio celebrata est,* must be understood in this sense, *celebrari cœpta est,* as Vinnius explains them, in his note on this title; and these, *is qui recusat adimplere contractum,* in this sense, *id est qui recusat perficere contractum.* In the case of earnest given at the time of a contract only projected and not concluded, it is clear, that the buyer, who refuses to conclude the bargain, is discharged from his obligation, by a loss of the earnest, and that he cannot be constrained to a payment of the price, since the bargain not being yet concluded, he has not yet contracted the obligation to pay it. For the same reason, we can demand nothing more than double the earnest, of the party who receives it, since he is not yet obliged to a delivery of the thing; but it ought to be otherwise, when the earnest is given after the conclusion of the bargain. The buyer may, in that case, be constrained to a payment of the price, since he is under an obligation to pay it; and, for the same reason, the seller may be constrained to deliver the thing, and in default of being able to deliver it, may be condemned in all the expenses, damages and interests of the buyer; and neither of the parties can be discharged from his obligation, though the one offers to lose the earnest, or the other to pay double the amount. As the earnest in this case is given in order to confirm the contract and to render it more certain and known, it would be absurd to give it an effect to destroy the contract, by destroying the obligations, rights, and actions which result from it. Vinnius, who is of this opinion, says, upon the authority of Pacius, that the contrary is practised upon in France. I am not informed of any such practice; and I think, that these authors, having little means of knowing our practice, have erred in the fact, upon this point. Despeisses, a French author, follows the opinion of Vinnius.

509. Though the buyer, who, after the conclusion of the bargain, gives earnest, refuses to execute the bargain, and to pay the price; if he is, notwithstanding, constrained to pay and does pay it, he ought not to lose the earnest; which ought to be restored to him, or if it consist of a sum of money, to be deducted from the price; for it is only in case of a non-execution of the bargain, by his refusal, that he ought to lose it; but when he pays it, though by constraint, the bargain is executed.

There is more difficulty, when the seller does not really execute the contract, but is condemned, in default of executing it, to the damages and interests of the buyer. I think, that even in this case, the buyer can claim nothing more than a return of the earnest, and not a restitution of double the amount; for the restitution of double the earnest being a penalty, which stands in the place of the damages and interests resulting from the non-execution of the contract, the buyer would cause himself to be twice paid for the same thing, if, after being fully satisfied for his damages and interests, he could also compel a restitution of double the earnest; contrary to this rule of equity: *Bona fides non patitur ut bis idem exigatur;* D. 50, 17, 57.

510. The following question remains to be considered. When it is uncertain whether the contract, in which earnest is given, is a contract concluded, or only projected, what ought to be presumed? I answer: Though earnest is given in proof of a contract concluded, *in argumentum venditionis contractæ;* yet, as it is also frequently given on account of contracts only projected, it cannot of itself, and in the absence of other concurring proofs, constitute a sufficient proof of the conclusion of the bargain. This must nevertheless depend upon circumstances; the earnest, which is given in the case of a bargain merely projected, being given only with a view to engage the parties to execute it, namely, the giver, by the fear of losing it, and the receiver, by the fear of rendering double the amount; it follows, that when that, which is given as earnest, is a thing of no value, we can scarcely regard it as the earnest of a bargain only projected, but on the contrary, we ought to consider it as earnest of the second kind, which is given to serve as the proof and testimony of a bargain concluded. And, therefore, when, in our country, the peasants give, as the earnest of their bargains, a *sou marqué*, or, sometimes even a *liard* only, which they call the *money of adieu*, such earnest ought to be considered as earnest of the second kind.

All that is above said of the earnest, which intervenes in the contract of sale, may be applied to that which intervenes in other contracts.

CHAPTER II.

OF FORCED SALES, LICITATIONS, AND JUDICIAL SALES.

§ I. Of forced sales.

511. A sale is forced, when the seller, previous to the contract of sale, has contracted the obligation to sell. This obligation may result from a promise to sell, which is treated of in the preceding chapter. It may also result from a testament. When a testator orders his heir or legatee to sell Peter a certain thing; whether it makes a part of the succession, or belongs to the heir or legatee, the latter, by accepting the succession or legacy, contracts an obligation to sell the thing to Peter, for the price stated in the testament, or if no price is stated, for that which shall be determined; D. 30, 1, 49, § 8, 1°.

512. A sale may also be forced by reason of public necessity, or even by reason of public utility only. For example, in a case of public necessity, as in a scarcity of grain, those, who have more than a sufficiency for their own use, may be compelled by the judge of police, to carry their grain to the market and sell it at the current price. It is the same in regard to all provisions, which are necessaries of life, when there is a scarcity of them, as may happen in the case of a siege.

The proprietors of houses or other estates may also be constrained to sell them for some purpose of public utility, as to make a street or public place, for fortifications, or for some public work. For example, by an ordinance of Philip the Fair, in 1303, it is ordained, that the proprietors of ground necessary for the building of parish churches and presbyteries, and for cemeteries, shall be obliged to sell the same for the just price. According to letters patent of Francis the first, which are in the treasury of the university of Orleans, the bailly and provost of Orleans are directed to constrain the proprietors of certain houses near the school of law, to sell them for the advancement of that school.

513. If the proprietor, who is compelled to sell his estate, for some purpose of public utility, to the king, to a city, or to an university, agrees upon the price himself, with the commissioners of the king, or with the city or university; this agreement is a true contract of sale. If he will not agree upon any thing, and suffers himself to be constrained to abandon the estate, for the price determined by experts, there is not properly, in this case, any contract of sale, inasmuch as there is no agreement; but the decision or sentence, rendered against him, stands in the place of it.

514. When a thing, which is sold for some purpose of public utility, is made *divini aut publici juris;* as when it is used for a cemetery, a street, or public place, it is evident, that all hypothecations or other charges, to which the thing is subject, are extinguished; saving to creditors and others, having rights in the thing, a reimbursement out of the price, according to the order of their hypothecations and privileges; from which it follows, that such sale does not give rise to any obligation of warranty.

515. We may not only be forced to sell for some purpose of public utility, but also on account of individual necessity. For example, if I have an estate, surrounded in such a manner, by an estate belonging to my neighbor, that I cannot go to it by any other way than through his land, I may constrain him to sell me, *justo pretio,* a right of way in that direction which shall be least inconvenient to him; *arg.* D. (11, 7, 12). The same point is established by decisions reported by Louet and Brodeau; *l. c. art.* 1, 2; Mornac, *ad. d. l.* 12.

§ II. Of licitations.

516. When several persons succeed in common to an estate or other thing, which cannot be divided without being depreciated, or acquire it in common, by some title, whatever it may be, as by purchase, legacy, donation, &c., any one of them may oblige the others to sell by licitation, that is to say, by suffering the whole to be adjudged to him among them, who will give the highest price for it. This licitation is made by the coheirs or coproprietors, in presence of a notary. If any one of them proves that he has not the means of bidding, and demands, in consequence, that the offers of strangers should be admitted, and that he may put up notices, informing the public of the day and place of adjudication, his demand ought to be allowed. When some one of the coheirs or coproprietors is a minor, it is necessary to the validity of the licitation, that the offers of strangers should be received; and the licitation ought also, in such case, to be made before the judge, who should adjudge the estate to the highest and last bidder. It is also necessary to the validity of a licitation, when there is a minor among the coheirs or coproprietors, that it should be made to appear, by the visit and report of experts appointed by the judge, that the estates in common cannot be divided without being depreciated, and consequently, that the licitation ought to be directed by the judge, as the only convenient mode of putting an end to the community. We may however dispense with the visit, when, by the nature of that which is to be divided, or by the report of a member of the coproprietors, it is evident, that a division cannot be conveniently made; as when, in a succession, there is but one house, or but a single farm, having a moderate quantity of land dependent upon it. When, upon a licitation, in which strangers are admitted to bid, the estate is adjudged to a stranger, the licitation is a true contract of sale, which the parties make of the estate

licited; a contract which produces on both sides all the obligations produced by a contract of sale. But when one of the coheirs or coproprietors is the adjudicatory, the licitation is regarded as a kind of division or act dissolving the community, rather than as a sale. These licitations are considered in the seventh part, and the differences between this act and a contract of sale are there exhibited.

§ III. Of judicial sales.

517. Immovables and movables are sometimes sold judicially. A sale of movables is made in this manner, either when it is made by the judge in court, or when it is made upon public outcry, by an officer of justice, as a sergeant; and may be either forced, like that which a creditor makes of the goods of his debtor which he has seized; or it may be voluntary, like that which the heirs of a succession make of the movables belonging to it. In regard to immovables, we have already seen one case, in which they are sold judicially, namely, that of a licitation, when there are minors amongst the coheirs or coproprietors. If an estate, in which a minor has an undivided interest, cannot be sold but by a judicial sale, there is still stronger reason, that the sale should be made only in that manner, when an estate belongs wholly to a minor, and, upon the advice of relatives, the judge permits a sale of it, as he may, when a sale is necessary to pay the debts of the minor and to prevent a seizure of his goods.

The principal kind of judicial sale is the sale, by decree, of estates actually seized by hypothecary creditors, against their debtor, who is the owner; against the curator to a vacant succession; or against the curator appointed to an estate abandoned by a third person, who was in possession of it. We shall not speak here of this kind of sale; it merits a treatise by itself, and is considered in the introduction to the twenty-first title of the custom of Orleans.

518. Judicial sales are either pure and simple, or made subject to the condition that no higher offer is received. The last are called *delays*, *adjudications saving*. In decrees, the adjudication pure and simple ought to be preceded by three delays, or adjudications saving a fortnight, that is to say, adjudications subject to the condition that no higher offer is received within a fortnight. These adjudications saving are also practised in the other kinds of judicial sales, such as licitations, when the parties require it. These sales are similar to those, which are called in the law *addictio in diem*, and of which we have already treated, in the fifth part.

519. The condition, upon which these sales are contracted, is suspensive, in which they are different from those mentioned above; and therefore they are not put into execution, before the expiration of the condition; the property of the estate thus adjudged is not transferred, nor is the adjudicatory put into possession of it. Neither is he obliged, *pendente hac conditione*, to pay the price.

If higher bidders appear, and the adjudicatory saving a fortnight, bidding over them, still remains the adjudicatory; in this case, the first adjudication, made to him, does not subsist, but is destroyed, *defectu conditionis*, by the offers which are received; the last only subsists, and it is in virtue thereof, that he is the buyer, and becomes the proprietor of the estate. This doctrine is implied in the law 6, § 1, D. *de in diem addict.* (18, 2, 6, § 1).

520. It is to be observed, that, in sales which are called *addictio in diem*, it is sufficient for the first buyer to offer as much as the party who bids over him, in order to be preferred in the second sale, as we have seen, *supra*, n. 453; but in our *adjudications saving*, it is necessary, that the adjudicatory, who is overbid, should himself overbid the other.

521. There is a more essential difference between the *adjudication saving* and the *addictio in diem* of the Roman

law. By the Roman law, if no higher bidder appeared, within the time limited by the agreement, the magistrate did not adjudge the thing sold to the buyer anew; the first sale was of full right confirmed; and the seller could not, without a breach of his engagement, sell the thing to a higher bidder. On the contrary, according to our usages, upon the last day of the fortnight, the estate is cried anew, and if no higher bidder appears, he, who pursues the sale, may obtain from the judge a new delay, which does not deprive the adjudicatory of his right as such, but gives him a right to demand a discharge from his offer or adjudication.

522. When, in default of a higher bidder, the estate is adjudged unconditionally to him, to whom it has already been adjudged saving a fortnight, this new adjudication is only a confirmation of the first, in virtue of which the adjudicatory will acquire the estate. These adjudications saving a fortnight are very different from a simple offer; which is not a sale, but a mere promise, or engagement, by which the bidder does not actually purchase, but engages to purchase, in case his offer is not covered; and therefore the thing bid upon is not at his risk; *supra*, n. 402. On the contrary, the adjudication saving is a sale, not, in truth, pure and simple, but suspended by a condition; and the thing is at the risk of the adjudicatory.

523. The engagement, contracted by a simple offer,—and that, which results from an adjudication saving, have this in common, that they are both dissolved of full right, as soon as another offer is accepted by the judge. This takes place, even when he who covers the first offer is unable to pay; for it is not the less true that there is an offer accepted, and, consequently, that the condition, upon which the preceding bidder contracted, has failed, namely, that no higher bidder should appear. It would be otherwise, if the offer were null, through defect of form, or by reason of incapacity in the bidder to contract; as when the bidder is a woman, who

makes an offer without being authorized by her husband, or a minor, without the authority of his tutor; such offers, though accepted by the judge through error, do not discharge the preceding bidder; for an offer which is null is not an offer.

524. This rule, that the bidder is of full right discharged by another offer accepted by the judge, is subject to exceptions. For example, by the ordinance concerning waters and forests, a bidder, and even an adjudicatory, may, within twenty-four hours, by paying the sum, in which his bid exceeds the preceding, renounce his offer or adjudication, and remit the adjudication to the preceding bidder, notifying him within the said time; and the latter may do the same thing in regard to his predecessor, and *sic deinceps* to the first bidder. From which it follows, that, in the courts of waters and forests, a bidder is not of full right discharged by an offer made above him. By the ordinance of 1681, concerning the farms of the king, it is provided, that, if the adjudicatory do not give a sufficient surety, within the time prescribed, the adjudication may be made to the preceding bidder; and this also furnishes an exception to the principle above stated.

CHAPTER III.

OF THE SALE OF RIGHTS OF SUCCESSION, AND OF OTHER RIGHTS ATTACHED TO THE PERSON OF THE SELLER.

525. The inheritance of a person deceased may be sold either in whole or in part.

§ I. What inheritance may be sold.

526. It is necessary, that the person, whose inheritance is sold, should have existed and should be dead; for there can be no inheritance of a man, who never existed, or who

is yet living; D. 18, 4, 1 & 7. And, therefore, if one, by error, sells the inheritance of his relative, whom he believes to be dead, but who is in fact living, the sale is null and produces no obligation on either party; D. 18, 4, 1. If the buyer, in such case, pays the price, by error, he is entitled to a repetition of it *condictione sine causa;* for it is paid without cause, since there is no sale. He is also entitled to a repetition of the expenses of making such false sale; for the seller, who leads him into error, by selling what is not in existence, ought to repair the wrong which is thereby occasioned. All this is conformable to the law 8, D. *de hæred. vend.* (18, 4, 8).

527. Can the future inheritance of a person be sold? The reason for doubting is, that it is established in the first part of this treatise, n. 5, that we may sell things whose future existence we expect, as when we sell, before harvest, the wine which we may make; and the question is to be decided in the negative, for the reason, that the rule stated admits of an exception in regard to things, which, it is contrary to decency and good manners to expect; as a future inheritance, which we cannot expect, but by expecting the death of the person, which is necessary to give an opening to it, which good manners do not permit. Our decision agrees with that of the Roman jurisconsults, who condemned, as contrary to good manners, all kinds of agreements concerning future successions; C. 2, 3, 19 *et fin.* According to the Roman laws, these agreements were forbidden, even in contracts of marriage; C. 2, 3, 15. In our law, the favor, with which it regards the latter contracts, permits these agreements to be inserted in them; but they are not allowed in others. See the Tr. on Obl. n. 132.

528. The sale of an inheritance is not valid, if it does not yet exist. But it is not necessary to the validity of a sale, that the inheritance should belong to the seller; for, according to the principles established in the first part of this

treatise, n. 7, the sale, which one person makes of a thing belonging to another, is valid; *res aliena vendi potest.* It is for this reason, that he, who sells rights of succession, which do not belong to him, as, for instance, because he is not within the proper degree to succeed, or is not the heir, except for a small part, of what he sells, contracts a valid engagement, and is obliged to cause the buyer to have the value of the inheritance, that is to say, all that he would have had, if it had really belonged to him; D. 18, 4, 8.

529. If one does not sell precisely the inheritance of a person, but only his claims to it, to be exercised by the buyer at his own risk, and without warranty to the buyer, that the inheritance really belongs to him; in this case, if it is adjudged, against the buyer, that the inheritance did not belong to his assignor, the latter will not be liable to any thing in favor of the buyer, not even to a restitution of the price; for it is not, in strictness, the inheritance which is sold, but the claims of the seller, such as they are, well or ill founded; *non hæreditas, sed incertum hæreditatis veniit;* it is a chance, which makes the object of the contract, as when one purchases the cast of his net of a fisherman; D. 18, 4, 10 & 11.

If however the seller sells his claims, with a knowledge that they are ill founded, though with an express declaration, that he does not intend to warrant that the inheritance belongs to him, he will be liable, on account of his deceit, to a restitution of the price; and he ought besides to indemnify the buyer for his expenses; D. 18, 4, 12.

§ II. What is included in the sale of an inheritance.

430. When one sells an inheritance, it is not the title and quality of heir which he sells; this title and quality are attached to the person of the heir, and cannot be separated from it; from which it follows, that they cannot be sold; for as no person can oblige himself to do what is impossible,

I cannot engage, in favor of another person, to cause him to have a thing, which, by its nature, cannot subsist in any other than my own person.

What is sold, when we sell the inheritance of a person deceased? We sell all that has accrued or may accrue from it. When I sell my rights in the inheritance of any one, I sell all the emolument, which I have already received, and all that I may receive from it; in a word, every thing to which it is entitled, upon condition that the buyer discharge me from and indemnify me against all the debts and charges to which the inheritance is subject.

From these principles, it follows, that the heir, who sells his rights of succession, does not the less remain the heir, and that he is not, by this sale, discharged from the engagements, contracted on his part, by accepting the succession; he remains, consequently, obliged in favor of the creditors of the succession, and in favor of legatees, and he may be pursued by both, saving his recourse against the buyer, who is bound to indemnify him; C. 4, 18, 2.

§ III. What are the engagements of the seller.

531. The sale of rights of succession or of an inheritance, according to the principles established in the preceding paragraph, comprising all that has accrued or may accrue therefrom, that is to say, all the emolument, which the seller has already received, or may afterwards receive, from the succession; it follows, that his engagement requires him to deliver to the buyer every thing which he has derived from the succession, not only those things which existed at the time of the falling thereof, and belonged to the deceased, but also every thing since born and accrued from those things, that is to say, every thing which has been exacted of debtors, and all the fruits, natural and civil, which the heir who is the seller has derived from the things belonging to the succession. This is the decision of Ulpian, in the law

2, § 1, D. *de hæred. vend.* (18, 4, 2, § 1). *In hæreditate vendita utrum ea quantitas spectatur, quæ fuit mortis tempore, an ea quæ fuit, quum aditur hæreditas, an ea quæ fuit quum hæreditas venundaretur, videndum erit? Et verius est hoc esse servandum quod actum est; plerumque autem hoc agi videtur, ut quod ex hæreditate pervenit in id tempus, quo venditio fit, id videatur venisse.*

532. The seller contracting an engagement to deliver to the buyer all the things in his possession, accruing from the succession, at the time of the contract of sale, it follows, that he is obliged to preserve all these things for him. He cannot, therefore, dispose of them, without contravening his engagements; yet, as the heir, who sells his rights of succession, remains the proprietor of the things belonging to it, until he delivers them to the buyer; if he disposes of them, contrary to the faith of his engagement, he transfers the property to those for whose benefit he alienates them, but he remains the debtor of the buyer of his rights of succession, in the same manner precisely, as if he had not otherwise disposed of the things belonging to it; and, in default of being able to deliver them, in consequence of the disposition he has made of them, he will be condemned in favor of the buyer, for his damages and interests; C. 4, 18, 6.

533. If the thing, which the seller sells to a third person, subsequent to a contract of sale of his rights of succession, afterwards perishes by accident, can the buyer of the rights of succession claim the price, which the heir receives of such third person? The reason for doubting is drawn from the principle above established, that the heir, who sells the thing, remains the debtor of it, as before the sale, since he cannot, in selling, change his obligation by his own act. The buyer of the rights of succession, being therefore the creditor of the thing, rather than of the price, it would seem that his credit ought to be extinguished by the extinction of the thing, according to the principle, *obligatio extingui-*

tur rei debitæ interitu. Such are the reasons for doubting, which Paul proposes, and notwithstanding which, he decides, that the buyer of rights of succession may, in this case, demand the price, for which the thing perished is sold. The reason is, that he, in truth, remains the creditor of the thing itself, notwithstanding the sale made of it by the heir; and he is also a creditor of the price, in such a manner, however, that he cannot exact both the thing and the price. Why is this? It is, that the heir is the debtor, in favor of the buyer of his rights of succession, of all that he acquires as heir: now, it is as heir, that he sells the thing and receives the price of it; and he is therefore the debtor of the price to the buyer.

In this respect, the seller of rights of succession is different from the seller of particular things; for if you sell me a particular thing, which you afterwards, contrary to the faith of the contract of sale, sell and deliver to a third person, and the thing perishes by accident, you are entirely discharged from your obligation, and I cannot demand the price received by you of the second buyer; for there was nothing due to me but the thing itself.

It is to be observed, that, on your part, you cannot demand the price, for which you sell me the thing, and that I am even entitled to reclaim it, if it is already paid; for, being under an obligation to pay you, only so far as you are faithful, on your part, to your engagement, and that being contravened, by the sale made to another of the thing previously sold to me, you thereby discharge me from my engagement.

534. It remains to be observed, that, in regard to things which are found amongst the effects of the succession, at the time of the sale made by the heir of his rights of succession, he warrants only against his own acts, in relation to the said things; for, in selling the inheritance, he sells these things only so far as and in the manner that they belong to the inheritance. This is the decision of the law

2, D. *dict. tit.* (18, 4, 2). *Venditor hæreditatis satisdare de evictione non debet; quum id inter ementem et vendentem agatur, ut nec amplius nec minus juris emptor habeat, quam apud hæredem futurum esset: plane de facto suo venditor satisdare cogendus est.*

535. We have seen how far the engagement of the seller of rights of succession extends, in reference to things which exist at the time of the contract of sale. In regard to things, which do not exist at that time, we must distinguish between those, which he has disposed of or which he has consumed by use, and those which are destroyed. As to those, which he has disposed of, if he has sold them, there is no doubt, that he ought to allow the buyer the price; for he ought to account to the buyer for all the profit, which he derives from the succession. He ought also to account to the buyer, for the value of things, which he has disposed of by donation, and of those which he has consumed by use: *Rerum ante venditionem donatarum prætia præstari æquitatis ratio exigit;* D. 18, 4, 2, § 3. The reason is, that he ought to account to the buyer, for every thing, which accrues to him from the succession: *Hoc agi videtur, ut quod ex hereditate pervenit in id tempus quo venditio fit, id videatur venisse;* D. 18, 4, 2, § 1. Now these things accrued to him, though he ultimately disposed of or consumed them. In regard to those, which perish before the sale, the heir is not liable for them to the buyer; for the loss of effects belonging to the succession ought to fall upon the buyer; the loss as well as the profit concerns him. We ought not to distinguish, in this case, whether the things perish with or without the fault of the heir; for, as he is the proprietor of the things, and does not then owe them to any person, he is not obliged to take any care of them, and consequently cannot commit any fraud in respect to them.

536. If the heir, though before the sale of his rights of succession, has accepted the succession of some one of the

debtors of the inheritance which he has sold, though this debt was extinguished, at the time of the contract of sale, by the confusion which was thereby made of it, the heir is not discharged from his liability to account for this debt to the buyer; for he is considered to have received payment of it, by the succession of the debtor, which he has accepted: *Aditio hæreditatis pro solutione cedit;* D. 46, 3, 95, § 2. This takes place, even when the debtor, whose succession has been imprudently accepted, died insolvent; for every succession is considered to be solvent, when it is accepted: *Solvendo hæreditas est, quæ inveniat hæredem;* D. 38, 6, 36.

537. In regard to the active debts of the succession, which are not yet paid, the heir, who sells the succession, is liable to nothing more in favor of the buyer, than to remit to him the titles of the said debts, in order that the buyer may obtain payment of them at his own risk, as the assignee of the heir, by notifying the debtors of the assignment to him. The heir is not liable to the buyer for the insolvency of the debtors, except when a debtor becomes insolvent, after the heir is put in delay to deliver the buyer the titles necessary to enable him to obtain payment, and such delay of the heir prevents the buyer from procuring payment, while the debtor is yet solvent.

538. If the heir is the debtor in favor of the deceased, whose inheritance he sells, ought he to account to the buyer of his rights of succession, for the debt due by him to the deceased? Yes; it is so decided in the law, 20, § 1, D. *de hæred. vend.* (18, 4, 20, § 1). The reason is, that he ought to account for all that accrues to him from the succession; now the discharge of his debt is an emolument, which accrues to him from the succession, since it is the succession which procures it. Mornac, *ad. dict. l.*, is nevertheless, but improperly, of the contrary opinion. For the same reason, if the estate of the heir is subject to a right of servitude in favor of the estate of the deceased, the heir

ought to re-establish the right, which is confused and extinguished, by his acceptance of the succession; for he ought to account to the buyer, for all the profit, which accrues to him from the succession; now the discharge from the servitude is a profit, which accrues to him from the succession, and which he cannot better account for to the buyer, than by re-establishing the right as before.

539. If the heir receives a sum of money of a person, who is falsely persuaded that he owes it to the succession, whether he receives it before or after the contract of sale, he is not obliged to account for it to the buyer; for, though the sum accrues to the heir, by means of the succession, yet it does not accrue to him from the succession, to which it was not due; he receives it rather from the error of him who paid it than from the succession. This is the decision of the law 2, § 7, D. *de hæred. vend.* (18, 4, 2, § 7), in which it is said, *hoc servari, ut hæres emptori non præstet, quod non debitum exegerit.* Observe, that this decision does not hold *in praxi*, except when the heir, having discovered the error, repays the sum to the party who has unduly paid it. If he retains it, he cannot be allowed to maintain that it was not due to the succession; for, if so, we may ask him, why then do you retain it?

540. It happens sometimes that an heir, in the sale of his rights of succession, reserves certain of the effects, as, for example, an estate. There is no doubt, that the buyer cannot demand the effect or the estate, which is excepted, nor the fruits, which the heir receives after the contract of sale; but can he demand those which are received previously? Labeo (D. 18, 4, 25) decides that he can. The reason is, that these fruits, by their perception, acquire an existence distinct and separate from the estate, out of which they are gathered; and, consequently, they are not included in the exception of the estate, of which they cease to be a part.

§ IV. What are the engagements of the buyer.

541. The buyer of rights of succession is obliged to pay the price agreed by the assignment. Besides this, he is obliged to indemnify the heir, from whom he purchases, for all the expenses incurred, and for all that may be incurred, by reason of the succession; for example, for the expenses of the funeral, payments made to the creditors of the succession, and to legatees, for the hundredth penny, for the profits, repairs, &c. He is not only obliged to reimburse all these expenses, but he is obliged to exhibit and report to him a quittance or discharge from the creditors of the succession, towards whom, the heir, as already observed, remains liable, notwithstanding the sale of his rights of succession. The time, within which he ought to report this discharge, is in the discretion of the judge, to be regulated by circumstances.

542. If the heir, either before or after the contract, becomes the heir of some one of the creditors of the succession, or of some one of the legatees, the buyer ought to pay him such debt or legacies. So decides Labeo (D. 18, 4, 24). The reason is, that by accepting the succession of a creditor of the succession which I sell you, I pay the debt of the latter at my own expense. This may be made clear by an example. I sell you my rights of succession in the succession of Peter; and I become the heir of James a creditor of Peter, in the sum of 10,000 livres. James, at the time of his death, has 100,000 livres of property, including this credit of 10,000 livres. In becoming the heir of James, there results a confusion and extinction of this debt of 10,000 livres, which I owe as the heir of Peter, to the succession of James, of which I also become the heir. By means of this confusion, I find no more than 90,000 livres in the succession of James, instead of the 100,000, which I should find, if I were not the heir of Peter, and if there were no confusion of this

debt. The confusion and extinction of this debt therefore cost me 10,000 livres, and consequently the buyer of my rights in the succession of Peter, who receives the benefit of this extinction, ought to reimburse me that sum.

543. When the heir is the creditor of the deceased, whose inheritance he sells, the buyer ought, in like manner, to make him an allowance for his credit, which is confused and extinguished, by accepting the inheritance; for he ought to remunerate him for all that the succession costs him. Now it costs him the extinction of this credit; D. 18, 4, 2, § 18. Mornac, *ad. h.* §, however, is of the contrary opinion; but he is wrong. It is otherwise, when the debt of the deceased is one, for which he is liable only during his life, as where he is a surety for some one, upon the condition that his liability as such shall extend only during his life; the creditor of such a debt, who becomes the heir of his debtor, is not entitled to a reimbursement of it, from the buyer of his rights of succession; for it is the death of his debtor, and not the acceptance of the inheritance, which extinguishes his debt.

544. If an estate, belonging to the succession, is subject to a servitude, in favor of an estate belonging to the heir, the buyer of his rights of succession, to whom the first estate is delivered, ought to re-establish the servitude; D. 18, 4, 2, § 19; D. 8, 4, 9; for as the heir loses it, by the confusion resulting from his acceptance of the inheritance, he is entitled to receive an indemnification for it from the buyer, who is bound to indemnify him for all that his character of heir costs him.

545. If the heir pays what he is falsely persuaded to be due from the succession, he is not entitled to a repetition of it against the buyer of his rights of succession. This is the decision of the law 2, § 7, D. *de hæred. vend.* (18, 4, 2, § 7). *Hoc servari, ut hæres emptori non præstet quod non debitum exegerit, neque ab eo consequatur, quod non debitum*

præstiterit. Nevertheless, if he is condemned by a sentence, in his quality of heir, to pay a sum, the buyer is obliged to reimburse him, though the condemnation is improper, and the sum is not in fact due; for he ought to be indemnified for all that his quality of heir costs him; and the buyer cannot object, as in the preceding case, that the money is paid by the heir in his own wrong, since being condemned, he cannot avoid payment. This is decided in the said law 2, § 7, above cited: *Si condemnatus præstiterit, hoc solum hæredi sufficit, esse eum condemnatum sine dolo malo suo, etiamsi maxime creditor non fuerit is, cui condemnatus est hæres.* This decision holds, especially, when the condemnation intervenes previous to the contract of sale; when the heir is not summoned until afterwards, he ought to put the buyer into the cause.

§ V. If, after the assignment, which an heir in part makes of his rights of succession, his coheir renounces the succession, does the part of the latter accrue, as well for profit as to charges, to the assignor, or to the assignee?

546. This question is difficult, and much controverted among the doctors. Bartolus, *ad. l. re conjuncti*, Duaren, *Tract. de jure acer.* 16, 6, and some others, hold in favor of the assignee. Their reasons are, first, that he, who sells a thing, sells every thing that makes a part of, and is a natural and essential dependance upon it. Now when I accept a succession, which is conferred upon me in part, the right of succession, which I acquire by my acceptance, includes the right of having the portion of my coheir by accretion, in case he repudiates the succession. This right of accretion makes a part of my right of succession, and is a natural and inseparable dependance upon it; it ought therefore to be considered as comprised in the sale, which I make of my right of succession.

There is so much the more reason for deciding the question thus, that the portion of my coheir, which accrues to me by his renunciation, is considered to be acquired to me, not only from the time of his renunciation, but from the instant of the death of the deceased, who, by means of this renunciation, is considered to have invested me alone with the entire succession. And, therefore, this part, which accrues to me by the renunciation of my coheir, already belonged to me, at the time of the sale, which I make of my right of succession; we cannot doubt, therefore, that it then made a part of it, and consequently that it is comprised in the sale.

Second. It is a principle established, *supra*, § 3, that he, who sells his right of succession, is bound to account to the buyer, generally, for every thing which afterwards accrues to him, by virtue of the right of succession so sold: *Non solum quod jam pervenit, sed et quod quandoque pervenerit restituendum est;* D. 18, 4, 2, § 4. Now, it is in virtue of the right of succession, which I sell, that the part of my coheir, who renounces, comes to me, by right of accretion; and the buyer is therefore well founded in requiring me to account for it to him.

It is also a principle established, *supra*, § 4, that he, who sells his right in a succession, is entitled to be acquitted by the buyer, generally, from all that he may afterwards be obliged to pay, in reference to the succession: *Si quid venditor nondum præstiterit, sed quoquo nomine obligatus sit propter hæreditatem, nihilominus agere potest cum emptore;* D. 18, 4, 2, § 20. Therefore, when I sell my right of succession, I am well founded to demand that the buyer shall acquit me from the debts of the succession, not only for the part, which first came to me, but also for the part, which accrues to me by the renunciation of my coheir in the succession, offering, on my part, to abandon to the buyer all that accrues to me from that part.

Third. It is a principle, that, in successions and in legacies of the property of a thing, the portion of the coheir or colegatee, who renounces, accrues to the portion of him who accepts, rather than to his person; different from the legacy of a usufruct, in which the accretion is made to the person of the legateee: *Portio fundi* (*legati*) *velut alluvio portioni, personæ fructus accrescit;* D. 7, 1, 33, § 1. Therefore, when I sell my right of succession, the accretion of the part of my coheir, who renounces, ought to be made to the buyer, with whom is found the part to which it ought to accrue. This argument appears to Duaren a demonstration, against which, in his opinion, nothing reasonable can be opposed. It is in vain, says he, to object, that he, who sells his right of succession, still remains the heir; that he is even considered as still preserving the hereditary portion which he sells; since he has the price of it paid to him by the buyer; this price represents the thing, in such a manner, that it is said in the law, 4, D. § *fin. si quis omissa caus. test.* (29, 4, 4, § *fin.*) *Si quis vendiderit hæreditatem, utique possidere videtur;* for the jurisconsult, having compared this accretion to the natural accretion of an alluvion, shows clearly enough, that it ought to be made, not to the seller, with whom the part, to which the part of the coheir who renounces ought to accrue, is considered to be, *fictione quadam et interpretatione juris*, but to the buyer, with whom, this portion is really and actually found to be. We cannot refuse, to a buyer of rights of succession, a natural accretion, which is made by alluvion, to an estate belonging to the succession; neither ought we to refuse him the accretion of the part of the coheir, who renounces, since the jurisconsult says these accretions have the same effect.

In order to confirm more and more his principle, that it is not to him, who preserves only the title of heir, but to him, to whom the rights of succession of this heir are really conveyed, that the portion of the coheir, who renounces, ought to accrue, Duaren refers to the case of an heir, who is constrained by the prætor to accept a succession, at the risk of a fidei-commissary, in whose favor he is charged to restore the portion for which he is instituted. The law, 34, D. *ad senat. cons. Trebell.* (36, 1, 43), supposes it to be the established doctrine, that the part of a coheir renouncing accrues to the fidei-commissary. He also alleges the case of an heir, whose rights of succession are confiscated, on account of his unworthiness; it is not to him, though he preserves the title of heir, but to the treasury, that the part of his coheir, who repudiates the succession, accrues; D. 29, 2, 83.

The contrary opinion has been embraced by Cujas, *Obs.* xii. 13, and followed by many other doctors cited by Fachineus, *controv.* 5, 101. The principal reason, upon which it is founded, is, that every bargain and every agreement includes only those things, which the contracting parties have in view, and concerning which, it is probable they have an intention to treat; D. 2, 15, 9, § 1. Now, when an heir in part sells his rights of succession, before his coheir renounces, it is probable, that the contracting parties do not intend to treat for any thing more than the portion, which the seller then appears to have in the succession. This is evident, especially, when the contract of sale imports that the heir sells *his part* in the succession of such an one; for these terms, *his part*, make it appear plainly enough, that the parties did not intend to treat but for one *part*, namely, that which the seller has in his own right in the succession; and that they do not intend to treat for the whole of the succession, though it may happen, that, by the renunciation of his coheir, the entire succession will ultimately belong to the seller.

Even when they do not use, in the contract of sale, the term *part*, but it is said, in general terms, that the heir sells *his rights in the succession of such an one;* even in this case, it is probable, that the parties regard only the part, which the heir appears to have in the succession, at the time of the contract of sale, which he makes of his rights of succession, and not that which accrues by the renunciation of his coheir; for the parties not being able to conjecture, at the time of the contract, that the coheir will afterwards renounce the succession, not expecting this renunciation, and not foreseeing it, it follows, that they treat only for the part, which the heir then has, and not for that which afterwards falls to him, by the renunciation of his coheir; *Neque enim pacto continetur, id de quo cogitatum non docetur:* D. 2, 15, 9, § *fin.*

In regard to the reasons alleged in favor of the other opinion, they answer to the first, by saying: I agree, that the renunciation of my coheir has a retroactive effect; that I am considered to be seized, from the time of the death of the deceased, of the part which accrues to me by his renunciation; and that consequently it makes a part of my right of succession, at the time of the contract of sale, which I make of it; but it does not follow, from this, that I sell this part; for it makes a part of my right of succession, without my knowing it, at the time; and I intend to sell only that which I know I have, and not that which I have without knowing it.

They answer to the second reason, that the law objected, which says: *Quod quandoque pervenerit restituendum est,* is to be understood, *de eo quod pervenerit ex ea hæreditatis parte quæ veniit.* In like manner, what is said concerning the obligation of the buyer of rights of succession to indemnify the seller, *Si quoquo nomine obligatus sit propter hæreditatem,* must be understood, *propter eam hæreditatis partem quæ veniit.*

To the third reason, they answer, that when one sells his right of succession, or his part in a succession, it is not so much the right itself, as the emolument, which has already accrued, or may afterwards accrue from it, that he sells, subject to the charge of an indemnification by the buyer; for this right of succession being attached to the person of the heir, and being so inseparable from it, that, notwithstanding the sale, he always remains the heir, and, in that quality, liable to the creditors of the succession, it follows, that the right in itself cannot pass to the buyer. From which it also follows, that, according to the maxim, *Portio repudiantis portioni accrescit*, the accretion of the portion of the coheir renouncing ought to be made to the heir who sells, in whom, notwithstanding the sale, his part in the succession remains, and not to the buyer, who has it not.

In regard to the objection drawn from the supposed analogy between this and the case of a usufruct, mentioned in the law 33, D. *de usufr.* (D. 7, 1, 33, § 1), they answer, that analogies, especially in law, are not ordinarily sufficient. The jurisconsult intends to remark a difference between the accretion, which takes place between coheirs or colegatees in property, and colegatees in a usufruct. The accretion in the latter case is made *personæ;* though a legatee loses his part in the usufruct bequeathed, he is not thereby prevented from being admitted to the accretion of the portions, which afterwards fall in, because this accretion is made *personæ;* whereas between coheirs and colegatees in property, the accretion is made *rei.* And, therefore, if, after I renounce a succession, one of my coheirs renounce it, his part accrues only to those of my coheirs, who have accepted; it does not accrue to me, who have repudiated my own, because the accretion is made *rei,* like an accretion made by alluvion; so far the analogy holds good. But, in other respects, these accretions are different. The accretion of an alluvion is a physical accretion, which can be made only to a real being; but the accretion of the part of a coheir, who renounces, is a civil and moral accretion, which is made to a civil and moral being, such as is my part in the succession, which is considered to remain in me, notwithstanding the sale which I make of my right.

In regard to the objection drawn from the law, 43, D. *ad. senat. cons. Trebell.* (36, 1, 43), which refers to the case of an heir, constrained by the prætor to accept a succession, Cujas answers, that if the heir, in this case, as to the part, in which he is instituted at the risk of the fidei-commissary, in whose favor he is charged to restore it, is deprived of the part, which accrues by the renunciation, it is by a peculiar reason, founded upon this, that having contemned the honor, which the deceased had done him, in appointing him his heir, he ought not to retain any thing in the succession, and ought to restore the whole to the fidei-commissary. But this decision ought not to be drawn into precedent; and Cujas maintains, that if the heir had voluntarily accepted, and had restored, *ex Trebell. senatus-consulto*, the part in which he had been instituted, and which he was charged to restore, the decision would have been otherwise. Cujas answers, in the same manner, the objection drawn from the case of the unworthy heir, that it is by a particular reason drawn from his unworthiness, that he is not allowed to enjoy the right of accretion.

ARTICLE II.

Of the sale of a right of usufruct, and of other rights attached to the person of the seller.

547. The right of usufruct of a thing may be sold; 1, by the proprietor of the thing; 2, by the usufructuary to the proprietor; and, 3, by the usufructuary to a third person.

§ I. By the proprietor of the thing.

548. There is no doubt, that the proprietor of a thing may sell to any one the usufruct of it, and may dispose of it by whatever title he pleases. How, it may be asked, can this be done? for a usufruct, according to the definition given of it, being the right of enjoying the thing of another, *jus*

utendi, fruendi re aliena, this right cannot subsist in the person of the proprietor. How then, can he sell and dispose of that which he has not? The answer is, that the right of usufruct, considered in its form of a right of servitude, cannot, in truth, subsist in the person of the proprietor; but the foundation and substance of this right, which consists in that of enjoying the thing, and receiving the fruits of it, subsist in the person of the proprietor, and are included in his right of property, so long as it is not yet detached from it. When therefore the proprietor disposes of the right of usufruct in favor of any one, he disposes of a right, which he really has. It does not, in fact, exist in him, in the form of a right of usufruct, *non habet usumfructum formalem;* but under another form, as included in his right of property, *habet usumfructum causalem.* When he sells the usufruct of a thing, it is the right which he has to receive the fruits of the thing, which he sells, and which he detaches from his right of property; and this right, by its separation from the right of property, takes the form of a right of usufruct; it becomes *jus fruendi re aliena*, and passes under this form to the acquirer.

§ II. By the usufructuary to the proprietor.

549. When the usufructuary sells his right of usufruct to the proprietor, he thereby makes a release of his right, which operates as an extinction and a reunion of it to the property from which it was separated; the proprietor, who repurchases the usufruct, is deemed the rather to discharge his estate from the servitude, than to acquire the right of an usufruct, which cannot subsist in the person of the proprietor: *Quum res sua nemini servire possit, adeoque nemo possit usumfructum rei suæ habere.*

§ III. By the usufructuary to a third person.

550. A usufructuary may also sell his right of usufruct to a third person; but this sale is rather of the emolument,

which the right of usufruct may produce, than of the right itself; for this right, being a right attached to the person of the usufructuary, cannot be ceded. The right of usufruct therefore subsists in the person of the usufructuary, notwithstanding the sale made of it. The buyer acquires only the emolument of this right, and the faculty of taking the fruits in the place of the usufructuary, during the existence of the usufruct, subject to the charges upon it, from which he ought to acquit the usufructuary.

From whence it follows, that a usufruct, though sold, is extinguished by the death of the usufructuary, who has sold it. On the contrary, the death of the assignee does not extinguish the usufruct, and his heirs may continue to enjoy it, as he would himself have enjoyed it, during the life of the usufructuary.

It follows, also, from these principles, that the usufructuary, by the sale made of his right, is not discharged from his obligation in favor of the proprietor, to leave the estate, of which he has the usufruct, in a good condition; it is to his succession, that the proprietor has a right to address himself, for a reparation on account of deteriorations, though occasioned by the assignee of the usufruct, saving to the succession a right of recourse against the assignee. Besides, the proprietor, *celeritate conjungendarum actionum*, may also, if he thinks proper, *omisso circuitu*, prosecute the assignee.

CHAPTER IV.

OF THE SALE OF ANNUITIES AND OTHER CREDITS.

ARTICLE FIRST.

How an annuity or other personal credit may be transferred; and of the difference between such transfer, and that of simple delegation or indication.

551. A credit being a personal right of the creditor, a right inherent in his person, it cannot, considered only ac-

cording to the subtlety of the law, be transferred to another person, nor consequently be sold. It may well pass to the heir of the creditor, because the heir is the successor of the person and of all the personal rights of the deceased; but, in strictness of law, it cannot pass to a third person; for the debtor, being obliged towards a certain person, cannot, by a transfer of the credit, which is not an act of his, become obliged towards another.

The jurisconsults have nevertheless invented a mode of transferring credits, without either the consent or the intervention of the debtor. As the creditor may exercise against his debtor, by a mandatary, as well as by himself, the action which results from his credit; when he wishes to transfer his credit to a third person, he makes such person his mandatary, to exercise his right of action against the debtor; and it is agreed between them, that the action shall be exercised by the mandatary, in the name indeed of the mandator, but at the risk and on the account of the mandatary, who shall retain for himself all that may be exacted of the debtor in consequence of the mandate, without rendering any account thereof to the mandator. Such a mandatary is called, by the jurisconsults, *procurator in rem suam*, because he exercises the mandate, not on account of the mandator but on his own.

A mandate, made in this manner, is, as to its effect, a real transfer, which the creditor makes of his credit; and if he receives nothing from the mandatary, for his consent that the latter shall retain to his own use what he may exact of the debtor, it is a donation; if, for this authority, he receives a sum of money of the mandatary, it is a sale of the credit. From which, it is established in practice, that credits may be transferred, and may be given, sold, or disposed of by any other title; and it is not even necessary, that the act, which contains the transfer, should express the mandate, in which, as has been explained, the transfer consists.

552. We must take care not to confound the transfer of assignment (*transport-cession*) which is here treated of, with the transfer of simple delegation or indication. The transfer of assignment contains a sale of the debt which is transferred; and, consequently, the insolvency of the debtor falls upon the assignee, to whom the transfer is made, as will be seen afterwards, if the assignor is not made to warrant his solvency by a special clause. The transfer of simple delegation does not contain a sale; it is a mere indication, which I make to my creditor, *unde ipsi solvam*, by pointing out to him one of my debtors, and giving him power to exact, in my name, that which the debtor owes me, to be by him received in deduction from that which I owe him. By this delegation, I continue to be the owner of the credit delegated, until it is extinguished by payment; and consequently if my debtor becomes insolvent, the loss falls on me; and my creditor, who continues to be such, until he receives payment, may cause himself to be paid out of my other goods.

553. This is a delegation of simple indication, and must not be confounded with a delegation, which is a novation, and which is made, when, in order to discharge myself from what I owe you, I delegate to you my debtor, who, in order to discharge himself from what he owes me, becomes obliged to you. By this kind of delegation, the debt, which the delegator owes to him, to whom he makes the delegation, and that which the debtor delegated owes to the delegator, are entirely extinguished; and, in the place of them, a new debt, on the part of the debtor delegated, is contracted in favor of him, to whom the delegation is made. It is evident, that this delegation is entirely different from that of simple indication. It is also different from a transfer of assignment; for in the latter there is no novation; it is the old debt, which was due to the assignor, which subsists, and which is transferred from the person of the assignor, *non quidem ex juris subtilitate, sed juris effectu*, to the person of the assignee.

554. The transfer of assignment is also very different from a subrogation, as will be seen in the treatise on that subject.

ARTICLE II.

Of the effect of the transfer, and of the notice which ought to be given of it.

555. The transfer of an annuity or other credit, before notice of it is given to the debtor, is what the sale of a corporeal thing is, before the delivery; in the same manner, that the seller of a corporeal thing, until a delivery, remains the possessor and proprietor of it, as has been established in another place; so, until the assignee notifies the debtor of the assignment made to him, the assignor is not divested of the credit, which he assigns. This is the provision of art. 108, of the custom of Paris: "a simple transfer does not divest, and it is necessary to notify the party of the transfer, and to furnish him with a copy of it."

556. From which, it follows, first, that before notice, the debtor may legally pay to the assignor his creditor; and the assignee has no action, in such case, except against the assignor, namely, the action *ex empto, ut præstet ipsi habere licere;* and, consequently, that he should remit to him the sum, which he is no longer able to exact of the debtor, who has legally paid the debt to the assignor.

557. Second, that before notice, the creditors of the assignor may seize and arrest that which is due from the debtor whose debt is assigned; and they are preferred to the assignee, who has not, before such seizure and arrest, given notice of the assignment to him; the assignee, in this case, is only entitled to his action against the assignor, namely, the action *ex empto*, in order that the latter *præstet ipsi habere licere;* and, consequently, that he should report to him a removal of the seizures and arrests, or pay him the sum, which, by reason thereof, he is prevented from obtaining of the debtor.

558. Third, that if the assignor, after having transferred a credit to a first assignee, has the bad faith to make a transfer of it to a second, who is more diligent than the first, to give notice of his assignment to the debtor, the second assignee will be preferred to the first, saving to the first his recourse against the assignor.

559. Though the assignee notifies the debtor of the assignment to him, the assignor, in strictness of law, remains the creditor, notwithstanding the transfer and notice; and the credit continues to be in him. This results from the principles established in the preceding article; but, *quoad juris effectus*, the assignor is considered, by the notice of the transfer given to the debtor, to be devested of the credit which he assigns; and is no longer regarded as the owner of it; the assignee is considered to be so; and therefore the debtor cannot afterwards legally pay the assignor; and the creditors of the assignor cannot, from that time, seize and arrest the credit, because it is no longer considered to belong to their debtor.

Nevertheless, as the assignee, even after notice of the transfer, is only the mandatary, though *in rem suam*, of the assignor, in whose person, the credit, in truth, resides; the debtor may oppose to the assignee a compensation of what the assignor was indebted to him, before the notice of the assignment; which however does not prevent him from opposing also a compensation of what the assignee himself owes him; the assignee being himself, *non quidem ex juris subtilitate, sed juris effectus, creditor.*

ARTICLE III.

In what consists the obligation of the seller, who transfers an annuity or other credit.

§ I. Different kinds of warranty.

560. The obligation of the seller of an annuity or other credit consists in a delivery of the titles to it, and in a war-

ranty of it. We distinguish two kinds of warranty of annuities and other credits; namely, warranty of law, and warranty of fact. The warranty of law is so called, because the seller is liable to it, of full right, without any agreement, and by the nature itself of the contract; it consists in an undertaking that the credit sold is actually due to the seller, and in defending the buyer against the demands of those who revendicate the property against him, or who claim any hypothecary rights in it. The warranty of fact is so called, because the seller is not liable to it of full right, and by the nature itself of the contract, but only when he obliges himself *of fact*, and by a particular clause of the contract. There are three kinds of this warranty; the warranty of fact simply so called; the warranty to furnish and make valuable; and the warranty to make valuable after a simple command.

§ II. Of the warranty of fact simply so called.

561. The warranty of fact, simply so called, is that by which the seller promises that the credit is good and that the debtor is solvent. This warranty is of fact; for, of law, if the parties are silent, the seller is not liable to it; he sells the credit such as it is, good or bad: *Si nomen sit distractum, Celsus scribit locupletem esse debitorem, non debere præstare;* D. 18, 4, 4. *Qui nomen, quale fuit, vendidit, duntaxat ut sit, non etiam ut exigi aliquid possit, et dolum præstare cogitur;* D. 21, 2, 74, § *fin.*

562. It is a question, whether this warranty of fact ought to be considered as stipulated, when the seller promises *to warrant against all troubles and hindrances whatsoever.* The reason for doubting is, that this clause may be understood of the warranty of law, which consists in defending the buyer against demands in revendication, hypothecary, and other similar demands, on the part of third persons, who pretend that the thing belonged or was hypothecated to them. Loy-

seau nevertheless decides, that this clause includes a warranty of fact as well as of law. The reason is, that general terms, made use of in an agreement, ought to include all the particulars comprised under the generality of the terms; now these terms, *all troubles and hindrances whatsoever*, are general and comprise both those troubles which are brought upon the possession of the annuity sold by third persons, and that which is brought upon its payment, by the insolvency of the debtor.

563. The seller, by this clause, promises nothing more than the present solvency of the debtor, and does not make himself a warrantor against any future insolvency, which may arise subsequent to the contract; for the thing sold ought to be at the risk of the buyer after the contract, unless the contrary is expressly agreed.

§ III. Of the warranty resulting from the clause to furnish and make valuable.

564. The second kind of warranty of fact is that which results from the clause *to furnish and make valuable*, by which the seller of an annuity or other credit is under an obligation *to furnish it, and make it of value, that the debtor is solvent, and that the annuity shall be duly paid.*

There have been different opinions concerning the interpretation of this clause, as well as the preceding. Some have pretended, that the preceding included only the ordinary warranty of law, and that by this the seller promised only the present, but did not make himself responsible for the future solvency of the debtor. On the contrary, Loyseau decides, that the preceding clause includes the warranty of fact, by which the seller promises the present solvency of the debtor, and that by this clause, he promises not only that the debtor is solvent at the time of the contract, but that he shall continue to be so, during the existence of the annuity; that is to say, by this clause, he makes himself the surety, and renders himself responsible for the perpetual solvency of, the debtor of the annuity. Loyseau establishes his opinion, by inquiring into the proper signification of the terms, *to furnish* and *to make valuable*. *To furnish*, says he, is to supply, to complete that which is wanting; as when we say, to furnish a company of soldiers, to furnish materials for a building, &c. Therefore, *to furnish an annuity*, is to supply and to make up what the debtor cannot pay; it is to make himself a surety for the annuity. In like manner, the terms, *to make valuable*, signify, *in se recipere*, to *take upon one's self*, to be responsible that the annuity shall be paid, so long as it shall endure. Loyseau also draws an argument from the terms, *promises to furnish and make valuable*. The infinitives, says he, do not of themselves denote any time, but must be referred, for their time, to the verb which governs them. Now the verb, *to promise*, which, in this phrase, governs the infinitives *to furnish and make valuable*, is a verb, which, in its nature, denotes the future time, for we promise for the future; consequently, this clause, by which the seller of an annuity promises to furnish and make it valuable, contains, not a mere assurance of the present solvency of the debtor, but a promise that the annuity shall be duly paid for the future. This clause, *to furnish and make valuable*, meets with still less difficulty, when we add, *as well in principal as arrearages*; for the term *arrearages* being susceptible only of meaning the *future*, since the future only are assigned, it follows that the seller warrants the payment of the annuity for the future. The clause is still more clear, when we add the term, *forever*, which is often inserted.

565. From what is above stated, touching the sense of the clause, to furnish and make valuable, it follows, that, in default of payment of the annuity, there results from this clause, to the benefit of the buyer, an action of recourse against the seller. But, in order that the debtor may be admitted to this

action, it is not sufficient, that the buyer should be put in delay, by a command issued against him, but it must be proved that he is insolvent; for, by this clause, the seller does not promise that the debtor shall always *be willing*, but that he shall always *be able* to pay, or, in other words, that he shall be solvent. If several persons are bound to the payment of the annuity, it is not sufficient that one of them should be insolvent; they must all be so, as well the principals obliged as the sureties.

566. It is also necessary, that the annuity should fail, without the act or the fault of the buyer. If, therefore, the buyer releases some one of the debtors of the annuity or their sureties, or if he discharges hypothecations; he cannot exercise the action of warranty against the seller; for he is not receivable to complain that the annuity has ceased to be good, since it has ceased to be so by his own act.

Is it the same, if he suffers the hypothecations to be barred by prescription, either by the lapse of time, or by neglecting to object to the decrees of goods hypothecated? There is more difficulty in this question; for it is not by his act, but by his negligence, that the annuity fails. Can it not be said, that the seller ought not to be received to object this negligence to the buyer, since it is common to them both, and he as well as the buyer might have taken care to interrupt the prescription, and to oppose the decrees?

We must however decide, with Loyseau, that the buyer in this case, in like manner, loses his action of recourse against the seller. The buyer, by the assignment, being the mandatary, though *in rem suam*, of the seller, is, by the nature of a mandate, himself obliged to these pursuits. If he is obliged, as we are going to see, to discuss the goods of the debtor, before recurring to the assignor, for the same reason, he is obliged to oppose himself to the decrees of the said goods; which is easier than it is to discuss them.

567. We cannot prove the insolvency but by a discussion

of the goods of the debtor. This discussion is made by a seizure of the movables which are found at his domicil, or by a proces-verbal, which establishes that there are none to be found there; which is called a proces-verbal for want of movables. The buyer, not being obliged to know whether the debtor of the annuity has other goods, may, after this discussion, bring his action of recourse against the seller. But if the seller point out to him other goods, either movable or immovable, he will be obliged to discuss them. He is not obliged to discuss those which are out of the kingdom. There are some who have thought, that he was not obliged to discuss goods situated out of the jurisdiction of the baillage, or at least out of the jurisdiction of the parliament, in which the debtor has his domicil; but this opinion has been rejected. It is necessary also to make an exception of goods which are in litigation, and the debtor's property in which is contested.

568. The seller is not allowed, after the buyer has commenced a real seizure of the goods pointed out to him, to point out others, the buyer not being under any obligation to make several seizures; but so long as the thing is entire, and the buyer has not yet commenced his pursuits, there is nothing to prevent the seller from pointing out to him other goods of the debtor, which have come to his knowledge since the indication of the first.

569. Lastly, the buyer is obliged to discuss those goods only, which are in the possession of the debtor of the annuity; and, the seller, who sells with the clause, to furnish and make valuable the annuity, cannot be obliged to discuss those which the debtor has alienated. This agrees with the novel 4, and with the opinion of Loyseau, who considers the question.

570. It remains to be observed, that the discussion is made at the risk and expense of the indicator. The jurisprudence of decisions has introduced the rule, that he, who is sent

back to a discussion, may demand that he, who opposes it to him, should furnish the money necessary for the purpose.

571. If, after this discussion, the buyer is unable to obtain payment of the annuity, the seller, who has sold with the clause to furnish and make valuable, cannot avoid being condemned to pay, in the place of the insolvent debtor, the arrearages of the annuity, and to continue such payment for the future. Loyseau requires however that we should leave the seller the choice of preferring a dissolution of the contract; in which case, he will be liable to restore to the buyer the price of the sale of the annuity, with interest, from the day of the failure of payment. This choice is useful to the seller, either when the annuity sold is an annuity issuing out of land, not redeemable, or when it is sold for a price less than its principal. The choice is founded upon this, that, by the clause to furnish and make valuable, the seller, in case of failure, constitutes an annuity for a price in money; and, it is just that he, who has constituted it, should be able to repurchase it for the price which he has received.

ARTICLE IV.

Of the warranty which results from the clause to furnish and make va lu able after simple command.

572. This warranty differs from the preceding, in this, that the assignee is not obliged to any other pursuits and diligence against the debtor, than a simple command. From which it follows, 1, that he is not obliged to discuss the goods of the debtor, and that it is sufficient if he is put in delay to pay, by a simple command, to entitle him to commence his action of recourse against the assignor, and to cause him to be condemned to pay, in the place of the debtor; and, 2, that he is not obliged to oppose himself to decrees of the goods of the debtor; for, in stipulating the warranty after simple command, he exonerates himself from the exercise of any other diligence.

573. If the seller of an annuity, after obliging himself to furnish and make it valuable, adds, *and to pay it myself in default of the debtor*, is this clause equivalent to the clause to furnish and make valuable, after simple command, which dispenses with discussion? or does it add nothing to the clause to furnish and make valuable? It appears, by what Loyseau reports, that the question has been strongly controverted, and that it has been determined by a decision in red robes, that this clause is only explanatory of the clause to furnish and make valuable, and that it does not exclude discussion.

ARTICLE V.

Of the obligations, which result from good faith, in the contract of sale of an annuity or other credit.

574. Good faith obliges the seller, in this contract, as in the contract of sale of corporeal things, to dissemble nothing of that which he knows, and of which the buyer has an interest to know, concerning the credit which he sells.

And, therefore, if it is proved, that the seller of a credit, at the time of the contract, had knowledge that the debtor was entirely insolvent; as, for instance, if the debtor has been discussed in all his goods, movable and immovable, and that the creditor made opposition and was unable to obtain any thing; this creditor, who, afterwards, sells the credit, by concealing the insolvency, of which he cannot be ignorant, from the buyer, who has no knowledge of it, sins against the good faith, which ought to govern in the contract of sale; and is obliged, in favor of the buyer, to take back the credit, and to restore the price, though there is no clause in the contract, by which he is obliged to a warranty of fact.

Further; as in the sale of corporeal things, the express clause, by which the seller declares, that he does not warrant against such a defect, does not discharge him, if it is proved that he has a perfect knowledge of this defect; so, in the sale of a credit, the express clause, that the seller does not warrant the present solvency of the debtor, does not discharge him, when it is proved that he has knowledge of the entire insolvency of the debtor.

ARTICLE VI.

Whether we may buy a credit of a certain sum for a less price, or an annuity for a price less than its principal.

§ I. Whether we may buy a credit for a price less than the sum due.

575. It is not to be doubted, that, in the exterior forum, we are permitted to buy a credit of a certain sum of money, for a price less than such sum, when the sale is not made with the clause to furnish and make it valuable, and the seller does not warrant the solvency of the debtor.

This is even permitted in the interior forum, provided, that, at the time of the contract, the solvency of the debtor is doubtful. And, therefore, if I purchase of you, for the sum of 600 livres, a credit of 1,000 livres; though in the end, I receive the entire sum, I am not obliged in conscience, to restore you the 400 livres, which I receive more than what I give you as the price of this credit, provided, that at the time of the contract, the solvency of the debtor is doubtful; for the surplus is the price of the risk which I run of not obtaining any thing, or of obtaining much less than the price, of the debtor.

The author of the *Morale de Grenoble*, t. 1, tr. 3, chap. 2, no. 7, is of the contrary opinion. He pretends that the buyer of a debt, however doubtful it may be, for a price less than the sum due, is obliged, if he receives the whole, to render to the seller the surplus of what he receives beyond the price, and that the risk, which he runs of the insolvency of the debtor, cannot be a sufficient reason to entitle him to receive more than he gives. This opinion seems to me to be destitute of foundation. It is true, that I cannot compel my own debtor, with whom I contract, to pay me for the risk which I incur of his insolvency, nor exact of him, on account of such risk, any thing more than what I lend him. The reason is, that his poverty, which causes the risk, should induce me to relieve and comfort, rather than to charge and oppress him. But there is nothing contrary to justice, in exacting payment of him, who sells me a credit against a debtor whose solvency is doubtful, for the risk, with which I charge myself in his place, of the solvency of the debtor, who is a third person, by purchasing this credit of him for a price less than the sum due; this risk is as capable of estimation, as the risk of the loss of a vessel, which the assurers, in the contract of maritime assurance, exact payment of, from those who have an interest in the vessel.

I agree also, that, in order to entitle me in the forum of conscience, to exact payment of him who sells me a credit, for the risk of the debtor's solvency, with which I charge myself in his place, and in order that I may consequently buy the credit for a price less than the sum due, it is necessary that there should be a real risk, and, that, at the time of the contract, the solvency of the debtor should be really doubtful. But if, at that time, the solvency of the debtor is known to me, or if it is easy to be known by informing myself, in such case, it is not permitted me to buy the credit for a price less than the sum due; for the credit of a sum, in regard to which, the debtor is notoriously solvent, is worth that entire sum; and, therefore, to buy it for less than the sum due is to buy a thing for less than its value, which is not permitted in the forum of conscience, as we have already seen, *supra*, n. 300; it is taking advantage of the seller's need of money, to make a profit at his expense; it is not to be doubted, therefore, in this case, that the buyer is obliged to a restitution in favor of the seller.

576. In a pressing need of money, you sell me, for 500 livres, a very good credit of 1000 livres, payable in three

months. I know the debtor to be a very rich merchant, who owes very little, and who has in lands, houses, and effects of trade, thirty times as much as is necessary to pay his debts. There is no doubt, that this credit of 1000 livres is worth 1000 livres, and that in purchasing it for 500 livres, the half of its value, I am guilty of a crying injustice against you, which at that time I am under an obligation to repair. But it happens, shortly after the contract, and before the expiration of the term limited for the payment of the credit, that, in consequence of accidents, which he could not foresee, the debtor, so rich at the time of the contract, becomes insolvent. There happens an inundation, which overwhelms his lands, or the lightning strikes his houses in the city, in the night, and burns them, with more than a hundred thousand crowns worth of merchandise, which they contain, so, that, from the credit of 1000 livres, which I purchased for 500, there is no reason to hope to obtain more than three or four hundred. It is demanded, whether, in this case, I cease to be obliged in your favor to a restitution. The reason for doubting is, that, by this event, the bargain between us does you no injury; but is even advantageous to you, since you would otherwise obtain less for your credit, than the price of five hundred livres. The reason for deciding, on the contrary, that notwithstanding these events, my obligation to restore continues, is, that, by the bargain between us and at that time, you suffer a true and real injury, and a diminution of your patrimony, by alienating, for the sum of 500, what is then worth 1000 livres. I, at that time, contract towards you an obligation to repair the injury; and being from that time subject to this obligation, I cannot discharge myself from it, but by payment, or by some of the other modes by which obligations are extinguished; the unforeseen events, subsequently occurring, cannot discharge me. If this credit, which is good at the time of my acquisition, afterwards becomes bad, it is a loss which ought to fall on me, and not upon you, since, as I become the proprietor of it by the acquisition, it is at my risk.

It remains to inquire, in what the restitution, to which I am obliged in your favor, ought, in this case, to consist. It seems, at first, that I am obliged to restore you the sum of 500 livres, which is the sum wanting to the just price, for less than which it is not permitted to buy. We may however maintain, that it ought to be sufficient, in this case, for me to restore you a moiety of the credit itself as it exists, in order that you may recover a moiety of what may be obtained from it. The reason is this. In making the unjust bargain, I contract an obligation to repair the injustice, and the injury which I thereby commit. This reparation may then be made in two manners; either by paying you 500 livres as the supplement of the just price of the credit, which I am not at liberty to buy entire, for less than 1000 livres, which is its just value; or by re-assigning to you a moiety of the credit itself, it being a moiety only, which I can lawfully purchase for 500 livres, which is the price only of a moiety. It is evident, that, immediately upon the contract, I can repair the wrong, in this second manner as well as in the first. The obligation to repair the wrong, which I contract in making the unjust bargain, consists therefore in the alternative of two things, namely, either to pay you the sum of 500 livres, or to re-assign to you a moiety of the credit itself as it exists. Now, it is a principle, in regard to alternative obligations, that it is in the choice of the debtor, to pay either of the two things which he pleases, though, since the contracting of the obligation, one of them is considerably deteriorated, provided it be not by the act or fault of the debtor; in this case, therefore, I ought to be permitted to acquit my obligation, by restoring you a moiety of your credit, though it is become bad.

This rule must, however, be subject to a limitation,

which depends upon two principles. The first is, that, when the loss or deterioration happens after the debtor is in delay, the debtor ought to indemnify the creditor, in case the creditor would not have suffered, if the debtor were not in delay, *si res non fuisset æque apud creditorem peritura*. The second is, that in the forum of conscience, he, who is obliged to repair a wrong, is deemed to be always in delay. According to these principles, I ought not to be permitted to acquit my obligation towards you, by re-assigning to you a moiety of the credit itself, except, in case you have not had occasion to reject better conditions in respect to it; otherwise, I ought to make you an allowance for what you might have received of another person, before the derangement of the debtor's affairs, and in reference to this, I ought to receive your declaration.

577. The distinction, which we have made, between the case, in which the solvency of the debtor is perfectly known to the buyer of the debt, and that in which it is doubtful, is not admitted in the exterior forum; it would there be the occasion of too much discussion and inconvenience; and, in the exterior forum, it is sufficient, that a credit is sold, without the clause of warranty of the debtor's solvency, in order that it may be lawfully purchased for a price less than the sum due.

578. When the seller of a credit warrants that it shall be duly paid, it cannot, in that case, either in the forum of conscience or in the exterior forum, be lawfully purchased for a price less than the sum due. Such a purchase ought not to be lawful any more than an usurious loan; for when I sell you, for 900 livres, a credit of 1000 livres, which I myself engage to acquit, if the debtor does not pay it, it is evidently the same thing, as if you lend me 900 livres, upon condition that I render you 1000 at the end of a certain time.

If the credit sold, however, is payable in another place

than that in which the contract is made, and the price paid; and, if, at the time of the contract, bills of exchange upon the place of payment, according to the course of exchange, are at a discount, the purchase of this credit for something less than the sum due may be lawful, provided the difference does not exceed the discount upon the said bills of exchange, according to the course of the place.

§ II. **Whether we may buy an annuity for a price less than its principal.**

579. It is not to be doubted, that, in the exterior forum, when an annuity is sold, without the clause to furnish and make valuable, it may be purchased for a sum less than its principal, though it is at the rate of one to twenty, which is the highest rate at which annuities may be constituted.

It is not always necessary to decide in the same manner, in the forum of conscience; for an annuity due at the rate of one to twenty, by a good debtor, and accompanied by good hypothecations, being an annuity which is certainly of the value of its principal, to purchase it for less is sinning against good faith, which does not permit the buying of things for less than their true value.

580. When the seller, in the sale of an annuity created at the rate of one to twenty, promises to furnish and make it valuable, and to cause it to be duly paid for ever, the annuity cannot be lawfully purchased, even in the exterior forum, for a sum less than its principal. For example, when an annuity of 50 livres, upon a principal of 1000 livres, is sold with the clause to furnish and make valuable, it cannot be lawfully purchased for 800 livres. The reason is, that, by the clause to furnish and make valuable, the seller of the annuity constitutes himself the debtor of it, conjointly with the debtor. It is consequently the constitution of an annuity of 50 livres against him for the sum of 800 livres, which he receives; now this constitution exceeds the legal rate; it is therefore usurious, as well as the contract in which it is included.

From which it follows, that the seller, who, in the sale of an annuity due at the rate of one to twenty, promises to furnish and make it valuable, has a right to demand to take it back, by rendering the buyer the sum paid, and that he may even deduct from the principal all the arrearages received by the buyer.

581. When the annuity is at a rate lower than that of the ordinance; as, for instance, at the rate of one to forty, thirty, twenty-five, &c. though it is sold with the clause to furnish and make valuable, it may be purchased for a price less than its principal, provided, however, that it is not less than the sum necessary to constitute the principal of a like annuity, created at the rate of one to twenty. For example, if one sells an annuity of forty livres, upon a principal of 1000 livres, which is at the rate of one to twenty-five, though it is sold with the clause to furnish and make valuable, it may be purchased for a less sum than its principal of 1000 livres; as, for example, for the price of 900 livres. But it cannot be lawfully purchased for a price less than eight hundred livres, which is equal to the principal of a rent of forty livres, when it is created at the legal rate.

582. It is to be observed, that, when one sells an annuity, the rate of which is low, for a sum less than its principal, with the clause to furnish and make it valuable, he ought to be permitted to repurchase and take it back, when it shall seem good to him, by restoring to the buyer the sum received of him as the price of the annuity, if the buyer do not prefer to keep it, and to discharge the buyer from the warranty which results from the clause to furnish and make valuable. The reason is, that the annuity, of which the seller constitutes himself the debtor to the buyer, by the clause to furnish and make valuable, is an annuity constituted for the price of a sum of money, which he receives; and it is of the nature of all annuities, constituted for the price of a sum of money, that the debtor may discharge

himself from them, by rendering the sum of money received as their price.

According to this principle, even when the annuity, which I sell with the clause to furnish and make valuable, is an annuity issuing out of land and not redeemable, it ought always to be permitted me to repurchase and take it back, by restoring to the buyer the sum received of him as the price, if he does not prefer to discharge me from the clause to furnish and make valuable; for though this annuity, in respect to the principal debtor, is an annuity issuing out of land and not redeemable, yet, in respect to me, who am constituted the debtor of it, jointly with the principal debtor, it is an annuity constituted for a price of money, from which I may consequently discharge myself, by restoring the sum received as the price.

583. When an annuity at a low rate is sold, with the clause to furnish and make valuable, for a sum less than its principal, and the buyer afterwards, by the repurchase of it by the debtor, receives the entire principal, is the buyer obliged to account to the seller for the difference between the price paid him and the principal? I think it is necessary to inquire, whether the price, for which the annuity is sold, with the clause to furnish and make valuable, does or does not exceed the principal of a like annuity created according to the legal rate. For example, if an annuity of 100 livres, at the rate of one to fifty, upon a principal of 5000 livres, is purchased for 2000 livres, which is the principal of an annuity of 100 livres, at the rate of one to twenty, I think, that in this case, the buyer, to whom this annuity is reimbursed by the debtor, ought to render to the seller the difference between the price paid and the principal received. But I think it should be otherwise, if the annuity is sold for a price, which is, in truth, less than its principal, but which is yet much greater than that of a like annuity, created at the legal rate. For example, if one purchases

for 3,500 livres, an annuity of 100 livres upon a principal of 5000 livres, I think if he receives, contrary to all expectation, a reimbursement of this principal of 5000 livres, he is not obliged to render to the seller the 1500 livres, received over and above the 3500 given by him as the price of the annuity. The reason is, that the advantage which the buyer receives from this reimbursement, which depended upon a very uncertain event, is sufficiently paid for by the disadvantage which he suffers, by the acquisition of an annuity of only 100 livres for a sum of 3500 livres, which, at the legal rate, ought to produce an annuity of 175 livres.

But, in the first case, in which the buyer gives, for an annuity of 100 livres, which the seller is obliged to furnish and make valuable, only a sum of 2000 livres, which is the lowest price, for which one can acquire an annuity of 100 livres, the advantage which he would derive from a reimbursement of the annuity, by receiving 3000 livres more than the price paid for it, is an advantage which the seller is not paid for, and for which consequently the buyer ought to account to him.

ARTICLE VII.

Of the sale of litigious credits, and other litigious rights.

§. Of the nature and of the obligations of this contract.

584. We denominate *litigious credits* those which are, or which may be, contested, either in whole or in part, by him whom we pretend to be the debtor of them, whether the process is already commenced, or whether, not being yet commenced, there is ground to apprehend it. When a credit of this nature is sold to any one for a certain price, in order that the buyer may make it valuable at his own risk and expense, and without being warranted to him, this is what we call a sale of *litigious rights*, or of a *litigious credit.*

By this sale, it is not so much the credit itself, that we sell, as it is the uncertain event of a process undertaken or to be undertaken in reference to this pretended credit: *Venditur dubius litis eventus.* It is for this reason, that the buyers of litigious rights are called *litium redemptores.*

585. From thence arises this difference between these sales, and the ordinary sales of credits. In the latter, the seller is bound to warrant that the credit, which he sells, exists and belongs to him; that the thing or sum is really due to him; *debet præstare emptori debitum subesse.* In the former, the seller does not warrant that the credit exists; he sells his claims such as they are, well or ill founded. *Non tenetur præstare emptori debitum subesse, tenetur tantum præstare bonam fidem.*

586. This good faith obliges him not only to remit to the buyer all the titles and documents which he has, but also to give him all the instructions in his power, concerning the credit which he sells. It also obliges him not to conceal from the buyer any thing which he may know to the disadvantage of the pretended credit, and which might deter him from buying or from buying at so great a price.

587. The good faith, which the seller is bound to observe in this contract, does not require, that he should be certain and fully persuaded, that the right which he sells is well founded; for he sells it only as doubtful and uncertain. It is sufficient, therefore, that he should be uncertain concerning the justice or injustice of his claim, in order that he may lawfully sell it; but if he knows that his right is ill founded, he cannot sell it without wounding good faith.

588. There is no doubt, that the bad faith which the seller commits, by selling a claim which he knows to be ill founded, obliges him in the forum of conscience, in favor of the debtor, to a restitution of the price received; for an ill founded claim and known as such is of no value; the seller

is consequently unable, without injustice, either to stipulate or to receive any thing as the price of such a claim.

Does this bad faith of the seller oblige him, also, in the forum of conscience, to restore to the buyer the expenses of carrying on the process in which he fails? I think, that if the seller simply exposes to the buyer what his claim is, without concealing from him any thing which concerns it, and without employing any artifice or any discourse to persuade him that it is good; though he is guilty of deceit in selling him a claim which he knows to be bad, yet he is not obliged to indemnify him for the expense of the process. The reason is, that, by the nature of the contract of sale of a claim which is sold as doubtful, it is left to the examination of the buyer himself, to determine whether he will carry on a process or not. It is upon his own proper examination, that the buyer determines to carry it on; he himself, therefore, is the cause of the damage which he suffers from the process, when he fails in it; he ought to take the loss upon himself, and is not consequently entitled to an indemnification from the seller.

But if the seller, in selling a claim which he knows to be bad, by his discourse, persuades the buyer, that it is maintainable, this bad faith obliges him to a reparation of the wrong which he causes the buyer who follows his counsel, and consequently to indemnify him for what it costs him to carry on the process. This decision is founded in the law 47, D. *de reg. jur.* (50, 17, 47): *Consilii non fraudulenti nulla obligatio est; cæterum si dolus et calliditas intercessit, de dolo actio competit.*

If the seller, touched with repentance, afterwards declares to the buyer, that he retracts all that he has said to him to persuade him of the goodness of his claim, and offers him a restitution of the price, together with his expenses, if the process is already commenced, and the buyer obstinately persists in the suit, the seller will not be liable to indemnify him for what it may cost him after that time.

589. We observe, by way of digression, that the seller, who sells to a third person a claim which he has against me, and which he knows to be ill founded, contracts also *ex delicto*, in the forum of conscience, an obligation in my favor, by which he is liable *in solido* with his assignee, to a reparation of all the damage which I sustain from the unjust process brought against me by the assignee, and which he has excited by making the assignment to the latter. He is liable for this damage, whether the process remains undecided; whether I gain it, and by the insolvency of the assignee am unable to obtain payment of the expenses, to which he is condemned in my favor; or, whether, by the injustice of the judge, the process is decided against me.

590. We have seen what are the obligations of the seller; those of the buyer are, first, to pay the agreed price as in other contracts of sale. If the credit sold is not of a nature to produce interest, the buyer owes the interest of the price only from the day of the demand of the seller. If it is of a nature to produce interest, he owes it, from the time, when, according to the law of the assignment, the interest of the credit sold ought to run for his benefit. The buyer is obliged, secondly, at least in the forum of conscience, to conceal nothing of what he knows, to the advantage of the credit, which is assigned to him, which might induce the seller to sell for a higher price.

§ II. Of the effect of the assignment of litigious rights against the debtor.

591. The laws, in order to put a bridle upon the cupidity of the buyers of litigious rights, and to put a stop to suits, ordain that the buyers of litigious rights shall not be able to exact of the debtor any thing more than what they give as the price of the assignment, with interest, and that the

debtor shall be discharged from the remainder. This is established by Anastasius, in the law *per diversas*, C. 4, 35, 22, and confirmed by Justinian, in the law *ab Anastasio*, C. 4, 35, 23. The equity of these laws, which is evident, has caused them to be adopted even in that part of the kingdom, which is not subject to the Roman law. This is attested by Mornac, *ad d. l.*, who cites a decision of 1586, pronounced in red robes, which fixes the jurisprudence in this respect.

592. The law of Anastasius is only directed against those assignments of litigious rights, which are made by a title of sale. He declares expressly, that he does not intend to affect those, which are made by a title of donation; and therefore the donee of a credit, though litigious, may exact of the debtor all that his assignor might exact. But it is necessary for this, that the donation should be honest and true. What if the act of assignment of a litigious credit import, that the creditor sells to such an one his credit, to the amount of a certain sum, for the said sum, and that he makes him a donation of the residue? Justinian, in the law *ab Anastasio*, (C. 4, 35, 23) decides, that, in this case, the donation must be presumed to be feigned and made in fraud of the law; and, consequently, that, without having any regard to it, the assignee cannot exact any thing more of the debtor than the sum given as the price of the assignment. This is very just; otherwise the law would always be eluded, and the clause of donation as to the surplus would become the established form. Justinian decides the question in the same manner, whether this pretended donation of the surplus is made to the buyer, or to some person by him supposed.

593. If the act of assignment appears to contain a donation for the whole of the litigious credit, and it is proved by other evidence, that the assignor has secretly received something of the assignee as the price of the assignment,

the donation will also in this case be declared to be made in fraud of the law, and the assignee will consequently be deprived of the power of exacting any thing more of the debtor than the price paid the assignor; C. 4, 35, 23.

594. The emperor Anastasius has excepted, in certain cases, from the penalty of his law, the assignments of litigious rights, though they are not made by a gratuitous title, namely: 1, those which are made to a coheir or coproprietor by his coheirs or coproprietors, of a litigious right which they have in common; 2, when a creditor receives from his debtor, in payment of what is due to him, some right of litigious credit, or other litigious right, which his debtor has against a third person; 3, when a legatee receives of the heir, in payment of his legacy, some litigious right belonging to the succession; and, 4, when the possessor of an estate procures the assignment to himself of some litigious right in it, which is necessary to assure him of its free enjoyment. Justinian, by a Greek constitution, which is not in the editions of the Corpus Juris Civilis, but which is found in the Basilics, and which Cujas has inserted in his Observations, *lib.* 16, *art.* 16, abrogates, in this respect, the constitution of Anastasius, and ordains, that, in every case, in which the assignment is not made by a title entirely gratuitous, the assignee of litigious rights can claim nothing more of the debtor than the price paid for the assignment.

This constitution of Justinian is not equitable, and ought not to be followed. The law of Anastasius, which deprives the assignees of litigious rights of the power to exact any thing more than the price of the assignment, is founded only upon the hatred which is merited by the buyers of suits, who appear to have no other motive than a love of litigation for the acquisition of the litigious rights, which they cause to be assigned to them; and, consequently, there ought to be no ground for the penalty inflicted by this law, whenever the assignment of litigious rights is made for a just cause.

When an heir or other person, who already has, in his own right, a part in a litigious credit, or other litigious right, acquires, for the price of a sum of money, the parts of his coheirs or coproprietors, it is evident, that this assignment is made for a just cause, namely, to dissolve the community. The assignee cannot therefore in this case pass for a buyer of process, and ought to be admitted to make valuable, in all their extent, the rights which make the object of the assignment. Mornac, as above cited, says that this was the opinion of the most skilful advocates of his time.

When a creditor, in payment of what is due to him, receives an assignment of a litigious credit, which his debtor has against a third person, we may distinguish two cases. If such creditor may easily obtain payment of his debt, otherwise than by this assignment, I think he should be subject to the penalty of the law, and regarded as the buyer of process; but if it appears, that he can with difficulty obtain payment in any other manner, and is obliged to take in payment this litigious credit, which his debtor offers him, the assignment, in this case, has a just cause, which prevents the assignee from being regarded as a buyer of process; and, therefore, he ought to be permitted to make the credit ceded to him valuable in its whole extent.

When the possessor of an estate, pursued by a pretended hypothecary creditor of the seller of the estate, purchases this credit, for a price less than the sum which makes the object of it, it is also necessary to distinguish whether the possessor has a good warrantor, and, instead of summoning his warrantor to defend him against this pretended creditor, he purchases the credit for a low price, in order to prosecute a suit afterwards against the seller; in which case, I think the seller comes within the law and that he cannot exact any thing more than the price paid. But if the possessor has a bad warrantor, and purchases this credit in order to preserve possession of his estate, I think, that, as the assignment in this case has a just cause, he may, if prosecuted by subsequent creditors, make his credit valuable against them in its whole extent.

595. We may also conceive of other cases, in which the cession of litigious rights must appear to be made for just cause, and not to be subject to the disposition of these laws.

The following is mentioned by Brunneman, *ad h. l.*, namely, where the assignment is made to any one, by reason of the sale of some other thing to him, *in consequentiam alterius rei venditæ.* For example, you sell me a piece of land, with all the credits, which you have against the farmers of the different farms which depend upon it; though, amongst these credits, there is a litigious one, which is sold to me at the same time with the land, but for a separate price, and much inferior to the sum which makes the object of it, this assignment ought not to be subject to the disposition of the law above cited; for, in this case, there can be no suspicion against me of seeking the acquisition of a suit. If I make a purchase of this litigious credit, it is in consequence of the acquisition of the land; and because the seller, in selling me his land, is not willing to make a reservation of any part of what may be due to him from his farmers. It would be necessary to decide otherwise, if, the land being sold by itself, I should purchase the litigious credit, after a certain interval of time, because in such case I should have no inducement to buy it.

596. Another case, according to Brunneman, who cites the doctors *ad has leges*, is, when the right, which is sold as litigious, is sold by a judicial sale, *si nomen sub hasta venditum.* For example, if an annuity, which is in litigation between me and my debtor, who maintains that it is barred by prescription, which is denied by me, is licited

between my heirs, and adjudged to a stranger, subject to the condition that he shall charge himself with the event of the suit; though this adjudication includes the sale of a litigious right to a stranger, yet it will not be subject to the disposition of the law, because the adjudicatary cannot, in such case, be regarded as an odious buyer of process, who seeks the acquisition of a suit, since, by the notice and proclamations, he is in some sort invited by the law to make the acquisition.

597. With the exception of these cases, the disposition of the law takes place, without any regard being had to the quality or dignity of the person of the buyer as an exemption from it, which, in the opinion of J. Faber, was allowed, but which opinion, Mornac, with reason, rejects. It is immaterial, whether an assignment of litigious rights is made for money or for some other thing. The assignee is not allowed to demand any thing more than the value of the things given for the assignment; Brunneman, *ad. d. l.* Neither is it of any consequence, whether the litigious rights are prosecuted against the debtor in the name of the assignee, or in that of the assignor. The debtor, in the latter case, proving, by the report of the assignment, that the assignor is only lending his name to the assignee, ought to be received to demand a discharge from the suit by offering to pay the price of the assignment. Even in case he is unable to report the assignment, he may put the demander upon his oath in this respect.

598. The right, which is accorded, by these laws, to the debtor of a litigious debt, ceded to a third person, is a kind of right of redemption of the debt, which is allowed him against the assignee. The debtor, by reimbursing the assignee, is permitted to take his bargain. The purchase, made of the debt by the assignee, is destroyed in his person and passes to that of the debtor, who is himself considered to repurchase his debt of the creditor, and

to transact with him for it for the sum mentioned in the assignment.

This redemption is very equitable. The good of peace requires that the debtor, who, in taking the bargain upon himself, extinguishes the process, to which the debt will give rise, should be preferred in the bargain, to an odious buyer of process.

The debtor, in order to exercise this redemption, ought to reimburse the assignee the sum paid by him to the creditor as the price of the assignment, and to furnish him with an acquittance or discharge of what he is under an obligation to pay, and which is not yet paid; he ought also to pay the interest of the sums paid by the assignee. The law, *per diversas* (C. 4, 35, 22), declares expressly: *Usque ad ipsam tantummodo solutarum pecuniarum quantitatem et* USURARUM *ejus actiones exercere permittatur.* But the interest cannot be claimed by the assignee, until after he has notified the debtor; who might say, that if he had given him notice sooner, he would have paid sooner, and thereby prevented the interest from running. The debtor ought also to reimburse the assignee for the expenses of the transfer, notice, and demand; for it is a principle, common to all kinds of redemption, that the party redeeming should indemnify the party against whom the redemption is exercised.

The debtor is admitted to this redemption, and to offer the assignee a reimbursement of the price of the assignment, even after the cause, upon the demand of the assignee, has been contested. This is the opinion of Brunneman, *ad. d. l.* However, if the assignee, after a long instruction, and after having removed all doubts concerning the legality of the credit assigned, by his cares and discoveries, has put the cause into a situation to be determined, I do not think that the debtor, on the eve of judgment and on the point of failing in his cause, ought to be admitted to this redemption, and to offer a reimbursement of the price of the assignment; for the case is no longer the same. The debts, of which the laws accord a redemption to the debtor, against the assignee, are those which are liable to difficulty, and which give rise to suits; but when the assignee, by the instruction of the process, has removed and cleared up all the difficulties, in regard to the legality of the debt, it is no longer within the case of those, of which the laws accord this redemption. Besides, the laws accord the redemption to the debtor, only for the purpose of preventing the process to which the debt may give rise; it is contrary to the spirit of the laws that the debtor, who is willing to sustain the process to the end, should be admitted, upon the eve of a judgment, to exercise this redemption; above all, if the judgment which ought to intervene, is a judgment in the last resort, which ought to put an end entirely to the process.

599. The debtor, by reimbursing the assignee the price of the assignment, does not discharge himself, in the forum of conscience, from the sum due, when he knows that it is due, or when he is deceived by his cupidity into the belief that it is not due. The debtor, by this redemption, which puts him in the stead and place of the assignee, is considered as purchasing the debt of his creditor, for the sum imported by the act of cession. But a debtor, who makes a composition with his creditor, of a litigious debt, for a certain sum, is not discharged towards him, in the forum of conscience, for the surplus, when he knows it is due.

The debtor, who knows that he owes the whole debt, does no wrong to the assignee, by reimbursing him only the price of the assignment; for the latter acquires the credit subject to this redemption, which the law accords the debtor. The debtor has a great interest in exercising it; for if he pays the entire debt to the assignee, he will not cease to be bound, in the forum of conscience, towards the creditor, to a reparation of the injury done him in obliging him to sell his credit at a loss, by the unjust refusal on his part to pay it.

600. It is to be observed also that these laws are made in favor of the debtor and not in favor of the assignor, who will not be admitted to reclaim the credit which he sells, by offering the assignee a reimbursement of the price which he has paid; Despeisses, *p.* 1, *tit.* 1, § 2.

PART SEVENTH.

OF ACTS AND CONTRACTS RESEMBLING THE CONTRACT OF SALE.

The acts and contracts, which resemble the contract of sale, are, 1, a gift in payment; 2, a remuneratory donation; 3, a burdensome donation; 4, a donation upon a life annuity; 5, the contract of exchange; 6, divisions; 7, licitations; and, 8, transactions. These are treated of and the differences between them and the contract of sale remarked in the following articles.

ARTICLE FIRST.

Of a gift in payment.

601. A gift in payment is an act by which a debtor gives a thing to his creditor, who is willing to receive it, in the place and in payment of a sum of money, or of some other thing, which is due to him. This act very much resembles the contract of sale. The thing which is given in payment stands in the place of the thing sold; and the sum, in payment of which it is given, stands in the place of the price; and therefore it is said in the law, 4, C. *de evict.* (8, 45, 4): *Dare in solutum, est quasi vendere.* Nevertheless, a gift in payment is not altogether a contract of sale; and it is not the same thing, for a debtor to agree with his creditor to sell him a certain thing, for the sum of so much, to be received in compensation of what he owes him, and to say, that the debtor gives his creditor such a thing in payment of such a sum, which he owes him.

602. First, the contract of sale is a consensual contract, which is perfect by the mere consent of the parties before

any delivery. A gift in payment is made only by the delivery, and it is even necessary that there should be a transfer of the property of the thing given in payment.

603. Second, when I sell you a thing for the sum of so much, to go in compensation of a like sum which I think I owe you, if I afterwards discover that I do not owe it, or do not owe so much, I cannot reclaim the thing sold, but only the price, which, by mistake, I compensate with a sum which is not due to you. The action, which I have against you, is the action *ex vendito, quæ datur ad pretium consequendum.* On the contrary, when I give you a thing, in payment of a sum, which, by mistake, I believe I owe you, I have a right to reclaim the thing itself of you; for my action, in such case, is that which we call *condictio indebiti per errorem soluti*, or *condictio sine causa*, the object of which actions is to reclaim the thing paid.

In like manner, when I give you a thing in payment of a sum of 200 livres, which I believe myself to owe you, though I owe you only 100; I cannot reclaim the 100 livres, but the thing, which I am bound to reclaim entire, by offering to pay you the 100 livres which I owe; for I cannot oblige you to become an owner in common with me of the thing, which you would not have received in payment, if you had not expected to have it entire: *Condictio rei integræ manet et obligatio incorrupta; ager autem retinebitur, donec debita pecunia solvatur;* D. 12, 6, 26, § 4. What if you are willing to retain the thing, and to pay me the 100 livres, which I do not owe you? Dumoulin, *de contr. us.*, *q.* 14, *n.* 182, decides that I may, in the same manner, oblige you to a restitution of the thing, by offering to pay you, because I would not have given it in payment, if I had known that I did not owe you the whole sum. He makes an exception in case I have exposed the thing to sale.

604. Third, he who sells a thing in good faith, believing himself the proprietor of it, is not strictly obliged to transfer

the property of it to the buyer, as we have already seen, *supra*, n. 1; and the buyer, so long as he remains undisturbed in his possession of the thing, cannot pretend that the seller does not fulfil his obligations. On the contrary, a gift in payment is valid only so far as the debtor transfers to the creditor the property of the thing, which the creditor consents to receive in payment of the sum due him; for there can be no real payment without a transfer of the property, according to this rule of law: *Non videntur data, quæ eo tempore, quo dantur, accipientis non fiunt;* D. 50, 17, 167. And, therefore, if the creditor, who has received a thing in payment of a sum of money, which was due to him, discovers that his debtor was not the proprietor of it, and consequently that he has not transferred the property of it to him, though he has not suffered any trouble on the part of the true proprietor, he may demand of his debtor the sum which he owes him, by offering to restore him the thing which he has received in payment, such a payment being null and insufficient to discharge the debtor. See the Treatise on Obligations, part 3, chap. 1, art. 3, sect. 3.

605. Notwithstanding the differences above mentioned, we must admit that a gift in payment bears much resemblance to the contract of sale. It is in consequence of this resemblance, that the creditor, when he is evicted of a thing given him in payment, has an action against the debtor who gives it in payment *ad instar* of that, which a buyer has against his seller, *utilem actionem ex empto;* and, in the same manner, that the buyer, in case of eviction, concludes against the seller to a restitution of the price, and for his damages and interests, *si quid supra pretium ejus intersit rem habere licere*, as we have seen, n. 68 and 131; so the creditor concludes by this action against his debtor, that he should be held to pay him the sum, in payment of which the thing, of which he is evicted, is given him, the payment of this sum being analogous to a restitution of the price of

the sale; and also that he should be held to pay him his damages and interests, *si quid supra hanc summam ejus intersit rem habere licere.* This results from the law 24, D. *de pignorat. act.* (13, 7, 24), and from the law 4, C. *de evict.* (8, 45, 4), which expressly give in this case *utilem actionem ex empto.*

It is to be observed, that besides this action, *utilem ex empto*, the creditor, in case of eviction of the thing, which is given him in payment, has also the action which results from his credit, from which the debtor is unable to discharge himself, by a payment which is found to be inefficacious; D. 46, 3, 98. But the action *utilis ex empto* is frequently more advantageous to him, because it comprises his damages and interests, *si quid supra intersit.*

606. It is not in the case of eviction only, that he, who gives a thing in payment to his creditor, contracts towards him the same obligation of warranty which a seller contracts. He is, in like manner, liable, *utili actione ex empto*, to warrant him, to whom he gives a thing in payment, against real charges, which are not declared to him, and against redhibitory defects with which the thing is found to be affected, in the same manner that a seller is liable. He is also liable, the same as a seller, *utili actione ex empto*, for the damages and interests of the creditor, to whom he gives a thing in payment, when it has not the entire quantity, or all the qualities, which he has declared to him that it has.

607. Lastly, good faith imposes upon the parties, in the case of a gift in payment, the same obligations which it imposes in the contract of sale. He, who gives a thing in payment, not only must not be guilty of any falsehood, in order to induce the buyer to accept it; but he must not even make use of any concealment of the defects of the thing, which may prevent his creditor from accepting it in payment. Neither ought he to give it in payment for a price greater than its just price, unless the creditor, having know-

ledge of the just price, consents, through his liberality, to take it at a price greater than its value. *Vice versa*, the creditor, on his part, ought not to receive the thing in payment, for a price less than it is worth. When, on the part of either, the lesion exceeds a moiety, the party injured is entitled to the same rescissory action, which takes place in the contract of sale. It is also in consequence of the resemblance which a gift in payment bears to the contract of sale, that it gives rise to a profit of sale, and to redemption.

ARTICLE II.

Of the remuneratory donation.

608. When a remuneratory donation is made as a reward for mercenary services susceptible of appreciation in money, and for which the party rendering them is entitled to an action to recover a recompense; if the value of the things given does not exceed that of the services, such a donation, though called by that name, in the act by which it is made, is a donation only in name; it is a true *gift in payment*, to which, all that is said in the preceding article, on the subject of a gift in payment, may be applied.

609. When the value of the things given exceeds that of the services, the donation, made as a reward for these services, is, in this case, an act of a mixed nature; it is a gift in payment, and equivalent to a sale, to the amount of the value of the services; it is a donation, for the amount in which the things given exceed the value of the services.

610. From whence, it follows, that if I give you an estate of the value of 30,000 livres, as a recompense for services worth 20,000, the act being a gift in payment, and consequently standing in the place of a sale for two thirds, and being a true donation for the other third; if you suffer an eviction of the estate, as the seller for two thirds of it, I am

liable for two thirds of the eviction, and for the resulting damages and interests.

If you suffer an eviction of a third, or of a less portion only, I am not liable; for being considered the seller of only two thirds of the estate, my obligation is fulfilled, so long as you have the two thirds; you can only demand, in this case, that I should be held to take back the two thirds, which remain to you of the estate, and to pay you for your services; because you probably would not have been willing to acquire the estate in part, and consented to take the two thirds in payment of your services, only in so far as you had the other third by a title of donation. This is an instance of the action, which is called in the law, *condictio causa data, causa non secuta.*

611. There is more difficulty in the case, in which you suffer an eviction of a piece of land which is one of the integral parts of the estate. Though this piece is not a third, at the most, or is even much less than a third of the whole estate; *stricto jure*, I ought to be liable to you, for the two thirds of this eviction and the damages and interests resulting from it; for, in the remuneratory donation, which I have made to you of the estate, not having distinguished what integral parts of the estate I gave in payment of your services, and what other parts I gave you in addition, I am considered to be the seller for the two thirds and the donor for the other third, of each of the integral parts which compose the estate, as I am considered to be of the whole estate; and, consequently, as the seller, I am liable for the two thirds of the eviction of each of the said parts. It must be acknowledged, however, that equity, in this case, seems to resist the rigor of this principle.

612. When the remuneratory donation is made as a reward for services, which are not of a nature to be appreciated at a price in money; for which, he, who renders them, is not entitled to any action to demand a recompense; and for

which, he, who receives them, is bound only to the duties of gratitude; a donation, made as a recompense for such services, however important they may be, is a pure donation, which has nothing in it analogous to the contract of sale.

ARTICLE III.

Of burdensome donations.

613. A burdensome donation is the donation of a thing, which is made subject to certain charges, which the donor imposes upon the donee. If these charges are appreciable at a price in money, and are equal in value to the thing given, such a donation is a donation only in name, and is equivalent to a contract of sale. The donor stands in the place of a seller, and contracts towards the other party the same obligations, which a seller contracts towards a buyer; and the donee, on his part, contracts the obligations to acquit the charges imposed upon him. This donation, like the contract of sale, gives rise to redemption and to seignorial profits.

614. If the charges are, in truth, appreciable at a sum in money, but of a less value than the thing given; for example, if I give you an estate of the value of 3,000 livres, subject to charges appreciable at 2,000 livres, the act will be of a mixed nature; it will be a sale of two thirds and a donation of one third, and consequently, the donor will be liable for the two thirds to the obligations of a seller, as we have already explained in regard to a remuneratory donation.

615. When the charges are not appreciable at a price in money, the act is a true donation, which has nothing in common with the contract of sale. The donee, in case of eviction, has no recourse against the donor; he is merely quit of the charges, if he has not already acquitted them; and if he has, he cannot claim any recompense.

ARTICLE IV.

Of donations upon a life annuity.

616. We must distinguish, in regard to this act, whether the life annuity is an annuity which very much exceeds, or does not exceed, the revenue of the estate. When it very much exceeds the revenue of the estate, so that it may appear to include the price of it, the act, in such case, has only the name of a donation. It is a contract similar to the contract of sale, which produces the same obligations, and which, in the same manner, gives rise to redemption and seignorial profits. When the annuity is scarcely equal to the revenue of the estate, the donation is then a true donation; the annuity appearing to be rather the price of the enjoyment of the estate, which the donor may reserve by the donation, than the price of the estate itself. And, therefore, the donor, in case of eviction, cannot claim any thing more than to be quit of the annuity for the future, either wholly or partially, according as the eviction is of the whole or of a part; and he cannot claim any damages and interests against the donor.

617. By an edict of the month of August 1661, his majesty, in order to restrain the cupidity of the clergy, and to prevent them from despoiling families, has prohibited the giving in mortmain of estates, or of life annuities greater than the revenue of the thing given; and even the giving of money for a life annuity greater than the rate of the ordinance; under the penalty of a nullity of the contracts, confiscation of the things given, and a thousand crowns by way of amends, against the communities; the whole to be disposed of, one third to the informer, and the surplus to the hospitals of Paris. These hospitals were excepted by the edict from this prohibition. But, by another edict, of the month of January 1690, they were made subject to its provisions.

ARTICLE V.

Of the contract of exchange, and of the acts which resemble it.

618. The contract of exchange is a contract, by which one of the contracting parties obliges himself to give a thing to the other, in the place immediately of another thing, which the other contracting party is obliged on his part to give him. I say *immediately*, for if we agree together that I shall give you such a thing for such a price, in payment of which, you shall, on your side, give me another thing, this agreement is not a contract of exchange, but it includes a sale of my thing, and a gift of yours in payment of the price of mine.

619. It is necessary, also, to the contract of exchange, that each of the contracting parties should compare the value of the thing which he gives with that of the thing which he receives, and that he should have an intention to acquire merely as much as he gives. But if two friends mutually give each other, the one one thing, and the other another thing, without regard to their value, this is a mutual donation which they make; it is not a contract of exchange.

620. The contract of exchange bears some resemblance to the contract of sale. It held the place of that contract, before the use of money, which gave birth to the contract of sale; for which reason, the Sabinians thought that an exchange was a true contract of sale; D. 18, 1, 1. The opinion of the Proculeians, who decide that the contract of exchange is different from the contract of sale, is more correct. The principal difference is, that, in the contract of sale, we distinguish the thing and the price; we distinguish between the contracting parties, one of whom is the seller and the other the buyer. On the contrary, in the contract of exchange, each of the things is both the thing and the price; each of the contracting parties is both seller and buyer; D. 18, 1, 1, § 1; D. 19, 4, 1.

621. Though the contract of exchange is different from the contract of sale, yet as it produces, in each of the contracting parties, the same obligations of warranty, which the contract of sale produces in the seller, we cannot deny that the contract of exchange is one which resembles the contract of sale, and partakes of the nature of that contract: *Permutationem vicem emptoris obtinere non est juris incogniti;* C. 4, 64, 2: *Permutatio vicina est emptioni;* D. 19, 4, 2.

622. According to the principles of the Roman law, the exchange was not a contract purely consensual. The mere agreement of exchange, by which two persons were agreed to exchange one thing for another, so long as it was not yet executed on the part of either of the parties, was only a simple pact, *nudum pactum*, which, according to the principles of the Roman law, did not produce any civil obligation; for there was only a certain number of agreements, which, without having as yet received any execution, and without being clothed with the form of a stipulation, were allowed to produce a civil obligation; the civil law having attributed to them their appropriate actions, on account of which these agreements were called *named contracts.* A sale was of the number of these *named contracts;* but an exchange, according to the opinion of the Proculeians, which had prevailed, being an agreement different from a sale, was only a simple pact, which, not being clothed with the form of a stipulation, did not produce any civil obligation. Nevertheless, if, in execution of this agreement of exchange, one of the parties had given to the other the thing, which he had promised to give him in exchange, the agreement, by the commencement of its execution, became a contract without a name, *do ut des*, from which resulted an action *præscriptis verbis*, by which the party, who had executed the agreement on his part, might constrain the other to the execution of his own. And, therefore, the contract of exchange, according

to the Roman law, was a real contract; C. 4, 64, 2; D. 19, 4, 2. This distinction, between contracts and simple pacts, having no foundation in reason and natural equity, and being a mere political invention of the patricians, in order to render the practice of the law difficult, and thereby to retain the people in dependence, has, with reason, been rejected in our law, as we have seen in our Treatise on Obligations. For this reason, with us, the agreement of exchange, before it has received any execution, and as soon as the consent of the parties intervenes, produces in both a civil obligation, and is a consensual contract, like the contract of sale.

The Roman jurisconsults took notice of another difference between the contract of sale and that of exchange, which, appearing to have its foundation in the nature of these contracts, may be admitted into our law. In the contract of sale, it is the buyer only, who is obliged precisely to transfer to the seller the property of the money, which makes the price of the sale: *Emptor nummos venditoris facere cogitur;* D. 19, 1, 11, § 2. But the seller, when he sells a thing, which he believes, in good faith, to belong to him, is not obliged precisely to transfer to the buyer the property of the thing sold; he is only obliged to defend him, when he shall be disturbed: *Hactenus tenetur ut emptori rem habere liceat, non etiam ut ejus faciat;* D. 19, 1, 30, § 1. On the contrary, as, in the contract of exchange, each thing is both the thing and the price, and each of the contracting parties is both seller and buyer, each of them is obliged precisely to transfer to the other the property of the thing which he gives him. And, therefore, the contracting party, who receives the thing, which is given him in exchange, though he do not yet suffer any disturbance in his possession of the thing, is not obliged, on his part, to give that which he has promised, if he discovers that the property of that which he receives is not transferred to him, and that it did not belong to the other party. All that the latter can claim is, that he should be restored that which he has given; D. 19, 4, 1, § 4. It is in this sense, that Pedius *ait alienam rem dantem nullam contrahere permutationem;* D. 19, 4, 1, § 3.

623. In the contract of exchange, each of the contracting or exchanging parties is obliged towards the other to deliver him the thing, which he promises to give him in exchange, and to warrant him against evictions, as well as real charges, and redhibitory defects; and if he does not satisfy this obligation, he is liable in his favor, for the damages and interests resulting from its non-execution, as, in the contract of sale, the seller is liable in favor of the buyer.

624. The copermutant, to whom I fail to deliver the thing, or to whom I fail in warranty, has his choice, either to conclude against me to a condemnation for his damages and interests, *actione utili ex empto*, or to reclaim the thing, which he gives me in exchange; C. 4, 64, 1. This law however made a distinction, in this respect, which does not appear to be founded upon any solid reason; and, therefore, I think, that this choice ought to be granted indifferently to the party evicted.

625. All that is said, in regard to the contract of sale, touching the obligations, resulting from the good faith, which ought to govern in that contract, and those which result from clauses concerning the quantity or quality of the thing sold, the place or the time of delivery, is entirely applicable to the contract of exchange.

626. The thing, which each of the contracting parties promises to give in exchange to the other, is at the risk of him, to whom it is promised to be given, as the thing sold is at the risk of the buyer, in the contract of sale; and if it perishes without any act or fault of him who promises, and before he is in delay to give it, he is discharged from his obligation, without the other party, to whom it is promised, being able to reclaim that which he has given on his part, and without being able even to discharge himself from his

obligation to give it, if his obligation is not yet performed; the same, as in the contract of sale, the buyer cannot, in such case, reclaim the price paid, or avoid payment of it, if it is not yet paid. The reasons, upon which we have established this principle, in regard to the contract of sale, *supra*, part 4, are of equal force in regard to the contract of exchange. The limitations to that principle are also applicable in regard to this contract.

627. He, who gives movables in exchange for some other thing, cannot attack the contract, whatever lesion he may pretend to suffer in the estimation of the said movables; for the rule of our French law, contained in article 445 of the custom of Orleans, which rejects the benefit of restitution in the alienation of movables, is a general rule, which includes exchange as well as sale. But he, who gives an immovable in exchange for things, the value of which is less than a moiety of the just price of such immovable, may, the same as a seller, demand the rescission of the contract, if the other copermutant does not prefer to supply what is wanting to the just price.

628. It remains to us to observe, on the subject of the contract of exchange, that, when it is of an immovable for another immovable, the one for the other, and without any return in money or other movable things, it is not subject by the customs either to the profit of sale or to redemption. If there is any return, the party, who makes the acquisition by means of it, owes the profit of sale for this return and to its amount. In regard to redemption, according to the most common law, the return in money or other movable things does not render the contract of exchange subject to it, except when the return exceeds a moiety of the value of the estate for which it is given. There is however in this respect a great diversity in the customs.

629. When the exchange is of an estate for movables,

it gives rise, the same as the contract of sale, to seignorial profits and to redemption; it is, in this respect, considered as a contract equivalent to a sale; otherwise nothing would be more easy than to disguise all contracts of sale under the appearance of such exchanges, in fraud of the lords and parties entitled to redemption.

630. We must not omit one of the principal effects of an exchange; which is, that the thing, received by me in exchange for that which I give, is subrogated of full right to the latter, and, takes the extrinsic qualities which that loses by the alienation; from which results this rule, *subrogatum capit naturam subrogati.*

Observe, however, that it is necessary, for this purpose, that the thing, which I receive in exchange, should be of a nature to be susceptible of the qualities of that which I alienate. For example, if I receive a constituted annuity in exchange for an estate, which came to me by descent in the paternal line, by the subrogation, this annuity will acquire the quality of being proper in the paternal line of the succession to which the estate alienated belonged, because it is sufficient, that the annuity should be immovable, in order that it may be susceptible of the quality of being proper to the succession; but it will not acquire the quality of being proper to the redemption belonging to the estate alienated, because annuities constituted are not susceptible of this quality. If it is for movables, that I exchange an estate descended to me in the paternal line, these movables will not acquire the quality of being proper to the succession, nor to the redemption belonging to the estate, because movables are susceptible of neither of these qualities.

It is evident, that the thing, which I receive in exchange for that which I give, cannot, by this subrogation, receive any other qualities than those which that thing has, and such as it has them. And, therefore, if I acquire an estate, in exchange for a constituted annuity, which came to me by descent in the paternal line, this estate will have the quality of being proper in the paternal line to the succession to which the annuity belonged, but it will not have the quality of being proper to the redemption, though it is of a nature to be capable of that quality; for, being subrogated to a constituted annuity, it cannot acquire the quality of being proper to the redemption, which quality the annuity had not and could not have.

It is also evident, that the thing, which I receive in exchange, cannot, by the subrogation, acquire any but the extrinsic qualities belonging to the thing which I give, and which that thing loses by the alienation; such are the qualities of being proper in such or such a line. But the subrogation cannot cause the qualities of feodal or censual, belonging to the estate which I alienate, to pass to that which I receive in its place, for these are intrinsic qualities, which cannot pass from one estate to another.

It is the same, in regard to charges of hypothecation, of substitution, and of others similar, to which one of the estates exchanged may be subject; they remain upon the estate, notwithstanding the alienation, which I make of it, and do not pass to that which is given me in exchange for it. If the latter also become hypothecated to my creditors, it is for another reason, which is, that I hypothecate to them all my goods present and future.

ARTICLE VI.

Of divisions.

631. According to the principles of the Roman law, different in this respect from those of our law, a division, among coheirs or other coproprietors, was regarded as a kind of contract of exchange, by which I was considered to exchange the undivided portion, which I had in the things

which fell to your share, for the undivided portion, which you had in the things which fell to mine. For this reason, a division is called *permutatio* in the law, 77, § 18, D. *de legat.* 2°, (31, 1, 77, § 18, 2°); and it is said in the law 1, C. *comm. utriusq. judic.* (C. 3, 28, 1), that *vicem emptionis obtinet.*

It is upon this principle, that Ulpian, in the law 6, § 8, D. *comm. dividund.* (10, 3, 6, § 8) decides, that my creditor preserves his hypothecation upon the part, which I had before the division in the things, which belong to your share, because, being considered to hold and to have acquired this part of me by the division, you could not acquire it in any other manner than as I had it, and charged with the hypothecations of my creditors.

According to the principles of our French law, quite opposed to those of the Roman, divisions bear no resemblance to the contract of exchange; they are not acts, by which the parties acquire, or are considered to acquire, any thing from each other. A division, according to our principles, is nothing more than an act, which determines the indeterminate part, which each coheir, before the division, had in the mass which is divided, to the particular things which fall to his share.

Before the division, each of the parties has a part or a moiety in the mass which is to be divided, which part is not certain or determined in regard to that of which it ought to be composed; it is by the division only that it is determined to the particular things assigned to the party; and it is considered to have been composed of these things from the beginning, and never to have comprised any of the things which fall to the other shares.

For example, when several coheirs divide the goods of a succession amongst them, the division determines the part of each of the heirs in the succession, to the things which fall to his share, in such manner, that each of the said heirs is considered to succeed the deceased, from the instant of his death, to the said things for the whole, and not to have succeeded to any part of what falls to the other shares.

In like manner, when several persons are made legatees conjointly of an estate, or when they purchase it in common, and they afterwards divide it, each of them is considered to have been the sole legatee or sole buyer of what falls to his share, and not to have been the legatee or buyer of any part of what falls to the other shares.

This takes place, though the division is made with a return in money or annuities. He, to whom the larger share falls, is considered to have been the heir, legatee or buyer of all that it contains, charged with a return; and he, to whom the smaller share falls, is considered not to have been the heir, legatee or buyer, for any more than the things, which fall to it by means of the return, which the other parties make to him.

It is evident, according to these principles, that a division is an act, which has no resemblance to the contract of exchange, and still less to the contract of sale, whether it is made with or without a return in money; for, according to these principles, the division is not a title of acquisition; by the division which I make with my coheirs or coproprietors, I do not properly speaking acquire any thing; its only effect is to render determinate to certain things, the indeterminate right which I previously had.

632. It is in consequence of this principle, that our custom of Orleans, art. 15, followed, in this respect, in those which have no contrary disposition, decides, that there is no profit of fief due on account of a division, though there is a return of money or other things. The article 113 contains nothing to the contrary, though it is said at the end of that article, that between persons who are not coheirs, a profit is due for the return; for the terms *other persons* must be understood to refer to the case of a third person, who pur-

chases the part of one of the heirs, and, in his character of assignee, makes a division with his coheirs. Such third person owes a profit for the returns, with which the share, which falls to him by the division, is charged; but he does not owe this profit for the returns by reason of the division, which, not being considered as a title of acquisition, cannot give rise to profits; but he owes it, by reason of the sale, which is made to him of the part of this coheir, these returns being an augmentation of the price of this part, of which he owes the profit.

633. The parties, by the division, contract the reciprocal obligation to warrant the things which fall to their respective shares; but this obligation is different from that which a seller contracts in favor of a buyer, or which any other assignor contracts in favor of the assignee. The seller or other assignor, by an onerous title, in consequence of the obligation which he contracts *præstare rem habere licere*, is liable in favor of the buyer, in case of eviction, not only to a restitution of the price, but for all the damages and interests, which the buyer suffers from the eviction, over and above the price, on account of intrinsic or extrinsic augmentations happened to the thing, *in id omne quod supra pretium emptoris interest rem habere licere*, as we have already seen, *supra*, n. 146. On the contrary, when a coheir or other copartner suffers an eviction of a thing fallen to his share, the other parties are only liable to make him an allowance for the sum, for which that thing is given him in the division, which allowance they are bound to make, each for his own part, the share evicted remaining confused; but they are not liable for the damages and interests resulting from the eviction, on account of an augmentation happened since the division in the thing evicted. This is the doctrine of Dumoulin in his *Tr. de eo quod interest*, n. 143, *et seq.*

For example, if there are four heirs of us, who divide a patrimony of 100,000 livres, and I suffer an eviction of a house given me in the division for 8000 livres, each of my coheirs will be liable to make me an allowance of 2000 livres only, though the house, at the time of the eviction, is worth 12,000 livres, because the quarter, where it is situated, is become a much better place for trade than it was at the time of the division. In this respect, these coheirs differ from a seller or other assignor, by an onerous title; for if one sells me a house for 8000 livres, and the price of the house rises to 12,000 livres, he will be liable in case of eviction, for my damages and interests amounting to 4000 livres beyond the price of 8000, which he ought to restore, as we have already seen, *supra*, n. 133. The reason of difference is, that my coheirs or other copartners cannot be considered as my assignors, in relation to the thing of which I suffer the eviction, since, according to the principles of our law, the parties, by the division, do not cede any thing, and do not hold any thing from each other. The sole reason, upon which the warranty among copartners is founded, is, that the equality, which ought to govern in divisions, being wounded by the eviction which one of the parties suffers of some one of the things fallen to his lot, the law, which exacts this equality, obliges each of the parties to re-establish it. Now, it is sufficient for this, that each of the parties should make an allowance, each for his part, of the sum for which the thing evicted is given in division. For example, in the case above supposed, when I suffer an eviction of a house which I have in my share for 8000 livres, in order to re-establish equality, it is sufficient for each of my three coheirs to make me an allowance of 2000 livres. By this, my share of 25,000 livres, which, by the eviction, is reduced to 17,000 livres, is re-established at 23,000 livres, and is consequently made equal to those of the other parties, which, by means of the sum of 2000 livres, paid me by each of them, are in like manner reduced to 23,000 livres.

Dumoulin goes farther, and is of opinion, that, even according to the principles of the Roman law, by which my copartners were regarded as the assignors of their portion in the things fallen to my lot, they were not liable for an eviction of those things, except on account of the sum for which they were given in exchange, and not on account of the damages and interests which I might suffer beyond that sum, by reason of any augmentation happened to the said things subsequent to the division. The reason, upon which he founds his opinion, is, that a seller or other assignor, by an onerous title, who sells, even in good faith, a thing which does not belong to him, is the only person, who draws the buyer into error, and who consequently ought to be liable for the damages and interests which the buyer suffers from the eviction: *Solus totam rem suam asserit, solus autem in totum decipit;* whereas, in a division, it is no more by the act of my copartners than my own, that the thing, fallen to my share, and of which I suffer the eviction, is improperly put into the mass of the goods which are to be divided among us. I cannot impute any thing to them, which they cannot impute to me, and consequently I ought not to be allowed to claim damages and interests against them: *Neuter magis asserit, neuter magis decipit quam alter; immo dicitur res evinci facto vel culpa communi, et sic nulla debet esse inter eos obligatio in id quod extrinsecus interest, sed ut mutuo compensent;* Dumoulin, *ibid.* n. 145. The law, 66, § *fin.* D. *de evict.* (D. 21, 2, 66, § *fin.*), appears to be opposed to this opinion. Dumoulin answers, that this text ought to be restrained to the case, in which I suffer an eviction, by the particular act of my copartner, on the part of his hypothecary creditors. This question, which Dumoulin discusses, is superfluous in our jurisprudence, for the reasons above explained.

From this principle, that the warranty, which is due to a copartner, on account of an eviction of some one of the effects fallen to his share, is limited to a re-establishment of the equality, which is injured by the eviction, Dumoulin draws the conclusion, that if my coheir suffers an eviction of an estate, given him in the division for a certain sum, say 3000 livres, and I suffer by lightning, or by some irresistible force, a loss of a like sum of 3000 livres in the estates fallen to my lot; though this loss does not give me an action of warranty against him, because the estates, which fall to a copartner by partition, are afterwards at his risk; yet I may oppose this loss to him, by way of compensation, and exception against the action of warranty resulting from the eviction suffered by him, because, as there is nothing more remaining to me in my share, than there is remaining to him in his, there can be no claim to the re-establishment of equality: *Quinta quæstio*, says he, *si cohæres qui nunc convenitur de evictione vel ad supplementum, possit deducere quod sibi interim de rebus in suam partem adjudicatis casu fortuito deperiit, ut sic licet non possit agere de casu fortuito, possit tamen excipere?* And he answers: *Ad quintam quod sic, ne ad summum in plus teneatur quam ad novam de integro divisionem; Tr. de eo quod int. n.* 146. This decision of Dumoulin is not free from difficulty. If admitted, it forms a second difference between the warranty of divisions, and the warranty which takes place in contracts; for, in the contract of exchange, for example, if my copermutant suffers an eviction of some one of the things given him in exchange, I cannot oppose against his action of warranty a compensation for the loss, which I suffer by some accident, in the things received in exchange of him.

634. There is a third difference between the warranty of copartners, and that of a seller. When an annuity is sold, the warranty of the seller consists only in defending the buyer against evictions on the part of third persons, who pretend that the annuity belongs or is hypothecated to them; but the seller does not warrant against the insolvency of the

debtor of the annuity, especially when it takes place subsequent to the contract, unless he is expressly obliged to do so, by the clause to furnish and make valuable; *supra*, part 6.

On the contrary, copartners are warrantors of each other, against the insolvency of the debtors of annuities fallen to their respective shares, so long as the annuities subsist, even when the insolvency does not happen until more than a hundred years after the division. For example, if there are four heirs of us, who divide a succession, and there falls to my share an annuity of 40 livres upon a principal of 800 livres, due from Peter; however good this annuity may be at the time of the division, if it afterwards fails by the insolvency of Peter, provided this failure does not occur through my fault, as, by suffering hypothecations to be prescribed against, or by suffering them to be set aside by decrees, which I do not oppose, I may, by proving the failure by a discussion of Peter's goods, if my copartners oblige me to do so, exact of them, that they should, each one for his part, continue to me 10 livres of the annuity, in the place of the annuity of 40 livres, against the failure of which they are my warrantors. The perfect equality, which ought to govern in divisions, is the foundation of this warranty. An annuity is a successive being, the real existence of which consists in all that may become due from it, until the repurchase; and, therefore, when, by the insolvency of the debtor, I cease to be able to receive what becomes due from an annuity fallen to my share, I am deemed not yet to have received the entire thing fallen to me, and not to be equal to my copartners, who have received the whole fallen to their shares; from whence it follows, that, in order to establish equality, they are bound to make up my deficiency.

635. There is a fourth difference between the obligation, which results from contracts of sale or exchange, and that

which results from divisions. When several persons sell or exchange with me a thing, each of them is liable in warranty to me, in case of eviction, for his part only; and neither of them is in any manner liable for the insolvency of his cosellers, unless they are bound to the warranty *in solido* by a particular clause of the contract. It is otherwise between copartners. If four of us divide a succession, and I suffer an eviction of a part of my share valued at 12000 livres, and one of my copartners is insolvent, the loss, which I suffer from his insolvency, must be borne by the two who are solvent and by me; and, therefore, each of the two, who are solvent, besides the sum of 3000 livres, which he owes for himself for his fourth part of the eviction of 12,000 livres which I suffer, owes me also the sum of 1000 livres, for his third part of 3000 livres, for which the insolvent is liable to me, and which his insolvency causes me to lose; this loss being borne by me and my two copartners who are solvent. This is founded upon the equality, which ought to exist between copartners, and which would otherwise be injured.

636. It remains to us to take notice of another and the last difference between these divisions, and contracts of sale, exchange, and others similar. In the latter, lesion is not sufficient to cause a decree of rescission, if it does not exceed a moiety. For example, he, who sells an estate of the value of 20,000 livres, cannot complain of lesion, unless the price, for which he sells it, is less than 10,000 livres; but in divisions, a more exact and scrupulous equality is required, and if one of the copartners is injured for more than a fourth part of what ought to come to him, it is sufficient to authorize him to demand a rescission of the division. For example, if the part of the common goods to come to me ought to be of the value of 20,000 livres, and I receive less than 15,000, it is sufficient to enable me to rescind the division.

637. In conclusion, the warranty which takes place in divisions has this in common with that which takes place in the contract of sale, that the mere fear only of an eviction does not give rise to the warranty. This is the decision of Dumoulin, *d. n.* 146 : *Secunda quæstio an in divisione possit agi de evictione ante rem evictam ;* and he answers : *Ad secundam quod non, nisi res tempore divisionis esset ab extraneo possessa.*

ARTICLE VII.

Of licitations between coheirs or coproprietors.

638. Licitation comes from the Latin term *liceri*, which signifies to put a price upon a thing, to make a bid for a thing exposed for sale, and from its frequentative verb *licitari*, which signifies to make several bids one above another; Calvin and Calepin, *in verb. liceri et licitari.* We understand by *licitation* an act, by which coheirs or other coproprietors of a thing in common and undivided between them put it to bid between them, to be adjudged and to belong to the highest and last bidder, upon condition that he pay to each of his coproprietors a part in the price, equal to the undivided part, which each of the said coproprietors had in the estate licited, before the adjudication.

639. When one of the coheirs or coproprietors, between whom the licitation is made, is the adjudicatary, the licitation is not a contract of sale, though it has the appearance of one. This licitation holds the place of a division, and, like a division, is nothing more than an act which dissolves the community.

In the same manner, that, in a division, which is made with a return in money or in annuities, the coheir, to whom the largest share falls, is considered to succeed to all that falls to his share, charged with the return, and to acquire nothing of his copartners; so, in licitation, the coheir is considered to be sole seized by the deceased of the whole of the estate, of which he renders himself the adjudicatary by the licitation, and to derive no part of it from his coheirs, towards whom, the law which calls them with him to the succession only charges him to pay, out of the sum to which the estate may be carried by the licitation, a part equal to that for which the said coheirs are called with him to the succession. This sum, as to the part, which the heir who is the adjudicatary owes to each of his coheirs, is similar to the return upon a division, which he is charged with in favor of each of them; and the part, for which each of them is called with him to the succession, is, by the licitation, determined to this sum, in such a manner, that they are considered never to have been seized of any other thing.

It is the same, in regard to other coproprietors. When several legatees or several acquirers dispose in this manner of an estate, which is bequeathed to them in common, or which they acquire in common, the party, who becomes the adjudicatary, is considered to have been directly the legatee or acquirer of the whole of the estate, subject only to the charge of making an allowance to his colegatees or coacquirers of their share in the price, to which the estate may be carried by the licitation to be made between them.

640. It follows from these principles, that the licitation between coheirs or other coproprietors is not, in our law, a contract of sale, which the liciting parties make of their share in the estate licited to him among them who becomes the adjudicatary, since, according to the above stated principles, the adjudicatary does not properly speaking acquire any thing from his coheirs or coproprietors.

641. From which, it follows, 1, that these licitations do not give rise to any profit of sale; 2, that they do not give rise to redemption; and, 3, that the adjudicatary is not bound by the hypothecations of the individual creditors of his colicitants. The particular creditors of each of the parties can

only intervene to the licitation and seize the right of their debtor, for the purpose of receiving in his place the part, which will come to him in the price of the licitation; but if they suffer it to be received by the debtor, they cannot demand any thing of the adjudicatary, who is not considered as acquiring any thing from his colicitants.

642. From which it follows, also, 4, that as the colicitants of the adjudicatary are not properly sellers of their part, they are not liable to the same warranty to which a seller is liable in favor of a buyer; but they are liable to one another only in the warranty to which copartners are respectively liable; which consists in nothing more than a restitution of what each of the colicitants has received from the price of the licitation, either for the whole, if the adjudicatary suffers an eviction of the whole, or for a part, if he suffers an eviction of a part only of the estate.

643. This decision ought to take place even when the licitation contains an express clause of warranty; for, in this case, such a clause ought to be understood to refer only to a kind of warranty, which agrees with the nature of the act, that is to say, a warranty, which takes place between copartners in divisions, the licitation being an act which stands in the place of a division.

644. When an act is passed without licitation between two heirs or other coproprietors who have a common title, by which act it is said, in express and formal terms, that the one of them sells to the other, for a certain price, his part in the succession, or in a certain estate, which is in common and undivided between them, it would seem, that we ought not to consider it doubtful whether such an act constitutes a contract of sale. Nevertheless, as in acts, we ought not to stop at the terms, but to look for the intention of the parties, and for the act which they intend to do, the jurisprudence has established, that notwithstanding the term *sale*, in which this act is conceived, it ought not to be con-

sidered as a contract of sale, but as an act standing in the place of a division, and dissolving the community previously existing between the parties, because there is ground for presuming, that the principal intention of the parties, in making this act, is to dissolve the community. And, therefore, all that has been stated in regard to licitation may be applied to this act; it neither gives rise to a profit of sale, nor to redemption.

645. The coheir or coproprietor, to whom it is said by the act, that the other coheir has sold his part, is not considered to have truly purchased and acquired of his coheir; but the whole is considered to remain to him by way of division, charged with a return of the sum agreed. And, therefore, as in a licitation, the adjudicatary is not bound by the hypothecations of particular creditors of his coheir, he ought to be equally discharged from them by this act, which is not different from a licitation. Lastly, this act ought not to give rise to the warranty of a seller, but to that to which copartners are respectively liable.

ARTICLE VIII.

Of transactions which have some resemblance to the contract of sale.

646. When, by a transaction, in order to induce you to desist from a demand which you have commenced, or which you are about to commence against me, I give you a certain thing, this contract is different from the contract of sale. It is of the class of contracts *do ut facias;* whereas the contract of sale is of the class of contracts *do ut des.* Nevertheless, this contract in some things resembles the contract of sale; the seller receives of the buyer a price, which is an equivalent for the thing which he sells him; and in consequence of this equivalent which he receives, he is bound to a warranty in favor of the buyer. So, in this transaction, I receive of him with whom I contract an equivalent

for the thing which I give him, namely, an abandonment of the demand which he has commenced, or which he was about to commence against me, which abandonment is a thing appreciable, and is really appreciated between us, at the value of the thing which I give him for it. I ought therefore, by this transaction, to contract the same obligation of warranty, in favor of the party to whom I give the thing, as the seller contracts in favor of a buyer; C. 2, 4, 33.

647. It would be otherwise, if, by a transaction, and in consideration of a sum of money, which I receive of you, I yield up to you the thing itself, which makes the object of the process between us, by an abandonment, in consideration of the said sum, of the demand which I had commenced against you for the same thing. I am not, in this case, obliged to a warranty of the thing in your favor; and if you suffer an eviction of it, you can demand nothing of me, not even a restitution of the sum which you have given; for, by this transaction, I do not cede to you that thing, I leave it with you such as you have it; I only desist from the uncertain claims which I have upon it, and from the demand which I have commenced against you; the money which I have received of you is not the price of this thing, but the price of my abandonment. This is also decided in the law above cited; C. 2, 4, 33.

In like manner, in the inverse case, if you abandon to me the thing which I revendicate, in consideration of a sum of money which I give you, you are not obliged in my favor to a warranty of this thing; and if I am evicted of it, I cannot reclaim of you the sum given; for you do not intend to cede me the thing, but only to desist from your uncertain claims upon it.

648. But if, by the act, it is declared, that I acknowledge that the thing, which makes the object of our contestation, belongs to you, and that it is agreed between us, that you

cede it to me for a certain sum, there is no doubt in such case, that the agreement is a true contract of sale, which obliges you to a warranty.

We have spoken here only of what may be found in a transaction which has some resemblance to a contract of sale: we shall elsewhere treat separately of this kind of agreement.

INDEX.

[The figures refer to the numbers of the paragraphs.]

F.

G.

I.

J.

L.

T.

U.

W.

ERRATA.

Page 96, line 12 from top, for "concern" read "concerns."
" 121, " 14 from top, for "as" read "for."
" 242, " 8 from top, for "is" read "are."